The Age of the Borderlands

The Age of the Borderlands

INDIANS, SLAVES, AND THE LIMITS OF MANIFEST DESTINY, 1790–1850

Andrew C. Isenberg

THE UNIVERSITY OF NORTH CAROLINA PRESS

Chapel Hill

Designed by Jamison Cockerham
Set in Arno, Scala Sans, and Fell English
by codeMantra

Cover art: *Fur Traders Descending the Missouri*, 1845. Painting by
George Caleb Bingham. Morris K. Jesup Fund (1933), Metropolitan
Museum of Art, New York. Courtesy of Wikimedia Commons.

Manufactured in the United States of America

Portions of chapter 2 appeared as Andrew C. Isenberg, "The Market Revolution
in the Borderlands: George Champlin Sibley in Missouri and New Mexico,
1808–1826," *Journal of the Early Republic* 21, no. 3 (Fall 2001): 445–65.
Portions of chapter 3 appeared as Andrew C. Isenberg, "An Empire of
Remedy: Vaccination, Natives, and Narratives in the North American
West," *Pacific Historical Review* 86, no. 1 (February 2017): 84–113.
Portions of chapter 5 appeared as Andrew C. Isenberg, "'To See inside of
an Indian': Missionaries and Dakotas in the Minnesota Borderlands," in
Conversion: Old Worlds and New, ed. Kenneth Mills and Anthony Grafton
(Rochester, NY: University of Rochester Press, 2003), 218–40.

LIBRARY OF CONGRESS CATALOGING-IN-PUBLICATION DATA
Names: Isenberg, Andrew C. (Andrew Christian), author.
Title: The age of the borderlands : Indians, slaves, and the limits
of manifest destiny, 1790–1850 / Andrew C. Isenberg.
Other titles: David J. Weber series in the new borderlands history.
Description: Chapel Hill : The University of North Carolina
Press, 2025. | Series: David J. Weber series in the new borderlands
history | Includes bibliographical references and index.
Identifiers: LCCN 2024045149 | ISBN 9781469685052 (cloth) |
ISBN 9781469683843 (epub) | ISBN 9781469685069 (pdf)
Subjects: LCSH: Borderlands—United States. | Manifest Destiny. | United
States—History—1783–1865. | United States—Territorial expansion.
Classification: LCC E179.5 .I85 2025 | DDC 973—dc23/eng/20241029
LC record available at https://lccn.loc.gov/2024045149

For

AMY

CONTENTS

List of Illustrations   ix

Acknowledgments   xi

Introduction   *1*

1   MAROONS   *27*

2   TRADERS   *63*

3   VACCINATORS   *99*

4   COLONIZERS   *125*

5   CONVERTS   *157*

Conclusion   *187*

Notes   *203*

Bibliography   *237*

Index   *271*

ILLUSTRATIONS

FIGURES

William Augustus Bowles, 1791   45

Abraham, 1848   60

An Osage Indian Lancing a Buffalo, 1846–1848   70

Braves' Dance, Ojibwa, 1835–1837   118

Benjamin Lundy, ca. 1820   138

Medicine Dance of the Dahcotah or Sioux Indians, 1848   173

MAPS

The North American borderlands before 1845   2

East and West Florida before 1821   31

The US-Mexico borderlands, 1835   145

Dakota country, 1830s–1840s   168

ACKNOWLEDGMENTS

This book took shape accidentally. I stumbled across many of its subjects—maroon settlements in Florida, the factory system for regulating trade with Indigenous people, the federal program to vaccinate Native Americans, the effort to make Texas into a haven for freed slaves, and the work of the Lac qui Parle missionaries—while pursuing research on other projects. At first, I saw these subjects as intriguing anomalies in the relentless expansion of the United States in the first half of the nineteenth century. I could not get them out of my mind, however, and I began writing about some of them, initially telling myself that the journal articles and book chapters I produced were merely exceptions to the rule that in the nineteenth century, the United States was North America's surpassing power and was determined to expand across the continent. Over time, however, I came to think that there were so many exceptions to that rule that there was not much left of the rule itself, and that it was time to rethink the nature of the US borderlands. This book is the result of that realization.

I am grateful to the many people who critiqued all or part of the manuscript, both in its current form and in earlier, piecemeal incarnations as conference papers, journal articles, and book chapters: Beth Bailey, Josef Barton, Matthew Beil, Amy Berkley, Kent Blansett, Samuel Davis, Andrew Denning, David Farber, Petra Goedde, Nicholas Guyatt, Stephen Hausmann, Frederick Hoxie, Michael Hill, William Chester Jordan, Larry Kessler, Deokho Kim, Janne Lahti, Patricia Limerick, Nancy MacLean, Arthur McEvoy, Laura Mielke, Kenneth Mills, Harvey Neptune, James Oakes, Thomas Richards, Justin Roberts, Louis Warren, Elliott West, Sean Wilentz, and two anonymous readers for the University of North Carolina Press. At the University of North Carolina Press, I am grateful to Val Burton, Debbie Gershenowitz, Andrew Graybill, Chuck Grench, Cate Hodorowicz, and Benjamin Johnson.

I am indebted to many archivists for helping me locate documents. I offer particular thanks to Peter Blodgett of the Huntington Library in San Marino, California; James Cusick of the P.K. Yonge Library of Florida History at the University of Florida in Gainesville; and Paul Huffman of the Mary Ambler Archives at Lindenwood University in St. Charles, Missouri.

I received financial support from many institutions to pursue this project. I am particularly grateful to Princeton University for a Christian Gauss Fund Research Leave; to the College of Liberal Arts at Temple University for a Sabbatical Research Leave and Summer Research Grant; to the Huntington Library for an Andrew W. Mellon Foundation Fellowship; and to the Hall Center for the Humanities at the University of Kansas for a Humanities Residential Fellowship.

The friends and family who supported me while I was writing this book were many. They include Michael Angell, Beth Bailey, Kent Blansett, Bruce Buttny, Bill Deverell, Frederick Ellis, Jessica Ellis, Luca Ellis, David Farber, Tom Faszholz, Jean Faszholz, Tristan Fogt, Richard Godbeer, Jen Harper, John Hillman, Lynn Hillman, Elena Isenberg, Emily Isenberg, Eric Isenberg, Joan Isenberg, Kai Isenberg, Noah Isenberg, Deokho Kim, Savanah Low, Paige Mansfield, Arthur McEvoy, Elaine Nelson, Marc Rodriguez, Edwina Schorn, Joel Schorn, James Sprague, Kim Sprague, Louis Warren, and Adam Wilson. I am grateful to them all.

Above all, I thank Amy, to whom I owe everything. This book is for her.

The Age of the Borderlands

Introduction

On May 25, 1836, John Quincy Adams addressed the US House of Representatives in an hour-long oration. Eight years earlier, when Adams was still president of the United States, an address of such length by the erudite Harvard
graduate would have been unremarkable. But by 1836, Adams was no longer
president. He had been defeated for reelection by Andrew Jackson in 1828;
left the White House in 1829 without attending his successor's inauguration;
quickly grown restless in retirement as he observed with dismay Jackson's
populist, expansionist, and proslavery policies; and returned to Washington
in 1831 as a member of the House. The nominal issue that inspired Adams's
sprawling speech in 1836 was a resolution authorizing the distribution of relief
to settlers who had fled their homes in Alabama and Georgia following a series of violent altercations with Indigenous people. Adams used that conflict
as an opportunity to embark on a wide-ranging discourse. As a *Congressional
Globe* journalist archly put it, the ex-president addressed the chamber "on the
state of the Union."[1]

Although Adams expounded on numerous subjects, he focused on the
most pressing issue of the moment: the rebellion in the Mexican province of
Coahuila y Tejas (or, as Americans called the northern part of the province,
Texas). Beginning in October 1835, "Texians," as expatriate American settlers

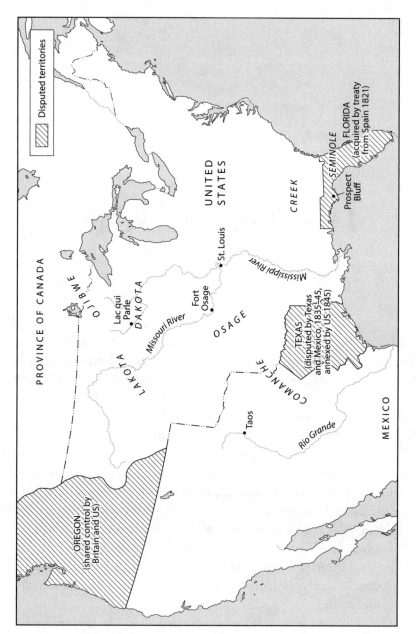

The North American borderlands before 1845.

in Texas were known, had revolted against Mexican rule. By April 1836, the Texians had unexpectedly defeated the Mexican force sent to subdue them, achieved a fragile independence, and appealed to the United States for annexation. Jackson plainly favored annexation, and Adams accused numerous House members of "thirsting" to annex Texas as well.

In dire terms, Adams warned against expanding the boundaries of the United States to include Texas. His opposition to annexation may have surprised some of his colleagues in the House. As a US senator from Massachusetts in 1803, he had been the only Federalist to vote in favor of Thomas Jefferson's acquisition of the Louisiana Territory. In 1818, as secretary of state during the administration of James Monroe, he had defended Andrew Jackson when Jackson, then an army general, had invaded Spanish Florida. In 1821, Adams acquired Florida for the United States from Spain in return for setting the southwestern boundary of the United States at the Sabine River—the border between the modern states of Louisiana and Texas. With that agreement in place, Adams believed that US expansion had gone far enough. Before the House in 1836, he argued that to extend the already "over-distended dominions" of the United States beyond the Sabine would be an untenable overreach. "Are you not large and unwieldy enough already?" he asked proponents of annexation. "Is your southern and southwestern frontier not sufficiently extensive? Not sufficiently feeble? Not sufficiently defenceless?" Annexation, he predicted, would precipitate a war with Mexico that the United States might well lose. Adams warned that Mexico had "the more recent experience of war" and "the greatest number of veteran warriors." He reminded the House of ongoing US military stumbles in Florida, where the United States had struggled to establish its control since acquiring the peninsula from Spain: "Is the success of your whole army, and all your veteran generals, and all your militia-calls, and all your mutinous volunteers against a miserable band of 500 or 600 invisible Seminole Indians, in your late campaign, an earnest of the energy and vigor with which you are ready to carry on that far otherwise formidable and complicated war?" Not least of all, he warned that if Mexico were to carry the war into the United States, the invader would find numerous allies among slaves and especially among the Indigenous people whom the United States was in the process of removing to the Indian Territory on the border with Texas. "How far will it spread," Adams asked, should Mexico invade the United States, "proclaiming emancipation to the slave and revenge to the native Indian"? In such an instance, "Where will be your negroes? Where will be that combined and concentrated mass of Indian tribes, whom, by an inconsiderate policy, you have expelled from their widely distant habitations, to embody them within a small compass on the very borders of Mexico, as if on purpose to give that country a nation of natural allies in their hostilities against you? Sir, you have a Mexican, an Indian, and a negro war upon your hands, and you are plunging yourself into it blindfold."[2] Adams's speech sparked a debate that consumed five hours, causing the House to stay in session long into the evening. That night, Adams, in his inimitably cramped handwriting, recorded the day's events in his diary. He congratulated himself that he had succeeded in sapping the House's enthusiasm for annexation.[3] Indeed, Adams and his like-minded colleagues in Congress managed to deter annexation for nine more years.[4]

On that day in 1836, Adams articulated a reality about the United States that reflects the central argument of this book: as a slaveholding republic born in the age of empire, a relatively weak United States found itself engaged with powerful European imperial competitors, even more powerful Indigenous societies, and formidable enclaves of fugitive slaves in a complicated struggle for sovereignty in several regions along its borders. Sometimes, as when Jackson invaded Spanish Florida in 1818, seeking to deal blows all at once to the Spanish, the British, the Seminoles, and communities of escaped slaves, the United States asserted itself *vertically* in the borderlands by trying to impose its will through violence or the threat of violence. More often, however, the United States was too weak to impose itself and so instead reached out into the borderlands *horizontally*, seeking influence through diplomacy or commerce. In practice, US expansion slanted in complex and contradictory diagonals into the borderlands. Each of those angles represented different narrative visions for the borderlands. "Manifest destiny," the most strident of those visions, was but one of many ways early nineteenth-century Americans imagined the future of their borderlands.

In Adams's view, the United States, which between 1783 and 1836 had expanded its territory northwest into the Great Lakes region, west into the Great Plains, and south to the Gulf of Mexico, had swollen beyond its capacity either to exercise effective sovereignty over border regions or to defend its extended borders against imperial competitors. The US presence in the borderlands, a multilateral and multiethnic region, was tenuous: until the 1840s, Britain dominated the region between the western Great Lakes and Oregon, while Spain and, later, Mexico controlled the region between Texas and California. The success of the Seminoles together with the escaped slaves who were allied with them in resisting US forces in Florida was hardly exceptional. In the western Great Lakes region, the Ojibwe dominated. The British liberally supported the Ojibwe and other Indigenous nations in the Great

Lakes region. In the event of another war with Britain, the natives were likely to once again be British allies as they had been in the War of 1812.[5] As for the horse-mounted natives of the Great Plains such as the Comanches and the Lakota, the United States in 1836 could not even begin to imagine challenging their control of the grasslands. Likewise, the fear that an invasion by a foreign power on the southwestern border might spur a slave revolt was quite real; by promising freedom, the British had encouraged thousands of enslaved people to join them in fighting against the United States in both the Revolutionary War and the War of 1812. In the first decades of the nineteenth century, numerous slaves fled from Georgia and Louisiana to Florida and New Spain; once in Spanish territory, maroon communities encouraged further flight and, slaveholders feared, rebellion. In short, Adams was entirely correct that in the first decades of the nineteenth century, the United States maintained a relatively weak presence on its borders where it had to contend with powerful, autonomous native groups, fugitive slaves, and competing imperial powers.[6]

Leaders such as Adams who in the first decades of the nineteenth century pondered the weaknesses of the United States in its border regions were in many respects confronting a new problem. Before 1800, the most profitable imperial holdings in the Americas were of two types: sugar plantations in the Caribbean and coastal Brazil; and Spain's silver mines at Potosí in the Andes and the Bajío in Mexico.[7] Almost everywhere else, until the end of the eighteenth century, the British, French, Spanish, and Portuguese empires in continental North and South America were primarily commercial and tributary rather than territorial. European imperial settlements on the American mainland, with the notable exceptions of the Spanish silver mines and a few other places such as Mexico's Central Valley, hugged the coastlines. European empires primarily claimed sovereignty over vast interiors of the Americas based on the reciprocal exchange of gifts and tribute with native leaders and by virtue of commerce in animal products and slaves that European merchants carried on with the Indigenous people of continental interiors. Thus, throughout much of British, French, and Spanish North America, European imperial claims to territory depended on the commercial and diplomatic loyalties of Indigenous people. European military forces occasionally launched punitive expeditions into the interior against natives who resisted these commercial and diplomatic arrangements but rarely managed, or even tried, to establish an enduring military presence.[8] Imperial boundaries, in this scheme, remained only loosely defined.

This system, in which Indigenous people held considerable influence, began to change in the late eighteenth and early nineteenth century, as

European empires shifted away from defining sovereignty in terms of relationships with Indigenous people and toward negotiating imperial boundaries with each other.[9] In 1777, for instance, Spain and Portugal agreed in the first Treaty of San Ildefonso to create a joint boundary commission to survey the border between their South American empires, marginalizing the Indigenous nations who lived in those lands.[10] When the United States and Spain agreed to a border between Georgia and Spanish Florida in 1795, they did not consult with the Seminoles who inhabited the territory. Indigenous people were similarly excluded in 1818, when the United States agreed to a treaty with Britain establishing the northern boundary of the United States and providing for joint Anglo-American occupation of Oregon. They were likewise left out in 1821, when Adams negotiated with Luis de Onís, a Spanish minister, establishing the border between the United States and New Spain at the Sabine River. All these agreements belonged to a larger European-US effort to sideline Indigenous people and negotiate imperial boundaries among themselves. European- and American-made maps reflected the shift in imperial mentalities: in the seventeenth and eighteenth centuries, when imperial claims depended on alliances with Indigenous people, maps of the North American interior abounded with the names of Indigenous nations. By the nineteenth century, similar maps had erased references to Indigenous nations and showed only empty space.[11]

Yet while European powers and the United States could erase Indigenous nations from their maps, they could not so easily dispense with the necessity of dealing with autonomous and powerful Indigenous nations on the outskirts of their territories. In the first decades of the nineteenth century, the old, somewhat unpredictable system of imperial sovereignty contingent upon diplomatic and commercial relations with Indigenous people persisted even as the new territorial system based on diplomacy (and sometimes war) between empires was ascending. For example, when the United States achieved its independence from Britain in 1783, it acquired—on paper at least—an extensive territory between the Appalachians and the Mississippi River. In 1783, however, the borders spelled out in treaties remained less meaningful than commercial and diplomatic relations with Indigenous people. While the British formally ceded the trans-Appalachian region to the United States, they maintained for decades merchant outposts in what was nominally US territory. The US explorer Zebulon Pike encountered one such outpost on the Upper Mississippi River in January 1806: a North West Company trading post. Seeing "the flag of Great Britain" over the post in what was nominally US territory, Pike wrote, "I felt indignant." But there was little he could do to assert US authority.[12] More than just flying their flag in US territory, the British, through their trade, retained the commercial and diplomatic allegiance of Indigenous people in the new US Northwest Territory. When the United States and Britain went to war six years after Pike stumbled across the British trading post, most of the Indigenous people in the Northwest Territory sided with the British. To the south, the Spanish had seized Florida from Britain during the American Revolution; the Florida peninsula almost immediately became a haven for fugitive slaves from the United States. The Spanish, who also controlled New Orleans, periodically inconvenienced American merchants by closing the mouth of the Mississippi River to commercial travel. Between 1803 and 1821, the United States acquired both Florida and New Orleans by treaty. The United States thus removed those territories from the control of an imperial competitor but in so doing took on an extensive territory where it struggled to establish its sovereignty.

Understanding the early nineteenth-century United States as weak relative to Indigenous people, escaped slaves, and imperial competitors contradicts both the popular and the scholarly view of the United States in this period. Most historians of what the historian Arthur M. Schlesinger Jr. once called "the age of Jackson" depict US expansion not only as inexorable but as one of the defining characteristics of the period.[13] According to this view, the United States in the first half of the nineteenth century was like a seething boiler that could barely contain the outward economic and cultural pressures within it: a virulent, racist hatred of Indigenous people; an all-but-insatiable desire for land; a dynamic, profitable, and expanding slave-based plantation system; an explosive market economy; and a self-righteous American missionary Protestantism that saw itself as a reforming beacon to the world. As the following chapters will show, however, all these outward pressures for expansion were more complex and contested than they seem on the surface; they all stumbled in the early nineteenth-century borderlands. By the end of the nineteenth century, of course, the United States had expanded to the Pacific, relegated most Native Americans to reservations, and emerged as a wealthy, imperial power. For historians who view these outcomes as virtual inevitabilities, US ascendancy was foreordained from the beginning of the century. Yet in the first half of the nineteenth century, the United States' place in the borderlands was weaker—and more complicated. US expansion in the first half of the nineteenth century was uneven, contested, and marked by frequent setbacks.

Expansion was not a national consensus. Rather, slaveholders in the US South drove much of the outward movement in the period as they sought more land for the production of agricultural commodities and the incorporation of the free territories on their borders into the system of slavery to eliminate them as places to which slaves might flee. Indeed, slavery loomed over expansion so thoroughly that what American historians rather loosely call "western expansion" should properly be called "southern expansion" between 1803 and 1845. In 1803, the United States initially sought to purchase the Louisiana Territory from France not to gain extensive territory in the trans-Mississippi West but to take possession of New Orleans so that planters in Kentucky, which was rapidly becoming an outpost of slavery, could have an outlet for their commodities.[14] The first three states to join the Union from the Louisiana Territory—and the only three to be admitted from the Louisiana Territory before 1846—were all admitted as slave states: Louisiana in 1812, Missouri in 1821, and Arkansas in 1836. In the decades that followed the Louisiana Purchase, the only territories the United States annexed were all for slavery's expansion: West Florida in 1812, East Florida in 1821, and Texas in 1845.[15] Support for the annexation of Louisiana, the Floridas, and Texas; the admission of Louisiana, Missouri, and Arkansas as states; and for good measure the removal of Indigenous nations such as the Cherokees and Creeks from Georgia and Alabama, came largely from slaveholding interests; the most concerted opposition came from antislavery advocates.

However, many historians have downplayed the partisan and regional nature of expansion in the first half of the nineteenth century in favor of depicting expansion as a national consensus, opposed only by a handful of crabbed elitists such as Adams. They note that Jackson, who made his political reputation during and after the War of 1812 battling Indigenous people, escaped slaves in Florida, and imperial competitors of the United States, won the most popular votes for president in three successive national elections in 1824, 1828, and 1832. Moreover, he won states in both the North and the South.[16] Yet, the expansionism that Jackson advocated was always a politically divisive and contested issue. In 1819, by a vote of 107–100, Jackson only narrowly escaped censure in the House of Representatives for his unauthorized attacks against Spanish outposts and British subjects during an invasion of Spanish Florida the previous year; in 1830, Jackson's Indian Removal Act barely passed the House of Representatives, 101–97; in 1832, an anti-Jackson coalition won a majority of the Senate; and beginning in 1836 and lasting for the next nine years, Adams and his congressional allies successfully deterred Texas annexation. Adams was one of numerous elected leaders—many of them Northeasterners who eventually coalesced into the Whig Party—who advocated strengthening US commerce, manufacturing, and infrastructure within existing US boundaries rather than overstretching US power by sprawling across the continent.[17]

Indeed, Americans were at odds about expansion. As citizens of a federal republic divided over slavery and relations with Indigenous people, Americans engaged in the struggle for sovereignty in the borderlands unevenly. Split over what the nature of the US republic should be—agrarian or market-oriented, slaveholding or emancipationist, pious or free-thinking—Americans often could not agree what the nature of US sovereignty in the borderlands should be, either. Even when US authorities were united in pursuit of specific aims in the borderlands, the United States usually did not have enough power simply to work its will.

To make sense of this confusion, this book makes three interconnected arguments: first, in the first half of the nineteenth century, the US position in the borderlands was *weak* relative to its imperial competitors and Indigenous people; second, because of this weakness, Americans did not impose themselves in the borderlands as much as they improvised through a series of commercial, diplomatic, political, cultural, and scientific *experiments*; and third, these experiments each reflected a *narrative* vision in a multifaceted American culture in which a diversity of competing visions vied for supremacy. In the mid-1840s, one of the most bellicose of those visions—manifest destiny—emerged triumphant, but its victory, like the eventual sweep of US sovereignty across the continent, was not inevitable. Alternative narrative visions for what the United States could be—visions that challenged American racial and economic hierarchies—did not disappear but remained embedded in a diverse American culture, emerging at unexpected moments in the second half of the nineteenth century to buttress the emancipation of slaves and sovereignty for Indigenous people.

WEAKNESS

The borderlands were born of imperial *weakness*. One of the main arguments of this book is that if one is to understand the history of the US borderlands in the first half of the nineteenth century, one must begin, as Adams did in 1836, by acknowledging the limits of US power. That acknowledgment runs counter to an argument that several American historians have advanced in recent years that the US federal government was a powerful force from its inception. These historians have pointed variously to the postal system, the federal courts, and to the federal powers to impose tariffs, regulate commerce, and finance debt as examples of the powers of the nineteenth-century federal state. Such arguments, seeking consistency between the nineteenth and twentieth centuries, tend to have more salience in the second half of the nineteenth century, particularly after the Civil War. In projecting the power of the twentieth-century United States into the first decades of the nineteenth century, these arguments make little concession to historical change; rather, they assert that the United States did not become powerful over the course of the nineteenth century; it was simply born powerful.[18]

Whatever power the federal government possessed dwindled as one moved from the settled East to the southern and western borders of the United States, however. Before 1850, the United States claimed sovereignty over an increasingly immense territory, but it effectively controlled only a small portion of it. In the first half of the nineteenth century, the US borderlands, sweeping in a broad crescent from East Florida to Texas to the Lower Missouri River to the western Great Lakes, and from the Mississippi River west to the Pacific Ocean were, by definition, places where the imperial authority of the United States, as well as that of Britain and Spain, waned. For instance, in the 1820s, though the United States claimed sovereignty over the Great Plains by virtue of the Louisiana Purchase of 1803, it had no real authority there. Americans did not envision settling in the Great Plains; in 1820, the US explorer Stephen Long called the region an uninhabitable "Great American Desert." Fully aware of the weakness of the United States relative to Britain and Spain, Long saw the utility of the Great Plains not as a place of settlement but as a natural obstacle to invasion by imperial competitors. "This region," Long wrote, "may prove of infinite importance to the United States," because it would "secure us against the machinations or incursions of an enemy that might otherwise be disposed to annoy us in that part of our frontier."[19] Just a few years later, in 1823, the American explorer William Keating described the impenetrable marsh west of Lake Superior in similar terms. "The nature of the country is such as affords a more formidable barrier to the invasions of an enemy than any *cordon* of posts that art could devise," Keating wrote.[20]

Americans looked to such natural obstacles to protect their western settlements because the United States could project little military power into the borderlands. Before the War of 1812, the US Army never numbered more than 7,000 men. In most of the years between the end of the War of 1812 and the beginning of the US-Mexico War in 1846, the army consisted of fewer than 10,000 men. In 1845, on the eve of war with Mexico, the US Army had just 7,300 men under arms. By comparison, Belgium, with a population one-fifth that of the United States, maintained an army of 30,000.[21] Americans did not imagine that with their small force they could expand into the borderlands. Rather, the United States focused on protecting its frontier of settlement. Calculating that most of the region in the trans-Mississippi West would remain in the hands of Indigenous people for the foreseeable future, the United States constructed a series of defensive military fortifications on its frontier, extending from Fort Snelling at the juncture of the Mississippi and Minnesota Rivers south to Fort Jessup on the Sabine River. The forts did little to demonstrate US power. In the 1820s and 1830s, US military power on the Upper Mississippi was so feeble that post commanders relied on local natives, the Sauk, to track down and return deserting soldiers.[22] In 1840, the secretary of war, Joel Poinsett, requested from Congress almost $900,000 to repair and extend the then thirty-year-old network of forts, and to increase the number of soldiers stationed at the existing forts and at two new ones he proposed building to 5,000. Had Poinsett's proposals for more troops been approved, it would have been a significant increase over the 1,651 men stationed at the five posts in the southern half of the network of borderlands posts at the time. Yet it would have paled in comparison to the 61,000 Indigenous "warriors" Poinsett estimated lived "within striking distance of the western frontier."[23]

Even when the United States concentrated its forces and took offensive military action in the borderlands, it struggled to establish its authority. When Jackson invaded Spanish Florida in 1818, he destroyed the Seminoles' villages and cornfields; but the Seminoles melted away deeper into the Florida swamps, only to reoccupy their villages once US forces had withdrawn. After touring several Indigenous villages in the Great Plains in 1810, George Sibley, a US Indian agent and contemporary of Jackson, wrote of the futility of such tactics.

> I have heard wise Men, members of Congress, Senators, prescribing "effectual means" for punishing and Subduing the Indians; and their grand *infallible* method was, to Send a Strong cavalry force, to dash into their towns and "burn them with fire," destroy their growing crops, and drive the inhabitants out; Such portion as they could not capture or kill. Such an assault, if properly conducted, would certainly cause much distress to the Indians *for a little while.* The Towns could be easily burned, and their little crops cut down and destroyed. It is highly improbable, however, than any of the Indians would be caught or killed.[24]

When the United States acquired Florida from Spain three years after Jackson's invasion, it was not by conquest but by diplomacy: Adams, as secretary of state, traded US claims to Texas in return for Florida. Fifteen years after that agreement, as Adams noted in his speech to the House in 1836, the Seminoles remained in Florida and continued to resist US authority.

Florida was a borderland where neither Europeans nor the United States could establish sovereignty; in this vacuum, Indigenous people and escaped slaves endured. Elsewhere on the continent, Indigenous nations did more than simply endure; the Comanches, for instance, were the dominant power in the southern Great Plains. The Creeks on the South Atlantic coastal plain, the Osages in the Lower Missouri region, the Ojibwe to the west of the Great Lakes, the Lakota in the northern Great Plains, and the Navajo in New Mexico exercised a similar dominance over those regions. Borderlands emerged not only between European and US empires but between Indigenous polities and colonial empires as well.[25]

The perspective of this book is from those borderlands—the peripheral, unintended creations of empires where imperial authority waned. One of the central arguments of this book is that precisely because imperial authority in the borderlands was weak, early nineteenth-century borderlands empowered the marginalized.[26] In the borderlands, Indigenous people and escaped slaves possessed agency: the ability to effect historical change. In recent years, some historians have critiqued the idea of agency for overestimating the ability of slaves to resist an institution designed to deny them their self-determination or for Indigenous people to resist settler colonialism.[27] Those critiques, this book argues, have overstated the power of the United States in the borderlands. The borderlands were places where slaves could self-emancipate and defy slavery's denial of their humanity and where Indigenous people possessed autonomy. Such freedom and autonomy threatened white, landed Americans. White Americans near borderland regions were uneasy about powerful and autonomous Indigenous societies; slaveholders could not abide free territories on the borders that beckoned to slaves to escape to freedom. Ironically, though advocates for US territorial expansion typically depicted the United States as the surpassing power in North America, the primary US motive for expansion was often to clear the borderlands of autonomous Indigenous nations and self-emancipated former slaves whose very presence exposed the reality of US weaknesses.

One of the most important developments in the first half of the nineteenth century, and one that is particularly important to this study, is how American society and culture became progressively and often violently racialized. In the US South, proslavery advocates increasingly justified the institution of slavery in terms of the alleged racial inferiority of the enslaved; in the

North, native-born Americans articulated a white identity so exclusive that it counted out some European immigrants such as the Irish.[28] Expansionists, especially proslavery white southerners who advocated the annexation of the Floridas and Texas, sought to extend US rule to the borderlands where, they imagined, they could eradicate Indigenous people and expand the institution of slavery. Yet, because the borderlands empowered non-white peoples, such visions for the borderlands were far easier to imagine than to actualize. What expansionists imagined they could do in the borderlands and what they could actually do were very different things. Racism is an expression and structuring of white privilege and power; because US power atrophied as it reached the borderlands, racialization in the borderlands was incomplete: the close association between a racial hierarchy and white political and economic power that characterized the settled parts of the United States—where whites dominated politically, militarily, economically, and demographically—did not prevail in the borderlands. Instead, in the borderlands, as the following chapters explore, Indigenous outcasts and escaped slaves found asylum in Florida in a space that neither the Spanish nor the Americans controlled; the United States created a space at a trading post on the Missouri River where, through subsidized trade, they sought the good will of local Indigenous people; American physicians on the Upper Missouri, in the Great Lakes region, and elsewhere set up temporary spaces where they administered life-saving vaccine to Indigenous people; an American antislavery advocate sought to create a space in Mexico that would be a refuge for free Blacks; and Presbyterian missionaries on the Minnesota River created a space where both they and their Indigenous converts could keep secular American society at a distance. Such experimental spaces could exist in the borderlands where emerging American racial hierarchies did not hold full sway.

Indeed, in the borderlands, non-whites could sometimes transcend American racial hierarchies. In borderlands Florida, for instance, John Horse, a Black Seminole slave, emerged as one of the Seminoles' military leaders in their conflicts with the United States in the 1830s. He surrendered to the United States in 1838, but only in return for acknowledgment of his status as a free Black—a remarkable instance, prior to the Civil War, of an African American securing freedom through violence against the state. Following his surrender, he acquiesced to removal to the Indian Territory but returned briefly to Florida in 1839 when the United States proved unable to complete the conquest of the remaining Seminole belligerents and needed the assistance of Seminole military auxiliaries. In 1850, concerned that the persistence of slavery in the Indian Territory threatened the status he had won as a free

Black, he removed, at the invitation of Mexico, across the Rio Grande to Coahuila to become, as Juan Caballo, one of the leaders of a colony of Indigenous and Black Seminoles. He became a captain in the Mexican Army whose writ included defending Mexico against Indigenous and white incursions from Texas.[29] The borderlands, in short, empowered Horse; in regions where sovereignty was contested, he could play competitors off against each other to defy racial hierarchies.

Some of the chapters in this book demonstrate similar complexities of race in the borderlands, where some white Americans were partly absorbed into Indigenous societies or into one of the imperial competitors of the United States and sought to advance the prospects of free Black or Indigenous people. One chapter demonstrates how fugitive slaves in Spanish Florida became allies of the Seminoles, and having acquired arms from Britain during the War of 1812, posed such a challenge to US pretensions on its southern border that the United States made repeated incursions into Florida to try to quell the perceived threat. A chapter that follows investigates a white abolitionist who in the 1830s made a pact with the Mexican government to establish a colony of freed slaves in northern Mexico. While the colony failed, the abolitionist helped to stymie the admission of Texas to the Union for several years. Another chapter analyzes a cadre of Presbyterian missionaries to the Dakota in the 1830s and 1840s who steeped themselves in the language and culture of the natives and sought not to assimilate the Dakota into white culture but to protect Dakota cultural autonomy. In the short term, each of these experiments fell short of success. Both the US state and American racial hierarchies were incompletely realized in the borderlands, but they were not powerless, either. Yet none of these experiments was an utter failure. As the conclusion will show, these experiments bore fruit later in the nineteenth century in unexpected ways, as slaves engineered their own freedom during the Civil War and as Indigenous people transformed reservations meant to be prisons into cultural homelands.[30]

While the United States remained too weak to extend much power into borderland regions for much of the first half of the nineteenth century, it nevertheless strived to do so. Indeed, borderland expansion was, for some Americans, a cultural and political imperative. Even Adams, as secretary of state between 1817 and 1825, sought to extend US territory and influence. Too often, however, historians have mistaken expansionists' strident proclamations of their intentions as evidence of what actually happened.[31] Such proclamations are better understood as aspirational. For instance, as national political parties struggled in the 1820s and 1830s to emerge from a confused and competing array of state and regional parties, they looked to the borderlands to find a unifying national political identity. Beginning in 1828, the major parties nominated for national office a series of officers from the War of 1812 who had made their reputations fighting Indigenous people. Andrew Jackson was the Democratic Party nominee for president in 1828 and 1832; Richard Mentor Johnson (who claimed to have killed the Shawnee war leader Tecumseh at the 1813 Battle of the Thames) was the Democratic nominee for vice president in 1836; and William Henry Harrison (the US commander at the Battle of Tippecanoe in 1811 and at the Thames in 1813) was the Whig Party nominee for president in 1840. The actual military records of these officers in their conflicts against Indigenous people were mixed, but as in other emerging nation-states in the nineteenth century, the projection of military and political power into borderlands was a source of nationalist identity in the United States—even though US sovereignty in the border- lands was more aspirational than actual.[32]

That aspirational version of US national identity was explicitly racial; some historians have aptly described the United States in the first half of the nineteenth century as a "Herrenvolk democracy": democratic and egalitarian for white men and oppressive for all others.[33] As the United States haltingly extended its power into the borderlands over the course of the century, it brought with it this racialized thinking, but because imperial power in the borderlands was limited and contested, it did so in complex and oblique ways. Racial identities in the borderlands, where cultural borrowing, inter- racial marriage, and adoption were common, were complex and malleable. For Indigenous nations, adoption and intermarriage were strategies to draw whites into their societies to bolster their strength to resist conquest.[34] Adop- tion and intermarriage meant that conflict in the early nineteenth-century borderlands was complex; it can rarely be described accurately as simply a clash between whites and Indigenous people, or between whites and fugitive slaves. For instance, on the US side of the Florida border in the late eighteenth and early nineteenth century, several notable Creek leaders such as Alexander McGillivray, William McIntosh, Peter McQueen, and William Weatherford, were the sons of white fathers and Creek mothers. In 1813, McIntosh and other Creeks fought alongside Jackson, the Tennessee militia, and Cherokees against another Creek faction that included Weatherford and McQueen. As Americans pressed into the borderlands, some Indigenous groups adopted American racial categories: McGillivray, McIntosh, and Weatherford were slaveholders; and Creeks recaptured fugitive slaves for white slaveholders in Georgia. Jackson and other white slaveholders had cordial relations with

Creek slaveholders, with whom they were allied against Seminoles who harbored fugitive slaves.[35]

That white slaveholders relied on Creeks to help them police slaves, and that the United States relied on some Indigenous people (Cherokees and McIntosh's Creek faction) to help them fight other Indigenous people (Seminoles and Weatherford and McQueen's Creek faction) points to the limits of the power of both the United States and white Americans in the borderlands. Throughout the borderlands, the United States needed Indigenous allies because it was too weak to assert its authority in the borderlands without them.[36] So, ironically, in conflicts with Indigenous people, white Americans often used racist and eliminationist language against their foes, and yet they relied on Indigenous allies in those conflicts. Often, once the United States had defeated Indigenous enemies, it abandoned eliminationist rhetoric and tried to convert former enemies into allies. During a war against the Seminoles in the 1830s, Americans collected Seminole skulls and shipped them to phrenologists so those pseudo-scientists could expound upon the presumed racial inferiority of Indigenous people.[37] Yet at the same time, the United States made headway in the conflict only by employing as military auxiliaries and diplomatic intermediaries Seminoles such as John Horse and officers such as David Moniac, a Creek nephew of Weatherford who graduated from West Point in 1822. In short, as the United States gradually pushed into the borderlands, it brought with it American racial hierarchies and the precepts of Herrenvolk democracy; yet in the borderlands, manifest US weaknesses undercut that ideology.

EXPERIMENTS

Violence such as the US wars against the Seminoles punctuated the history of the early nineteenth-century borderlands. The United States also conducted a series of campaigns in the Northwest Territory in the early 1790s; battled the Shawnees, Creeks, and other native groups during the War of 1812; and fought with the Sauk and Meskwaki in 1832, among other conflicts.[38] These campaigns demonstrated, if nothing else, the determination of many Americans to extend US sovereignty into the borderlands. Yet in most instances, despite the rise of political leaders such as Jackson and Harrison who had made their reputations battling Indigenous people, the United States did not possess enough strength simply to impose its will in the borderlands. At no point before the US-Mexico War did the United States exercise effective control over even half of the territory that it claimed. In most cases, the United

States relied on diplomatic overtures toward borderlands Indigenous people. The balance of power in the borderlands was thus markedly different from, for instance, that of the southern states of Georgia, Alabama, Mississippi, and Tennessee in the early 1830s. Those areas had been borderlands in the seventeenth and eighteenth centuries, but by the 1830s, white settlers and the US Army combined to remove the Cherokees, Choctaws, Creek, and Chickasaws to the Indian Territory.[39]

While by the 1830s the United States could coerce Indigenous people in areas where whites dominated politically and demographically, in the borderlands it was another matter. In the borderlands, the United States often had to improvise. One of the following chapters investigates a federally subsidized trading post in western Missouri in the 1810s that sought to attach the commercial loyalties of local natives, the Osages, to the United States. Another tells of the extensive US medical diplomacy in the 1830s to vaccinate Indigenous people against smallpox. The imperial competitors of the United States—Spain and Britain—also subsidized trade and offered the smallpox vaccine to Indigenous people. Like the United States, they understood that so long as no empire was powerful enough to take command of disputed borderlands, empires held sway there not by eliminating or removing Indigenous people but by winning their allegiance.

The US borderlands in the first half of the nineteenth century, in other words, were the sites of numerous projects. In the interstices between empires, Indigenous people and escaped slaves adapted and improvised: they played competing empires against each other, bolstered their populations by adopting Black, white, and Indigenous outsiders, and formed alliances to check US power. Some American projects, such as the attempt to create a colony of ex-slaves in Mexico, or the evangelization of Indigenous people, arose when missionaries or reformers took advantage of the absence of US authority to pursue their own visions. Others happened as US government officials sought creative means, such as subsidized trade or medical diplomacy, to win the good will of Indigenous people or to assert the influence of the United States in regions where military control eluded them. In any case, another central argument in this book is that one of the important characteristics of borderland regions is that they were (and are) sites of *experimentation*.[40]

Borderlands projects were diverse because, as social and cultural historians have shown over the past five decades, American society in the first half of the nineteenth century was richly complex, contradictory, and rapidly changing. In the first fifty years of the nineteenth century, the US economy transformed, shucking off the century-old apprentice system of production to develop a manufacturing sector and shifting, though incompletely, from subsistence-oriented to commercial agriculture. Along the way, Americans developed not only canals, railroads, and cities but also industrial pollution, labor unions, and new laws hostile to those unions and friendly to manufacturers. Greasing the wheels of this new business activity, a thriving cottage industry in counterfeit currency arose. The number of slaves quadruped in the first half of the nineteenth century, while the number of free Blacks rose by a factor of eight. Free Blacks created a determined abolitionist movement and shuttled thousands of fugitive slaves to freedom. White Americans uprooted themselves and scattered across the country; by 1850, roughly one-quarter of native-born white Americans lived outside of the state of their birth. Hundreds of thousands of immigrants poured into the United States, many of them Catholics from Ireland and Germany, making Catholicism the largest denomination in the United States by 1850 and prompting a burgeoning nativist movement. A Protestant religious revival swept through the United States, spinning off a dizzying number of social movements, including temperance, Sabbatarianism, vegetarianism, and abolitionism. Americans revolutionized family life in the first part of the nineteenth century: the size of families dropped precipitously; middle-class women found themselves shunted into a cloying and straitened sphere of household duties and child-rearing; children experienced the innovations of birthday parties, Christmas gift-giving, and Sunday schools. More than 100 utopian communities—variously embracing philosophies of socialism, transcendentalism, celibacy, experimental open marriages, and millennialism—arose between the Revolution and the Civil War. An erupting print culture buoyed these new cultural trends, not least a highly partisan participatory politics that exploded in the first half of the nineteenth century. Political parties—the Whigs, the Free Soil Party, the Liberty Party, the Anti-Masonic Party—arose and collapsed rapidly while women and African Americans clamored for inclusion in the body politic.[41] Forays into the borderlands—US efforts to impose sovereignty, diplomatic and commercial experiments to win the good will of Indigenous people, and private missions by Americans—reflected all these dense complexities of nineteenth-century American society and culture.

The chapters that follow connect some of these complexities of American culture and society to the borderlands. The US government agent who managed trade with the Osages near the juncture of the Missouri and Kansas Rivers in the 1810s was torn between condemning the market and hoping to become wealthy himself through commerce. The abolitionist who attempted to establish a colony of freed slaves in Mexico in 1835 reflected the incongruities of the antislavery movement: while calling for the end of slavery he applauded the idea of removing all people of African descent from the United States and thus creating an all-white republic. The Presbyterian missionaries who evangelized the Dakota in Minnesota in the 1830s were both critics of American society—they thought it was beyond redemption—and, somewhat unwittingly, products of the reformist bent of American culture. In short, white Americans brought the complexities of early nineteenth-century American culture and society with them when they came to the borderlands.

NARRATIVES

The observation that American expansion into the borderlands reflected the complexities of US society might seem obvious, but historical accounts of US expansion rarely reckon with the richness of American social, cultural, or political history. Most histories of territorial expansion maintain a kind of fiction that whatever the complexity of American culture and society in the first half of the nineteenth century, when it came to the borderlands, Americans put those complications aside and found common ground in a dedication to conquest and expansion.[42] That fiction has a name: "manifest destiny."

In 1845, a partisan Democrat and newspaper editor, John L. O'Sullivan, wrote that it was "our manifest destiny to overspread the continent allotted by Providence for the free development of our yearly multiplying millions."[43] O'Sullivan did not invent the term "manifest destiny" himself: he appropriated it from an earlier article by one of his journal's staff writers, Jane McManus Storm Cazneau.[44] Few terms in American history resonate as forcefully as "manifest destiny," and few are as nebulous. For generations, American historians have invoked the phrase to explain the transformation of the United States from a moderately-sized republic at the outset of the nineteenth century to a continental empire by the end of the century. In 2012, the historian Amy Greenberg summarized the explanatory power that many historians believe manifest destiny possesses:

> The long process of American territorial expansion was both facilitated and justified by the mid-nineteenth-century ideology (or national vision) known as Manifest Destiny. In the 1840s, Manifest Destiny accelerated western settlement and provided a rationale for continued continental expansion. It cast western expansion as natural and predetermined and legitimated a policy of brutal, racially based warfare against both Indians and Mexicans. Starting in the late 1830s,

American politicians asserted, and many citizens believed, that God had divinely ordained the United States to grow and spread across the continent. The course of American empire, supporters insisted, was both obvious (manifest) and inexorable (destined).[45]

Greenberg, like many historians who have invoked manifest destiny to explain US expansion, immediately qualified this generalization, writing, "Not everyone believed that the United States had a manifest destiny, of course, but by the 1840s the majority of Americans seemed to agree that the growth of their nation to the Pacific Ocean was natural and inevitable."[46] Indeed, most historians who have invoked the notion of manifest destiny to explain US expansion have been vague about who believed in the idea and how such believers turned the idea into action. The reason for such vagueness is that it is not at all clear that a majority of Americans supported manifest destiny. In the 1830s and 1840s, the removal of Indigenous people and the annexation of Texas were highly divisive and closely contested issues that only narrowly passed Congress. The expansionist James K. Polk, who engineered the annexation of Oregon and war with Mexico in 1846, won the presidency in 1844 only because a third-party candidate of the antislavery Liberty Party, who received only 2.3 percent of the vote nationally, drew a few thousand votes away from Polk's main opponent, Henry Clay, in New York, tipping that state's electors, and thus the Electoral College, to Polk.

Understood in its original context, O'Sullivan's notion of manifest destiny was no more of a consensus that Polk's election was a landslide; instead, O'Sullivan's manifest destiny article was a partisan screed written in a divided political moment. The issue that consumed political leaders' attention in 1845 was the same one that had consumed them when Adams made his hour-long speech to the House in 1836: the annexation of Texas. In 1845, the issue remained as divisive as it had been nine years earlier. The Senate had rejected an annexation treaty with Texas in June 1844. However, nine months later, in February 1845, Congress reversed itself and narrowly passed a joint resolution for annexation. The vote in the Senate was as close as it could possibly be: 27–25. Acting on this slim majority, President John Tyler offered annexation to Texas in early March. O'Sullivan wrote his manifest destiny editorial while the United States was awaiting a reply from the Republic of Texas to its offer. Despite his grandiose rhetoric, O'Sullivan plainly feared that—as the joint resolution had passed the Senate in February by only the slimmest of margins—continuing divisions within the United States over the wisdom of the annexation of Texas might scuttle the project. For its part, Texas might have resolved to remain independent. In the 1840s, thousands of Americans who had migrated west to California, Oregon, and Utah took concrete steps toward following the example of the Texians to form independent republics.[47] In other words, the US potential to overspread the continent was not providentially destined but rather, given the divided politics of the 1840s and the tenuous attachment of American settlers in the West to US citizenship, quite uncertain. O'Sullivan's sweeping hyperbole, with its declaration of the inevitability of US dominance over much of North America, was not a distillation of an American consensus but a fustian effort to overawe uncertainties and resistance to annexation. "It is now time for the opposition to the Annexation of Texas to cease," O'Sullivan wrote. "In regard to Texas, enough has now been given to party. It is time for the common duty of Patriotism to the Country to succeed."[48] Like Jackson, Polk, and other advocates for empire, O'Sullivan understood that territorial expansion required bullying not only the United States' neighbors but also the domestic opponents of empire.

Eventually, historians took manifest destiny out of O'Sullivan's originally limited and quite partisan context and promoted it to a consensus among mid-nineteenth-century Americans—though it took nearly a half-century for that to happen. As a result, O'Sullivan now enjoys a currency in modern American history textbooks that eluded him during his lifetime. He died in 1895, having faded into irrelevance after 1845. He lost control of his journal, the *Democratic Review*, within a year of his manifest destiny editorial; he later became a filibuster in Cuba, a propagandist for the Confederacy, and a spiritualist who claimed to be able to communicate with the dead.[49] For most of the second half of the nineteenth century, US history textbooks had little to say about territorial expansion and even less to say about O'Sullivan or "manifest destiny." When historians discussed territorial expansion, they treated it not as providential destiny but as a matter of political contestation. In his 1856 text, *American History*, for instance, Marcius Willson described the US-Mexico War as "opposed as impolitic and unjust by one portion of the American people, and . . . cordially approved by the other." William Swinton's 1872 *First Lessons in Our Country's History* argued that Mexico's abolition of slavery made it "an easy place of refuge for fugitive slaves" and thus contributed to the outbreak of war; he did not mention manifest destiny. Edward Ellis's 1896 schoolbook, *Epochs in American History*, virtually ignored US territorial expansion; the only subjects Ellis included between the ratification of the Constitution and the onset of the Civil War were the inventions of the cotton gin, steamboat, and telegraph. Like Willson and Swinton, Ellis did not mention manifest destiny.[50]

The term "manifest destiny" survived in American public discourse in the second half of the nineteenth century, but there was little consensus about its meaning. When journalists and public intellectuals used the term—and they did so relatively infrequently—they employed it as often to condemn empire as to endorse it. In the 1880s and 1890s, editorialists who opposed the US secretary of state James G. Blaine's interventionist policies in Latin America, for instance, used "manifest destiny" as a term of opprobrium to critique policies they predicted would involve the United States in costly and fruitless wars. There was little sense that the United States alone possessed a manifest destiny: editorialists critiqued imperial expansion by Britain, Russia, the Ottomans, and Japan by labelling it as those nations' "manifest destiny." The term was so plastic and versatile that pundits wrote of Chicago's "manifest destiny" to rebuild following a fire that destroyed much of the city center in 1871; New York City's "manifest destiny" to build a bridge across the East River; and the Republican Party's "manifest destiny" to endorse the prohibition of alcohol.[51]

It was not until the late 1890s, after the surprisingly rapid consolidation of large parts of western North America into the United States and at a time when the United States was asserting its power in the Caribbean, the Pacific, and elsewhere—in short, at a time when the United States was emerging as a global empire—that historians embraced O'Sullivan's idea that the United States had always been destined to dominate North America and anointed manifest destiny with its aura of consensus. The late nineteenth-century historian Theodore Roosevelt was instrumental in this reinterpretation of the past. In his popular four-volume work, *The Winning of the West*, published between 1889 and 1896, he cast the emergence of an overseas US empire in the 1890s as the inevitable outcome of the progressive extension of US sovereignty into the borderlands that he dated to the founding of the American republic. He did not employ the term "manifest destiny," but he came close: "The winning of Louisiana," he wrote, for example, "followed inevitably upon the great westward thrust of the settler-folk; a thrust which was delivered blindly, but which no rival race could parry, until it was stopped by the ocean itself."[52] Like other historians of his era who shared his belief in white supremacy, such as Woodrow Wilson and William Dunning, Roosevelt saw the emergence of US overseas empire as an unbroken (and wholly justified) continuation of the US defeat of Mexico and subjugation of Indigenous people.

In 1900, he wrote a new foreword to *The Winning of the West* that unapologetically connected earlier American conquests to the recently concluded Spanish-American War. "The backwoodsmen had pushed the Spaniards from the Mississippi, had set up a slave-holding republic in Texas, and had conquered the California gold-fields, in the sheer masterful exercise of might," he wrote. "In the year 1898 the United States finished the work begun over a century before by the backwoodsman, and drove the Spaniard outright from the western world."[53] Frederick Jackson Turner's well-known 1893 essay, "The Significance of the Frontier in American History," was less overtly racist and less celebratory about empire than Roosevelt's work, but Turner subscribed to the same teleology: in the contest for sovereignty in North America, the United States was destined to prevail. For Turner, the "Great West" was "free land" (no Indigenous people or competing empires offered any resistance worth dwelling upon) that was in "continuous recession" under the pressure of American settlers.[54] In effect, Roosevelt and Turner reinvented the history of the North American borderlands. When they looked at the United States in the first decades of the nineteenth century, they did not see a state hemmed in by relatively powerful Indigenous nations and imperial competitors but the continent's dominant power, the expansion of which was a foregone conclusion.

The concept of manifest destiny smoothed this reinvention of the past. In the first decades of the twentieth century, as Roosevelt and Turner's notion that US empire was foreordained became orthodoxy among professional historians, scholars began to argue routinely that most nineteenth-century Americans had always shared the belief that it was the manifest destiny of the United States to expand its territory.[55] By that time, historians had forgotten whence the term had come; it was not until 1927 that a University of Buffalo historian, Julius Pratt, identified O'Sullivan and his 1845 editorial as the popularizer of the term.[56] Somewhere along the way, historians began to capitalize "Manifest Destiny": a sure sign that the term had become, like the "Great Awakening" or the "Progressive Era," a way for historians to paper over a paradigm's inconsistencies and explanatory inadequacies to lend a facile sense of coherence to a complex history.[57]

Since then, many Americans historians have succumbed to the temptation to pronounce O'Sullivan a true prophet of US expansion (usually ignoring his other prognostications from his 1845 editorial, such as his prediction that the United States would annex Canada, and that California would, like Texas, achieve its independence from Mexico before being annexed to the

United States around the year 1945). By contrast, historians have relegated Adams's 1836 address to the House of Representatives, with his warnings about the limits of US power, to the margins. In fact, neither Adams nor O'Sullivan was wholly correct: Mexico did not invade the United States allied with Indigenous people and spark a slave rebellion, as Adams feared, nor did the United States annex Canada, as O'Sullivan predicted. The way to understand North American borderlands in the first half of the nineteenth century lies somewhere in between: the United States was stronger and more determined to expand than Adams imagined, but it struggled to impose its will in the borderlands and frequently resorted to diplomatic suasion and various experiments; the desire for expansion that O'Sullivan articulated was quite real, but desires butted up against US weaknesses and the realities in the borderlands; expansion was not a consensus but rather a hotly contested issue; even those who favored expansion could not agree about where, how, or when it should happen.

O'Sullivan did not articulate an American consensus on expansion; rather, he offered a prospective *narrative* for the US borderlands. In the diverse and complex society and culture of the United States in the first half of the nineteenth century, when both government officials and private citizens pursued a variety of experimental projects in the borderlands, his was just one of many borderlands narratives. This book relates some of those competing visions, long obscured by historians' overweening attention to manifest destiny. O'Sullivan's is now the most well-known narrative, but in the first half of the nineteenth century, competing narratives abounded. These narratives variously predicted that a slave revolt, a smallpox epidemic, or a military defeat at the hands of Indigenous people would emerge from the borderlands.[58] Still other narratives posited that Americans would move west and establish independent polities; that if the United States and Mexico went to war, Mexico would both ally with Indigenous people and foment a destructive slave rebellion; that emancipated slaves would establish a refuge in the borderlands; that Christianized Indigenous people would establish autonomous polities; that Americans would introduce camels to North American deserts and adapt Arabic customs. In the first half of the nineteenth century, many of these narratives seemed more plausible to many Americans than manifest destiny.[59]

To find such narratives, we must look beyond O'Sullivan. His views have too long dominated our understanding of the borderlands in the first half of the nineteenth century. Records such as runaway slave advertisements or the writings of Indian agents or missionaries were—unintentionally—narratives, no less so because they were written by white Americans typically unsympathetic to slaves or Indigenous people. By placing these texts in historical, ethnographic, and sometimes environmental context, we can try to discern the perspectives of Indigenous people and slaves who left relatively few written records of their own.

Drawing on such sources, this book thus challenges the notion, embodied in the concept of manifest destiny, that the territorial expansion of the United States was an American consensus and an inevitability executed by the continent's greatest power. Throughout the borderlands, the United States had to accommodate itself to the presence of powerful Indigenous societies and other imperial competitors. American weaknesses and fears in the region encouraged the federal government to experiment, win alliances and reach accommodations with Indigenous people, and adapt to the environment. The imperial power vacuum in the borderlands opened the way for private citizens to put their alternative ideas for American society into practice. Rather than a place where the United States realized a purportedly inevitable destiny to overspread the continent, the North American borderlands were sites of experimentation. Such experimentation existed precisely because US sovereignty in the region was tenuous: the United States could rarely impose its will; this created a space where improvisation reigned.

Rather than focus on a handful of privileged voices in the eastern United States such as Jackson and O'Sullivan, this book surveys Indigenous people, free Blacks, missionaries, and reformers across a broad swath of the borderlands. In so doing, the book defines the first half of the nineteenth century as the age of the borderlands, when an ambitious yet relatively weak US state sought to expand into its borderlands—only to encounter there its own weaknesses. Early nineteenth-century borderlands such as East Florida in the 1810s or the Upper Great Lakes in the 1830s were places where US authority waned; they were thus places that empowered Indigenous people and escaped slaves. In the borderlands, Indigenous groups maintained their autonomy and fugitive slaves found refuge. American critics of the market-oriented, expansionist, slaveholding society in the United States saw the tenuousness of US power in the borderlands as attractive; they saw the borderlands as a grand laboratory where, free from the constraints of the dominant culture or under the protection of Indigenous nations or one of the United States' imperial competitors such as Mexico, they could experiment with their particular visions for society. Those experiments included vaccinating Indigenous people against smallpox and helping them to establish autonomous enclaves or resettling freed slaves in the borderlands. In

short, in the first part of the nineteenth century, borderlands were characterized not merely by US ambitions for expansion but by experimentation,
political accommodation, cultural malleability, and the empowerment of
Indians and slaves.

CHAPTER ONE

Maroons

On the night of May 18, 1789, under a waning moon, two teenaged slaves, Patty and Daniel, took flight from Bewlie, a plantation near Savannah, Georgia. Daniel was just fifteen years old. Patty was nineteen; as she fled, she carried in her arms her nine-month-old son, Abram. Peter Henry Morel, the slaveholder who called Patty, Daniel, and Abram his property, described Patty in the runaway slave advertisement he placed in the *Georgia Gazette* as "a young likely wench" and Daniel as "a young lad . . . of a yellowish cast." Peter Morel and his older brother, John, shifted their hundreds of slaves among Bewlie and several nearby Morel properties seasonally: planting rice and cotton on mainland plantations in the early spring, moving to Ossabow Island on the Atlantic coast to cut and process indigo in the late spring, returning to the mainland in the fall to harvest rice and cotton, and going to the coast in late fall to cut timber. At some point during their movements between Morel properties, Patty and Daniel had encountered Titus, an older slave belonging to John Morel. Titus, according to Peter Morel, "enticed [them] away." Peter Morel placed an advertisement offering a reward of twenty dollars in silver for the fugitives only two days after they had fled, yet he despaired that the slaves had "gone to Florida," at the time a Spanish territory fewer than ten days' travel to the south. In 1789, Georgia was a border state, and Morel knew as well as Patty and Daniel that with a few days' head start and a bit of luck, a determined flight might result in freedom.[1]

In fleeing south to Spanish Florida, Patty and Daniel followed the path of thousands of escaped slaves. Yet fugitives to Florida have received relatively little attention from American historians, most of whom have centered their studies on fugitives who fled to northern states and Canada.[2] In the first decades after the American Revolution, however, those who fled to Florida may well have outnumbered those who fled to the north. Indeed, by the late eighteenth century, fugitives dominated Florida both numerically and politically. These fugitives included not only African slaves but Native Americans who had broken away from the powerful Creek confederacy. Black fugitives who reached Florida typically formed communities that allied themselves with fugitive Indigenous people.

Indigenous and Black fugitives joined together in Florida to find refuge from the slavery, captive-taking, and slave trading that were overriding features of the South Atlantic coastal plain in the eighteenth and early nineteenth century. The most powerful sovereignties in the region, the Spanish, English, and Creek—two European colonial powers and the region's most powerful Indigenous confederation—enslaved both Africans and Indigenous people alike. Yet enslaved people such as Patty and Daniel could escape bondage if they could flee to the Florida borderland between Spanish, English, and Creek control. Those three polities shared versions of a derogatory term for such fugitives. The Spanish called them *cimarrónes*, a word that likely derived from *símara*, meaning "wild" or "gone astray" among the Taino natives of the Greater Antilles. The English borrowed the word as "maroons." The Creek called both Black and Indigenous refugees in Florida *Seminoles*—a word they also borrowed from cimarrónes.[3]

Marronage—the act of fleeing slavery—dominated the Florida borderlands, but it was not unique to that region. Indeed, it was found everywhere in the Americas where slavery abutted borderlands. Beginning in the sixteenth century and continuing until the nineteenth, slaves fled to borderlands in Spanish America, the French and British Caribbean, and the Guianas, where they created rebel communities that were enduring thorns in the sides of slaveholding empires. In sixteenth- and seventeenth-century Hispaniola, Panama, and New Spain, African slaves who had fled to form their own communities forced the Spanish to concede to them their freedom. Rebellious maroon communities in the bayous of eighteenth-century Louisiana were a persistent threat to the French system of slavery. In eighteenth-century Jamaica, maroons battled British forces to a standstill, forcing the British to acknowledge their autonomy. While marronage was a form of resistance to slavery, few—least of all the maroons themselves—imagined that it would lead to universal emancipation. Indeed, maroons sometimes won acknowledgment of their autonomy from slaveholders by agreeing to act as slave-catchers for other fugitives.[4]

If the status of maroons in Florida was uncertain, so too was imperial dominion over Florida. Florida was nominally a European colonial possession—changing hands from Spain to Britain in 1763, then back to Spain in 1783, then to the United States in 1821. The Creeks, whose primary territory straddled present-day Georgia and Alabama, episodically claimed Florida as theirs as well. Yet by the beginning of the nineteenth century, Indigenous and Black Seminoles were the true rulers of East Florida. In 1818, even before it took possession of Florida from Spain by treaty, the United States together with hundreds of Creek allies invaded Florida in a vain attempt to destroy it as a site of Indigenous autonomy and magnet for fugitive slaves. For generations, American historians have maintained that the invasion compelled Spain to cede Florida to the United States a few years later.[5] While Spain indeed transferred Florida to the United States by treaty in 1821, the invasion had little to do with the cession. In military terms, the invasion accomplished nothing: Black and Indigenous Seminoles withdrew before the invaders and disappeared into Florida's canebrakes and swampy interior. Indeed, they remained in Florida until the 1850s, defying repeated US efforts to assert its sovereignty. For its part, Spain was glad to be rid of Florida: the Spanish had tried to trade Florida to Britain for Gibraltar in 1720; they offered it again to Britain for Gibraltar in 1783. The Spanish were only too happy for the United States to take Florida off their hands in 1821 in exchange for US recognition of Spanish sovereignty in the far more valuable territory of Texas.[6]

In acquiring Florida, the United States took on a territory dominated by maroons: self-exiled Indigenous people and self-emancipated people of African descent. We do not know if Patty, Daniel, and the baby Abram were among the maroons in Florida at the time the United States took possession of the province more than thirty years after their flight from Bewlie. Whether they made it to Florida or not, however, their flight, and in a larger sense, marronage itself, was an act of resistance to slavery.

INDIGENOUS OUTCASTS AND ESCAPED SLAVES

Spain established a settlement in Florida, at St. Augustine, in 1565, more than a century before slaveholding English planters from Barbados settled the Province of Carolina, about 275 miles north of St. Augustine, in 1670. In 1687, the first group of fugitive slaves from Carolina reached St. Augustine, and groups of escapees continued to arrive in almost every succeeding year. Although Spanish colonists held slaves throughout their empire, Spanish slavery in many parts of the Americas was less onerous than enslavement on a plantation in an English colony and provided a more accessible path to freedom.[7] Late seventeenth- and eighteenth-century Spanish law protected slaves in ways that Anglo-American law did not. In 1784, for instance, two white men attacked a Florida slave named Frank by setting a dog on him and beating him. Within a month, Spanish officials brought the men before a judge and charged them with assault and battery.[8] By contrast, in the mainland North American British colonies and, later, in the United States, while courts occasionally indicted whites for assaulting slaves whom they did not own, legal repercussions for assaulting a slave were rare.[9] A South Carolina physician who visited Florida in the early nineteenth century noted the difference, remarking upon the Spaniards' "indulgent treatment of their slaves, by which the Spaniards are so honourably distinguished, and the ample and humane code of laws which they have enacted, and also enforce, for the protection of the blacks, both bond and free."[10]

In Florida, Spanish authorities eventually adopted a policy of freeing Carolina escapees and enlisting them in the St. Augustine militia. The policy did not emanate from Madrid; it was a local initiative that Spanish officials in Florida developed to protect and extend their border with the Carolinas.[11] By the 1720s, ex-slaves who had become soldiers in the Spanish militia regularly raided South Carolina (North and South Carolina had officially divided in 1712). British authorities colonized Georgia in 1732 in large part to create a buffer to protect South Carolina from attack and to deter further fugitives.[12] Initially, Georgia disallowed slavery because it was too easy for slaves to slip away to Florida; but eventually slaveholding planters from South Carolina, including the Morels, expanded across the Savannah River into the northeastern part of Georgia. For their part, English settlers in the Carolinas and Georgia, usually accompanied by Indigenous allies such as the Creeks, raided Florida in return, with the explicit purpose of recapturing fugitive slaves and capturing and enslaving Indigenous people.[13] Yet the English settlers in South Carolina and Georgia could do little to stem the tide of escapees to Florida.[14] In 1738, the Spanish established a military outpost just north of St. Augustine, Gracia Real de Santa Teresa de Mose, manned by 100 free Blacks. By 1746, one-third of the 1,500 inhabitants of St. Augustine were Black.[15]

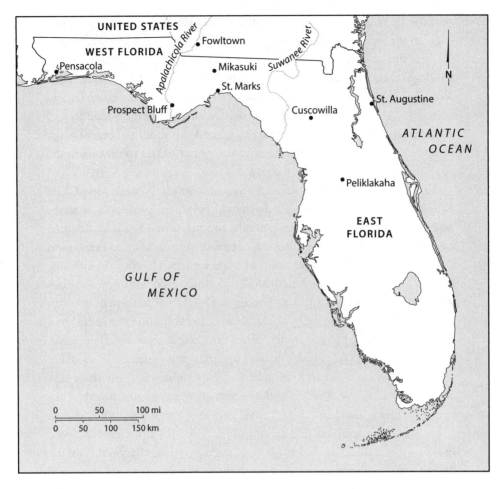

East and West Florida before 1821.

Slaves regularly fled the English-speaking colonies for Florida until 1763, when Britain acquired Florida from Spain as part of the settlement ending the Seven Years' War. Spain relocated most of Florida's free Blacks to Havana before formally ceding the territory to Britain. The British imported slaves to Florida and tried to establish there the plantation system that was so profitable in the Chesapeake, the Carolinas, and—especially—the Caribbean. Yet the British held Florida only briefly; Spain re-acquired Florida in 1783 after opportunistically declaring war against Britain during the American Revolution.[16] Under Spanish rule once again, Florida reemerged as the objective for fugitive slaves from the US southern states, with Pensacola surpassing St. Augustine as a destination for fugitives. As a nineteenth-century abolitionist wrote, slaves in the southernmost US states "had full knowledge" of the freedom that fugitives in Florida had attained, and their example "was thus constantly exerting an influence upon those who remained in bondage."[17] In Florida, Spain also inherited thousands of free Blacks who, according to a Spanish official in 1784, "in the course of the late War had resorted to the British standard and were on that account deemed free."[18] By the early nineteenth century, free Blacks made up about 20 percent of the inhabitants of Pensacola and a significant number of the volunteers in the Spanish battalion stationed in the city.[19]

Yet in Spanish Florida, freedom remained tenuous. When it suited their diplomatic interests, Spanish officials could be ardent protectors of slaves who had self-emancipated. For example, in 1784, when Spain and Britain were working to mend their relations, a Spanish official, Antonio Fernández, assured the British that former slaves who had won their freedom by enlisting in British forces during the American Revolution would remain free in Florida.[20] Likewise, in 1792, Spanish officials in Florida refused a petition from the United States (delivered by a delegation of Creeks, who often recaptured fugitives for a price) to restore free Blacks to their former American slaveholders.[21] Yet in 1784, Spanish officials imposed a pass system in Florida that required free Blacks to carry certificates of manumission—something that all escapees and most veterans of the British army lacked—or be subject to re-enslavement. That same year, a royal decree reduced the duty on slaves imported into Spanish ports in an effort to increase the commerce in slaves. In 1790, Spain ended its policy of offering sanctuary to fugitive slaves from the United States—although Florida officials made little effort to track down and return fugitives.[22] In these inconsistent approaches to slavery, the Spanish resembled the British, who insisted that the Spanish recognize the freedom of former slaves who fought for the British during the American Revolution, but also demanded that the Spanish protect Anglo slaveholders from white, Black, and Indigenous "banditti" who stole slaves from British planters who remained in Florida after 1783.[23]

Despite the ambiguous state of freedom in Spanish Florida, runaway slave advertisements in the 1780s testified to Florida's drawing power for South Carolina and Georgia slaves. In June 1783, Raymond Demere, a planter in Burke County south of Augusta, Georgia, placed an advertisement in the Savannah *Gazette* stating that three slaves, Peter, Cowley, and Caesar, all men in their mid-twenties or early thirties, had fled from his plantation and "may probably attempt to make off towards East Florida." In October 1786, William Clark advertised the flight of ten slaves. Isaac, "a tall black slim fellow, about

35 years of age," and his wife, Juba, "a sensible country born wench," were one of three couples who had fled. The others were Pate, "a stout well made fellow . . . about 25 years of age," and his wife, Phebe, "a short well made Mulatto wench"; Battes, "a Cooper by trade," and his wife, Quahobe, "a short black wench, about 20 years old"; and Ned, "a stout well made fellow," and Sue, "his wife, a small well made wench," who "carried her two daughters with her, one named Cloe about 6 years old, and Sue, a suckling child, about 10 months old." All the adults, Clark noted, had "lived many years in West-Florida" during the period when it was British territory and had likely fled in that direction. Two years later, six men, all between their twenties and early forties, fled Strathy Hall, a coastal Georgia plantation, for Florida. In December 1789, a couple, Ben and Nancy, both 25 years old, fled from Savannah and "crossed the Ogeechee ferry with some other negroes, probably with the intention of making the Spanish settlements."[24]

Although the slaveholders who placed these notices did not intend to leave a record of slave agency, by repeatedly suggesting that Florida was the likely destination for fugitives, runaway slave advertisements attested to how keenly slaves saw the promise of freedom in the Florida borderlands. When one reads runaway advertisements closely, patterns emerge. Most fugitives were young adults: old enough to plan and execute a flight, yet young enough to yearn to live the years ahead of them as free people. Many were familiar with Florida, having either traveled there or been enslaved there when it was British territory. Many fled as couples, and many women carried young children with them, risking the severe punishments meted out to recaptured fugitives to try to spare their children from slavery and live as a family without slavery's daily threats of violence, degradation, and separation.

Enslaved people of African descent were not the only people to flee south to Florida in the late eighteenth century. Since the settling of Carolina by the English, disease, war, and the slave trade had destabilized the Indigenous nations of the South Atlantic coastal plain; in the last half of the eighteenth century, thousands of Indigenous people broke off from the dominant Indigenous polity in the region, the Creek confederacy, and sought refuge from the maelstrom in Florida. The Indigenous slave trade was the primary catalyst for the chaos. Between 1670, when planters founded the Carolina colony, and 1715, the English enslaved between 30,000 and 50,000 Indigenous people of the South Atlantic coastal plain. As in West Africa, where European slave traders relied on Africans to supply them with captives from rival villages, the English in Carolina relied on Indigenous people to supply them with captives from other Indigenous nations.[25] For their part, the Indigenous people of the Atlantic coastal plain had long engaged in the practice of captive-taking. Among Indigenous nations of the region, captive men usually faced ritual torture and death; women and children were likelier to be enslaved or adopted. By the time the English arrived in Carolina in 1670, Indigenous people on the Atlantic coast had already begun to sell captives to English slave traders in Virginia. The Carolina planters, however, intensified the Indigenous slave trade far beyond the scale practiced in Virginia. The Westos were early allies and suppliers of slaves to the Carolinians; only to find themselves supplanted in the late 1670s by others, notably the Yamasees. Those enslaved included the Apalachees, Timucuas, Arkansas, Tunicas, Taensas, Tuscaroras, Choctaws, Savannahs, Cherokees, and at times the Westos and Yamasees themselves. Eventually, the Creeks emerged as frequent allies and commercial partners of English enslavers. In a notable slave-catching expedition in 1704, for instance, James Moore, the Carolina governor, led a force of English settlers and Creeks to Florida, captured roughly 4,000 Apalachees, and had them sold into slavery in the sugar-producing islands of the English Caribbean.[26] The English exported most of the Indigenous slaves they acquired to planters in the Caribbean, but a sizable number remained as slaves in Carolina. In 1708, the population of the province was 9,580; of these, roughly 4,000 were African slaves and 1,400 were Indigenous slaves.[27]

The extensive slave trade radiating out from Carolina facilitated the transmission of smallpox. For most of the seventeenth century, Indigenous people in the South Atlantic coastal plain were fortunate to have avoided the epidemic diseases that originated in Europe; but the slave trade enabled the transmission of smallpox and other diseases by bringing Indigenous people and English settlers into frequent close contact. In 1696, a smallpox epidemic that began along the James River in Virginia reached Carolina. Carried along by the Indigenous slave-trade network, smallpox ravaged numerous Indigenous nations, reducing the populations of the Sewees, Santees, Congarees, Winyaws, Cusabos, and Eitwans, among others, to small remnants. The Creek confederacy lost perhaps two-thirds of its population.[28] Smallpox returned to the South Atlantic coastal plain in 1711, 1738, and 1759, afflicting those who had been born since the last epidemic and thus had no acquired immunity.[29]

The depopulation of the South Atlantic coastal plain beginning in 1696 transformed the dynamics of the Indigenous slave trade. By 1715, so few Indigenous people remained in the region that nations such as the Yamasees and the Creeks, who had been suppliers of slaves to the English in Carolina, were no longer able to procure the volume of captives that the English demanded. In their weakened state, they began to fear that the English might turn the tables and enslave them. In the spring of 1715, the Yamasees and Creeks launched a series of preemptive attacks on the English. Within a year, most of the other Indigenous nations in the region had joined them. By 1718, about 400 Carolina colonists had been killed—about 7 percent of the English settler population in Carolina. The conflict ended only when the Carolinians convinced the Cherokees to side with them against the alliance of other native groups.[30]

Despite the decades of disease, slave raids, and war, by the 1730s, white colonists remained a minority in the South Atlantic coastal plain. In South Carolina, the Black population had surpassed the white population well before 1710, and by the beginning of the decade of the 1730s, the 22,000 African slaves in the colony far outnumbered the 12,000 whites.[31] Only about 1,000 English settlers populated Georgia by the end of the 1730s. Spain, which struggled throughout the eighteenth century to induce anyone other than missionaries to inhabit the northern periphery of its North American colonies, had settled only about 2,000 Spaniards in St. Augustine. Most of the Spaniards in Florida were either soldiers or government officials. In the first decades of the eighteenth century, the dominant power in the South Atlantic region was neither the British nor the Spanish but the Creeks. In the 1730s, despite the ravages of smallpox and the slave trade, the Creek confederacy numbered between 8,000 and 20,000 people inhabiting between forty and sixty towns.[32]

Yet the Creeks were decentralized: divided not only by village and clan but by language. Most Creeks spoke a variant of Eastern Muskogean: Upper Creeks on the Coosa, Tallapoosa, and Alabama Rivers spoke the Koasati and Alibamu languages; Lower Creeks on the Chattahoochee River spoke Hitchiti or Mikasuki. All these languages belonged to the Eastern Muskogean language group, yet they were different enough from each other that the Hitchiti-speaking Oconee called the Upper Creeks *Uchize*, meaning People of Another Language.[33] For their part, Koasati-speaking Upper Creeks called the Hitchiti *At-pasha-shliha*, or Mean People.[34] The Upper Creeks' disdain reflected imbalances of power and prestige within the Creek confederacy. Three Upper Creek towns—Tukabatchee, Abihka, and Kashita—and one Lower Creek town, Coweta, dominated smaller, peripheral towns in the confederacy.[35] On the farthest periphery of the Creek confederacy were non-Muskogean speakers: a village of Shawnees (who spoke an Anishinaabe language) as well as the Natchez and Yuchi (whose languages are linguistic isolates).[36]

Buffeted by violence and disease and under pressure from English, Spanish, and (from the west) French colonists, the linguistically divided and politically decentralized Creeks struggled to hold their confederacy together in the eighteenth century. For a time, they succeeded: in the years after the defeat of the Creeks and their allies in the Yamasee War, Brim, a *mico* (leader) of the primary Lower Creek town Coweta, briefly imposed his authority on most of the Creek confederation and successfully advanced Creek interests by playing the English in Charlestown, the Spanish in St. Augustine, and the French in Mobile against each other. In 1704, the Lower Creeks had joined Carolinians in their raids on the Spanish and their Indigenous allies in Florida; and in 1711, Brim allied himself with the English in Carolina against the French in Mobile. And yet in 1715, the Lower Creeks had joined with the Yamasee against the Carolinians. By the 1720s, under Brim's leadership, the Lower Creeks, having demonstrated to the various European imperial powers the costs of being the Creeks' enemies, dangled the prospect of alliance before all of them.[37]

Such alliances were as much commercial as diplomatic. As the Indigenous slave trade declined, a trade in deerskins arose to replace it. Seeking the best terms, the Creeks traded immense numbers of deerskins to the English, French, and Spanish. The Carolinians alone shipped roughly 20,000 skins annually across the Atlantic in the late 1710s. That volume rose to 60,000 annually in the 1720s, and 80,000 annually in the 1730s. By the middle of the eighteenth century, 150,000 deerskins left Charlestown for England every year.[38] To the west of Creek country, another Muskogean nation, the Choctaws, traded most of their deerskins to the French; by the end of the eighteenth century they had nearly eliminated white-tailed deer from their territory, and traditional Choctaw subsistence strategies in which hunting supplemented agriculture were no longer viable.[39] In return for deerskins, the Creeks and other Indigenous nations in the South Atlantic coastal plain received woolens, linens, and cotton; leather saddles and shoes; muskets, lead, and powder; copper, brass, and tin kettles; iron knives, pins, fishhooks, scissors, and other tools; and not least, as one prominent merchant in Florida called it, "cheap rum."[40] Integration into the commercial exchanges of the eighteenth-century British Atlantic world transformed the Indigenous economies and societies of the South Atlantic coastal plain, drawing them even closer into a colonial world predicated on slaveholding, commerce, and the accumulation of property.[41]

The commercial pursuit of diminishing populations of deer drew some Lower Creeks into northern Florida in the mid-eighteenth century. Around 1750, an Oconee leader, Ahaya, called by the English "Cowkeeper," moved to Florida permanently: he and his followers broke off from the Creek confederacy, migrated to Florida, and established a village at Cuscowilla (near present-day Gainesville). Ahaya's motivations were complex. Abundant populations of deer were a lure, but as Ahaya's English name implied, even more important were Florida's extensive canebrakes and lush savannas, which could serve as grazing lands for Oconee cattle herds. Over the course of the eighteenth century, Indigenous people such as the Oconee had increasingly borrowed colonists' land-use strategies and had taken to raising livestock. The migrants to Cuscowilla adopted Spanish techniques for raising cattle, notably by herding their stock from horseback.[42] Ahaya's followers called the savanna near Cuscowilla *Waucahutche*, meaning "cow pen" in Mikasuki.[43] Apart from the material advantages offered by northern Florida, cultural and political differences split the Oconee from the Creek confederacy. The Mikasuki-speaking Oconee were always somewhat loosely attached to the largely Muskogean-speaking Creek confederacy. In addition, Ahaya bristled under the leadership of Brim's successors in Coweta. While Ahaya was staunchly loyal to English traders and loathed the Spanish, Coweta leaders insisted on playing the intricate game of borderlands diplomacy, flirting alternately with the English, the Spanish, and the French. Such tactics, common to Indigenous diplomacy in the borderlands, worked—when in the hands of a skilled diplomat and leader such as Brim. In the decades after Brim's death in the early 1730s, however, and under the enduring pressure of diminishing supplies of game and the epidemics that continued to whipsaw through the South Atlantic coastal plain, parts of the loose, interethnic Creek confederacy began pursuing their own interests. Over the next decade, both Mikasuki and Muskogean speakers followed Ahaya out of the Creek confederacy and into Florida. By the mid-1760s, the Creeks who remained in the north called the polyglot, multiethnic Indigenous migrants to Florida *Seminoles*. By the 1790s, there were between 2,000 and 3,000 Seminoles in northern Florida.[44]

In Florida, the Seminoles enjoyed material comfort as well as a distance from Indigenous and European enemies and thus security from attack not available in Creek country to the north. The itinerant naturalist William Bartram described Cuscowilla in the 1774 as "on the most pleasant situation that could be imagined or desired, in an inland country; upon a high swelling ridge of sand hills, within three or four hundred yards of a large and beautiful lake." Each household kept "a small garden spot" of "Corn, Beans, Tobacco, & Citruls [*sic*]." However, the town derived most of its agricultural production from an enclosed "plantation . . . worked and tended by the whole community," about two miles from the village. Boys spent their days in the field to protect the crops from birds, "whooping and hallooing, to chase away crows, jackdaws, blackbirds, and such predatory animals. . . . The men in turn patrole the corn fields at night, to protect their provisions from the depredations of night rovers, as bears, raccoons, and deer." Cuscowilla's leader at the time of Bartram's visit, also named Cowkeeper by the English and a descendant of the Cowkeeper who had led the Oconee to Florida, maintained large herds of cattle in the neighborhood of the town. According to Bartram, "the cattle were as large and fat as those of the rich grazing pastures of Moyomensing [sic] in Pennsylvania."[45]

In the imperial vacuum of northern Florida, the Seminoles carved out an existence that was both independent and prosperous. Bartram captured the state of the Seminoles by describing them—more than a little incongruously—as both "treacherous" and the "picture of happiness." (He similarly described Cowkeeper as "very affable and cheerful . . . yet ferocious.") By "treacherous," Bartram meant that the Seminoles were independent: Seminoles who continued to trade deerskins played British and Spanish traders against each other to extract the best prices. Moreover, they had detached themselves from the Creek confederacy. "The Siminoles," Bartram wrote, are "a treacherous people, lying so far from the eye and control of the nation with whom they are confederate." Yet he marveled that "they seem to be free from want or desires. No cruel enemy to dread; nothing to give them disquietude, but the gradual encroachments of the white people. . . . The visage, action, and deportment of the Siminoles, form the most striking picture of happiness in this life; joy, contentment, love, and friendship, without guile or affectation, seem inherent in them."[46] Their prosperous, neat, and well-populated villages stood in stark contrast to Spanish settlements. In 1801, John Devereux DeLacy, an Irish naturalist traveling in Florida, wrote to Thomas Jefferson that Pensacola was "going to decay," its few residents moving away, and "the buildings going to ruin." Just twenty miles away from Pensacola, however, he found Seminole villages "which display an astonishing degree of taste and industry in the arrangment [sic] and management of their farms more by far than a great many of the American or Spanish planters."[47]

Most slaves who fled from colonial settlements in South Carolina or Georgia to Florida eventually found their way to one or another of these tidy and prosperous Seminole villages. Slavery was not unknown there: the Seminoles, like other Indigenous nations of the South Atlantic coastal plain, kept both Indigenous captives and Blacks as slaves. At Cuscowilla, for instance, the Seminoles held Yamasee slaves. Yet Bartram was surprised to note that Indigenous slavery lacked the overt cruelty and violence of chattel slavery in the

Chesapeake and the Carolinas. "I saw in every town," he wrote, "more or less male captives, some extremely aged, who were free and in as good circumstances as their masters; and all slaves have their freedom when they marry, which is permitted and encouraged, when they and their offspring are every way upon equality with their conquerors."[48] Most Black fugitives in Florida became free: by the 1830s, there were about 1,200 free Blacks living among the Seminoles in Florida. There were, as well, about 200 Black slaves (making the free and slave Black population of the Seminole villages equal to about 50 percent of the Indigenous population).[49] Yet slavery among the Seminoles was markedly different from chattel slavery in the US South. William Simmons, a South Carolina physician, wrote after touring northern Florida in 1822 of the Seminoles' "great indulgence to their slaves." They neither "impose[d] onerous labours on the Negroes" nor sold them. Simmons continued, "The Negroes uniformly testify to the kind treatment they receive from their Indian masters, who are indulgent, and require but little labour from them. . . . The Negroes dwell in towns apart from the Indians, and are the finest looking people I have ever seen. They dress and live pretty much like the Indians, each having a gun, and hunting a portion of his time. Like the Indians, they plant in common, and form an Indian field apart, which they attend together."[50]

Indeed, Seminole slavery more closely resembled tenancy than the chattel slavery of the US South. A nineteenth-century chronicler of Florida wrote that among the Seminoles one found "the slave usually living with his own family and occupying his time as he pleased, paying his master annually a small stipend in corn and other vegetables. This class of slaves regarded servitude among the whites with the greatest degree of horror." Free and enslaved Blacks lived together in Seminole villages, "separate and apart from their masters." Free Blacks, like slaves, paid "a certain quantity of vegetables annually" to the Seminoles, for the right to occupy the land.[51] James McCall, a US Army officer who visited a Black settlement near a Seminole village in 1826, wrote that "they are chiefly runaway slaves from Georgia, who have put themselves under the protection" of the Seminoles, "to whom for this consideration, they render a tribute of one-third of the produce of the land." Apart from this rent, McCall wrote, "they are free to come and go at pleasure, and in some cases are elevated to the position of equality with their masters."[52]

AN ANGLO-SPANISH IMPERIAL VACUUM

In the multicultural, multiethnic, and multiracial Seminole villages, cultures were permeable and identities malleable. Although Ahaya, the first leader of the Seminoles of Cuscowilla, was largely hostile to the Spanish in St. Augustine, the culture of the Seminoles, according to Bartram, was "tinctured with Spanish civilization." He observed that "there are several Christians among them, many of whom wear little silver crucifixes, affixed to a wampum collar round their necks, or suspended by a small chain upon their breast. These are said to be baptized; and notwithstanding most of them speak and understand Spanish, yet they have been the most bitter and formidable Indian enemies the Spaniards ever had."[53] Black Seminoles generally spoke English, Spanish, and either Muskogean or Mikasuki or both.[54] English fur traders residing among the Seminoles often married Seminole women. In Cuscowilla, Bartram observed that "the white traders are fully sensible how greatly it is to their advantage to gain [the] affections and friendship [or Seminole women] in matters of trade and commerce."[55] The Spanish governor of East Florida wrote in 1784 that "from the alliances" that English traders had "contracted with the Indian women has come a large number of half-breed and some quarter-breeds." William Augustus Bowles, a British adventurer in Florida, married a daughter of a Lower Creek *mico* around 1779; Osceola, a Seminole war leader in the 1830s, was the son of a Seminole woman and a white trader. Black and Indigenous Seminoles frequently intermarried; Osceola's wife was the daughter of an Indigenous Seminole man and a Black Seminole woman.[56]

While European cultures, commercial goods, and genes diffused into Seminole country, neither the Spanish nor the British ever exercised effective political control over Florida. By the time Spain ceded Florida to Britain at the end of the Seven Years' War in 1763, the Spanish controlled little more than the near vicinity of St. Augustine. In 1766, the Philadelphia naturalist John Bartram (the father of William Bartram), toured Florida; it was only three years after Britain had taken possession of the province from Spain. In the elder Bartram's view, the "Creek" (the term by which most English writers at the time referred to the Seminoles) were the true rulers of Florida. The Spanish, he wrote, had "quarreled with ye creek indians which of late years cubed them up within thair fortifications beyond which if thay ventured without A strong guard thay was in danger of being killed even in sight of ye town." As a result, the forest had overtaken abandoned Spanish plantations: "All thair improvements ruined & now where thay had cleared & planted even within A few miles of ye town there now grows large evergreen oaks & pines."[57] Another English traveler in Florida, William Stork, concurred, writing in 1767 that "the peninsula of Florida is a country very little known in Europe: even the Spaniards, who from indolence, and a fear of the Indians, seldom ventured beyond the lines of St. Augustine, made themselves but little acquainted with it."[58]

Stork and other British colonists believed that, unlike the Spanish, they could extend their dominion over Florida and exploit its potential. James Grant, the British governor of East Florida between 1763 and 1771, was effusive about the profits to be made in Britain's new colonial province. "The lands are rich and fertile in the interior parts of the province," he wrote.

> Fruits and grains may be raised with little labor . . . the breeder here
> will be under no necessity of laying up fodder for the winter; for there
> is at all times sufficient quantity of pastures to maintain his cattle. The
> indigo plant remains unhurt for several years. Wild indigo is found
> here in great abundance. . . . All the fruits and productions of the
> West-Indies may be raised here. . . . Oranges, limes, lemons, and other
> fruits, grow spontaneously over the country. This province abounds
> with mahogany, and all kinds of lumber.[59]

Stork agreed, praising Florida's potential for commodities such as white pine, mahogany, rice, sugar, and cotton. "I am much disposed to prognosticate," he wrote in 1769, "that cotton will, in time, be a staple commodity in Florida."[60]

Yet the British struggled as much as the Spanish to colonize Florida. William Bartram, who as a young man in 1766 had accompanied his father to Florida, returned in 1774 to find that, after an initial influx of settlement, the English had retreated and their sovereignty in Florida was little distinguished from Spanish rule. On arriving at St. Simon, an island on the border with Georgia, he wrote that "A very large part of this island had formerly been cleared and planted by the English, as appeared evidently to me, by vestiges of plantations, ruins of costly buildings, highways, &c. but it is now overgrown with forests." As for mainland Florida, the younger Bartram wrote that the Seminoles had "effectively cut off their communication" between St. Augustine on the Atlantic coast and St. Mark's on the Gulf of Mexico, a distance of 180 miles. The "ancient highway" between the two settlements "is grown up in many places with trees and shrubs." Bartram found that Florida had defied the ambitions of Stork; only five years after Stork enthusiastically predicted the success of British colonization of Florida, the younger Bartram stumbled across "a deserted plantation, the property of Dr. Stork, where he once resided." Rather than the British, the Seminoles, Bartram concluded, dominated Florida. Though "but a weak people with respect to numbers," he wrote, the Seminoles possessed "a vast territory; all East Florida and the greatest part of West Florida, which being naturally cut and divided into thousands of inlets, knolls, and eminences, by the innumerable rivers, lakes, swamps, vast savannas and ponds, form so many secure retreats and temporary dwelling places, that effectually guard them from any sudden invasions or attacks from their enemies."[61] When John Le Conte, a US Army officer, explored Florida in 1822, he noted numerous deserted British settlements on the St. John's River, "sad monuments of the folly and visionary extravagance of the English when in possession of this country."[62] A German traveler who visited East Florida immediately after the American Revolution, as Britain was preparing to cede East and West Florida back to Spain, commented that "the Spanish cannot promise themselves any great advantage in receiving back the two Floridas."[63]

When the Spanish reclaimed Florida from Britain in 1783, they were no better able than the British to impose control on the province. The Spanish maintained four undermanned presidios in East and West Florida, at St. Augustine, San Marcos de Apalache (or, as the English called it, St. Marks), Pensacola, and Mobile. To extend their influence among the Seminoles, they relied on the diplomacy and commerce of non-Spaniards whose loyalty to Spain was tenuous: Alexander McGillivray, a Creek leader who was the son of a Scottish trader and Creek mother (Vicente Manuel de Zéspedes, the Spanish governor of East Florida, called him "an English mestizo"); and a British merchant firm, Panton, Leslie, and Company, which remained in Florida after the end of British rule.[64] McGillivray—a kind of successor to the early-eighteenth-century Creek *mico* Brim, who had successfully played competing European empires against each other to maintain the position of the Creek confederacy—kept in Spain's favor by preying on Spanish officials' fears of the newly independent United States. In 1785, McGillivray warned Zéspedes that the greatest threat to Florida was Americans, who "are proceeding in great Numbers to the Mississippi, with an Intent to establish themselves upon the Territory . . . at the risque of war." To counter that threat, McGillivray assured Zéspedes that the Creeks would prevent the expansion of the United States—so long as the Creeks could remain supplied with goods from Panton, Leslie, and Company (with whom McGillivray was a silent partner). If "the Indians are Certain of a permanent & well regulated Support of the Goods that they have been accustomed to," McGillivray concluded, they will "attach themselves to the Government which Supports them."[65] Shortly after reclaiming Florida from Britain, Spanish officials resigned themselves to keeping Panton, Leslie, and Company as their commercial representatives in the region. Zéspedes wrote to government officials in Madrid that "to win effectually the friendship of these Indians for ourselves, it would be risky to expel this firm."[66] Yet neither McGillivray (whose loyalties were to the Upper Creeks as well as to Panton, Leslie, and Company and who, after 1790, also held a commission as an officer in the US Army) nor William Panton and John Leslie (whose priorities were their firm's profits) had any real investment in Spanish rule in Florida. Panton and Leslie's loyalties were to whomever ruled Florida. In 1783, after news of Britain's cession of Florida to Spain had reached the British inhabitants of Florida, both Panton and Leslie had written to Patrick Tonyn, the British governor of the Bahamas, solemnly attesting "that we shall ever preserve our loyalty to the King."[67] Yet, within months, they wrote to the Spanish governor of their desire to "transfer" their attachment from the British king to "faithful adherence to the Spanish monarch."[68]

When Spain took nominal control of Florida from Britain, there were numerous signs that no European empire was capable of governing the peninsula. "The whole of the People in the Province are in the utmost Confusion," a British settler wrote to Robert Bissett, a British planter in Florida, in 1783. "The Cowkeeper and other Indian Chiefs," the correspondent continued, "say that whenever the English leave the Town and Province it belongs to them, that they will kill every Spaniard that offers to set his head out of the Lines of the Town."[69] In 1785, Francis Fatio, a Swiss planter who had settled in Florida in 1771 and who, like Panton and Leslie, had shifted his loyalties from the British to the Spanish, warned Spanish officials that the Seminoles were preparing to "renew their pillages and make dangerous all communication" between St. Augustine and the interior. He rued that "the few Spanish subjects" in Florida were "either in the service of the garrison, or live on a small liquor trade or other mercantile business of little consequence." As a result, Florida was little more than "an African presidio."[70] In the aftermath of the American Revolution, between 10,000 and 12,000 American royalists fled from the United States to Florida. Many of them, near poverty, congregated on the outskirts of St. Augustine in huts built of palmetto leaves.[71] A significant number of these "desperate exiled American royalists," as Zéspedes called them, turned to banditry. They plundered the plantations that British settlers were preparing to evacuate, making off with numerous slaves.[72] In 1785, some of these American royalists in St. Augustine, tempted by the obvious weakness of Spanish authority, openly contemplated rebellion against Spain.[73] In 1801, a visitor to Pensacola wrote that "there is no more than the bare site of the old forts and fortifications to be seen tho the spaniards make a shew of preserving them by keeping Centinels &c on duty at them."[74]

Spanish control of Florida was so feeble that one American royalist, William Augustus Bowles, briefly emerged as the plenipotentiary of a Euro-Indigenous-African confederacy in Florida that he styled the "State of Muskogee." Bowles was distinguished from other exiled royalists by his integration into Indigenous society: after being drummed out of the British army in Pensacola in 1779, Bowles married a Lower Creek woman and assimilated into Lower Creek and Seminole society. Subsequently, British colonial officials engaged him to act as a British agent in Florida; his charge was to become a counterweight to McGillivray, the half-Scottish leader of the Upper Creeks, and to entice the commerce of the Seminoles and Lower Creeks away from Panton, Leslie, and Company and toward British firms based in the Bahamas. While Bowles never ceased to act on behalf of Britain (or, for that matter, his own ambitions), he also repeatedly sought to force Spain, the United States, and not least McGillivray and the Creeks to acknowledge what Bartram and others had already realized: that the Seminoles were an independent nation and, in practical terms, the true rulers of Florida.[75]

Bowles went about that task by claiming the mantle of statehood for the Seminoles—not unlike the way that American colonists declared independence from Britain and thus transformed themselves from recalcitrant British taxpayers (whom the British Parliament could ignore) to rebels (whom the British Parliament could not).[76] In 1790, after having appointed himself "ambassador to the British king," from the "United Nations of Creeks and Cherokees" Bowles traveled to London with eight Indigenous people to petition the British government to support his efforts in Florida to create an Indigenous state that would be a British protectorate. Bowles designed a flag for his imagined state that borrowed elements from both the United States and British flags: a blue symmetric cross on a red field, with a yellow emblem of a sun on a blue canton.[77] Yet Bowles's independent nation had an inauspicious start. After he returned to Florida in 1791, he and his followers—some Seminoles, free Blacks, and a few American royalist bandits who still remained in Florida—focused on plundering Panton, Leslie, and Company's trading outposts.[78] Overestimating his influence in the borderlands, Bowles blundered into New Orleans to meet with the Spanish governor of Louisiana and West Florida, to whom he proposed an alliance against McGillivray's Upper Creeks and the United States. Instead, the Spanish imprisoned him. Bowles spent much of the next six years as a prisoner in Havana, Madrid, and the Philippines, before escaping and returning to Florida in 1799.[79]

Once back in Florida, he resumed his effort to create an Indigenous state. In late 1799, calling himself "Director General" of the State of Muskogee, he

William Augustus Bowles, 1791. Painting by Thomas Hardy, engraving by Joseph Grozer. National Portrait Gallery, Washington, DC.

ordered all Spanish and US officials to leave Florida. A flurry of pronouncements followed, most of which were published in the Bahamas to establish the State of Muskogee's legitimacy in the eyes of British colonial officers. Bowles declared as void a treaty that McGillivray had signed with the United States in 1790 that ceded some territory claimed by the State of Muskogee. Bowles protested a 1795 treaty between the United States and Spain that drew a boundary line between the United States and Florida; the Seminoles, through whose territory the boundary line ran, had not been party to the treaty and did not agree to its terms. He invited slaves in Spanish and US territory to escape to freedom in Muskogee, and he offered land grants of 100 acres to white Americans who would settle in his territory and become citizens of the State of Muskogee.[80] In April 1800, in response to Spanish attacks on Seminole villages, he declared war against Spain.[81] Taken as a whole, the pronouncements declared that the Seminoles were an independent people: Bowles and the Seminoles would decide who could and could not inhabit their territory; McGillivray and the Creeks could not negotiate on their behalf; Spain and the United States could not divide Seminole territory without their consent; Spain could not resort to violence against the Seminoles without consequences.

By mid-1801, he had attracted to himself adherents in "4 or 5 towns," according to a US Indian agent to the Creeks.[82] Bowles drew to his standard not only a large number of Seminoles and the remnants of white American royalists in Florida but also free Blacks. Yet while Bowles encouraged fugitive slaves to flee to his ranks, he distinguished between slaves who freed themselves and joined his banner and slaves captured in conflict: in 1802, for instance, he bragged that his forces had captured many "Prime Slaves" from the Spanish at St. Augustine, and he suggested that Americans might want benefit by "purchasing up the Negroes, Property & Plunder that may be taken by the Muskogeans."[83] Nevertheless, many free Blacks rallied to Bowles, and his immediate retinue included both Indigenous and Black Seminoles. Black men named Cudjo, Harry, and Esten served as interpreters for both Bowles and an allied Seminole leader, Payne, who had succeeded the second Cowkeeper as the *mico* of the Seminole town of Cuscowilla. Another Black Seminole, Billy, who like Bowles resided in the Seminole town of Mikasuki under its *mico*, Kinache, joined Bowles in several battles against the Spanish. When Bowles attacked the Spanish fort of San Marcos de Apalache in January 1802, his force consisted of several hundred Indigenous Seminoles and about forty Black Seminoles. In the first few years of the nineteenth century, when Bowles's influence was at its height, free Blacks in Seminole country conducted several raids on plantations to liberate slaves; still more slaves fled to Seminole territory of their own accord.[84]

Bowles established his capital at Mikasuki, a Seminole village just thirty miles from the Spanish fort at San Marcos de Apalache—Spain's reach was so limited that Bowles could center his activities so closely to the Spanish garrison with impunity. In April 1800, Bowles invested San Marcos with a force of between 200 and 300 Seminoles; after a 5-week siege, the 88-man Spanish garrison surrendered.[85] He resumed his attacks on Panton, Leslie, and Company and wrote to the *Nassau Gazette* in 1802 that his forces, having "marched to plunder, pillage & lay waste Augustine," came away from the campaign with "some considerable share of very valuable property." He created a navy—three ships—manned by diverse crews. The small Muskogee navy harassed Spanish merchant ships in the Caribbean, capturing twelve ships in 1801 and 1802. However much these actions made Bowles seem more like a brigand than a "director general," in the early nineteenth century, most nations allowed soldiers to plunder and awarded prize money to sailors— and Muskogee, in Bowles's mind, was an independent state.[86]

Bowles's reign as the leader of the State of Muskogee was brief; he was brought down by the same borderlands statecraft that he had once used to rise to power. In March 1802, the major European powers signed a treaty at Amiens in France; Europe was at peace for the first time since 1793, Britain and Spain began a strategic rapprochement as common enemies of France, and Bowles's utility to the British waned. Later that year, the primary Seminole leaders, including Kinache, made peace with Spain. Over a decade earlier, Bowles had blundered into New Orleans and found himself a Spanish prisoner; in May 1803, he made a similar mistake when he and his followers attended a conference in the United States. Some 400 Creeks and Seminoles attended as well as Benjamin Hawkins, a US Indian agent and former US senator from North Carolina; John Forbes, a Scottish merchant whose firm, John Forbes and Company, had succeeded to the Indigenous trade once controlled by Panton, Leslie, and Company; and Esteban Folch, the son of Juan Vicente Folch, the Spanish governor of West Florida. Hawkins and Forbes liberally distributed gifts to the Indigenous people at the conference; in return, a group of Upper Creeks who had once been closely associated with McGillivray seized Bowles and delivered him into the hands of the Spanish.[87] Hawkins mused that Bowles's fantastic ambitions clouded his judgment of how the situation in the borderlands had changed. "It was inconceivable to me that Bowles who understood a good deal of the Indian language," he wrote, "should not have been able to make the necessary determination between past and present." Instead, to the end, Bowles went on playing "his former part of Director General, untill he was apprehended in the midst of his guards and adherents . . . and quits the stage in Irons."[88] Bowles died in a Havana prison in 1805.

Bowles was a rash and quixotic freebooter, but his State of Muskogee was not the only would-be independent polity in Florida in the late eighteenth and early nineteenth century. In 1795, disaffected Anglo settlers on the St. John's River—some of whom had been settled in East Florida since it was a

British possession, some of whom were royalist exiles, and some of whom were recent immigrants from the United States—rebelled against Spain in a failed effort to create an independent state. (Bowles had once courted the failed rebels to join his State of Muskogee.)[89] In late 1810, around the same time that a Mexican priest, Miguel Hidalgo, led an uprising in a village in Guanajuato that eventually led to Mexico's independence from Spain, American settlers in several West Florida parishes revolted against Spanish rule and briefly established a US satrapy, the so-called Republic of West Florida. The United States, on the pretext that the rebellious parishes properly belonged to the Louisiana Purchase of 1803, annexed them.[90] In 1812, a group of Anglos from East Florida and Georgia including George Mathews, a former governor of Georgia, hoping to emulate the success of the West Florida rebellion and, like West Florida, be annexed to the United States, briefly established the Territory of East Florida along the Atlantic coast near the St. John's River. The East Florida republic endured for only a short time before Black and Indigenous Seminoles, led by Kinache, Payne, and Payne's brother, Bolek, attacked the Anglo forces and summarily defeated them.[91] The attack demonstrated to whites in Georgia that the Seminoles were the true rulers of East Florida. The brief history of the State of Muskogee and the even shorter history of the Territory of East Florida showed that while Black and Indigenous Seminoles were not powerful or numerous enough to elaborate their control of East Florida into an Anglo-American-style state, they could prevent anyone else from doing so.

AN AMERICAN QUAGMIRE

Though Black and Indigenous Seminoles successfully prevented either the United States or a European imperial power from establishing effective sovereignty in East Florida, many Americans, almost from the time the United States achieved its independence from Britain, nonetheless yearned to expand into the peninsula. In 1812, James Innerarity, a Scottish partner in John Forbes's trading company, predicted that the United States would attempt to "seize" both East and West Florida, "both provinces having long been objects of their ambition."[92] When the United States and Britain stumbled into war that year, largely over Britain's impressment of roughly 10,000 American sailors into the British navy during the first years of the nineteenth century, Americans who harbored ambitions to expand the boundaries of the United States saw their opportunity. In short order, the War of 1812 became a sweeping US expansionist venture—the largest such venture in the nineteenth century before the US-Mexico War in 1846. Unlike the war with Mexico, however, the War of 1812 ended without US boundaries changing.[93]

Indeed, in the borderlands, failure and defeat marked much of the US war effort. To the west, US military leaders calculated at the outset of the war that they would be unable to defend their outposts, and they ordered the evacuation of Fort Osage on the Missouri River, Fort Madison on the Mississippi River, and Fort Dearborn on the Chicago River; at Fort Dearborn, Potawatomis attacked and decimated the retreating US force a few miles outside of the fort. To the north, many Americans welcomed the war as an opportunity to conquer and annex Canada; yet US military capacity fell well short of those ambitions. Between the fall of 1812 and the spring of 1814, the United States launched a series of invasions into Upper and Lower Canada. US forces won several notable battles: at Fort George and York in the spring of 1813, and a naval victory on Lake Erie in the fall of 1813. Yet in each case, the US invasions ended with British regulars, Canadian militia, and Indigenous allies repulsing US forces. The United States won a defensive victory at Lake Champlain in the fall of 1814, which came while US and British diplomats were negotiating an end to the war and did nothing more than restore the status quo antebellum on the northern border.[94] The most notable outcome of the fighting in the northern theater of the war was the death of the Shawnee war leader Tecumseh at an otherwise strategically inconsequential battle in Upper Canada in October 1813.

In the southern theater, the greatest US triumph, at New Orleans in January 1815, was like the victory at Lake Champlain, a defensive victory against the British as the war was ending; it had no effect on peace terms. As in the North, the most important outcome of the violence in the South was the defeat of an Indigenous enemy of the United States: an Upper Creek faction, the Red Sticks, that had emerged a few years before the start of the war. The Red Sticks opposed changes in Creek society toward American-style farming, planting, commerce, and race-based slavery that had begun under the leadership of McGillivray. Yet the Red Sticks were not, strictly speaking, Creek traditionalists. Two of their leaders, Peter McQueen and William Weatherford, were like McGillivray, of both Creek and white descent; Weatherford, in fact, was McGillivray's nephew, and like him, was a slaveholder. Rather, like the Oconee in the eighteenth century when they had broken away from the Creek confederacy and migrated to Florida, the Red Sticks opposed the Lower Creek leadership in Coweta not because the leadership favored stock-raising and slaveholding like the whites in Georgia and the Carolinas but because the Lower Creek leadership had profited disproportionately from the new order.

The Creek confederacy had been fraught with division for over a century, but the Red Sticks' rupture with Creek leadership was profound.[95] Indeed, by 1813, it had evolved into a Creek civil war. In the summer of 1813, when a group of Red Sticks came into conflict with a group of Lower Creeks friendly to the United States at a settlement that also housed whites, the United States capitalized on the violence to intervene. Andrew Jackson, at the head of a force made up of Tennessee militia, Cherokees, and Lower Creeks, routed Red Stick encampments at Tallushatchee in November 1813 and at Horseshoe Bend in March 1814.[96] Many of the surviving Red Sticks fled to Florida to seek refuge among the Seminoles under the protection of the Spanish, who had armed and tacitly supported the Red Sticks during the Creek civil war.[97] Some joined with the British, who during the war with the United States had stationed troops in nominally neutral Spanish Florida.

For Jackson, the flight of the Red Sticks to Florida exposed a US vulnerability in the southern borderlands. In the view of Jackson and other American slaveholders, Spain and the Seminoles, with the connivance of the British Empire, weakened enslavers' power over the enslaved by harboring escaped slaves. Florida was such an abiding concern for Jackson that in November 1814, in the last months of the war, he attacked Pensacola with a force of militiamen, regular US soldiers, and Choctaws to dislodge about 100 British marines and several hundred Red Sticks who had fled to Spanish Florida for safety. He launched the attack in defiance of President James Madison's explicit orders that he take no action that might involve Spain, a neutral power, in the war. Jackson, however, pursued his own foreign relations; as far as he was concerned, by permitting Britain to land its forces in its territory, Spain was already a hostile power. He wrote to Madison's secretary of state, James Monroe, after the attack on Pensacola that he believed he had "convinced the Spaniards that we will permit no equivocations in a nation professing neuterality [sic]."[98]

While Jackson's attack forced the British to withdraw from Pensacola, they remained ensconced at a fort 120 miles to the east. The fort, built in mid-1814 overlooking the Apalachicola River on Prospect Bluff, had once been a Forbes and Company trading post. The structure was, according to one observer in 1815, a "starfort" with six faces, 25-foot high walls, and sixteen cannons. It was located about sixty miles southwest of the Spanish fort San Marcos and only seventy miles south of the US border. In the second half of 1814, the British had recruited a force of roughly 3,500 men to the fort including both Red Sticks and fugitive slaves from both Spanish Florida and the United States. The British formed the ex-slaves into a corps of colonial marines. Many of the Spanish fugitive slaves who joined the British at Prospect Bluff had fled there from Pensacola when Jackson had invaded the city.[99] When the British withdrew from Prospect Bluff in mid-1815 as part of the agreement ending the war, they officially demobilized the military unit they had created but left behind some Red Sticks and ex-slaves and a large supply of arms and ammunition at the fort.[100] According to Hawkins, who wrote to Jackson with information about the fort in August 1815, about eighty ex-slaves remained at the fort.[101]

The presence of even so small a group of armed ex-slaves so close to the US border terrified southern slaveholders.[102] A British-sponsored slave revolt had been an abiding fear of southern slaveholders during the war; rumors of such an undertaking had circulated through the US South. In June 1814, for instance, David Holmes, the governor of Mississippi, wrote to Jackson that he "had information from Pensacola" that the British had deposited on the coast "twenty thousand stand of arms and a large quantity of ammunition"— suggesting that "they will endeavor not only to engage the Indians, but the negroes in their cause." While Holmes suspected that the report was exaggerated, he nonetheless found it credible enough to pass the intelligence on to Jackson.[103] In early January 1815, a national journal, the *Niles Weekly Register*, republished an exaggerated report from a Georgia newspaper that a British fleet had landed *"fourteen thousand troops, and a considerable part of them blacks,"* at the mouth of the Apalachicola River. The British force, the report stated, had "built a strong fort at Forbes's store, and placed in it a garrison of 300 men" comprising Red Sticks and "runaway negroes." The author of the report predicted that while the main British force would carry out a "grand expedition" by invading Georgia, the garrison of *"savages* and *negroes"* would remain behind at Prospect Bluff, "with a full supply of arms and ammunition, for the purpose of murdering women and children on the inland frontiers of Georgia."[104] In short, the force of self-emancipated slaves at Prospect Bluff gave form to slaveholders' long-standing inchoate fears of slave revolt.

According to Jackson's own intelligence reports in mid-1816, however, the fort at Prospect Bluff posed little direct threat to the United States. While the very existence of the fort lured slaves in the United States to flee to it in search of freedom, the post itself was undermanned, and the armed ex-slaves there focused on preparing to fend off or escape an expected attack from the Americans.[105] Many of those within the fort were Spanish-speaking fugitive slaves from Pensacola; their leader was an ex-slave known as Garçon. A number of

English-speaking ex-slaves had settled around the fort on farms; their leader was a Black Seminole named Abraham. Yet when the British withdrew in 1815, most of the compound's population migrated under Abraham's leadership from Prospect Bluff to East Florida. Jackson's subordinate, Gen. Edmund Gaines, though crediting reports in 1816 that "upwards of three hundred men" remained at the fort, nonetheless conceded that "some of them are reported to have gone to St. Marks" in East Florida.[106] Likewise, another of Jackson's junior officers, Capt. Ferdinand Amelung, reported to Jackson in June 1816 that "about 20 choctaws, a number of Seminoles and a great number of run-away negroes are supposed to have been there some time ago but a great part of these Brigands have abandoned the Fort on account of scarcity of provisions and have gone to ... East Florida."[107]

Whatever number of maroons remained at Prospect Bluff, Americans nonetheless feared that the post was a magnet for further fugitives. In February 1816, Timothy Barnard, a trader who lived with the Yuchi Creeks, wrote to Hawkins that "I have several letters ... reporting runaway negros. ... If that fort is not broke up soon by the red people or white the citizens of Georgia will loose a number of their negros before the summer is over." Hawkins passed Barnard's warning on to William H. Crawford, the US secretary of war. Despite telling Jackson a year earlier that the fort was garrisoned by only eighty men, when Hawkins wrote to Crawford he inflated his estimate, writing that at the fort, "the whole number of blacks is 350."[108] Crawford passed these concerns to Jackson in March 1816, writing that "between two hundred and fifty and three hundred blacks" at what he called the "negroe fort" were "inveigl[ing] negroes from the frontiers of Georgia. ... This is a state of things which cannot fail to produce much injury to the neighboring settlements."

Yet Crawford was careful to restrain Jackson from taking action. Knowing that Jackson had already violated Spanish sovereignty during the war by invading Pensacola, Crawford instructed him to do no more about the fort than "to call the attention of the governor or military commander of Pensacola to this subject."[109] A month later, Jackson dutifully wrote to Mauricio de Zuñiga, the Spanish governor of West Florida: "I am charged by my government to make known to you that a Negroe Fort, erected during our late war with Britain ... is now occupied by upwards of two hundred & fifty negroes, many of whom have been enticed away from the service of their Masters, Citizens of the United States." He repeated Crawford's charge that the garrison at Prospect Bluff was engaged in "secret practises to inveigle Negroes from the frontier citizens of Georgia." Yet he also added a threatening codicil to the message that would have surprised Crawford, writing that "this Banditti's conduct will not be tolerated by our government and if not put down by the Spanish Authority will compel us in self Defence to destroy them."[110]

During the war, Spain had been powerless to prevent the British from conducting military operations in Florida, including establishing the fort at Prospect Bluff; in 1816, they were similarly powerless to prevent the United States from sending a force to Prospect Bluff to destroy the fort. Nonetheless, Zúñiga tried to deter Jackson from acting unilaterally. In May 1816, he responded to Jackson that the fort was an issue for Spain to resolve, writing that "the Negroes," many of whom had been slaves in Pensacola, were "natives of this place" and thus "vassals of the King." He deemed them "Insurgents or Rebels," and he pledged that Spain would deal with them. They were, in other words, just another group of maroons—the kind of irritants that the Spanish dealt with throughout their empire. He concluded his message to Jackson by writing that he trusted that "neither the Government of the US, nor Yr. Exy. will take any step to the prejudice of the sovereignty of the King."[111] Yet it was too late. Six weeks earlier, even before writing his message to Zúñiga, Jackson had already ordered Gaines into Florida. "Half peace and half war is a state of things which must not exist," Jackson wrote. He continued,

> If the fort harbours the Negroes of our citizens or friendly Indians
> living within our territory, or holds out Inducements to the slaves
> of our Citizens to desert from their owner's service, this fort must
> be destroyed. . . . If they are a Banditti assembled on the Territory of
> Spain or claim to be the subjects of any other power and are stealing
> and enticing away our negroes, they ought to be viewed as a band of
> outlaws—land pirates, and ought to be destroyed. . . . I have very little
> doubt of the fact that this fort has been established by some villains
> for the purpose of murder rapine and plunder and that it ought to be
> blown up regardless of the ground it stands on. . . . Destroy it and re-
> store the stolen negroes and property to their rightful owners.[112]

Jackson's reference to slaves who had fled to Florida from "friendly Indians within our territory" was telling. Slaveholding Creeks, especially those such as William McIntosh who had fought alongside Jackson against the Red Sticks in 1814, resented the existence of the fort at Prospect Bluff and its encouragement of marronage as much as slaveholding white Americans. Hawkins, the US agent to the Creeks, sought to capitalize on this alignment of US and Creek interests by convincing the Creeks to destroy the fort at Prospect Bluff and thus avoid having US troops enter Spanish territory. In April 1816, Hawkins wrote to Crawford that "the Chiefs of this nation" were soon to meet to discuss taking it upon themselves "to recover if practicable the negros in West Florida run from the United States." Hawkins encouraged the Creeks to act, writing that "something must be done, and very soon, or Georgia will soon be despoiled of all their negros on their frontiers."[113] Within weeks, Hawkins received word that the Creeks had resolved to attack the fort. He wrote to Tustunnuggee Hopoie, a prominent Creek leader, that "I rejoice to hear you say 'you are sure the Indians will be able to settle everything.' I wish they may. If they can take the negros from among them and deliver them up to their masters, who are Americans, Indians and Spaniards, they will do an act of justice which will be long remembered by the people of the United States." Hawkins promised a bounty of fifty dollars for every adult male fugitive the Creeks captured, and he offered smaller amounts for women and children. To placate Tustunnuggee Hopoie's concerns that the Creek would be encroaching on Seminole territory, Hawkins waved away the Seminoles' seven decades of autonomy in Florida: "The Muscogees and Seminoles are one people, their great national name is Muscogee."[114] At the same time, well aware that the Seminoles harbored hundreds of fugitives, Hawkins wrote to Jackson that he had "directed a deputation to the Seminoles to prepare them to be quiet in the present state of affairs."[115] Finally, Hawkins wrote to Zuñiga that "the runaway negro establishment in East Florida has been a nuisance to Spain and the U States, as well as to the Muscogee Indians divided by our line of demarcation, and the latter having requested me to aid them to brake them up, and to restore the negros to their masters, I have consented that the Indians by a combined effort, may effect this desirable object of themselves."[116]

Yet Jackson was unbothered that a US attack on maroons in Spanish Florida might spark war with Spain; indeed, he seemed to relish the idea. Thus, it was a combined force of about 300 men from the United States—about half white troops under Gaines, and half Lower Creeks under McIntosh—that descended on the fort at Prospect Bluff in July 1816. The invaders arrived at Prospect Bluff only shortly ahead of a force of Spaniards and Seminoles, dispatched there by Zuñiga and Kinache, that intended to conduct the fort's inhabitants either to safety among the Seminoles or back to slavery in Pensacola. The US attack on the fort was brief: Jackson had ordered a handful of gunboats from New Orleans to meet Gaines's troops; following a short skirmish between McIntosh's Lower Creeks and the fort's defenders, a volley of shots from the gunboats ignited a cache of powder behind the walls; the resulting explosion destroyed the fort. Most of the people inside the fort were killed, but the Americans' estimates of the number of dead varied considerably. One US officer put the number inside the fort at 325 and estimated the number of survivors of the blast as only 50. The commander of one of the gunboats initially estimated that 200 people had been in the fort at the time of the explosion and that only 25 survived; he later estimated that 300 people had been killed. Yet, prior to the brief battle, none of the Americans had reconnoitered the fort thoroughly enough to have an accurate sense of the strength of the garrison. Like US military officers in the Vietnam War who inflated body counts of enemy dead to give an impression of success, the officers who reported on the brief battle understood that the unauthorized use of US force in Spanish territory would be easier to justify if the number of maroons in the fort was significant. Yet, as Gaines and Amelung had earlier acknowledged, hundreds of maroons had already left Prospect Bluff for East Florida before the combined US-Creek force arrived. In all likelihood, only a relatively small force remained at Prospect Bluff at the time of the battle. Non-Americans with no interest in making the force at Prospect Bluff seem significant estimated the garrison to be far smaller. A Creek trader, Alexander Dumont, thought there were only about seventy men in the fort prior to the battle; John Innerarity estimated that about forty men died in the explosion.[117] These figures correspond to Amelung's estimate of eighty men in the fort prior to the battle.

Immediately following the attack, Gaines sent a message "to the Seminole chiefs" that closely resembled Jackson's threatening message to Zuñiga a year earlier. "You harbor a great many of my black people among you," he wrote to the Seminoles. "If you give me leave to go by you against them, I shall not hurt any thing belonging to you." Kinache's reply, like Zuñiga's the year before, showed he understood Gaines's message for what it was: an assertion that the prerogative to recapture slaves who had run away from US citizens transcended not only Spanish sovereignty in Florida but Seminole autonomy as well. "I harbor no negroes," he wrote. Moreover, "I shall use force to stop any armed Americans from passing my towns or on my lands."[118]

Unwilling—yet—to cross the border into Spanish Florida and potentially provoke a war with Spain, in October 1817, Gaines, with a force of about 250 troops, attacked Fowltown, a Seminole village on the Georgia side of the US-Florida border. The US pretext for the attack was that Seminoles at Fowltown had taken part in "the predatory war carried on for some time past against the Georgia frontier." Indeed, border raids had been common in the US-Florida borderlands since the end of the War of 1812: white Americans raided Seminole towns to steal cattle and enslave or re-enslave Black Seminoles; in return, Seminoles raided whites and slaveholding Lower Creeks such as William McIntosh.[119] A Senate committee concluded in early 1819 that by 1817, "a border warfare was commenced between the Seminole Indians and the frontier inhabitants of Georgia," though "it is difficult to determine with certainty who commenced those hostilities, or on whom the greatest injuries were inflicted."[120] At Fowltown, the Seminoles put up a brief defense—the town had only about sixty men capable of fighting—in order to allow the townspeople to withdraw to swampy ground outside of the village; the villagers then retreated entirely into Florida. Thus, like the Red Sticks in 1814, the Seminoles of Fowltown fled to Spanish Florida when confronted with superior US force; nevertheless, Gaines, in his report to Jackson, depicted the defeated and retreating natives as a continuing threat to the United States. The threat stemmed from the anxiety about fugitives that pervaded the thinking of US soldiers and officials. Gaines estimated that, with the new addition of men from Fowltown, "the number of hostile warriors," in Florida had risen to "more than two thousand, besides the blacks, amounting to nearly four hundred men, and increasing by runaways from Georgia."[121]

The attack on Fowltown was merely a prelude to a larger US invasion of Florida. In 1814 at Pensacola and again in 1816 at Prospect Bluff, Jackson had invaded Florida without authorization from the federal government. In both instances, Jackson had affected nonchalance toward the prospect that his actions might cause war with Spain. After Prospect Bluff, he wrote to Crawford that in the wake of the attack, "it would appear that a War with Spain may take place."[122] In 1818, however, the president, James Monroe and the secretary of war, John Calhoun endorsed a US incursion. Following the attack on Fowltown, Calhoun ordered Gaines "to penetrate to the Seminole Towns, through the Floridas" but to avoid violence against Spanish troops. Calhoun then ordered Jackson "to concentrate your forces and adopt the necessary measures" to support Gaines's offensive. Jackson leaped at the opportunity to invade Florida, but he chafed at the order to leave Spanish troops unmolested. He suggested to Monroe in January 1818: "Suppose the case that the Indians are beaten, they take refuge either in Pensacola or St. Augustine, which open their gates to them . . . ? Permit me to remark, that the arms of the United States must be carried to any point within the limites of East Florida, where an Enemy is permitted and protected or disgrace attends." Jackson's suggestion would mean war with Spain, and "the whole of East Florida seized." Jackson proposed to Monroe that "the possession of the Floridas would be desirable to the United States, and in sixty days it will be accomplished."[123]

Monroe approved of the invasion of Florida—he informed Congress in late March 1818, about two weeks after Jackson had marched south into

Florida, that he had ordered "the major general commanding the southern division of the troops of the United States . . . to the theatre of action" because Spain had failed to control the Seminoles, leaving "the United States . . . to pursue their enemy, on a principle of self-defence."[124] Yet Monroe forbade Jackson from directly engaging with Spanish troops. However feeble Spain's presence in Florida was, the Spanish possessed significant force in the Americas, if they could marshal it. Despite Jackson's confidence, Monroe knew that while the United States might overwhelm the token Spanish force stationed in Florida, Spain had dispatched thousands of soldiers to the Americas to put down independence movements—in 1818, roughly 10,000 Spanish soldiers were in Venezuela alone—and possessed enough ships to transport them to Florida.[125] Moreover, Monroe knew that should Jackson provoke Spain to declare war on the United States, "the adventurers of Britain & other countries, would under the Spanish flag, privateer on our commerce."[126] Monroe thus assured Congress, "Orders have been given to the general in command not to enter Florida, unless it be in pursuit of the enemy, and, in that case, to respect Spanish authority wherever it is maintained; and he will withdraw his forces from the province again as soon as he shall have reduced that tribe to order."[127]

Jackson blustered into Florida in the spring of 1818, initiating what historians call the First Seminole War. He targeted the towns of the two most prominent Seminole leaders, Kinache and Bolek. Jackson left Fort Scott in southern Georgia on March 10 and, taking the same route his forces had traveled in 1816 in their assault on the fort at Prospect Bluff, followed the Apalachicola River south. At Prospect Bluff, Jackson ordered the fort that he had destroyed two years earlier be rebuilt. From there, US forces followed a 75-mile path northeast to confront Kinache at his village, Mikasuki.[128] Along the way, Jackson's roughly 800 regular US Army troops were reinforced by McIntosh and a force of about 1,500 Lower Creeks and roughly 1,000 volunteers from Tennessee.[129] (Without congressional authority to do so, Jackson had called for the volunteers in January.) Just as at Fowltown, the Black and Indigenous Seminoles of Mikasuki briefly resisted Jackson's force before fleeing. After entering the vacated town—or, actually, the complex of towns encircling a lake—Jackson put 300 houses to the torch. In his report to Calhoun, Jackson—with an eye toward constructing a narrative that justified his actions—claimed that he had discovered "more than fifty fresh scalps" in Kinache's "Council houses," and that the Seminoles had fled to the Spanish garrison at San Marcos, where they "had received the means of carrying on the war."[130] Indeed, frustrated that the Seminoles and Blacks had eluded him at Mikasuki, Jackson immediately marched on San Marcos; he reached the post in early April and sent a brusque message to the fort's commander, Francisco Caso y Luengo, saying that the US president had "direct[ed] me to march my army into Florida" to "chastise a Savage foe" and "a lawless band of Negro Brigands"; Jackson accused Caso y Luengo of having provided "large supplies of munitions of war" to the "Indians & Negroes." He demanded that the Spanish permit Jackson to take possession of the fort. When Caso y Luengo stalled for time; Jackson took the fort by force.[131] While Jackson was taking San Marcos, a US Navy officer cruising the Florida coast hoisted a Union Jack to lure two Red Stick leaders aboard his ship, where he hanged them.[132]

From San Marcos, Jackson marched his combined American and Lower Creek force toward Bolek's Town on the Suwanee River; Bolek had removed there from Cuscowilla after the Seminoles' clashes with the "Patriots" of the Territory of East Florida. As at Fowltown and Mikasuki, a small force of Black and Indigenous Seminoles from Bolek's Town resisted Jackson's army long enough for the inhabitants of the town to flee. At Bolek's Town, however, Jackson found one further consolation: he captured Robert Armbrister, a former British marine officer who had served during the War of 1812 under Edward Nicolls, the British officer who had established the fort at Prospect Bluffs and its corps of colonial marines.[133] When he returned to San Marcos, Jackson subjected Armbrister and another captive, George Arbuthnot, a Scottish trader who had been at San Marcos when Jackson had seized the town, to a trial by a military tribunal. The court convicted both men of being, as Jackson put it, "exciters of this Savage and Negro War"; Jackson had both men executed.[134] He told Calhoun, "I hope the execution of these two un-principled villains will prove an awfull example to the world, and convince the Government of Great Britain" that supporting the Seminoles through "unprincipled Foreign, or private Agents" would spur US "retribution."[135] Finally, Jackson marched from San Marcos to Pensacola, where he accused the Spanish governor of West Florida, José Masot, of harboring "no less than 500 Indians in Pensacola many of them known to be hostile to the U States." Therefore, Jackson wrote, "I deem it politic and necessary to occupy Pensacola."[136]

Shortly thereafter, Jackson declared the campaign against the Seminoles ended and decamped for Tennessee—but his efforts to provoke war with Spain continued. In August, Jackson tried to order Gaines "to take and gar-rison St. Augustine, the capital of East Florida." Following the tactic he had employed at San Marcos and Pensacola—accusing the Spanish of harboring Seminoles to justify his attacks—Jackson warned Gaines that "it will be necessary to obtain evidence" substantiating that Spanish authorities in St. Augustine were arming the Seminoles. In November, he proposed to Calhoun that the United States invade and occupy Tampa Bay, because "The Savages & Negroes . . . have fled east of the Suwaney river, and . . . settled in the Alatchaway plains, near St. Augustine, or more southwardly."[137] Jackson's efforts to urge Gaines and Calhoun to make further attacks revealed how little his invasion, lasting only from early March to late May 1818, had actually changed. When the brief campaign was done, the Black and Indigenous Seminoles reoccupied their villages or built new ones; the Spanish and British lodged diplomatic protests but otherwise ignored Jackson's provocations; Florida remained a Spanish possession. In 1819, Jackson faced the prospect of congressional censure for his conduct in Florida.

Jackson's invasion, far from encouraging Spain to cede the Floridas to the United States, merely delayed the diplomatic negotiations about the transfer. In January 1818, before Jackson embarked on his invasion of Florida, the secretary of state, John Quincy Adams, and the Spanish envoy to the United States, Luis de Onís, had outlined the general terms of a treaty according to which Spain would cede Florida to the United States in return for the United States ceding some part of its claim to territory west of the Mississippi. In July 1818, when Onís learned the details of Jackson's invasion, he ceased negotiating with Adams about a new border to demand that US troops withdraw from Pensacola and San Marcos. Negotiations resumed after Calhoun wrote to Gaines (Jackson had since departed for Tennessee) that "the President is determined to restore St. Marks and Pensacola . . . to the Spanish authority." He ordered Gaines to surrender Pensacola to the Spanish and evacuate the city immediately.[138] In October 1818, Adams and Onís agreed to a treaty by which Spain would cede the Floridas to the United States in return for US recognition of Spanish sovereignty in Texas.[139]

If the invasion only hindered rather than facilitated the US acquisition of Florida, what, then, did it accomplish? Jackson's invasion resulted in the deaths of roughly sixty Black and Indigenous Seminoles.[140] Yet, by the end of 1818, some Seminoles moved back into the villages that Jackson had destroyed, while others retreated into the interior of the Florida peninsula.[141] In 1823, Horatio Dexter, a merchant, estimated that more than 400 "Negroes" remained in Florida—as many as Gaines had estimated to be in Florida in 1817. According to Dexter, more than eighty alone inhabited the town of

Abraham, 1848.
Engraving by N. Orr.
From John T. Sprague,
*The Origin, Progress,
and Conclusion of
the Florida War*
(New York: D.
Appleton, 1848).

Angola, south of Tampa Bay, "where they are employed by the Havanna fishery smacks & pass to Cuba frequently." Moreover, "the Micosukys with their chief, the son of the late Kenhijah & his Negroes have returned to near their old town."[142] Archaeological records indicate that African American villages in Florida in the early 1820s included Angola; Nero's Town on the Suwanee River; and Pilaklikaha (also known as Abraham's Town) on the Withlacoochee River, which had been founded by Abraham, one of the leaders at Prospect Bluff.[143]

In January 1819, a committee of the House of Representatives recommended censuring Jackson for his illegal trial and execution of Ambrister and Arbuthnot (in the end, the full House declined to censure Jackson by a vote of 107–100). A Senate committee agreed with the House committee that the executions had been illegal. It further concluded that in taking it upon himself to call for volunteers from Tennessee to aid the invasion of Florida, "the committee are compelled to declare that they conceive General Jackson to have disregarded the positive orders of the Department of War, the constitution, and laws." Above all, the Senate committee concluded that Jackson, in attacking San Marcos and Pensacola, intended "to involve the nation in a war without her consent." The committee concluded that "were this nation subject to the will of a military despot, and there were no constitutional barriers to the inordinate exercise of military ambition, more than this could scarcely have been expected."[144]

For historians who adhere to the manifest destiny paradigm, there is little place for the Senate's condemnation of Jackson. They depict Jackson's invasion of Florida as a sanguine example of US expansion. In their view, Jackson conquered the Seminoles and bullied the Spanish into ceding Florida to the United States; if some Americans disapproved of Jackson's methods, they certainly could not argue with his results. As one such historian put it, Jackson's "murderous 1818 raid into Pensacola convinced Spain to cede the territory to Washington."[145] Yet it is not at all clear that Jackson's raid had anything at all to do with Spain's cession of Florida to the United States in 1821. Spain formally protested Jackson's invasion, but having struggled for decades to establish their rule in Florida, the Spanish more than anyone understood how little Jackson's raid against the Seminoles accomplished. Spain was far more concerned with maintaining good relations with the United States so that the United States would continue to withhold recognition of the ongoing independence movements in the provinces of Rio de la Plata, Chile, New Granada, Venezuela, Guatemala, New Spain, and Santo Domingo. While Spain hoped to maintain its sovereignty in those territories, it had long sought to rid itself of Florida. Indeed. Spain had made overtures to the United States, offering to exchange Florida for recognition of Spanish sovereignty in Texas as early as June 1817.[146] Jackson's invasion of Florida merely delayed that accord between the United States and Spain.

Thirty years before Jackson's invasion, the Georgia slaves Daniel and Patty, carrying Patty's infant son, Abram, had fled from Georgia toward Florida. If they reached Florida, they may well have been living when Jackson invaded, when he withdrew, and when Black Seminoles reoccupied the villages that Jackson had briefly taken. Indeed, the Black Seminole Abraham who founded Pilaklikaha and who was sometimes known as Abram may well have been the Abram whom Patty carried to freedom in Florida in 1789. Little is known of Abraham's youth other than that he was born between 1787 and 1791—as was Patty's Abram. According to the abolitionist legislator Joshua Giddings, who wrote an account of the Seminole wars in 1858, Abraham's "parents had fled from Georgia, and died in their forest-home."[147] Giddings, an ardent abolitionist, imagined Abraham to be as inveterate an opponent of slavery as himself. Yet in the Florida borderlands, maroons such as Abraham could not afford to take a strict ideological position on slavery if they hoped to maintain their autonomy. Like Spaniards, Seminoles, and the followers of William Augustus Bowles, all of whom had alternately held slaves and welcomed fugitives, Florida maroons such as Abraham, like maroons elsewhere in the Americas, sometimes accommodated to slaveholders. In 1822, according to a white settler in Georgia, an "Indian negro, named Abraham," returned to slaveholders in Georgia "some slaves that had been plundered by the Seminole Indians."[148] By that time, Abraham had become an interpreter for Micanopy, a Seminole leader who succeeded his uncle, Bolek, to the leadership of the Cuscowilla Seminoles. Abraham's status among the Seminoles was high enough that he married one of Bolek's widows. In 1826, Abraham accompanied Micanopy to Washington as an interpreter. He just missed Jackson, who, after losing the presidential election in 1824, had resigned his seat in the US Senate and returned to Tennessee. Abraham was one of "the three principal men" of Pilaklikaha, according to James McCall, an army officer who visited the village in 1826.[149] According to Giddings, "He appears to have been a man of unusual influence."[150] Though Jackson claimed victory over the Seminoles and their Black allies in 1818, and returned to Florida as territorial governor for a brief eight months in 1821 after the United States formally acquired the territory, it was Abraham, and the thousands of Black and Indigenous maroons like him, who remained the true rulers of borderlands Florida.

CHAPTER TWO

Traders

The year 1803 was pivotal for the United States and for the Native Americans who lived in the border regions of the early republic. The most consequential event of the year was the US purchase of the Louisiana Territory from France. Yet the Louisiana Purchase began as peradventure. US envoys embarked for France in 1803 hoping for nothing more than to acquire the city of New Orleans and its surrounding area, for which they were prepared to offer $10 million. They were willing to settle for navigation privileges on the Mississippi and commercial rights in New Orleans, which they anticipated might cost them $2 million. However, representatives of the French First Consul, Napoléon, surprised the US envoys by offering the entirety of French Louisiana to the United States for $15 million. Reeling from the loss over the previous two years of tens of thousands of troops in Haiti—they had died of yellow fever and in battle against the ex-slaves who had ruled Haiti since overthrowing their French enslavers in 1791—Napoléon had resolved to divest his empire of its American holdings.

Historians have often remarked that the purchase doubled the territory of the United States. "In a stroke, Jefferson had doubled the size of the United States," Eric Foner wrote in 2006. "Overnight, the size of the United States more than doubled," John M. Faragher echoed in 2020.[1] Yet, at the time, no one could agree about the borders of the purchase. In 1803, Spanish officials disputed the extent of Louisiana, arguing that the territory—which Napoléon had bullied Spain into ceding to France in a secret treaty in 1800—amounted to nothing more than a narrow strip of land on the west bank of the Mississippi River between St. Louis and New Orleans.[2] US officials themselves were unclear about the boundaries of the province. An early US report in 1803 could say only that "the precise boundaries of Louisiana, westwardly of the Mississippi, though very extensive, are at present involved in some obscurity. Data are equally wanting to assign with precision its northern extent."[3] Britain, for its part, did not recognize the legality of the Spanish retrocession of Louisiana to France in 1800, and thus questioned the legitimacy of the US purchase altogether. In short, the purchase into which the United States stumbled in 1803 did not guarantee its control of the West. Rather, through the purchase, the United States entered into a complex competition for sovereignty in the trans-Mississippi borderlands with Britain and Spain and with the sovereign Native American nations who shifted their commercial and political allegiances among these imperial powers.

Some Americans in the early nineteenth century imagined that they possessed an important advantage in this scramble for the Louisiana Territory: the booming American economy. Within just a few years of the US acquisition of Louisiana, the United States embarked upon a rapid economic transformation, as manufacturing and commercial agriculture began to displace cottage industries and subsistence farming. The number of federal patents issued doubled in every five-year period between 1790 and 1814. The number of banks rose from 4 in 1791 to 246 in 1816. The volume of internal trade increased from about 100,000 tons in 1790 to roughly 500,000 tons in 1815. Investors founded 44 textile mills before 1812, and a further 96 between 1812 and 1814. Manufacturing begat urbanization: between 1790 and 1810, the population of Philadelphia doubled from 45,520 to 91,874, while that of New York tripled from 33,131 to 96,373. Urban populations and industry created unprecedented demands for raw materials and commercial agricultural products. To supply New York City with lumber, loggers deforested southern New York state in the years after 1800. They supplied other cities as well: in 1812, seven-eighths of the commercial timber in Baltimore (which itself nearly tripled its population between 1790 and 1810, from 13,503 to 35,583) came from the state of New York.[4] In his 1809 message to Congress, James Madison wrote that "The face of our country everywhere presents the evidence of laudable enterprise, of extensive capital, and of durable improvement."[5]

American historians refer to this broad transformation as the "market revolution."[6] Yet, like "manifest destiny," the term "market revolution" obscures as well as reveals. The expansion of the commercial economy was not unheralded; the consumer revolution of the eighteenth century anticipated the market revolution of the nineteenth. Colonial Americans were avid consumers of manufactured goods: their consumption of British imports increased from £1 to £2 per capita between 1720 and 1760. By the 1780s, judging by probate records, even settlers in the backwoods of Kentucky possessed numerous manufactured goods such as silverware, looking glasses, table linen, and mattresses.[7]

Although the new market economy was not unprecedented, some early nineteenth-century US policymakers nevertheless envisioned that the expansion of commerce would carry the United States into the Louisiana Territory. In 1808, Albert Gallatin, the secretary of the treasury, recommended to Congress $20 million worth of internal improvements to spur manufacturing and commerce; his proposal included turnpikes to link cities on the Atlantic coast with New Orleans and St. Louis, the two largest cities in newly acquired Louisiana.[8] In particular, the planned road to St. Louis would facilitate the most profitable commerce in the Missouri River region: the trade in furs with Indigenous people. The fur trade was an immense commercial enterprise. In the first years of the nineteenth century, Britain imported $160,000 worth of beaver pelts alone from the Great Plains every year. The wealthiest American in the early republic, John Jacob Astor, who was worth roughly $20 million when he died in 1848, initially made his fortune in the fur trade in the early nineteenth century. Between 1788 and 1803, St. Louis trading companies annually garnered about $200,000 worth of furs from Indigenous people on the Lower Missouri River; about half that sum came from the Osages, the preeminent Indigenous nation in the region.[9]

Aside from the profits to be made from the fur trade, some Americans envisioned that the fur trade would be a means of shifting lands from Indigenous to US control. Native people such as the Osages trapped beaver and muskrat and hunted deer for white traders in return for goods they obtained largely on credit. In February 1803, two months before finalizing the Louisiana Purchase, Jefferson wrote to William Henry Harrison, then governor of the Indiana Territory (which at the time extended west to the Mississippi River and thus bordered on the Louisiana Territory), suggesting that the United States would "be glad to see the good and influential Indians among them run into debt, because we observe that when these debts get beyond what the individual can pay, they become willing to lop them off by a cession of land." A few weeks earlier, he had written to Andrew Jackson that "obtaining lands" (together with "the preservation of peace") was a principal object of US policy toward Native Americans.[10] Suggestions such as these prompted the anthropologist Anthony F. C. Wallace to criticize "a degree of ruthlessness in Jefferson's dealings with the Indians, the ruthlessness of a benevolent zealot who would do virtually anything to insure that his new, free, American republic survived and grew."[11]

Yet in practice, the market revolution failed to advance US sovereignty in the Louisiana Territory in the first years of the nineteenth century. Despite—or because of—living in a consumer economy since the mid-eighteenth century, many Americans, including influential Americans such as Jefferson, harbored misgivings about the expansion of commerce. Instead, in the Louisiana Territory, Jefferson and his successor Madison made the pursuit of profit in the fur trade a low priority; in the first decades of the nineteenth century, the United States forbade alcohol from the fur trade and limited the number of traders in the borderlands through a license system. The primary US institutional effort to extend sovereignty into the borderlands was the so-called factory system, a network of federally owned trading posts, or factories, where federal factors exchanged manufactured goods with Indigenous people for furs.[12] Despite Jefferson's musings about debt and land cessions, the purpose of the factory system was not to extort land through ruinous debts but to win the good will of Indigenous people. Factors sold their goods at low cost; they sought only to cover the costs of their posts. They were expressly forbidden from selling goods to Indigenous people on credit.[13] Through the factory system, the federal government hoped not to detach Native Americans from their lands but to detach them from their commercial ties to private fur traders, most of whom were French-speaking merchants who had operated for many years in Louisiana under Spanish rule, and who had as little concern for the interests of the United States as they had had for those of Spain. However ruthless Jefferson's imaginings may have been, as he expressed them to Harrison and Jackson, in the multilateral borderlands of the Louisiana Territory where Native Americans, including the powerful Osages, could seek commercial and political alliance with Britain or Spain, compromise and accommodation was the rule; and both the United States and the Osages subordinated their commercial interests to diplomatic ones.

By the early 1820s, however, some US officials believed that the moment that Gallatin had anticipated in 1808 with his plan for roads connecting East and West had finally arrived. US policymakers decided that the factory system had outlived its usefulness in an age of increasing commerce. The

United States disassembled the factory system and appointed a team of federal agents to survey a road from Missouri through the southern Great Plains to New Mexico—the Santa Fe Trail—in order to facilitate the expansion of US trade into northern Mexico. By the time of the survey, most federal officials no longer regarded private commerce as a hindrance to US interests in the borderlands; instead, they viewed it as its vanguard. Yet this effort to spur commerce in the borderlands had unintended consequences: while it enabled a handful of traders to become wealthy, it did little to promote the expansion of US sovereignty. Indeed, the arrival of American merchants to the southern Great Plains in the 1820s augmented the power not of the United States but of an imperial competitor, the Comanches, who were the true rulers of the southern plains in the early nineteenth century. Thus, despite the vaunted transformative power of the market revolution, in the early nineteenth-century borderlands, the market revolution had little effect on US sovereignty in the western borderlands.

The initial conciliation and later ineffectiveness of US commerce in the Louisiana Territory was exemplified by George Champlin Sibley, Jefferson's chief factor in the region and later one of the commissioners who surveyed the Santa Fe Trail. Appointed in 1808 to manage the factory at Fort Osage on the Lower Missouri River, Sibley at first embraced important aspects of Jefferson's agrarian political economy: he believed that commerce between natives and unscrupulous fur traders—especially non-US citizens—corrupted the virtue of Indigenous people and the national interests of the United States. At Fort Osage, Sibley enthusiastically pursued his mission to regulate trade in order to stabilize relations between Indigenous people and white Americans in the Lower Missouri borderlands. Notwithstanding Jefferson's musings about land cessions, Sibley and most of his superiors in the factory system believed that US expansion into the Louisiana Territory would be best accomplished by a measured, peaceful progression of US influence in the region that integrated Indigenous people into the emerging US commercial economy, rather than by a headlong rush for the profits of the trade in furs and pelts. Yet Sibley gradually developed his own commercial ambitions, and like many white settlers in Missouri, by the mid-1810s, he had begun speculating in lands and dabbling in trade. By the early 1820s, he had largely accommodated to the economic mores of the emerging market society in the United States. Sibley, once an obstacle to unregulated commerce in the borderlands, became its apostle.

Yet while Sibley had succeeded as a factor, he floundered at business. In 1822, when the factory system ended, he borrowed heavily to buy the stock of goods at Fort Osage, anticipating that he could reap the profits of a trade in furs with the Osages that he had managed for over a decade on behalf of the United States. He quickly failed as a private trader, however, and discharged his debt only by selling some of the land he had purchased over the previous decade. Ironically, it was he, and not the Osages, who, to borrow Jefferson's phrase, had to "lop" off a fur trade debt by a cession of land. Sibley's failures mirrored those of the United States. Once the federal government opened the fur trade to private traders, its influence in the Missouri River borderlands waned.

CHILDREN OF THE MIDDLE WATERS

When the United States acquired Louisiana, the dominant power in the Lower Missouri River region was neither the French, who had sold the territory to the United States, nor the Spanish, who had nominally ruled Louisiana for most of the previous four decades, but the Dhegihan Siouan-speaking Osages, who called themselves *Ni-u-ko'n-ska*, or Children of the Middle Waters. During the century preceding the Louisiana Purchase, the Osages controlled a territory straddling woodlands to the east and prairie to the west, extending from the Missouri River in the north to the Red River in the south. They were the primary suppliers of furs and slaves to European traders in St. Louis. The Osages' commerce with Europeans made them wealthy, and their control of the three primary river arteries that flowed eastward from the Great Plains into the Lower Mississippi—the Missouri River, the Red River, and between them the Arkansas River—allowed them to interdict most European traders who tried to reach competing Indigenous groups to the west such as the Caddoan-speaking Pawnees and Wichitas. Preventing Caddoan groups to the west from acquiring firearms from European traders kept the Pawnees and Wichitas relatively weak, thus allowing the Osages, themselves armed with muskets acquired through trade, to raid Caddoan-speaking groups for captives with ease. Over the course of the eighteenth century, the Osages captured thousands of Indigenous people and sold them into slavery in the Illinois country, Lower Louisiana, and the French Caribbean. The Osages were a relatively small nation: probably no more than 12,000 people at the outset of the eighteenth century and, owing to the impact of disease, fewer than that by the end of the century, grouped into two, and later three subdivisions. Had their Indigenous and European enemies united against them, they would have easily outnumbered them; but the Osages successfully exploited the divisions among their rivals. By the beginning of the nineteenth century, the Osages had overawed their Indigenous neighbors, and European traders entered Osage territory warily.[14]

According to their own oral traditions, the Osages had migrated from the Ohio Valley to the Lower Missouri in the seventeenth century, as part of a larger Dhegihan Siouan group that eventually divided into the Osages, Kaw, Omahas, Poncas, and Quapaws.[15] The Osages separated themselves from the rest of the Dhegihan Sioux when they reached the juncture of the Missouri and Osage Rivers; whether by design or by happy accident, they placed themselves at the strategic, commercial, and ecological center of North America, in a borderland between forest and prairie, and between the French, Spanish, and British empires.[16] The Osages traveled widely over their territory to harvest resources from both the grasslands and the woodlands. According to the fur trader Auguste Chouteau, "Having sowed their corn in the month of April, they start in the first days of May for hunting buffaloes at the distance of about three hundred miles from their settlements and they do not return before the end of the month of August. In September they gather their corn and immediately after they start to hunt beavers, deers, and pass all the winter scattered in the woods and do not come back to their village before the 10th or 15th of March."[17] By the beginning of the nineteenth century, there were three large Osage villages: the Big Osage (the largest group) on the Osage River; the Little Osage on the Missouri River, and, beginning sometime in the 1760s, a third division, the Arkansas Band of the Osage, on the Verdigris River just north of the Arkansas River.

The Osages were able to range easily over their extensive territory because by the time Chouteau observed them, they had possessed horses for almost a century. Beginning in 1680, horses had diffused, through intertribal trade, northward and eastward from New Mexico after the Pueblos had revolted against the Spanish, driven out the invaders, and seized control of the Spaniards' livestock.[18] By the beginning of the eighteenth century, horses, or at least the knowledge of them, had spread into Osage territory: an equestrian pictograph on a rock wall near the White River, a tributary of the Mississippi between the Arkansas and the Missouri Rivers, dates to about 1700.[19] In 1719, Claude du Tisné, a French trader in furs and slaves, acquired horses from the Osages when he visited one of their villages on the Osage River.[20] The Osages traded horses to other Indigenous groups and to the occasional French visitor such as du Tisné; but they used them primarily to hunt bison in the grasslands several hundred miles west of their villages. Sibley participated in such a hunt in 1811 with a group of eighty Osage hunters. "The firing of 80 guns, the yells of the excited Indians, and the tremendous roaring of

An Osage Indian Lancing a Buffalo, 1846–1848. Painting by George Catlin. Gift of Mrs. Joseph Harrison Jr., Smithsonian American Art Museum, Washington, DC.

so many affrighted Buffaloes, many thousands, altogether, made up [the] scene." he wrote. "The valley was soon cleared; but the thundering of the retreating animals was heard for an hour afterwards. The issue of the affair was 27 Buffaloes killed."[21]

Osage territory was rich not only with bison but with other wildlife. The American explorer Zebulon Pike, traveling through the Osage prairie in 1806, remarked, "We were continually passing through large herds of buffalo, elk, and cabrie; and I have no doubt but one hunter could support 200 men."[22] The grasslands through which Pike traveled were only one part of the Osage territory; Osage woodlands contained black and brown bears, beavers, red and gray foxes, minks, muskrats, otters, and immense numbers of white-tailed deer.[23] Drawing from this region, in the decades before the Louisiana Purchase, the Osages provided St. Louis fur traders with well over half of the furs, pelts, and deerskins that they collected from Indigenous nations on the Missouri River. In 1794, when St. Louis fur traders met in order to divide the trade of nine Indigenous nations of the Missouri among themselves, they estimated the total value of the trade to be 175,000 *livres*; the

Chapter 2

Osages' share was 96,000 *livres*. The commerce of the Kaw, whose trade was the second largest on the Missouri, was worth only one-quarter of that of the Osages. In 1798, Zénon Trudeau, the lieutenant-governor of Upper Louisiana, wrote that the Osages used their preeminent position in the fur trade to dictate the terms of trade to the Europeans: "On many occasions they compel the traders to an unequal and unjust exchange, maltreating them if they resist. But these vexations do not prevent the traders from returning next year."[24]

The Osages tenaciously controlled their territory, preventing traders from passing through their land to trade with other Indigenous groups, and preventing any outsiders—Indigenous or white—from hunting in their territory. A St. Louis periodical reported in 1790 that traders who attempted to bypass the Osages to "go to the other nations" of the Missouri found that "before they return they will be stopped and pillaged."[25] In 1791, Manuel Pérez, the lieutenant-governor of Illinois, wrote to Esteban Rodriguez Miró, the governor-general of Louisiana, that 200 Osages had positioned themselves on the Missouri "to await the traders who were to ascend to the other nations." They halted one group of traders bound for the Kaw and took "the greater portion of the merchandise." When the traders remonstrated, the Osages told them they should consider themselves fortunate that they had been left with anything at all. "This incident makes it clear," Pérez wrote, "that the Osages are determined not to let traders pass to the other nations."[26] In a borderland where the Osage could play imperial competitors against each other, there was little the Spanish could do. The only effective course of action for the Spanish was to impose a trade embargo on the Osages. Were they to do so, however, Miró feared that English traders—who controlled the trade with Indigenous people of the Mississippi River above St. Louis—would move southward, "reach the Missouri by way of branches of other rivers," and "introduce themselves among the Osages."[27] Indeed, in 1791 a Spanish official warned that the English, "in order to tempt" Indigenous groups from the Missouri to trade with them, "give them merchandise at a very low price [and] hope to recover their loss in the future."[28]

If white traders could not pass through Osage lands to reach the Osages' Indigenous competitors, neither could white trappers operate in Osage territory. In the fall of 1802, Daniel Boone, who had moved from Kentucky to Spanish Louisiana in 1799, was trapping beaver on the Niangua River, a tributary of the Osage River. A group of Osages confiscated all his furs—and also forced Boone and his companions to cook a meal for them. The Osages confiscated the furs of Boone's son, Nathan, when he tried to return to the Niangua in 1803 and again in 1804.[29]

The Osages sold not only furs and pelts to European traders but also Indigenous captives. In the early eighteenth century, French traders on the Lower Mississippi River began buying captives—usually Pawnees or other Caddoan-speaking natives—from the Osages. The French transported many of those slaves to New Orleans or to the English in Charlestown; from there, they shipped the slaves to one of the Caribbean sugar islands.[30] While most slaves went to the Caribbean, a significant number of Caddoan-speaking slaves remained in the French settlements in Illinois—so much so that among French settlers in Illinois, *Pani*, the French term for Pawnee, became a euphemism for "slave." A 1732 census of the Illinois country found 699 inhabitants of French settlements; 40 percent of those inhabitants were slaves: 119 Indigenous people and 165 Africans. By 1751, there were 1,380 inhabitants in the French settlements of the Illinois country. Almost 600 of those people were slaves; 149 of those slaves were Indigenous people. In 1769, five years after the Spanish had acquired Louisiana from France, the Irish-born Spanish governor-general of Louisiana, Alejandro O'Reilly, banned the trade in Indigenous slaves (though not Indigenous slavery itself). The illegal trade in Indigenous slaves continued nevertheless, with St. Louis as its commercial hub.[31]

Spain's failure to halt the trade in Indigenous slaves was instructive. In the Lower Missouri borderlands, the Osages, rather than the Spanish, were the true authorities. They held sway over most Indigenous nations in the region; only the Comanches to their southwest were their equals. French traders, who only glancingly acknowledged Spanish authority in Louisiana, were, to all purposes, the Osages' junior commercial partners in the region. In 1793, according to Trudeau, Spanish authorities tried to break the power of the Osages by inducing the Shawnees and Loup River Pawnees to join the Spanish in war against the them; the only result was to rouse the Osages to war so that "extreme terror seized on all of our settlements, and the inhabitants did not venture to go out except in armed parties of twenty or thirty men."[32] Trudeau warned the Spanish governor of Louisiana, Francisco Luis Héctor de Carondelet, that if the Osages decided to attack the European settlement, "they will tire out and kill the poor inhabitants, who, not being able to cultivate their lands, will be obliged to emigrate to the other towns of the province or to the American side" of the Mississippi.[33] Three years after the failed effort to organize an alliance against the Osages, the Spanish returned to placating them; Carondelet sent medals and Spanish flags to Osage leaders as a sign of Spain's good will.[34] In 1803, Nicolas de Finiels, a French engineer in the service of Spain, wrote that "despite the efforts that have been made to weaken" the Osages, "they continue to make the European settlements uneasy."[35]

When the United States acquired Louisiana from France in 1803, Americans quickly apprehended that the Osages ruled the Lower Missouri. "The truth is," Jefferson wrote to Henry Dearborn, the secretary of war, in July 1804, the Osages "are the great nation South of the Missouri, their possession extending from thence to the Red river, as the Sioux are great North of that river. With these two powerful nations we must stand well, because in their quarter we are miserably weak."[36] The Osages of the Arkansas River so disdained the United States that they could not believe that the United States had managed to acquire the Louisiana Territory. In late May 1804, as Meriwether Lewis and William Clark were leading their expedition up the Missouri River and had nearly reached the Osage River, they encountered a French trader who, according to Clark, had just returned from "that part of the Osarge nation settled on the Arkansa River." The French trader had carried to the Osages a letter from Pierre Chouteau informing them of the sale of Louisiana to the United States. The trader told Lewis and Clark that "his letter was committed to the flaims, the Inds. not believing that the Americans had possession of the Countrey."[37]

Yet the commerce that had levered the Osages to dominance exacted a price: contact with traders exposed the Osages to disease; traders interfered with traditional Osage governance; and the pressure of commercial hunters took its toll on wildlife. As a result, while the Osages remained a formidable regional power at the time of the Louisiana Purchase, their hold on the Lower Missouri was not as secure as it had been even a decade earlier. An epidemic of smallpox swept through the Lower Missouri in 1801–2, affecting the Osages as well as other Indigenous nations of the Lower Missouri.[38] The number of Osages who died in the epidemic is unknown, but according to Clark, the Osages' neighbors, the Omahas, lost 1,600 people, leaving them "to the insults of their weaker neighbours, which before was glad to be on friendly terms with them."[39] In April 1801, Charles de Hault de Lassus, the lieutenant-governor of Upper Louisiana, having learned that "the Mahas, Ayoas, and other Indians . . . have suffered last winter from the smallpox," ordered all fur traders returning that spring from the west, including Osage territory, to quarantine at Gabaret Island north of St. Louis.[40]

One effect of the epidemic may have been to leave the weakened Osages less able to defend their territory from attack. In fall of 1805, Potawatomis attacked the Little Osage village, killed thirty-four, and took sixty captives—an intrusion into Osage territory that would have been unthinkable a decade earlier. Osages, once the enslavers of their neighbors, had become the enslaved. It is possible, however, that the Potawatomis never intended to permanently enslave their Osage captives. Among Indigenous nations in the middle of North America, captors sometimes returned captives in an effort to establish good relations—indeed, sometimes the point of the raid was to obtain captives merely to return them.[41] US agents, also hoping to win the good will of the Osages, delivered about fifty of the Osage captives from the Potawatomis; Pike brought them to the Osages in the summer of 1806, at the start of his expedition into the southern Great Plains. James B. Wilkinson, an Army lieutenant who accompanied Pike into the southern Great Plains in 1806, described "wives throwing themselves into the arms of their husbands, parents embracing their children, and children their parents." As a diplomatic gesture, the return of the captives was a success for the United States. It demonstrated to the Osages that the United States could wield enough authority of its own in the borderlands for the Osages to consider them worthy diplomatic and commercial partners. For almost a century, the Osages had maintained their preeminent position in the Lower Missouri by virtue of their commercial and diplomatic relationships with the putative rulers of Louisiana—first the French, then the Spanish. According to the terms of that relationship, access to the commercial wealth of the interior depended on the good will of the Osages. In return, the Osages received preferential trade terms, which allowed them to maintain their dominance over their Indigenous neighbors. Whether or not the Osages saw the return of the captives as an opportunity to improve relations with the Potawatomis, they seized on the redemption of captives to attach themselves to the United States as they had once been attached to the French and Spanish. Sans Oreille, an Osage leader, praised the United States, saying, according to Pike, "Who did this? was it the Spaniards? No. The French? No. Had either of those people been governors of the country, your relatives might have rotted in captivity." However much the return of the captives was a diplomatic success, it ended with further tragedy. Shortly after the arrival of Pike with the redeemed captives, Wilkinson reported that the Osages "were seized with a species of influenza," which took 200 lives. Someone in Pike's party may have brought the disease to the Osages in the course of redeeming the captives. Or some of the Osage captives themselves may have carried the disease from the Potawatomis back to their home.[42]

While the effect of disease was obvious, traders, more insidiously, undermined traditional Osage political structures and encouraged division. A key moment of rupture occurred in 1802, when the French government of Louisiana abruptly decided to change the terms according to which it regulated trade with the Osages. As late as 1795, Zénon Trudeau, the lieutenant-governor of Upper Louisiana, believed that the half brothers Auguste and Pierre Chouteau, who together held the government monopoly on trade with the Osages, had a salutary influence on the natives.[43] Indeed, Trudeau and Carondelet relied on the advice of the Chouteaus, who understood the intricacies of Osage politics, to determine diplomatic priorities in the Lower Missouri borderlands. Seven years later, however, concerned that the control of the lucrative trade with the Osages had not only enriched the Chouteaus but made them more powerful in the Lower Missouri borderlands than the Spanish territorial government, Manuel de Salcedo, the governor-general of Louisiana, decreed that the Chouteaus' monopoly on the Osage trade was at an end. The monopoly would henceforth be held by a consortium headed by a competing St. Louis trader, Manuel Lisa, who not incidentally had paid a significant amount to the government to acquire the monopoly. According to Salcedo, the shift would "conciliate with the political views of this government" and ensure that "the profit from the said trades be divided among all."[44]

The Chouteaus did not meekly accept the loss of their monopoly. According to de Lassus, when he informed Auguste Chouteau of Salcedo's decision, Chouteau made "the most lively representation of prejudice and impairment that has resulted to him."[45] By the fall of 1802, the point at which the Chouteaus were obliged to deliver their trading posts near the Big and Little Osage villages to Lisa and his partners, they had engineered divisions and changes in leadership among the Osages that benefited their interests. Because Lisa's monopoly applied only to the Big and Little Osages and not to the smaller, outlying Arkansas Band, the Chouteaus persuaded a large group of Osages to move from the northern villages to join the Arkansas Band. Indeed, by the time of the Louisiana Purchase, perhaps half of all the Osages belonged to the Arkansas division. According to Wilkinson, these Osages migrated south "at the request of Pierre Chouteau, for the purpose of securing their trade." Pike added that Chouteau had encouraged the split "as a revenge upon Mr. Manuel [Lisa], who had obtained . . . the exclusive trade of the Osage nation." Still more damaging to the Osages, the Chouteaus interfered with Osage leadership structure. Traditionally, each Osage division had two leaders, known as *Ga-hi-ges*: one from each of the two Osage moieties, *Tsi-zhu* (which symbolized sky and peace) and *Honga* (which symbolized earth and war). Cashesegra, or Big Track, one of the leaders of the Arkansas Band, was loyal to the Chouteaus; he was not a *Ge-hi-ge*, however, but a prominent warrior who had received a medal from the Spanish at Chouteau's request. In 1800, when one of the Big Osage *Ga-hi-ges* died, the Chouteaus circumvented the usual succession system to elevate Pawhuska, or White Hair, another man friendly to their interests, to leadership. According to Wilkinson, Pawhuska was "a chief of Chouteau's creating, as well as Cashesegra." Among the Little Osage, Pierre Chouteau promoted Nezuma, or The Rain That Walks, to leadership by taking him along with a delegation of other Osages to visit Thomas Jefferson in Washington. Nezuma, Wilkinson wrote, "has no more command in the village than a child, is no warrior, and has not even the power to controul the will of a single man in his nation." Nevertheless, Nezuma, upon Chouteau's recommendation, received a medal from Jefferson, signifying his leadership status among the Little Osages. "Our grand medals have become so common," Wilkinson wrote, "that they do not carry with them the respect which they should."[46]

Apart from the effects of disease and the interference of the Chouteaus in Osage governance, the position of the Osages declined as fur traders apprehended that other borderland regions richer in game were more profitable than the Lower Missouri. In 1802, Louis Vilemont, a French traveler in North America, estimated that the Osage trade remained the largest on the Lower Missouri; it was worth almost 100,000 *piastres* annually. The combined volume of trade of the Kaw and the Omahas, the Osages' closest competitors, was only half that of the Osages. Yet, farther north, in the woodlands west of the Great Lakes, the Ojibwe traded almost 140,000 *piastres* worth of furs to the British every year. The Dakota added another 78,000 *piastres* worth of furs.[47] In 1804, Pierre Chouteau wrote to Albert Gallatin that while the Osage trade was worth over $40,000 annually, making it the most valuable on the Missouri, he anticipated that commerce with the Lakota on the Upper Missouri, though worth only $15,000 in 1804, would soon eclipse it. The Lakota trade, Chouteau wrote, promised to be "beaucoup plus considérable à l'avenir"—much larger in the future.[48]

Yet in 1803 the Osage trade remained large, and the Osages themselves still dominated the region. US officials were less concerned with the profits to be made from the trade than with the diplomatic benefits that might attach to a commercial relationship between American traders and the Osages. In 1804, when Jefferson met in Washington with a delegation of Osages (including Pawhuska, Sans Oreille, and Nezuma), he expressed to them his hope that commerce between Osages and Americans would build good relations. "You have furs and peltries which we want, and we have clothes and other useful things which you want. Let us employ ourselves then in mutually accommodating each other." He promised the Osages that the United States intended "to establish an Agent to reside with you," who would "be the guardian of our peace and friendship," and "maintain a good understanding and friendship between us."[49] Indeed, Jefferson tried to steer US officials in the Lower Missouri borderlands away from conflict and toward commerce. In July 1808, Meriwether Lewis, whom Jefferson had appointed as governor of Louisiana Territory, frustrated like Spanish governors of Louisiana before him with the autonomy of the Osages, wrote to William Henry Harrison, governor of the Indiana Territory, that he had invited the "Shawnees, Delawares, Kickapoos, Soos, Saues, Jaways, &c." to make war against the Osages. Lewis declared that the Osages were "no longer under the protection of the United States" and hoped that the Osages' enemies would "drive them from our neighborhood."[50] When Jefferson learned of Lewis's action, he quickly reminded him that the United States was not prepared to join the conflict. "Nothing ought to be more avoided than the embarking ourselves in a system of military coercion on the Indians," he wrote. Rather, "commerce is the great engine by which we are to coerce them, not war." Rather than military might—which the United States could barely effect in Louisiana anyway—Jefferson recommended to Lewis the regulated trade of the factory system: "As soon as our factories on the Missouri & Misipi can be in activity they will have more powerful effects than so many armies."[51]

TO SECURE THE FRIENDSHIP OF THE INDIANS

Only a month after Jefferson wrote to Lewis touting the advantages of the factory system in attaching the interests of the Osages to those of the United States, a unit of US Army troops arrived at a bluff overlooking the Missouri River, 330 miles upriver from St. Louis, to establish the post that would house the Osage factory. The US party in 1808 included William Clark, by that time a brigadier general and the principal US Indian agent for the Louisiana Territory; Reuben Lewis, Meriwether Lewis's younger brother and newly appointed as an Indian subagent; and Nathan Boone, Daniel Boone's son and a guide for the US party. Clark was not new to the area; he had seen the site, a few miles upriver from a place called Fire Prairie, in late June 1804, in the first weeks of the exploration he had led with Meriwether Lewis. He had described it in 1804 as a "commanding position" on a seventy-foot-high bluff on the south bank of the Missouri. Presciently, he had added, "this spot has many advantages for a fort and a trading house with the Indians."[52]

Fort Osage, the post that Clark helped to establish, included just such a "trading house," extending the US network of factories to its westernmost point. The United States had established the factory system twelve years earlier, modeling it on those of the French, British, and Spanish, who had facilitated their alliances with Indigenous people in the North American interior through a diplomacy of gift-giving and subsidized trade.[53] In 1796, the United States had established its first two factories: in Georgia (for the Creeks) and Tennessee (for the Cherokees). By 1802, the United States had added four more: Fort St. Stephen (for the Choctaws) and Chickasaw Bluffs (for the Chickasaws) in Mississippi Territory, Fort Wayne in Indiana Territory (for the Miamis), and Fort Detroit in Michigan Territory (for the Potawatomis). The US officials who had established the factory system during the administrations of George Washington and John Adams were mostly unenthusiastic about the program. The Federalist economic program focused on stabilizing the currency and solidifying the support of creditors and entrepreneurs for the new federal government. The factory system ran counter to Federalist economic policies that catered to investors and encouraged commerce; but Federalists grudgingly established factories to provide an alternative to British and Spanish commerce because they (correctly) feared that without a US trade presence in the borderlands, Indigenous people might form alliances with imperial rivals.

The election of Thomas Jefferson in 1800, however, brought into power an administration far more hopeful about a program designed to regulate commerce. For Jefferson, and for the members of his administration who shared his general beliefs, regulated commerce had the capacity to create a peaceful and democratic civil society; unregulated commerce had the potential— or even the likelihood—to corrupt. Shortly after the Louisiana Purchase, Jefferson's administration set about expanding the factory system. By the end of the first decade of the nineteenth century, in addition to the posts for the Miamis, Potawatomis, Choctaws, and Chickasaws, the system included factories not only at Fort Osage, but at Natchitoches; Chicago; and at Michilimackinac, at the northernmost tip of the lower peninsula of Michigan. The posts traced a crescent through the borderlands of Indigenous territory and the converging US, British, and Spanish empires, from the Great Lakes in the Northwest Territory to the Lower Missouri, to banks of the Mobile and Red Rivers.[54]

In exchange for furs, the factories provided Indigenous people with goods—among them firearms, ammunition, woven cloth, knives, and other tools—at cost. At Fort Osage, the factory added a mere 25 percent to the wholesale cost of goods in order to cover the costs of transportation and the maintenance of the post. The factories neither sold alcohol nor extended credit.[55] Embracing the Jefferson administration's suspicions about unregulated commerce, the directors of the factory system hoped to undercut private fur traders—many of whom in the Lower Missouri were, like the Chouteau brothers, French-speaking former Spanish subjects—and force them out of the market. John Mason, the first superintendent of the factory system, described private fur traders as persons "of desperate character, who are debasing the habits of the Indians—and at the same time cheating them of their little earnings by constantly dealing out to them spirituous liquors."[56] John C. Calhoun, the secretary of war under James Monroe, was particularly concerned about the effect of private trade in the Louisiana Territory, "the best region for furs and peltries on this continent." He wrote in 1818 that unregulated commerce in furs in the Louisiana Territory would be disastrous. "Each trader, or association of traders, would endeavor to monopolize the trade within certain limits, and would exert their cunning and influence to render the savages their partisans, and the enemy of their rivals in trade. . . . A state of disorder and violence would universally prevail."[57] For these reasons, in January 1803, Jefferson commended the purpose of the factory system to "undersell private traders . . . drive them from the competition," and thus, win "the good will of the Indians."[58]

Yet the purpose of the factory system was not simply to undersell private traders and thus limit what Jefferson and others saw as their baleful influence upon Indigenous people. In the same letter in which Jefferson wrote of the importance of the factories in winning the good will of Indigenous people, he wrote of how he hoped "to encourage them to abandon hunting" and become stock-raisers and farmers. For Jefferson, independent farmers formed the basis for a virtuous commonwealth; for him to imagine that Indigenous people might become independent farmers much like white yeomen meant that—rhetorically, at least—he could imagine their inclusion in the US body politic. Yet his ambition for Indigenous people to become farmers was not simply that he idealized agrarianism. It was intimately connected to the goal of US policies toward Indigenous people that Jefferson had articulated to Andrew Jackson in February 1803: "obtaining lands." Were Indigenous people to become farmers, he wrote, "the extensive forests necessary in the hunting life, will then become useless, and they will see advantage in exchanging them for the means of improving their farms."[59] Or, as he wrote elsewhere, "a single farm will show more of cattle, than a whole country . . . can of buffaloes."[60] In Jefferson's imagination, Indigenous people transformed into some version of yeomen farmers would willingly cede their extensive hunting territories to the United States—and those lands could be settled by white Americans. Jefferson's musings put a congenial gloss on dispossession: he imagined a colonization that benefited the colonized. Dispossession was thus at least a rhetorical goal of the factory system. When Clark came to establish Fort Osage in 1808, he negotiated a treaty with the Osages in which the United States agreed to establish a factory, while the Osages ceded to the United States their territory east of Fire Prairie and south of the Missouri River.[61]

The stated goal of the factories—to speed the transformation of Indigenous people into yeomen farmers—remained a part of the factory system until it was disestablished in 1822. Thomas McKenney, who assumed control of the factory system in 1816, wrote to all factors that year that "the Government, and Society in General, would be happy to learn that our border neighbors were quickening in their advances to a start of civilization."[62] McKenney encouraged factors to instill in Native Americans an appreciation for manufactured goods and a commercial economy in order to uplift them from their presumed savagery. "There can be no doubt but that time will be required to divert [Indigenous people] from the chase, and to introduce them into the practise of agriculture, and the arts of civil life," McKenney wrote. "But much may be done to facilitate the progress. It is certainly of importance to give them a just conception of the value of goods."[63] Calhoun imagined that the factories might eventually become centers of Indigenous settlement, "which, by giving greater density and steadiness to their population, will tend to introduce a division of real property, and thus hasten their civilization."[64] And yet, the stated beliefs of Jefferson, McKenney, and Calhoun—that the factory system would hasten the transformation of Indigenous people into yeomen farmers—was likely nothing more than useful rhetoric since all three men were doubtless aware that the system subsidized commercial hunting and trapping, hardly something the United States would do if it were genuinely committed to making Indigenous people into yeomen farmers.

While it was more aspirational than actual, the rhetoric about transforming Indigenous people from fur traders into yeoman farmers reveals something important about the factory system. The suspicion of commerce and the idealization of agrarianism that guided the factory system after Jefferson's ascension to the presidency were grounded in a set of beliefs that historians call "republicanism." The narrative at the heart of republican ideology held that virtuous republics must be based upon independent agriculturalists. Many republicans believed that only self-sufficient landholders who depended neither upon the patronage of rulers nor upon the whims of commerce could be virtuous citizens. Republicans looked—more than a little selectively—to ancient history to construct a narrative to bolster these beliefs, arguing that in democratic Athens and republican Rome, it had been independent landholders who had been responsible for maintaining republican virtue by acting in the best interests of the commonwealth. Republics were fragile, however; republicans believed that commerce raised human society above the level of savagery, but almost inevitably, commercialism and imperialism progressively engulfed republics by creating venal relationships of dependency: over time, both Athens and Rome became corrupt empires. The seventeenth- and early eighteenth-century English and Scottish political theorists who first articulated these ideas believed that Britain, its rulers in London having surrounded themselves with merchants, bankers, and stock-jobbers, had already descended into empire and corruption. During the course of the various political crises that preceded the American Revolution, many influential Americans—especially wealthy, slaveholding planters such as Jefferson who were flattered by the notion that landholding produced virtue—adopted many of these ideas eagerly.[65]

Yet republicanism was not a consensus. Late eighteenth- and early nineteenth-century Americans spoke, as the historian James Kloppenberg put it, "overlapping . . . political languages" derived from republicanism, classicism, liberalism, and Protestantism.[66] Nor was republicanism much of an obstacle to expanding commerce: the consumer revolution of the eighteenth century and the market revolution of the nineteenth century easily brushed past republican suspicions. When Jefferson entered the White House in 1801, his supporting coalition reflected these inconsistencies; his party included free traders as well as idealistic adherents to pastoralism. Despite Jefferson's seemingly unshakable commitment to pure agrarianism, in 1794, he established an industrial nailery at Monticello to manufacture nails both for use on the plantation and for sale.[67]

The factory system reflected the conflicted character of early nineteenth-century Jeffersonian political economy. The authors of the factory system, chagrined that the state monopoly they had created uncomfortably resembled British mercantile companies, made a gesture toward free trade by licensing private traders to operate alongside, and in competition with, the factories. One of those private traders was Pierre Chouteau; the United States not only granted him a license to trade, but in 1804 it conceded to his influence with the Osages by making him a federal subagent for the Osages.[68] Thus, within a year of the Louisiana Purchase, the Chouteaus had reestablished their position on the Lower Missouri: they were both the largest private traders and enjoyed a special influence with the imperial authorities who claimed to rule the region. That a federal agent to an Indigenous nation would also pursue his own commercial ambitions with that nation was a prescription for conflict of interest—yet it was also not unique in the Lower Missouri. William Clark, the supervisor of all Indian agents in the Louisiana Territory, was one of the founders of the Missouri Fur Company in 1809. His partners in the firm included the Chouteau brothers, Reuben Lewis, and Benjamin Wilkinson, the nephew of the territorial governor of Louisiana James Wilkinson. Indeed, despite republicans' solemn condemnations of corruption, self-dealing abounded in the borderlands of the early American republic. Territorial officials not only sought to profit from the fur trade, but government officials—including state legislators, territorial officers, cabinet secretaries, members of Congress, and Supreme Court justices—used their powers to facilitate spectacularly corrupt land speculation schemes from which they also profited.[69]

The blurred lines between public office and private interests did not trouble federal officials enough to put a stop to the practice, in part because officials' priority was to draw the Indigenous people of the borderlands away from the commercial influences of Britain and Spain—whether Indigenous people traded with US factors or with private American traders was a secondary concern. The commercial influences of Britain and Spain were extensive: in the late eighteenth and early nineteenth century, British merchants based in Montreal collected between one-half and two-thirds of their furs from Indigenous people in the United States.[70] The supervisors of the factory system feared that Indigenous peoples' extensive commerce with British traders undermined US claims to sovereignty. In a letter to all factors in 1811, John Mason warned that "British agents and Traders with the Indians may attempt to excite in their minds prejudices and hostile dispositions toward the United States." Therefore, "you will redouble your efforts to satisfy the wants and conciliate the minds of the Indians within your reach." US officials saw Spain as a threat as well; in the years leading up to the War of 1812, they predicted that Spain would join Britain in war against the United States in order to regain the Louisiana Territory. In 1811, Sibley reported ominously that the Pawnees had "been much courted by the Spanish authorities of New Mexico at Santa Fe."[71]

A slight, dyspeptic, New England-born bookkeeper, Sibley had accompanied Clark, Lewis, and Boone to Fort Osage in 1808.[72] The son of John Sibley, a restless planter who had settled in Louisiana prior to its purchase by the United States, and the maternal grandson of Samuel Hopkins, one of the most renowned Calvinist theologians in the United States, Sibley embodied the contradictions of early nineteenth-century US society and culture: he was both acquisitive and censorious. He was in this respect perhaps too well suited to the factory system, which incorporated within it an ideal of the public good while accommodating itself to private cupidity. In Sibley's youth, his father and maternal grandfather had presented him with contrasting models. Samuel Hopkins was an erudite and accomplished student of the leading New England theologian of the eighteenth century, Jonathan Edwards. A high-minded moralist, Hopkins advocated immediatism both for matters secular (he called for the immediate abolition of slavery) and spiritual (unlike traditional Calvinists, for whom seeking grace was an arduous, lifelong ordeal, Hopkins was a revivalist who believed in immediate conversion experiences).[73] Sibley's father, John, by contrast, was a faithless, pleasure-seeking, fortune-hunting wastrel. In 1784, the elder Sibley abandoned his wife, Elizabeth, two-year-old George, and George's infant brother, Samuel, and moved to Fayetteville, North Carolina, where he published a newspaper (he was a Democratic-Republican but also favored ratification of the Constitution) and invested in land and slaves.[74] Until he was six years old, George lived with his mother and brother in his grandfather's household in Newport, Rhode Island, where Reverend Hopkins preached at the First Congregational Church. In 1788, John Sibley sent for his wife and sons to join him in North Carolina; George, however, continued to correspond with his grandfather until 1797. In 1790, not long after joining her husband in North Carolina, Elizabeth Sibley died; before the end of the next year, John Sibley had remarried. In 1802, after fathering a son and a daughter with his second wife, he followed his earlier pattern and left her, too, embarking for French Louisiana. Eventually, John Sibley acquired a plantation, Grand Ecore, near Natchitoches.[75] As an adult, George Sibley was a curious combination of the traits of his father and grandfather: simultaneously earnest (sometimes to the point of being a scold) and desirous of comfort and quick wealth.

George Sibley struggled to reconcile these inconsistencies. He sometimes echoed his grandfather's antislavery sentiments. In 1813, for instance, he wrote to his brother, Samuel, who had joined their father in Louisiana, that he had no desire to relocate to Louisiana to be near his family at Grand Ecore because of "the great number of Slaves there." He wrote that "it does not by any means comport with my ideas of comfort and worldly happiness to be at all times Surrounded by a great majority of miserable wretches, who only want a safe opportunity to cut the throats of their master." Yet when Sibley wrote these words to his brother, he had already purchased three slaves in Missouri.

He tried to distinguish himself from his planter father, writing that his "few Slaves, who are all well fed & cloathed & kindly treated, are not So much employed to amass Wealth for their owner as to provide Substantial comforts, make domestic improvements, & render life easy, comfortable, and happy."[76]

Sibley was similarly contradictory about debt. He reflected typical republican beliefs in condemning debt as destructive of independence and virtue. He wrote to his brother in 1815 criticizing their father for having mortgaged Grand Ecore, thus entering "that cursed state of bondage which is ever produced by imprudently and unnecessarily contracting debt."[77] Yet since 1805, when he had first come to Missouri as an assistant at a factory near St. Louis, Sibley had owed $500 to his former employer in North Carolina. He had probably borrowed the money when he moved to Missouri in 1805 to post it as a bond as a condition for becoming a subagent at a short-lived factory near St. Louis. Though republicans deplored patronage and nepotism as enthusiastically as they did debt, Sibley nonetheless owed his position to his father, who had become an Indian agent at Natchitoches, and who used his connections to arrange a position for his son.[78] For four years, Sibley struggled to pay off his $500 debt, and frequently expressed anxiety about it. In 1806, for example, he wrote to his brother that the debt "hangs like a dead weight on my mind" and that he had fallen into "a kind of Melancholy about it."[79] Yet he seemed to have forgotten that gloom by 1822, when he borrowed $14,000 to purchase a stock of goods in order to become a merchant. He spent the next two decades struggling to repay that debt.[80]

For most of his first three years at Fort Osage, Sibley pitied his loneliness. He complained of being "buried alive in the woods with not a Soul about me who cares a fig whether I am comfortable or not, whether I be dead or alive."[81] To combat such loneliness (and to secure closer ties to the Indigenous people with whom they were trading) French fur traders often married Indigenous women. Such unions usually lasted only as long as the traders remained in the borderlands—a practice the French called *mariage à la façon du pays*—marriage in the custom of the country. Both Pierre and Auguste Chouteau entered into such marriages with Osage women in the eighteenth century.[82] Sibley intimated such a possibility to his brother not long after his arrival at Fort Osage in 1808, writing, "Some of the young Squaws may wean me from Society, if so, it may turn out that I shall remain here Several years." Sibley was perhaps still thinking in this direction in 1811 when he wrote to his brother of the Osage "princesses and young ladies of rank decked out in all the finery of beads red ribbons and vermillion" who sometimes visited the post. In the same letter, he mused of "taking a trip to Kentucky in quest of a Wife."[83] Instead of these options, Sibley improvised his own course. In mid-1812, he invited Ellen Lorr, the fifteen-year-old daughter of Pierre Lorr, a French interpreter at Fort Osage, to share his bed. The punctilious Sibley drew up a contract with Lorr: acknowledging that she had "freely and willingly placed herself under my protection, to live and abide with me," he promised to "maintain the Said Ellen decently and comfortably" and pay her $100 on January 1 every year, so long as she "Shall continue to conduct herself faithfully, honestly, and with Strict female propriety, towards me." Ellen, who could not speak much English and was illiterate in French, did not place her mark upon the agreement, but Francis Audrain, a sutler who supplied Fort Osage with provisions, and Isaac Rawlings, Sibley's assistant factor, witnessed the document.[84] The arrangement lasted only nine months: the United States shuttered Fort Osage during the War of 1812; when Sibley and Lorr returned to St. Louis, he quickly abandoned her.

An enslaver who criticized enslavement; a chronic debtor who preached against debt; a man who made an illiterate fifteen-year-old into his contractual concubine—Sibley was certainly no saint. However plastic his principles were on these subjects, he was scrupulously honest and generous in dealings with the Osages. When Sibley became the factor at Fort Osage in 1808, the factory system's superintendent, John Mason, wrote to him: "The principle object of the government in these establishments being to secure the Friendship of the Indians in our country . . . let every transaction with them be conducted as to inspire them with full confidence in its honor, integrity, and good faith." Mason counseled all his factors to "be conciliatory in all your intercourse with the Indians, and so demean yourself toward them generally and toward their chiefs in particular as to obtain and preserve their Friendship and to secure their attachment to the United States."[85] Sibley was almost unfailingly true to these instructions. One of his first acts as factor, within weeks of his arrival at Fort Osage, was a kindness to a grieving Osage man. He noted in his diary, "An old Osage came to me with Tears in his eyes, & begged for a little blue cloth to bury his wife in." The man could not afford the expensive cloth, but Sibley, "considering his age and distress as proper objects of favor" decided to "let him have 2 yds of Cloth and a Carrot of Tobacco and took the skins he offered in part payment."[86]

Not long after, Sibley had an opportunity to demonstrate his integrity toward the Osages. No sooner had Clark returned to St. Louis than the Osages immediately contested the treaty he had negotiated. Osages who had not been present at the negotiations objected to the cession of lands south of the Missouri River; those who had been present contended that they had not ceded the land to the United States but merely agreed to share it with Americans. Meriwether Lewis, governor of Louisiana Territory, rewrote the treaty—making clear that the land south of the Missouri was indeed ceded to the United States—and dispatched Pierre Chouteau, the federal agent to the Osages, together with Reuben Lewis, to Fort Osage to secure the Osages' agreement.[87] (That Chouteau needed to be sent to the Osages was somewhat unusual for an agent, most of whom resided among the nations to which they were posted; Chouteau, however, preferred to remain in St. Louis.) On November 7, 1808. Sibley recorded in his diary that Chouteau had arrived at the post "to conclude another Treaty with the Osages" though it "does not differ very materially from the one made by Genl Clark." Only Chouteau and Reuben Lewis treated with the Osages, but Sibley saw enough of the exchange to observe that Chouteau concluded the treaty "in great haste and made use of threats to make the Indians sign it." When it came time for the Americans at the post to affix signatures to the treaty as witnesses, the two ranking officers in command of Fort Osage, Capt. Eli Clemson and Lt. Louis Lorimer, dutifully signed the treaty as witnesses despite not actually having been present at the negotiations. Sibley wrote that "these Gentlemen Sign[ed] merely for form's sake which I was invited also to do, but peremptorily refused." His demonstration of honesty may have impressed the Osages, but it earned him the enmity of both Chouteau and Clemson; neither forgot the slight, as Sibley would learn five years later. As late as 1811, Sibley noted that the precise content of the treaty had "never yet been officially communicated to the Osages."[88]

By that time, Sibley had emerged as an unofficial advocate of the Osages. In February 1811, he wrote to Clark that the Osages, who "for the last two or three years faithfully observed the counsels they have received from the United States and strictly refrained from making war on the neighboring tribes," had complained to him that those neighbors were encroaching upon Osage lands. "I have repeatedly referred them to their agent Mr. Chouteau and told them . . . that I have no official right of interference on such matters yet they will continue to bother me with their complaints . . . and I am absolutely obliged either to listen to them or by refusing, give them great offense." In case Clark managed to miss Sibley's criticism of Chouteau, the factor made it explicit: "They address themselves to me as an agent of the United States (there being no one else here who will take any part in Indian Affairs of any kind; and no one appointed to attend to them here; and it being very inconvenient they say to wait upon their agent in St. Louis)."[89]

If Sibley was the antithesis of Chouteau, the federal agent to the Osages, he was also the antithesis of Chouteau the private trader. Sibley eagerly endorsed the anti-commercial principles of the factory system—particularly its demonization of private traders. He denounced "narrow-minded Peddlers" and their "groveling ideas."[90] He blamed violence in the borderlands on the machinations of fur traders such as Chouteau. "The extortion of the traders are always so exorbitant that 'tis not at all surprising the Indians sometimes resort to robbery," he wrote. However, "the Factory System as established by Jefferson, was designed to obviate this end, and to a great extent it has had that effect."[91] For the Osages, Sibley's factory was an institution designed to reward them for their commercial loyalty to the United States. There was little mystery to the Osages' position; according to Sibley, the Osages obtained goods at Fort Osage "at prices less than half what the traders extort from them."[92]

Just as the Osage trade had been the most valuable to fur traders in St. Louis in the eighteenth century, it was the most valuable in the factory system. Between November 1807 and September 1811, Sibley handled more merchandise than any other factor. McKenney rated Fort Osage, together with Tombibgy in the Mississippi Territory (where the deerskin trade flourished) and Prairie du Chien in the Northwest Territory (where muskrat pelts were the primary commodity of trade), as the most valuable posts in the system. Drawing on the vast resources of the Missouri and its tributaries, however, Fort Osage between 1817 and 1819 collected nearly twice as many beaver pelts—the most valuable commodity in the North American fur trade—as all the other posts in the factory system combined. At the same time, Fort Osage's deerskin trade expanded from just over 10,000 skins in 1816 to over 33,000 in 1819.[93]

Jefferson and some of his subordinates may have hoped that their policies would ultimately bring about the assimilation of the Osages and other Indigenous people and the settlement of their lands by white Americans, but they could not dictate the course of events in the contested borderlands. So long as British and Spanish competition provided the Osages and other Indigenous people with alternatives to US political and economic alliance, the United States could do no more than preserve their tenuous alliances with Indigenous people and their even more tenuous claims to sovereignty in the region through subsidized trade. Sibley grasped that maintaining good relations with the Osages was his primary mission. The factory system, he wrote in 1822, "is a benevolent and well-contrived scheme . . . to secure, in some degree, the good will of the Indians to our government and people."[94]

In 1811, Sibley undertook an extensive mission to promote good relations between the United States and Indigenous groups in the Lower Missouri region. Accompanied by several Osage leaders, Sibley embarked on a two-month tour of Kaw and Pawnee villages in the Lower Missouri River Valley. His mission, as he described it in his journal, was "to effect a peace between the Osages, Konsees, Pawnees and Ottoes."[95] Consciously aping the examples of the explorers Pike, Lewis, and Clark, Sibley not only covered some of the same territory that Pike had traced in 1805 but in his diary pointedly compared himself to the explorer. He saw his mission as an extension of his mandate as factor at Fort Osage: to demonstrate to the Kaw and Pawnees US sovereignty in the Louisiana Territory and to incorporate them into a commercial alliance.

When Sibley's party—twelve Osages (one of whom spoke Pawnee), Sibley's interpreter (who spoke French and Osage), and Sibley's Irish servant—reached the Kaw village on the Kansas River about sixty-five miles northwest of Fort Osage, they were, according to Sibley, "Received at the Village in the most friendly and Respectful manner, in the Indian Style; with all the courtly etiquette and Ceremony used by these people on what they consider great and very important occasions." After being escorted into the village by a "Mounted escort," the party was "conducted to the Lodge of the Grand Chief," for a feast. Sibley was "particularly gratified to observe Several Flags with the Stars and Stripes, flying in different parts of the Town, besides the large and very handsome one that gracefully waved over the Lodge of the Great Chief." To cement good relations with the Kaw, Sibley encouraged them to trade at Fort Osage to avoid the "exorbitant" prices of private traders.[96]

From the Kaw town, Sibley's party—now numbering twenty people with the addition of eight Kaw delegates—traveled about 100 miles west to the Pawnee villages on the Platte River. At the Pawnee town, they were received "with much ceremony and courtesy." However, Sibley soon discovered the fragility of the US claim to sovereignty in the region: a Spanish expedition had recently visited the region. Furthermore, the Pawnees showed Sibley letters, dated 1807, from the Spanish governor of New Mexico, "expressive of their Satisfaction of their loyalty," and accompanied by Spanish flags and medals.[97] Since the Louisiana Purchase, Spain had maintained—and would continue to maintain until the United States and Spain agreed to a border in 1821—that the territory the United States had purchased from France in 1803 barely extended beyond the west bank of the Mississippi, and that thus the Osages, Kaw, and Pawnees were part of the Spanish dominion in North

America. For its part, until 1821, the United States maintained that the Louisiana Territory extended to the Rio Grande.[98] Both Spain and the United States sponsored expeditions into the disputed territory as demonstrations of their sovereignty. The explorations of Pike on the Arkansas River, Lewis and Clark on the Missouri and Columbia Rivers, and Thomas Freeman and Peter Custis on the Red River all in the first decade of the nineteenth century were part of the competing efforts to exert authority over the contested borderlands. The Spanish party that visited the Pawnees, led by Facundo Melgares, distributed flags and medals—the usual symbols of allegiance in borderlands diplomacy—and secured the Pawnees' promise to protect the route to New Mexico from American incursions. Both the Spanish and the Americans understood that their claims to sovereignty depended on the allegiance of Indigenous people in the disputed region. The natives understood that as well: a Pawnee leader, Cher-a-ta-reesh, expressed his disappointment to Sibley that when Pike had visited in 1806, he had promised to return with medals and other tokens of allegiance but had never done so.[99]

The provident Sibley was prepared. "I had been careful to provide myself amply with American flags and medals," he wrote triumphantly in his diary.[100] He pronounced himself ready to make good upon Pike's promise. Cher-a-ta-reesh, in return, proclaimed Sibley to be Pike's "brother," and accorded him every diplomatic consideration. Sibley convened a "grand council" of Pawnees, Kaw, and his own delegation of Osages and distributed gifts as well as the flags and medals. "After I had fully Set forth the advantages that would inure to them from a free and uninterrupted intercourse for trade, with the US Factory at Ft. Osage," Sibley wrote, "they very Readily agreed to bury the tomahawk."[101] The Pawnees reciprocated Sibley's gifts with a gift of thirty horses to Sibley's party. Upon his return to Fort Osage, Sibley reported to William Clark that not only had he secured the formal allegiance of all the groups but that they had also sworn peace among themselves. The Osage, moreover, promised to permit the Pawnees and Kaw to traverse their lands to reach Fort Osage and take advantage of the subsidized prices there. The grand council was Sibley's greatest success during his tenure as factor at Fort Osage: the promises of peace that he secured in 1811 endured during the War of 1812, when most of the Osages, Pawnees, and Kaw remained neutral.[102]

MERCHANTS HAVE NO COUNTRY

Despite the success of Sibley's mission to the Kaw and Pawnees, the War of 1812 was a turning point for Fort Osage, the factory system, and Sibley himself. The Treaty of Ghent that ended the war initiated a rapprochement between the two Anglophone commercial economies on opposite sides of the Atlantic. Before the war interrupted all commerce between the United States and Britain, British textile manufacturers—who employed more workers than any other industry in Britain—had imported about half of their raw cotton from the United States. After the war, US exports of raw cotton not only resumed but increased. By 1826, the United States supplied three-quarters of Britain's raw cotton. The United States maintained that share of the market until the Civil War. Following the peace in 1815, the British significantly reduced their support for Indigenous people in the borderlands who resisted US claims to sovereignty. In 1818, American and British delegates cordially agreed to a border between the United States and Britain's North American territories. The postwar settlement thus largely removed the threat of an Indigenous-British military alliance, which had been one of the primary justifications for the factory system. The federal government, accordingly, began to shift from the accommodationist policy that had undergirded the factory system to a policy of removal of Indigenous people. In 1816, William Clark redrew the map illustrating Osage land cessions from the treaty of 1808, extending the claims both northward and southward.[103] The Senate first articulated a removal policy in 1817; political support for removal culminated in the 1830s with the forced migration of thousands of Indigenous people to reserves in the trans-Mississippi West.[104]

No longer easily able to pit the British against the United States in order to gain concessions, the Osages were unable to prevent the surge of white American settlers into the Lower Missouri borderlands. The population of Missouri mushroomed from roughly 25,000 in 1815 to over 66,000 by 1820.[105] The population increase created a rapid rise in land prices and opportunities for commerce. In 1813, Sibley, who had relocated to St. Louis during the war, reported to his brother that he had acquired 1,000 *arpens* (about 1,600 acres) near St. Louis, and that he would continue to devote as much of his salary to land purchases as he could afford. While avowing, "I do not mean tho by any means to become a land speculator," he reported triumphantly to his brother in 1816 that he had received an offer of eight dollars per acre for the lands he had purchased for a mere sixty cents an acre three years earlier.[106]

Legal trouble, however, derailed whatever plans Sibley harbored to profit from the market revolution. In June 1813, the United States had closed Fort Osage for the duration of the war. Sibley, together with the other residents of the post, including the Lorr family, were relocated to St. Louis. Ellen Lorr, who had shared Sibley's bed for nine months, seemed to have expected that

Sibley would marry her when they reached the city. Instead, he left her, and she promptly sued Sibley for breach of promise. She claimed in her suit, filed in July 1813, that she had only "suffered . . . Sibley to cohabit with her" on "promises and assurances of marriage being immediately carried into effect." She further claimed that "she was begotten with child by said Sibley" and that "he has utterly forsaken her." Eli Clemson, the Fort Osage commander who had often been annoyed by Sibley's piety about honest dealings with the Osages, submitted a deposition on Lorr's behalf, saying that he had "frequently heard it suggested that the Defendant had promised marriage to the plaintiff." Pierre Chouteau, who had no affinity for either Sibley or the factory system, supported Lorr's suit; in fact, it was his son-in-law, Louis LeBeaume, who had brought the lawsuit against Sibley, since Lorr, a female minor, did not possess the legal capacity under Missouri law to act on her own behalf.[107]

Chouteau's involvement in the suit revealed that *Lorr v. Sibley* was about more than an allegation of breach of promise. The Chouteau family, like other members of the old colonial elite in St. Louis, were leaders of the Missouri junto: Francophone holders of extensive French and Spanish land grants; many of them, like the Chouteaus or men such as Bernard Pratte, were also leaders of the fur trade. Following the Louisiana Purchase, the members of the junto feared that US authorities might void their land grants, and they resented the federal factory at Fort Osage that undersold their businesses. To protect their landholdings and to resist regulation of the fur trade, the junto enlisted the help of Anglophone migrants to Missouri such as Thomas Hart Benton, a newspaper editor, who became one of Missouri's first two US senators; Silas Bent, a lawyer, who became a territorial superior court judge; Edward Hempstead, a lawyer, who served variously as the territorial attorney general and speaker of the territorial assembly; Hempstead's law partner William Mears, who later became attorney general of Illinois; and William Clark, the former explorer and territorial governor, who hoped that the support of the junto might propel him to even higher office. To prosecute Lorr's suit, the Chouteaus hired Hempstead and Mears. Sibley, for his part, turned to prominent Anglophone political enemies of the junto to represent him: first Rufus Easton (who dropped out when he became Missouri Territory's representative to Congress), and then Easton's law partner, Charles Lucas.[108]

In the end, the court determined that Sibley was guilty of breach of promise. Lorr had sued for $10,000, but received only $1,000, which Sibley had posted as bond when the suit began.[109] The trial damaged the marriage prospects neither of Lorr nor of Sibley. During the course of the trial, Sibley met Mary Easton, the daughter of his first attorney, Rufus Easton. They married in

August 1815. Like Ellen Lorr, who had been fifteen years old when Sibley drew up his concubine contract with her, Mary was fifteen years old at the time of her marriage to Sibley.[110] In June 1817, Lorr married François Bonne and eventually had five children. While Sibley and Lorr seemingly put the trial behind them, the political contention between the junto and Anglophone settlers continued; indeed, it progressed to dueling, the ultimate extension of political contestation in early nineteenth-century America.[111] Two months after Lorr's marriage, Lucas goaded Benton, who had also been involved briefly in the Sibley trial, into insulting him. Lucas challenged Benton to a duel on an island in the Mississippi River claimed by neither Missouri nor Illinois. There, Benton killed him.[112]

As Lucas was both opposed to the junto and the son of a prominent judge who was also an enemy of the junto, the killing endeared Benton to the junto at a moment when they were looking for a new champion. The erstwhile political leader of the junto was the territorial governor and former explorer William Clark. As the United States prepared to admit Missouri as a state, members of the junto anticipated that Clark would continue to protect their interests as state governor. Yet when Clark lost to the anti-junto candidate in the August 1820 state gubernatorial election, the junto members feared that they had been eclipsed by the swarm of Anglophone settlers to Missouri in the years since the Louisiana Purchase. In late September, the leaders of the junto met in the Chouteau mansion in St. Louis to galvanize support for Benton's election to the US Senate and to bring reluctant state legislators into the fold. They succeeded in securing Benton's election in the legislature by one vote. After his election to the Senate, Benton repaid his elite patrons by securing the passage of a bill upholding the old French and Spanish land grants in Missouri.[113]

After securing the lands of the members of the junto, Benton turned to opening the fur trade to private enterprise. From the factory system's inception in 1795, the US Congress had rechartered it every two or three years. Sibley wrote to McKenney in 1819, "Like a wretch under sentence of death, it has been reprieved from year to year, still under sentence, growing weaker and weaker, while its enemies are acquiring fresh vigor from new hopes."[114] Alone among the factories, Congress accorded Fort Osage special status. The treaty with the Osages that Pierre Chouteau had negotiated in 1808 and that the Senate had ratified in 1810, guaranteed the continual maintenance of the post. In return for the cession of 200 square miles of land, the federal government had promised to pay the Osages an annuity of $1,500, and, at the factory, "permanently to continue, at all seasons of the year, a well-assorted store of goods, for the purpose of bartering with them on moderate terms for their peltries and furs."[115] When Chouteau negotiated the treaty, the agreement to maintain the factory must have seemed trivial; after all, the Office of Indian Trade had already decided to establish a post among the Osages. Within a decade and a half, however, the federal government regretted its decision to protect the fur trade of the Lower Missouri from the operations of the market.

In 1821, Thomas McKenney, the superintendent of the factory system, precipitated the conflict that ended with the dissolution of the factory system by proposing to raise the factories' capital from $300,000 to $500,000 in order to establish posts on the Upper Missouri. McKenney further recommended that more stringent restraints be placed on private trading outfits. He urged that the federal government impose a license fee of $200 on private traders, require a bond of $10,000, and effectively (rather than just nominally) ban whiskey from the trade. In response, Benton marshaled support from Ramsay Crooks, an executive in John Jacob Astor's American Fur Company, and Benjamin O'Fallon, an Indian agent appointed at Astor's insistence, to contest McKenney. The ensuing disinformation campaign charged the factories with corruption and inefficiency. Indigenous people were dissatisfied with the factories, Crooks maintained. The factors skimmed profits from the posts, O'Fallon asserted. The system's business practices were laughable, Benton claimed. When Benton's campaign caused the system to lose its charter, Crooks congratulated him: "You deserve the unqualified thanks of the community for destroying the pious monster."[116] In a letter to Sibley, McKenney rued that there were only five members of Congress who actively sought to destroy the factory system, "but these five had influence with the rest so as to secure their votes."[117]

The end of the factory system opened the fur trade to a handful of powerful firms. While Chouteau and other French colonial elites in St. Louis had anticipated that they would profit most from the deregulation of the fur trade, the primary beneficiary was instead the better-capitalized John Jacob Astor, who by the late 1810s had amassed millions of dollars first as a fur dealer in the United States for the Montreal-based North West Company, and later as a dealer in Chinese opium.[118] Astor's American Fur Company formed a Western Department to exploit the resources of the Missouri in 1822, shortly after the disestablishment of the factory system. By 1826 the American Fur Company had absorbed or underpriced its various rivals, among them the Missouri Fur Company; the French Fur Company of Bartholomew Berthold, Bernard Pratte, and Pierre Chouteau Jr.; Joseph Renville's Columbia Fur

Company; and Andrew Henry and William Ashley's Rocky Mountain Fur Company.[119]

The Osages greeted the disestablishment of the factories with dismay. When Congress voted to disband the factory system, Sibley wrote that the Osages "were very much dissatisfied and displeased." They had lost their "former unbounded confidence in us, in consequence of what they alleged to be a failure on the part of the United States to fulfill the treaty."[120] In 1822, Sibley wrote a long eulogy for the factory system for the *National Intelligencer*, a tri-weekly periodical that, like Sibley, gradually shifted from Jeffersonian to Whig partisanship over the first decades of the nineteenth century. The factory system, Sibley wrote, was "a benevolent and well-contrived scheme" to "prevent quarrels, and robberies, and bloodshed, along our frontier settlements; and to secure, in some degree, the good will of the Indians to our government and people."[121]

Privately, however, Sibley had been accommodating himself to commerce for years. In 1815, he wrote to his brother, Samuel, "I propose in about two years to commence the Dry Goods and Indian Trade business at St. Louis on a pretty extensive scale, in partnership with an old friend of mine, a wholesale merchant at Baltimore." Two years later, Sibley and his wealthy father-in-law tried to draw Samuel into a planned mercantile business in St. Louis, which they proposed to start with $30,000 worth of goods. In 1819, however, Sibley was still at Fort Osage, where he began raising hogs and cattle and constructing a saw- and grist-mill. "An outlet and good market for vast quantities of Flour, Pork and Whiskey will exist for many years to come among the numerous Traders, Garrisons, &c. on the Missouri, above this," he wrote. "As soon as I get my Stock Farm & Mills going, I shall hope to furnish from two to three thousand Doll's worth of Provisions which I shall count on Selling at my door."[122] In short, between the Treaty of Ghent and 1819, Sibley steadily accommodated himself to the demands and opportunities of a market society. In a letter to a fellow merchant in 1818, Sibley summed up the changes in his economic philosophy, articulating both his repugnance for commerce and his resignation to it. In response to his friend's lament that he was unfit for business, Sibley wrote: "You are too generous by half, and if I mistake you sell your Goods too low. You ought to consider yourself embarked in a very disagreeable and perilous trade. . . . There is a relation (or ought to be) between Man and Man that should divest itself of every interested motive. . . . But between Merchant and Merchant, Trader and Trader, interest and interest alone gives the nod."[123]

A few months after eulogizing the factory system in the *National Intelligencer*, Sibley together with two partners, Paul Baillio and Lilburn Boggs, agreed to pay the US government $14,383.60 for the stock of goods at Fort Osage. Baillio and Boggs had been, at different times, Sibley's assistants at Fort Osage; Baillio had also served as the assistant at the Chickasaw Bluffs factory. Having successfully managed the Osage trade in the service of the government, the three clerks anticipated that they would have little trouble turning a profit for themselves. Indeed, by the summer of 1823 Sibley claimed to have accumulated $10,000 worth of furs and pelts. Yet the partners proved unable to deliver their furs to St. Louis to sell them for a profit.[124] Unlike Astor's American Fur Company, which by the 1830s operated a fleet of steamboats on the Missouri River, Sibley and no easy way to transport his furs to the market. By 1825, Sibley's business had failed. "In 1822 I was induced to purchase on credit the Stock of Indian Goods then on hand at the US Indian Factory at Ft. Osage," he explained to a friend. "Owing to a variety of untoward circumstances, and some bad management on the part of my partners, we have failed to meet our engagement with the Govt." In 1825, the partners owed $12,176.70 to the federal government. Sibley estimated that if he disposed of his land, he might be able to discharge about $5,000 of his debt.[125]

Sibley's business failures left him eager to accept an unexpected appointment from the federal government to survey a road from Fort Osage to Santa Fe, New Mexico.[126] Senator Benton, who had been instrumental in destroying the factory system, was the principal sponsor of the bill authorizing the survey of the trail. The survey was, however, ideologically bipartisan; it combined the interests of emerging Jacksonian Democrats in western expansion with the National Republicans' interest in federally sponsored roadbuilding to promote commercial growth and economic integration.[127] It also marked a complete departure from the former policy of regulated trade. While the United States had once pursued a policy of restrained, state-controlled commerce to extend its sovereignty over the borderlands, by the 1820s it looked to the expansive energies of private traders to extend US influence.

Merchants had begun to filter from the United States into New Mexico shortly after Mexico became independent from Spain in 1821. By 1825, merchant caravans had marked the Santa Fe Trail with deep ruts that cut an unmistakable path through the southern plains. Rather than a survey of the already established road, Sibley's mission was, as Benton put it, to negotiate "a right of way through the countries of the tribes between Missouri and New Mexico."[128] Accordingly, near the site where he had convened his "grand council" of Osages, Pawnees, and Kaw in 1811, Sibley and the other commissioners met with the Osages and the Kaw in August 1825. Shone-gee-ne-gare, the Kaw leader with whom Sibley had treated in 1811, met again with Sibley in 1825. Fourteen years earlier, Sibley had persuaded the Osages to allow the Kaw and Pawnees to traverse their territory in the interest of restraining private traders. Now, in exchange for $800 worth of goods, he extracted from the Osages and Kaw a different concession: permission for private traders to traverse their territory in order to reach New Mexico.[129]

After the council, Sibley continued toward New Mexico. After biding his time for a week at the US-Mexico border, while Joel Poinsett, the US minister to Mexico, secured permission for the surveying party to cross into Mexico, Sibley arrived in Taos in October 1825. In Santa Fe, the New Mexican governor, Antonio Narbona, treated Sibley and his small party to a round of parties and fandangos. Sibley's sojourn in New Mexico was hardly the diplomatic success that his mission at Fort Osage had been, however. In Missouri, he had accommodated to the Indigenous practice of gift-giving in order to secure their alliance. In New Mexico, by contrast, he was contemptuous of the officials he met, repeatedly hectoring them for what he viewed as their petty corruption. Two minor conflicts between Sibley and his New Mexican hosts demonstrate the changes in his diplomatic demeanor.

The first occurred in March 1826. Sibley had contracted with a Taos ranchero for lodgings for himself and his men, and stables for his horses. Shortly after settling in, the alcalde (mayor) of Taos interjected himself into the arrangement, imposing an ad hoc fee. The alcalde insisted that the bargain be committed to paper by a New Mexican bureaucrat and authorized, a process that Sibley calculated would cost him two dollars. Upon meeting with the alcalde about the matter, "I immediately discovered that the plan was to get a fee out of me for the Alcalde," Sibley wrote in his diary in indignation. "I told them at once I would submit to no such imposition . . . & that I would sign no paper but of my own writing."[130] At Fort Osage, Sibley had regarded such transactions not as bribery but as diplomatic niceties. Indeed, at Fort Osage, all commerce was subordinated to diplomatic concerns. In New Mexico, however, he was determined that US interests lay not in accommodating to political regulation of business activities but in resisting them—even when the matter was as petty as a two-dollar fee.

Sibley's second conflict with his hosts occurred shortly before his return to Missouri in August 1826. The alcalde of Taos sent him a summons to appear before him to address the matter of a local man who had been beaten by one of Sibley's men. Sibley refused to appear and instead delivered a written account of the events to the alcalde: the local man had attempted to steal one of Sibley's horses from the pasture where the animal had been tied to graze. Sibley's man had tried to retrieve that horse, a fight resulted, and the local man "got what he richly deserved." Sibley closed his account of the events to the alcalde with a pointed assertion of the sacredness of property rights: "I will not suffer any person, Spaniard, French, or American, or Indian to take liberties with me or my Property."[131] As in the earlier case, Sibley's refusal to submit to any legal authority other than that of the United States was a pointed departure from the diplomatic compromises of the Lower Missouri borderlands.

While US authorities had imagined that opening a commercial avenue to New Mexico would not only speed American commercial expansion but solidify US sovereignty in the disputed borderlands, the trade primarily benefited a handful of American merchants and—ironically—an imperial competitor of the United States, the Comanches, through whose territory the Santa Fe Trail passed. Like the Osages on the Lower Missouri, the Co-manches had emerged in the eighteenth century as the dominant Indigenous power in their region. Like other nations that had once inhabited the fringes of the Great Plains such as the Kiowas and Cheyenne, the Comanches, who until the early eighteenth century had scraped out an existence in the foot-hills of the Rocky Mountains, reinvented themselves over the course of the eighteenth century as horse-mounted, bison-hunting nomads of the south-ern Great Plains. By the end of the century, they had become the scourge of northern New Spain, raiding as far south as Zacatecas, San Luis Potosí, and Guadalajara for horses and slaves. They traded both to Indigenous nations to their north, who used the horses to follow and hunt the bison and employed women captives to process bison robes for trade. In the 1830s and 1840s, tens of thousands of bison robes—processed by former Comanche captives and brought to market by former Comanche horses—found their way to Amer-ican Fur Company trading posts on the Missouri River.[132]

When American merchants arrived in Comanche territory, the Coman-ches seized on this new source of wealth. Beginning in 1821, hundreds of merchant caravans traveled the Santa Fe Trail from Missouri to New Mexico every year. Between 1824 and 1846 the value of American merchandise en-tering New Mexico averaged $190,000 a year.[133] Before American merchants could reach New Mexico, however, they had to compensate Comanche leaders for the right to pass through Comanche territory; every year, the Comanches collected thousands of dollars' worth of tribute. For instance, when the American trader Thomas James embarked for Santa Fe in 1821, he was intercepted by a party of Comanches who took $3,000 worth of his goods. Proceeding on to a Comanche village, James presented the leading men of the village with gifts of tobacco, powder, lead, vermilion, and calico worth $1,000. The Comanches, deeming the presents insufficient, appropriated another $1,000 worth of goods.[134] The thefts did not deter James from returning to Comanche territory in succeeding years to trade for horses. Indeed, the Comanches emerged in the 1820s and 1830s as the main suppliers of mounts to American merchants, selling them directly to American traders such as James and indirectly, through other Indigenous intermediaries, to the brothers William and Charles Bent, who established a trading post on the Santa Fe Trail in 1833.[135] James, the Bent brothers, and other merchants drove the animals to Missouri for sale. Although overland emigrants in the 1840s and 1850s did not know it, most of the horses and mules with which they outfitted themselves in Missouri before embarking across the Great Plains for California, Oregon, or Utah, had been procured by Comanche raiders somewhere in Mexico. The Comanches also supplied a large number of horses to planters and farmers in Louisiana.[136] In the end, though Benton and others hoped that with the factory system gone, unfettered commerce would speed the expansion of US sovereignty, in the decades that followed the end of the factory system, trade largely subsidized the Comanches and other Indigenous nations in the Great Plains as well as wealthy merchants such as Astor.

Five years after leaving office, Jefferson lamented the effect that the commercial revolution was having on US sovereignty. In March 1814, he wrote to a friend that "merchants have no country. The mere spot they stand on does not constitute so strong an attachment as that from which they draw their gains."[137] It was not always thus, however. For a brief moment, between the Louisiana Purchase and the War of 1812, the United States, bolstered by the prevailing political ethos, tried to bend the market revolution to the interests of borderlands diplomacy by restraining trade in the interest of securing the allegiance of Indigenous people in the borderlands. The multilateral competition for sovereignty in the borderlands set the terms for resistance to unregulated commerce in the borderlands. Ironically, when the success of the factory system helped to resolve the dispute for sovereignty in the borderlands in favor of the United States, the path was clear for the rise of the market.

CHAPTER THREE

Vaccinators

In early October 1832, an American physician, Meriwether Martin, met with a large group of Lakota at their camp southeast of the Black Hills and offered to vaccinate them against smallpox. During the course of his journey from St. Louis to the Lakota country, Martin had vaccinated more than 400 Indigenous people whom he had encountered at several Indian agencies and villages on the Upper Missouri River. At the Lakota camp, about 900 Lakota likewise agreed to the treatment. Martin administered the vaccine hurriedly, as the Lakota were eager to break camp and go in search of bison before the last remnants of the large summer herds dispersed for the winter. Their impatience notwithstanding, many stayed in camp long enough to be treated by Martin, who wrote that those who received the vaccine "appeared thankful for the opportunity of avoiding the fate of many of their neighbors."[1]

In the early 1830s, the Lakota were the most powerful Indigenous nation of the Upper Missouri River region. To a significant extent, they owed their dominance to their ability to adapt to the European economic and ecological invasion of North America. In the eighteenth century, they had migrated to the Great Plains from the Upper Mississippi River valley; acquired a European import, the horse; and transformed themselves from woodlands planter-gatherer-deer-hunters to horse-mounted bison hunters. They expelled the

Kiowas from the Black Hills region and dominated the Arikara, village-dwelling corn planters on the Missouri River. A French fur trader who resided among the Arikara from 1803 to 1805 called them "a certain kind of serf who cultivates for" the Lakota.[2]

Despite their preeminence in the region, many Lakota understood that there was good reason to receive the vaccine. In the first third of the nineteenth century, tens of thousands of Native Americans perished in smallpox epidemics that spanned the North American continent—part of a process of depopulation dating to the sixteenth century that the environmental historian Alfred Crosby termed European "ecological imperialism."[3] Lakota winter counts—pictographic records of the notable events of the year—record outbreaks of smallpox in 1779, 1780, 1798, 1801, 1810, and 1818.[4] Indeed, the 1779–80 smallpox epidemic had decimated the Arikara as well as other Missouri River village nations and had been one of the important factors in shifting power in the high plains from villagers such as the Arikara to semi-nomadic bison hunters such as the Lakota.[5] The Lakota were well aware that in 1830, two years before Martin's visit, roughly 10,000 Pawnees, the Lakota's neighbors (and often rivals) to the south, had died during a smallpox outbreak.[6] By 1832, the readiness of many Lakota to be vaccinated—embracing a European medical innovation to counteract the spread of an Old World disease—reflected their ability to adapt to and, thus, outlast European ecological imperialism.[7]

The Lakota were not the only Indigenous people to be vaccinated in the 1830s. Over the course of the decade, American physicians vaccinated at least 39,000 and perhaps as many as 54,000 Indigenous people (keeping count of the number who filed past physicians to receive the vaccine proved difficult). Altogether, physicians administered the vaccine to between 10 and 15 percent of the roughly 340,000 Indigenous people in the United States.[8] Nor were Americans alone in offering vaccine to native North Americans. The government of Mexico vaccinated California natives in the 1820s. The Hudson's Bay Company began vaccinating natives in British North America in 1837. Vaccination of colonized indigenes was not limited to North America. The Swedish government began compulsory vaccination of the Saami in 1816. On the northern Pacific island of Hokkaido, the Japanese government initiated a program to vaccinate the indigenous Ainu in the 1850s.[9]

Most Swedes and Japanese regarded the Saami and Ainu, respectively, as savages, just as most white Americans by the 1830s considered Indigenous people to be an inferior race. Indeed, the US vaccinations occurred while American scientists were embracing the ideas of phrenology, which held that the study of the shapes of skulls showed Indigenous people to be racially inferior to whites, and the United States embarked upon a program of removal of Indigenous people from areas east of the Mississippi River (just as in Sweden, the Saami vaccination program paralleled a policy of forced assimilation). In between military campaigns against the Shawnees, Sauk and Meskwaki, Seminoles, and others, the US government forcibly removed tens of thousands of natives, including the Cherokees, Choctaws, Odawa, and Potawatomis, from territories east of the Mississippi River to reservations in the trans-Mississippi West.[10] One might thus suspect that Martin and other physicians who vaccinated Indigenous people were isolated do-gooders operating outside of government authority. Yet, like the vaccinators in Sweden, Japan, and Mexico or George Sibley at Fort Osage, Martin was a government agent. He administered the smallpox vaccine under the auspices of an 1832 federal law directing the Office of Indian Affairs to vaccinate Indigenous people. The law stipulated that "it shall be the duty of the several Indian agents and sub-agents, under the direction of the Secretary of War, to take such measures as he shall deem most efficient, to convene the Indian tribes in their respective towns, or in such other places and numbers, and at such seasons as shall be most convenient to the Indian population, for the purpose of arresting the progress of small-pox among the several tribes by vaccination." The law further empowered the War Department "to employ as many physicians or surgeons, from the army or resident on the frontier," to vaccinate Indigenous people "who are infected, or may be in immediate danger of being infected."[11]

The incongruity between the US campaigns of war and removal, on the one hand, and the vaccination program, on the other, demands an explanation: Why would the US government carry out an extensive vaccination program when at the same time it sought to remove Indigenous people from the eastern United States to the trans-Mississippi West and project its sovereignty into the borderlands?

Understanding the vaccination program begins with recognizing the tenuousness of the US presence in the western borderlands in the 1830s. The removal policies of the 1830s certainly foreshadowed the eventual military defeat and legal subjugation of Indigenous people. Indigenous nations removed from east of the Mississippi River to the West—the Cherokees, Creeks, Choctaws, Chickasaws, Shawnees, Potawatomis, Miamis, Kickapoos, Lenape, Sauk, and Meskwaki among them—found themselves by the 1830s surrounded and often outnumbered by white settlers. To the West, however, it was another matter. In 1832, when Congress passed the Indian

Vaccination Act, the United States still maintained a relatively weak presence in the western borderlands. There, it was forced to contend not only with powerful, autonomous native groups such as the Lakota but with competing British and Mexican empires. Above all, Americans had to contend with smallpox itself—a fearful disease for Americans as well as for natives. For many Americans, the fear of smallpox outweighed the fear of Indigenous people. Moreover, vaccination was a way for the United States to win the good will of Indigenous people and thus to detach them from alliances with competing imperial powers. Not least, vaccination allowed Americans to shore up their own anxieties about their sovereignty in the borderlands and present themselves to natives (and to themselves as well) as beneficent. Cognizant of the United States' weaknesses, Americans' fears and sense of powerlessness in the face of natives, imperial competitors, and smallpox impelled them to vaccinate Indigenous people in the borderlands.

Most western and Native American historians have simply ignored the vaccination program. It does not fit neatly into the paradigms of manifest destiny and what has come in recent years to be called "settler colonialism" that dominate historians' understanding of the period.[12] Rather than explain the vaccination program in the context of American weaknesses and fears, the few historians who have sought to explain it have tried to align it with US expansion into the borderlands—a conquest that, they imply, though not complete until the 1890s, was already a foregone conclusion in the 1830s. Americans, according to this view, feared and hated Indigenous people; they welcomed their deaths by whatever means because the disappearance of Indigenous people opened the continent to white American settlement. Antebellum Americans supposedly shared the view of John Winthrop, the first governor of Massachusetts, who wrote in 1634, "The natives, they are all neere dead of the small Poxe, so as the Lord hathe cleared our title to what we possess."[13]

Certainly, some Americans in the first half of the nineteenth century adhered to Winthrop's view of smallpox as a providential scourge. In 1851, for instance, the popular historians John Warner Barber and Elizabeth Barber suggested that an illness, probably smallpox, had been visited upon the Indigenous people of Massachusetts in the early 1620s by an angry God as punishment for the natives' alleged practice of enslaving or killing shipwrecked European sailors.[14] In the opinion of the handful of historians who have studied the vaccination program, its intent was a cynical reflection of the views of Americans such as the Barbers. Russell Thornton, in his encyclopedic study of American Indian population decline since 1492, characterized the vaccination program as a failure, because of a "lack of interest on the part of United States officials" in truly seeing Indigenous people vaccinated.[15]

Yet the program's extent belies that claim. While the number of Native Americans vaccinated in the 1830s may seem small, it compares favorably to other medical programs that targeted remote and dispersed native populations. A smallpox inoculation program aimed at the children of Guanajuato, Mexico, in 1797, for instance, reached only 19 percent of the province's children, and less than 10 percent of the children in rural districts, where the population, like that of Native Americans in the United States, was scattered.[16] For a vaccination program to be successful, the vaccine did not need to reach everyone in any one group. The unvaccinated could be protected from contagion if they remained within a group in which many had been vaccinated—a form of protection epidemiologists call "herd immunity" or "community immunity."[17] For smallpox, at least one-half of a community would need to be vaccinated to achieve herd immunity. Taking into account the limited ability of nineteenth-century nation-states to vaccinate dispersed populations, the US program, like those of the British, Mexicans, Swedes, and Japanese, was a qualified success: communities such as the Lakota whom Martin vaccinated in 1832 likely achieved herd immunity and were well-protected, while communities in which only a few individuals received the vaccine remained vulnerable.

Straining like Thornton to fit vaccination within the larger context of American conquest, J. Diane Pearson has argued that federal officials withheld the vaccine from Indigenous people who resisted removal or were otherwise hostile to the United States. Yet US physicians routinely offered the vaccine to Indigenous people such as the Ojibwe whose relationship to the United States was icy; the purpose of the medical diplomacy was warmer relations. Moreover, Pearson's argument is largely based on her reading of a single sentence written by Lewis Cass, the secretary of war, in a letter to John Dougherty, an agent in the Office of Indian Affairs. After delegating Dougherty to direct the vaccination program on the Missouri River, Cass added that he should not "send a Surgeon higher up the Missouri than the Mandans, and I think not higher than the Aricaras." If that was all that Cass had written, then Pearson's interpretation of the purpose of the vaccination program might seem persuasive. Yet, Cass immediately followed the sentence by suggesting that Dougherty might later extend the vaccination program farther upriver. After writing that the vaccination program should stop at the Mandan villages in 1832, Cass wrote that in regard to further vaccinations, "The proper time for this service will be determined by you, and will depend upon the most convenient opportunity for finding the Indians collected together." Cass had good reason to suggest to Dougherty that in 1832 the vaccinations extend no farther than the Mandans. He had written to Dougherty about the vaccination program in early May, shortly after the passage of the act. He knew that by the time his instructions reached Dougherty, and the agent had organized a party to take a physician, a subagent, and an interpreter up the Missouri, most of the summer would have passed. Indeed, by the time Martin—the physician Cass appointed—reached the Lakota, it was already late October, and nearly time to descend the Missouri. Such practical concerns abound in the instructions Cass sent to his agents about the vaccination program: he mused about the virtues of ascending the Missouri by boat versus hiring horses and going overland; if Dougherty opted to travel by land, Cass reminded him that physicians were to provide their own horses; he further stipulated exactly when the physicians' compensation of six dollars per day should commence; and he clarified that "the vaccination of 100 Indians will be considered a day's service."[18]

If, according to these historians, Americans did not truly want to vaccinate Indigenous people, then according to others, such as Paul Kelton, Indigenous people did not truly want to be vaccinated, either. Kelton has argued that by the 1820s, vaccination was part of a "culture war" aimed at undermining the traditions of Cherokee healers.[19] Kelton applauded those Cherokees who declined to be vaccinated, while offering little explanation for the many who received the vaccine willingly. His perspective, in its reluctance to recognize fully the ways in which many natives incorporated some American medical practices—what historians of medicine call "hybridity"—casts native healing practices as culturally static.[20] Far from being static, native healers readily adopted remedies they perceived to be effective. Kelton himself notes that in the eighteenth century, the Cherokees and other natives in the South Atlantic coastal plain incorporated the practice of quarantine to arrest the spread of smallpox.[21] More poignantly, at Fort Clark on the Missouri River in August 1837, at the height of a smallpox epidemic among the Mandan, a trader, Francis Chardon, reported that one Mandan, desperate to prevent his child from falling ill, adopted the practice of inoculation from Americans and improvised a version of the procedure: "An Indian Vaccinated his child, by cutting two small pieces of flesh out of his arms, and two on the belly—and then taking a Scab from one, that was getting well of the disease, and rubbing it on the wounded part, three days after, it took effect, and the child is perfectly well."[22] The Mandan father, like the 900 Lakota Martin vaccinated in 1832, were among the many Indigenous people willing to risk incorporating a medical practice from a different culture if it promised to be effective against smallpox.

The vaccination program was neither so facile as to undermine native healers nor so cynical as merely to reward cooperative Indigenous nations and punish hostile ones. The vaccine program is best understood in light of manifold American weaknesses: the vulnerability of white Americans to smallpox and the inability of the United States to realize its claim to sovereignty in the borderlands. Americans articulated their fears of smallpox as well as their thwarted ambitions for expansion in stories they told of encountering smallpox in the borderlands. Narrative provided a structure that allowed Americans to give voice to their fears and at the same time contain them.[23] According to the literary critic David Shuttleton, eighteenth-century English smallpox narratives were a means of expressing and containing fears of the disease. Like captivity narratives, a genre that also allowed for the expression of fears of Indigenous people, smallpox narratives both articulated and resolved fears of the disease. Both captivity and smallpox narratives adhered to a pattern of torment, steadfastness, and recovery: a secularized version of the Christian narrative of redemption.[24] In the 1830s, narratives similarly became vehicles by which Americans expressed their fears of smallpox, natives, and their own expansion into the borderlands. Three such narratives of vaccination, all published between 1831 and 1839—a captivity narrative of a boy taken by the Kickapoos; a journal of an expedition to the Ojibwe; and a travelogue of a journey to California—both explained and shaped American actions.

Fear manifested itself in American smallpox narratives in three ways. First, smallpox was the scourge not only of Indigenous people but also of white Americans. While Indigenous people constituted the majority of smallpox victims in the first part of the nineteenth century, Americans who had long lived in isolation from Old World disease pools—especially settlers in the North American backcountry who had never been exposed to the virus—were just as vulnerable to the disease. Narratives emphasized this shared vulnerability and encouraged vaccination as a public health measure. Second, the United States had to contend for sovereignty not only with autonomous native groups but with competing European imperial powers. Journals and narratives highlighted this competition, encouraging Americans to recognize that in this multilateral borderland, the United States could not simply impose its will; rather, it should employ vaccination to try to win the allegiance of natives against competing imperial powers. Third, the United States embarked upon the vaccination program to rationalize its expansion into the borderlands. In vaccination narratives, Americans sought to convince not only the natives but themselves of their good intentions; they sought to show that they would be pacific and would bring benefits to the natives. Eager to draw a contrast between themselves and competing empires, Americans sought to vaccinate Indigenous people to protect themselves both from the virus and from the perception that, as conquerors, they were no better than Britain or Mexico. The US empire, Thomas Jefferson infamously declared in 1780, would be "an empire of liberty."[25] In the 1830s, it was also an empire of remedy: through vaccination, Americans hoped to convince themselves, in the face of removal and their encroachments into Mexican territory, of the safety, certainty, and benignity of the US presence in the borderlands.

SHARED VULNERABILITY

Smallpox is an affliction both deadly and relatively easily transmissible. The *Variola* virus that causes smallpox usually travels through the air and enters new hosts through the respiratory tract, but it can also spread if a potential host comes into contact with a fresh smallpox scab or pustule. Once the disease has found a new host, it incubates for ten to fourteen days before manifesting itself as intense pain, fever, an eruption of pox sores on the surface of the body, and depending on the severity of the variant of the virus, death. If one was fortunate enough to be afflicted with discrete smallpox, in which the pox sores were scattered over one's body and did not touch one another, the chance of survival was 90 percent. Half of the victims of confluent smallpox, in which one had so many pox sores on one's body that they clustered together, died. Almost all the victims of hemorrhagic smallpox, which caused subcutaneous bleeding, perished. The only carriers of smallpox are human beings, and because a significant proportion of smallpox hosts die before they can pass the disease along to someone else, the disease is endemic only in places where the population is relatively sizable and dense and where carriers of the disease who have not yet become symptomatic have a good chance of encountering as-yet-uninfected hosts and transmitting the disease to them. Early modern European cities were ideal places for smallpox to thrive. Between the sixteenth and eighteenth centuries, smallpox settled into early modern European cities and became an endemic childhood disease—80 percent of its victims were under ten years of age—yet smallpox accounted for less than 10 percent of all deaths. Most western Europeans were exposed to the virus as children; those who survived the exposure acquired lifelong immunity, though a bout of measles could wipe out immunities acquired by exposure to other diseases, including immunity to smallpox.[26]

Most European colonists who first arrived in the Americas possessed immunity to smallpox acquired in childhood. Yet natives, who had no previous exposure to the disease, died in large numbers when the smallpox virus arrived in the New World. Epidemics of smallpox recurred every few decades, afflicting everyone who had been born since the previous epidemic.[27] By the end of the eighteenth century, however, although Indigenous people still constituted many of the victims of smallpox in North America, many persons of European descent born in the Americas were, by virtue of their isolation from Old World disease pools, as vulnerable to smallpox as Indigenous people. This was especially true in the backcountry, where many Americans grew to adulthood without having been exposed to smallpox. Such settlers were, in an epidemiological sense, Native Americans. Between 1775 and 1782, the disease killed an estimated 130,000 North Americans—natives, colonists, and slaves alike—in outbreaks from the British Atlantic colonies to central Mexico, the Puget Sound region, and Hudson's Bay.[28]

The relative remoteness of eighteenth-century North Americans from the centers of exposure to smallpox in European cities disposed some to experiment with smallpox inoculation—a treatment that preceded vaccination. A physician inoculated a patient by making an incision in the patient's arm and introducing into the incision a small amount of fluid from the pustule of a smallpox victim. If the inoculation worked, the patient would develop a mild case of smallpox and acquire an immunity to even the most virulent strains of the disease.[29] Western Europeans had adopted the practice from Turkey in the early eighteenth century, demonstrating that, like Indigenous people a century later, they were willing to risk borrowing a medical procedure from another culture if it promised to protect them from smallpox.[30] Benjamin Franklin, impressed by the procedure, advocated for general inoculation in Philadelphia in 1759.[31]

Yet inoculation was a gamble. Sometimes, inoculated patients transmitted the live virus to new hosts, and thus contributed to the spread of smallpox rather than its containment. That was the case in Boston in 1721, when physicians resorted to inoculation to try to arrest the spread of the disease yet may have contributed only to its spread.[32] Moreover, introducing the live virus into the human body could lead to a deadly case of smallpox for the patient. In 1758, the theologian Jonathan Edwards, having recently accepted an appointment as the president of the College of New Jersey (later Princeton University), underwent smallpox inoculation to protect him from an outbreak of the disease. The fifty-four-year-old Edwards was either too weak to endure the inoculation or simply unlucky—he died within a month of the procedure.[33]

One early nineteenth-century captivity narrative simultaneously reflected Americans' fears of smallpox, inoculation, and Indigenous people. The *Narrative of the Captivity and Suffering of Isaac Knight from Indian Barbarity* casts the ten-year-old Knight as both a victim of captivity and an unintentional instrument of the transmission of smallpox. The narrative begins with a seemingly innocuous detail: in 1793, Knight's parents had their son vaccinated against smallpox when the disease appeared near their home in Henderson County, Kentucky. On the face of it, this important detail of the story could not be true. A physician vaccinated a patient by introducing via incision not *Variola* (smallpox) matter but *Vaccinia* (cowpox or kinepox). *Vaccinia* is not dangerous to humans but nonetheless confers immunity to smallpox. Edward Jenner, the English physician who discovered that an infection of cowpox makes one immune to smallpox, did not publish his first treatise on vaccination until 1798, and vaccinations did not reach the United States until two years later.[34] The author of Isaac Knight's narrative certainly meant inoculation, but many nineteenth-century Americans often used the terms interchangeably, and Knight dictated the narrative four decades after the events he described occurred, by which time vaccination had replaced inoculation.

Shortly after receiving the treatment, Knight together with four other boys were set upon by a group of Kickapoos and Potawatomis. For over a century, the Kickapoos, an Anishinaabe nation, had alternately employed diplomacy and violence to maintain their position in the complex borderland of the Great Lakes region. At the end of the eighteenth century, the Kickapoos inhabited the region around the Wabash and Vermilion Rivers, and the Illinois prairies to the west of those rivers. Like other Anishinaabe nations such as the Odawa, Potawatomis, Miamis, Sauk, and Meskwaki, they had sought refuge in this region in the seventeenth century from the Haudenosaunee (Iroquois), who had become powerful after acquiring guns from Dutch traders in return for furs. To defend themselves from the Haudenosaunee, as well as from Siouan-speaking nations such as the Dakota and Osages to their west and south, the Kickapoos usually maintained a close alliance with other Anishinaabe nations in the Great Lakes region. For similar reasons, together with other Anishinaabe nations they sought out and maintained an alliance with the French. Yet at times over the course of the eighteenth century, relations with other Anishinaabe groups and with the French soured and became violent. The Kickapoos joined with the British against the United States during the American Revolution, but by the time of Knight's capture in 1793, a small number of American settlers had migrated to the Wabash River region, and some bands of the Kickapoos sought to make some accommodations to white commerce and settlement in an effort to remain in their homeland. Other Kickapoos, especially those who inhabited the prairies west of the Wabash River—a group that included, presumably, those who took Knight captive, resisted US encroachments.[35]

The captors killed two of the boys and forced the other three, including Knight, to return with them in captivity to the Illinois country.[36] Between the early seventeenth and mid-nineteenth century, Indigenous people captured thousands of settlers. Depleted by epidemics of smallpox and other diseases, Indigenous people often adopted captured children in an effort to replenish their populations—and it appears from Knight's narrative that the Kickapoos intended to adopt him. As a result of over a century of captivities and intermarriages, by the late 1820s, the Great Lakes region had a Métis, or mixed-ancestry, population between 10,000 and 15,000. Yet there was no single pattern of captivity. Some captives might be ritually executed to atone for losses in conflicts with the colonists. While some children were awarded as replacements to households that had recently lost a child to disease, and young women captives might eventually marry within the village, other captives were kept as servants or held for only a short time before being ransomed. Many captives—particularly those who were especially young when captured or well-treated by their captors—resisted repatriation.[37]

Not so Knight. Although some of the Kickapoos treated him with kindness, he described his captivity as an ordeal. Such a description was typical of captivity narratives, one of the most popular American literary genres in the eighteenth and early nineteenth centuries.[38] Yet Knight's captivity narrative departs from the usual form in a significant way: within a week of his capture, Knight fell ill with smallpox. In a sense, for Knight to become symptomatic ten days or so after being inoculated showed that the inoculation worked as it should: he developed a mild form of the disease from which he was meant to recover and gain immunity. Yet as Knight's narrative reveals, it was this aspect of inoculation—intentional exposure to the disease—that made late eighteenth-century Americans wary of the procedure. Like anyone who had been inoculated, Knight might die of smallpox—or he might transmit a fatal case to someone else. Few of Knight's fellow Kentucky settlers may have known of the botched inoculation program in Boston in 1721 or the fate of Jonathan Edwards in 1758, but most had heard similar tales of inoculations gone wrong. Among the Kickapoos, Knight attempted to disguise the nature of his illness. He was spared when a grandmotherly woman in the village took pity on him and nursed him back to health. Yet shortly after Knight began to recover from his illness, the disease appeared among the Kickapoos.

Although the disease had broken out in the Ohio Valley generally and could have reached them by any number of means, Knight did not doubt that he was the source of the outbreak among the Kickapoos. One of his first victims was the woman who had nursed him back to health. He wrote: "The death of this humane and motherly old squaw gave the Author of this Narrative most unpleasant feelings, and was the cause of much distressing exercise of mind." The woman was an exception, however. In general, Knight relished having transmitted the virus to the Kickapoos, writing that he "hoped that some of the most cruel and barbarous of them would die with it." His only fear was that he might be discovered as the carrier of the illness.[39]

In a startling departure from typical captivity narratives, in which the captives are victims who are redeemed by their faith, in Knight's tale, the helpless captive became a remorseless bringer of death, and his captors became his victims. Knight was in effect an embodiment of the smallpox virus itself: a foreign presence within the village but largely unnoticed and seemingly too small to be the cause of such suffering. A gruesome incident in Knight's narrative both confirms his role as the secret bringer of death to the Kickapoos and firmly separates the narrative from the Indian captivity genre. With so many Kickapoos sick and dead, it fell to Knight to care for a year-old child. Although the baby was the grandchild of the woman who had herself cared for Knight, he nonetheless resented the extra responsibility, and when the opportunity arose, he suffocated the child with a blanket.[40] The episode inverts both the moral lesson of a typical captivity narrative and the sympathy of readers. In many other narratives, captives described (or invented, in order to emphasize the alleged perfidy of their captors) incidents in which Indigenous people murdered infant captives, either because the infant would slow them on their march, or because they reasoned the baby was ill. For instance, such a murder was included in the narrative of Sarah Ann Horn, a captive of the Comanches; her account was published in 1839—the same year that Knight's narrative appeared.[41]

On the surface, Knight's narrative seems to celebrate the extermination of Indigenous people in a manner little different from an infamous episode in eighteenth-century North American history: British officers' attempt to start a smallpox epidemic among their Indigenous enemies during the Seven Years' War. According to the historian Elizabeth Fenn, Anglo-American forces in the Seven Years' War employed the smallpox virus as an instrument of conquest, making gifts to natives of blankets that had been used by smallpox victims and that probably contained smallpox scabs, thus engaging in an eighteenth-century form of germ warfare. The question for Fenn was not whether the British wished for enemy natives to die of smallpox, but whether the British general Jeffery Amherst managed to transmit the disease to them successfully, or, as she put it, "Did he or didn't he?"[42] Knight was, likewise, an instrument of germ warfare. Yet a closer reading of Knight's narrative reveals deeper ambiguities. Knight's depiction of the Kickapoos is not uniform; some of them he presents in a sympathetic light. While readers of the narrative are initially encouraged to think that the Kickapoos are the villains of the story, within a few pages they are shown as victims who are far less frightening than the smallpox virus that Knight carries. The ambiguous depiction of the Kickapoos reflects the evolution of Knight's thinking. As a boy captive of the Kickapoos in the 1790s, Knight relished bringing death to them. Yet he experienced a religious awakening before dictating his story in the 1830s and came to regret his role in transmitting smallpox to the Kickapoos.[43]

Published in 1839, Knight's narrative reveals a quite different understanding of smallpox and Indigenous people than the views of the eighteenth-century British officers whom Fenn analyzed. Most British officers, born in Europe, had been exposed to smallpox as children and survived it. (A notable exception was Amherst's subordinate at Fort Pitt, Col. Henry Bouquet, who had never had smallpox. Although he may not have realized it, Bouquet, like Knight and other backcountry settlers, was as vulnerable to smallpox as the natives.) Although the Seven Years' War long preceded the advent of the germ theory of disease, the British knew from experience that a person once exposed to the disease was immune. Most—with the exception of Bouquet—could contemplate using the smallpox virus as a weapon against their enemies in the American epidemiological hinterland, secure in the knowledge that the disease would not rebound upon them.[44]

By contrast, the sense of shared vulnerability is the key to understanding Knight's narrative. Indigenous people were not the only North Americans to die in smallpox epidemics in the nineteenth century. In Philadelphia, more than 600 people died of smallpox between 1807 and 1817. In New York, nearly 300 died in an outbreak in 1815–16. Keenly aware of the threat of smallpox, early nineteenth-century Americans eagerly adopted Jenner's vaccine. On December 25, 1800, Thomas Jefferson wrote to Benjamin Waterhouse, one of the first professors at Harvard Medical School, that "Every friend of humanity must look with pleasure on this discovery, by which one evil more is withdrawn from the condition of man."[45] Waterhouse wasted no time in promulgating the treatment, vaccinating his children and three domestic servants in 1800. By 1801, he wrote to Jefferson that by shipping his vaccine to physicians around the United States, he had "planted the true vaccine disease directly in the Province of Maine, in New Hampshire; in the state of Vermont, Rhode Island, Connecticut, New York, Virginia, South Carolina, Georgia, Kentucky, and Tennessee; and in every part of Massachusetts, including the islands of Nantucket, and Martha's Vineyard. The physicians in the states of Pennsylvania, Delaware, North Carolina, and Maryland, were supplied from my stock."[46] Waterhouse also supplied Jefferson with vaccine. Jefferson's physician set about vaccinating Jefferson's family, neighbors, and slaves immediately upon receiving the vaccine. Ultimately, Jefferson wrote, at his Monticello plantation, "our whole experiment extended to about two hundred persons."[47]

To prevent a smallpox outbreak from spreading from Indigenous people to white Americans, the federal government began considering the vaccination of natives. In 1818, Lt. Col. William Trimble returned from a tour through Comanche territory and urged the federal government to vaccinate them.[48] In 1820, Josiah Meigs and other physicians petitioned Congress to create a "National Vaccine Institution." They emphasized that the disease was undiscriminating: "The rich and the poor, the old and the young, are alike liable to this disease. It is not confined to any particular place, but pervades alike our cities and villages." Moreover, Meigs and the other physicians added, the disease did not distinguish between Indigenous people and settlers: "Neither are the untutored natives of our land secure from this plague; it is frequently carried into their camps and villages."[49] In advocating widespread vaccination, the physicians understood that any effective program against smallpox must include Indigenous people, or else the virus would persist. Thus, in 1809, a St. Louis physician announced in the *Missouri Gazette* that he would vaccinate "indigent persons, paupers, and Indians" free of charge.[50]

In 1830, an outbreak of smallpox among several native communities that bordered American settlements and trade routes prompted the federal government to create its vaccination program. The disease devastated the Pawnees whose villages were located along the Republican River in the central Great Plains. John Dougherty, the Indian agent at Cantonment Leavenworth, described the suffering of the Pawnees in language similar to that of Knight's narrative. He wrote that the Pawnees "were dying so fast, and taken down at once in such large numbers, that they had ceased to bury their dead, whose bodies were to be seen, in every direction, laying about in the river, lodged on the sand bars, in the hog weeds around their villages, and in their corn cashes; others again were dragged off by hungry dogs into the prairie." The epidemic also spread to the neighboring Otoes, Omahas, and Poncas. At the same time, the disease erupted among the Odawa and Potawatomis of Ohio, according to James Jackson, an Indian agent on the Maumee River.[51] None of the affected groups lived in isolation from American settlements. The Pawnees' villages were near the heavily traveled Santa Fe Trail between western Missouri and New Mexico. By 1830, more than 10,000 settlers lived in Ohio, Indiana, and Michigan in the area near the Maumee River. When the Indian agents pressed their superiors for a vaccination program, their implication was obvious: an epidemic of smallpox in these regions threatened American settlement and commerce.

Like Knight, who called the Kickapoo woman who nursed him back to health "humane," Indian agents and missionaries who lobbied for vaccination couched their appeal in the language of humanity. In 1818, Trimble called the vaccination of the Comanches a course "dictated by humanity."[52] Douglas Houghton, a physician employed to vaccinate the Ojibwe in 1832, argued that "every motive of humanity toward the suffering Indian" argued for extending the vaccination program to further native groups.[53] Isaac McCoy, a Baptist missionary to the Potawatomis and Odawa, wrote to Secretary of War Lewis Cass that the "claims of humanity" demanded that the government rescue "thousands of men and women and children from this awful calamity."[54] Both McCoy and Cass were ardent proponents of removal. For them, "humanity" meant not that Indigenous people possessed rights, such as the right to remain in their homes, by virtue of being fellow human beings; rather, it was part of a vocabulary of sentimentality. Their humanitarian appeals were combined with graphic descriptions of bodily suffering in a form that was, according to the cultural historian Karen Halttunen, part of an emerging Anglo-American middle-class literary culture of sentimentality. Graphic descriptions of pain—the flogging of sailors or slaves, for instance—became an essential part of the literary genre of humanitarian reform.[55] Like familiar narrative genres, the language of humanity was a way for McCoy and others to express their own fears of smallpox. That they pressed for a vaccination program in the language of humanity hardly meant that the United States had abandoned its goals for removing natives from the path of American settlement. Rather, like Knight, they had come to understand that where the smallpox virus was concerned, Indigenous people and white Americans shared a common vulnerability.

MEDICAL DIPLOMACY

Following the passage of the Indian Vaccination Act, numerous physicians appointed by the federal government dispersed among dozens of Native

American groups from the Great Lakes to the Upper Missouri River to vaccinate them against smallpox.[56] The federal program sought to win the natives' good will and perhaps even their allegiance to the United States; but there was nonetheless nothing the United States could do to force natives to accept the vaccine. To understand how Indigenous people controlled the vaccination process, one must distinguish, as anthropologists do, between "directed" and "permissive" acculturation. The former type characterizes the forced assimilation of reservation boarding schools in the late nineteenth century, for instance. The latter type characterizes the adaptations natives made freely, such as accommodations to fur traders. The vaccination program belonged to the latter type. As long as Indigenous people remained autonomous, their acculturation was permissive: they could accept or reject what the Americans offered them.[57]

In administering the vaccine program, rather than directing his subordinates from Washington, the secretary of war, Lewis Cass, was forced to defer to his agents in the field. "Much dependence is placed upon your knowledge of the Country and the Indians," Cass wrote to Dougherty.[58] In turn, agents delegated the execution of the program to physicians who could do little more than administer the vaccine to the available and the willing. For instance, Meriwether Martin, after reaching Leavenworth on the Missouri River in August 1832, hoped to vaccinate the Shawnees but never reached them. Instead, after vaccinating some Iowas at the Leavenworth agency and a handful of Otoes he encountered at a trading post, he proceeded to the Lakota encampment near the Black Hills, where skeptical leaders permitted him to proceed with the vaccinations only after he had demonstrated the procedure on the children of his interpreter. When Martin visited the Dakota—kinspeople of the Lakota—they refused vaccination entirely. Through October, he visited several Lakota and Yanctonai bands but was frustrated that many of the members of the bands he visited were absent— they had gone deep into the Great Plains for the seasonal bison hunt.[59]

Physicians not only struggled to locate Indigenous people; the live vaccine itself was uncooperative. Martin was slowed by a shortage of vaccine and was forced to harvest new medicine from the arms of some of the children he had vaccinated. Indeed, in the early nineteenth century, the primary obstacle to an effective vaccination program was finding a way to transport the cowpox lymph over long distances without the lymph becoming inert. Harvesting the live virus from patients recently vaccinated proved to be the most reliable method.[60] Physicians harvested vaccine from their patients at any time from one to eight days after having initially administered it to them.

Jenner advised harvesting the vaccine by puncturing a cowpox pustule to let the vaccine "gradually ooze out." The virus could be preserved by setting a bead of it on a glass square to let it dry, and then sandwiching the dried bead between another square of glass. Even if dry vaccine matter retained its effectiveness, however, it needed to be delicately moistened with water before it could be administered. To be most effective, according to Jenner, the extracted virus should not be dried but rather should be "inserted immediately in its fluid state" into the arm of the next patient. To administer the vaccine, physicians gently punctured the patient's arm with a lancet that had the vaccine matter on its tip. "It is by no means necessary to draw blood in the operation," one physician advised. "On the contrary . . . the less injury to the tender extremities of the absorbents, the better." A small inflammation indicated a successful vaccination.[61]

While some native groups such as the Dakota refused the vaccine, many Indigenous nations eagerly received the medicine. Elbert Herring, the Commissioner of Indian Affairs, reported in December 1832, that the natives vaccinated by physicians in his bureau "have manifested an anxious desire to secure to themselves the benefits and protections of the process of vaccination."[62] Historians of medicine once argued that vaccination programs aimed as much to extend the power of the state as to prevent disease.[63] Certainly the vaccination program in the 1830s was part of an effort to incorporate natives, at least in a public health sense, into the American body politic: vaccinated natives would not spread smallpox to vulnerable American settlers. Yet Martin's experience also accords with the recent work of historians of medicine, who argue that nineteenth-century vaccination efforts cannot be seen as orderly, top-down programs; both local physicians and intended recipients of the vaccine, not to mention the microbe itself, exercised decisive agency and control over the process.[64]

Natives could either reject the vaccine or receive it without abandoning traditional medical practices. A smallpox outbreak near the Cherokees in 1824 is instructive: by the mid-1820s, Cherokee society was divided between those highly acculturated to American norms and others who adhered to Cherokee traditions—and a large number who fell somewhere between these two extremes. When smallpox threatened to appear in Cherokee country in the spring of 1824, some Cherokees sought protection by submitting to traditional cures—a series of rituals and the consumption of an herbal tea—while others, particularly those who attended a Moravian mission school, received the vaccine from the missionaries. Many Cherokees reasoned that the safest course of action was a hybrid one: to take the medicines offered by both the Moravians and those traditional Cherokees whom the Moravians called "sorcerers." The missionaries' journals made repeated references to converts who disappointed the Moravians by availing themselves of both Cherokee and American medicines.[65]

The refusal of some natives to be vaccinated reflected their faith in traditional native remedies. In many respects, that faith was well placed. Edward Jenner's innovation in the treatment of smallpox gave physicians in the 1830s an effective treatment for one of the most fearsome diseases of the era, but in other respects American physicians had little to offer patients. American medicine at the time remained dominated by the humoral paradigm that dated to Greek antiquity. Treatments for most ailments involved exorcising bodily "humours" through bloodletting, emetics, laxatives, or perspirants. In the 1830s, physicians ascribed outbreaks of diseases such as malaria and cholera to the atmosphere, or to intemperance, or both.[66]

The openness of many natives to smallpox vaccination became a key to US diplomacy in the borderlands. In the 1830s, Hudson's Bay Company fur traders based in Canada operated with impunity in US territory in the Great Lakes region and northern Great Plains. British commerce had a diplomatic as well as commercial purpose; like George Sibley's factory at Fort Osage, the Hudson's Bay Company sought to retain for Britain the diplomatic and military loyalties of its native trade partners. The United States, though it officially banned unlicensed foreign fur traders from its territory, was powerless to stop the commerce. Natives shifted their allegiances and played one imperial power against the other, hoping to maintain their autonomy by keeping all claims to sovereignty (other than their own) tenuous and dependent on their good will.

In this context, the smallpox vaccine had long been another gift intended to engender the good will of Indigenous people. In his instructions to Meriwether Lewis before he embarked on his journey into the West in 1804, Thomas Jefferson had emphasized that Lewis should do his utmost to sway the natives to the loyalty of the United States, and particularly to bring with him some vaccine. He wrote: "Inform those of them with whom you may be, of it'[s] efficacy as a preservative from the small-pox; & instruct & incourage them in the use of it."[67] In 1819, the secretary of war John Calhoun had referred the leader of another Missouri River expedition, Stephen Long, to Jefferson's instructions to Lewis; and in 1820, a private vaccination advocate shipped a box of vaccine to the Long expedition's physician, Edwin James, "for the purpose of introducing vaccination among the Indians."[68]

The passage of the Indian Vaccination Act in 1832 formalized the policy of medical diplomacy that Jefferson and Calhoun had urged on western explorers such as Lewis and Long. When an agent to the Ojibwe, Henry Schoolcraft, embarked on a diplomatic mission on the Upper Mississippi River in the summer of 1832, he brought the physician Douglas Houghton with him to offer vaccine to the Ojibwe under the terms of the new law. Schoolcraft hoped that the offer of vaccination would help detach the Ojibwe, whose territory west of Lake Superior straddled the border between the United States and Canada, from the competing influence of the British. The Ojibwe had been allies of the British in Canada before the War of 1812; they had fought alongside the British against the United States during the war; and in the years following the conflict, they continued to look to the north for material support, traveling every year to British garrisons where they received gifts of firearms and ammunition in return for promises of support. They were not firm allies of the British, however; rather, they successfully played the British and the United States against each other, extracting gifts and concessions from both. The British traders were both more experienced at dealing with the Ojibwe and more generous: they distributed twenty times more goods than the United States.[69]

The US and British claims to the western Great Lakes region were mere pretenses. The Ojibwe and allied Anishinaabe nations dominated the western Great Lakes. The Ojibwe were allied with two other large and powerful Anishinaabe nations, the Odawa and Potawatomis, to form a confederation, the Council of Three Fires. These three confederated nations had collectively controlled the lands bordering all the western Great Lakes since at least the seventeenth century. The Ojibwe, having supplied themselves with guns first from the French and later from the British, expanded this territory by repulsing the western advances of the Haudenosaunee in the late seventeenth century and pushing the Dakota southward and westward toward the Great Plains in the eighteenth century.[70] Thomas McKenney, the superintendent of Indian Affairs, visited the Ojibwe at Fond du Lac in 1826 to conclude a treaty with them. In his journal, he confessed that the Ojibwe, rather than the United States, controlled the Upper Mississippi: "The Indians, at these remote points, are out of the reach of the influence of the agency."[71]

Similarly, Houghton's 1832 journal of his vaccination mission was an unremitting tale of unease and powerlessness that reflected the weakness of the US position in the northern Great Lakes region. Houghton was overwhelmed by the marshy, densely wooded environment of the upper Great Lakes,

Braves' Dance, Ojibwa, 1835–1837. Painting by George Catlin. Gift of Mrs. Joseph Harrison Jr., Smithsonian American Art Museum, Washington, DC.

describing rapids that destroyed canoes, impassable forests, and portages through swamps where one was knee-deep in mud. Worst of all, "musqitoes attacked us in hordes," he wrote. Still more unnerving to Houghton were the customs of the Ojibwe he encountered. At Cass Lake, he witnessed a scalp dance: three Dakota scalps, "decked fantastically with the feathers of the war eagle ... were supported like so many flags upon sticks by three girls who continued dancing with all the relatives of the disceased." The Ojibwe "singing & dancing & their shouts together with the drum upon which they were constantly tapping were extremely annoying." Most frightening to Houghton were the reports that parties of Dakota, the enemies of the Ojibwe, were waiting at certain points on the Mississippi to ambush Schoolcraft's party.[72]

Houghton vaccinated over 2,000 Ojibwe, despite having little enthusiasm for the job. For a physician, he was surprisingly churlish about the popularity of vaccination among the natives. "I find the vaccination of the Indians an irksome task, chiefly in consequence of the great numbers," he wrote to his brother in June 1832. "When I commence operating they crowd around me with their arms ready, and anxiously wait their turn."[73] Anxiety, irksomeness, annoyance; real attacks by mosquitoes and imagined attacks by the Dakota— for Houghton, the upper Great Lakes borderland was an uneasy place.

Chapter 3

The conference with the Ojibwe did little to put Houghton at ease; rather, it reminded him of the limits of US power. The Ojibwe eagerly received the vaccine that Houghton offered but remained cool to Schoolcraft's diplomatic efforts. At Leech Lake, Houghton vaccinated roughly 400 Ojibwe during a council that Schoolcraft and an Army lieutenant, James Allen, held with the Ojibwe leader, Eshkibagikoonzhe, or Flat Mouth. Schoolcraft and Allen presented Eshkibagikoonzhe with cloth, knives, tobacco, and ammunition; and they implored him, according to Allen, to make peace with the Dakota and "endeavor to procure and enjoy some of the comforts of the whites, and learn to live like them." Eshkibagikoonzhe, who, according to Allen, already had adapted to many aspects of American material culture—he lived not in a traditional Ojibwe lodge but in a house "built of squared timber"—accepted the gifts but refused to accede to any of Schoolcraft's requests. While the Ojibwe continued to file past Houghton to receive their vaccinations, Eshkibagikoonzhe harangued Schoolcraft and Allen. The Dakota, Eshkibagikoonzhe maintained, had attacked the Ojibwe. In an attempt to enlist the United States in the Ojibwe reprisals against the Dakota, Eshkibagikoonzhe threw the US medals that had been presented to him at Schoolcraft's feet and threatened to seek the help of the British against the Dakota if Schoolcraft refused him. Eshkibagikoonzhe's intransigence reflected how little effective power the United States wielded in the multilateral borderlands. As Allen described, the Ojibwe "feel inaccessible and secure from any power whatever, even that of the United States."[74] The most the United States could muster in the contested region in return for the gift of vaccination was the tenuous allegiance of autonomous native nations.

The offer of vaccine as a tool of diplomacy was an increasingly common stratagem in the nineteenth-century borderlands. The Hudson's Bay Company began offering vaccine to the natives of Canada in 1837 in response to the US program.[75] The Japanese offered vaccine to the Ainu of Hokkaido as they jostled with Russia for control of the island and for the good will of the island's inhabitants.[76] In frontier regions where sovereignty was contested and the allegiance of native groups undetermined, the United States, like the British traders in Canada and the Japanese in Hokkaido, claimed to be not conquerors but healers. While many Americans harbored hopes that the United States could extend its sovereignty into the borderlands, the vaccination program was more medical diplomacy than medical imperialism. It was (for natives) a hybrid medical practice and (for the United States) an uncomfortable reminder of the limits of US power in the borderlands.

Vaccination of natives was also part of a paternalistic narrative that legiti-mized real and imagined US forays into the borderlands. Around the same time of the expeditions of Martin and Houghton, the vaccination initiative was realized in a literary sense in a frontier narrative published in 1831, *The Per-sonal Narrative of James O. Pattie of Kentucky*. By his own account, Pattie did more to save Indigenous people from smallpox than any other single person: he claimed to have vaccinated over 23,000 inhabitants of Mexican Califor-nia. His narrative tells the story of his six-year sojourn in Mexico, from his arrival together with his father as a trader in Santa Fe, New Mexico, in 1824, until his return to New Orleans in 1830.[77] Pattie's editor (and probably his ghostwriter) was Timothy Flint, a Massachusetts-born, Harvard-educated clergyman-turned-journalist who later achieved some renown for a biog-raphy of Daniel Boone.[78] Like Flint's biography of Boone, Pattie's narrative is rife with frontier exaggeration and invention. Pattie's account of having rescued the daughter of the governor of New Mexico from captivity among Indigenous people, for instance, reads like the plot of a nineteenth-century romance—indeed, the source may well have been Flint's own 1826 novel *Francis Berrian*, which tells a curiously similar story of an American fron-tiersman rescuing the daughter of the New Mexican governor from captivity among Indigenous people.[79]

The alleged rescue of the Mexican maiden was no less dubious, however, than Pattie's account of having vaccinated thousands of California natives against smallpox. The story of the vaccinations is perhaps more surprising, because Pattie and his father were hunters, trappers, and traders who har-bored no sympathy for Indigenous people generally. The Native Americans in Pattie's account are either naïvely feckless or treacherously cruel—usually the latter. In either case, their behavior is that of truculent children: impulsive, self-centered, and untrustworthy. Pattie's narrative recounts one instance after another of his exercise of stern parental authority over the natives. Not only does he rescue the captured daughter of the governor, but in two other episodes he reunites families, redeeming native children who had been cap-tured or lost. The restoration of children to their parents is a key theme of Pattie's narrative: he reorders familial lines of authority in a borderland dis-ordered by childish impetuosity in the absence of a strong patriarch.[80]

Pattie disparaged Mexicans even more than Indigenous people. According to Pattie, he and his fellow Americans rescued the New Mexican governor's daughter from the Indigenous people who had taken her captive because

Chapter 3

the Mexican forces in Santa Fe lacked the courage to confront the natives. Later in the narrative, after Pattie and other Americans repulse an attack by Indigenous people during a trapping expedition, the natives, once defeated, acknowledged that the Americans were "too brave, and too good marksmen, to be Spaniards." The Mexicans, according to Pattie, also lack industry. During a trip to Guaymas on the coast of the Gulf of California, he lamented that the region "would be among the richest of the Mexican country, if it were inhabited by an enlightened, enterprising, and industrious people." The Mexicans, moreover, are no less cruel than the natives: after trapping beaver along the Gila River, crossing the Mohave Desert, and eventually reaching San Diego, California, in March 1828, Pattie reported, he and his father were imprisoned by Mexican authorities as suspected spies. Within weeks, the elder Pattie died in his cell, a victim of "the cruelty of these vile people." In the narrative, the death of Pattie's father figures as the moment when Pattie realizes the borderlands as a place where, in the absence of US sovereignty, true patriarchal authority is undermined, leaving only Indigenous anarchy or Mexican tyranny. Following the death of his father, James Pattie remained in prison for nearly a year, suffering a series of arbitrary injustices from the Alta California's governor, José María Echeandia.[81]

Nearly a year after Pattie was first imprisoned, according to his own account, he negotiated his parole. A smallpox epidemic had broken out among the missions of California.[82] Pattie claimed to have some smallpox vaccine in his possession. Governor Echeandia grudgingly released Pattie on the condition that he vaccinate the inhabitants of California against the disease. Pattie told Flint that he began his program of vaccination in January 1829. Within a month he claimed to have vaccinated both the soldiers of the garrison of San Diego and the Indigenous acolytes of the nearby mission. After having somehow "procured a sufficient quantity of the vaccine matter to answer my purpose," he moved northward, vaccinating by his account thousands of Indigenous people at the coastal missions until he reached Los Angeles, where he administered the medicine to 2,500 townspeople. He continued northward, vaccinating the acolytes and soldiers of Santa Barbara and San Luis Obispo, finally reaching San Francisco in June. Altogether, he claimed to have vaccinated more than 23,000 people.[83]

The eminent historical demographer Sherburne F. Cook was dismissive of what he called "the Pattie vaccination legend." The number of people Pattie claimed to have vaccinated does not hold up under scrutiny. The total population of the missions, garrisons, and towns Pattie visited in coastal California, from San Diego in the south to the Russian sea otter hunting outpost of Fort

Ross in the north, was in all likelihood about 16,000—far fewer people than the number Pattie claimed to have treated. Nor is it credible that anyone could have managed to vaccinate so many people in only six months, while traveling altogether several hundred miles on horseback and foot. There is thus every reason to be skeptical of Pattie's story. Yet other aspects of Pattie's tale ring true. Epidemic disease did afflict California in late 1828—although it was neither the vast nor the virulent epidemic that Pattie described. Indeed, it may not have been smallpox at all, but measles. Although is inconceivable that Pattie, after languishing in prison for nearly a year, possessed enough vaccine to treat thousands of patients, he did have another source of medicine: Russian fur traders deposited stocks of vaccine at Monterrey and San Diego in 1829.[84]

Cook was right to cast a skeptical light on Pattie's story. Yet an important question is not simply whether Pattie's account is true but *why* Pattie would make such remarkable claims. In his account of his travels from Missouri to California, Pattie expressed little empathy for Indigenous people; instead, he depicted them as savages and reported frequent violent encounters with them. In California, however, Pattie cast himself as the savior of Indigenous people, juxtaposing the life-saving administration of his vaccine with the cynical baptisms of the corrupt Mexican friars. The mission natives, Pattie wrote, had been brought to the coast from the interior "by compulsion, and then baptised, which act was as little voluntary" as their capture.[85] The implication could not have been lost on Pattie's readers in the 1830s, a decade when thousands of Americans crossed international borders to settle in Texas and American traders traversed the Santa Fe Trail to trade with New Mexico: US sovereignty in the region would be more enlightened and benign than that of the "vile" and corrupt Mexicans.[86]

In truth, Spanish colonial authorities had embarked upon smallpox prevention programs in North America long before Pattie claimed to have introduced vaccination to California. In 1797, following an outbreak of smallpox in Tehuantepec, the viceroy of New Spain, Miguel de la Grua Talamanca Branciforte, ordered that inoculations begin in New Spain. As a result, extensive inoculation programs were conducted in Mexico City, Guanajuato, and other cities. Responding to an outbreak of smallpox in Bogotá, King Charles IV of Spain issued a proclamation on September 1, 1803, ordering that the smallpox vaccine be distributed throughout the Spanish-American colonies. When the king's officially appointed vaccinator arrived in Puerto Rico—his first destination— he found that local physicians had already begun to vaccinate patients.[87] Vaccination first reached California in 1821, when a physician administered the vaccine to forty children at Monterey. Whether Pattie knew of these efforts or not it would not have altered his impression of Mexicans as diffident, ignorant, and indolent. In his telling, life-saving vaccine was an American import.

The question whether James Pattie actually vaccinated anyone in 1829 curiously parallels the question whether Jeffery Amherst actually transmitted smallpox to Indigenous people via infected blankets in 1763. In either case, the question, as the historian Elizabeth Fenn put it with regard to Amherst—"did he or didn't he?"—can probably never be answered.[88] What is clear is that there was a significant change in the two-thirds of a century between Amherst and Pattie. In 1763, it seemed like a good idea to Amherst and many others to try to cause an epidemic of smallpox among the Indigenous people. In 1831, when Pattie's narrative was published, it seemed like a good idea to prevent such an epidemic. By the 1830s, Americans reasoned that an outbreak of smallpox among natives was a threat to all Americans. Moreover, in the complicated and unpredictable competition for political dominance in the borderlands, the diplomatic benefits of offering vaccination to autonomous native groups were paramount.

Thus, only a year after the publication of Pattie's narrative, the US government embarked on a vaccination program that, unlike Pattie's story, was indisputably real. Like Pattie's narrative, the vaccination program served for Americans as a kind of vindication and justification of their ambitions for the borderlands. The vaccination effort was an early public health program that, however rudimentary, transcended the fate of Indigenous people. Success in vaccinating Indigenous people would protect frontier settlers from an outbreak of smallpox that might begin among the natives. Moreover, the program was an extension of US influence—in this case, the power to cure ills—into a borderland where US power was limited and where its sovereignty was contested by Britain and Mexico. In its effort to accommodate to natives and to win their good will, the program reveals the antebellum United States not confident of its expansion but rather wary and improvisational in its forays into the borderlands.

CHAPTER FOUR

Colonizers

On March 10, 1835, in Ciudad Victoria, the capital of the Mexican state of Tamaulipas, Francisco Vital Fernández, the Tamaulipas governor, signed a contract with a United States citizen, Benjamin Lundy, establishing Lundy as a state *empresario*. The terms of the contract were straightforward. Lundy had two years to settle 250 families on thirty leagues (about 132,000 acres) in northern Tamaulipas; in return, Lundy would receive a large grant of land.[1] Over the previous decade, governors of Coahuila y Tejas, the Mexican state bordering Tamaulipas to the north, had similarly appointed over a dozen Americans as empresarios ("entrepreneurs" in Spanish). The expectations of these northern Mexican state governors were that the American empresarios would encourage other Americans to settle in sparsely populated northern Mexico. The American immigrants, state authorities hoped, would spark economic development and population growth in northern Mexico, provide a bulwark against Indigenous raiders such as the Comanches, and as naturalized Mexican citizens, participate in the democratic development of the decade-and-a-half-old Mexican Republic.[2]

Between 1825 and 1835, the most successful of these American empresarios, Stephen Austin, settled thousands of American émigrés in his colony in Texas, as Americans called the northern part of Coahuila y Tejas. When

Lundy signed his own empresario contract in Victoria, it seemed to some Mexicans that Austin's colony was a model for empresarial development: the Texas cotton economy had prospered, native raids had abated, and many Americans, including Austin, had become Mexican citizens and participated enthusiastically in state and federal politics. Yet to other Mexicans, Austin's colony posed a clear threat to the future of the Republic of Mexico. Many of Austin's settlers had brought with them to Texas a significant number of enslaved African Americans. These expatriate American slaveholders defied Mexico's antislavery political consensus. When Mexico had won its independence from Spain in 1821, there were only about 3,000 slaves in the new republic. Over the following decade, both the Mexican federal government and the state of Coahuila y Tejas enacted a series of antislavery laws. At every turn, however, Austin, the de facto leader of the expatriate American settlers in Texas, resisted these antislavery efforts. He preserved for his slave-holding colonists the right to import slaves into Texas, obstructed gradual emancipation laws, and in one instance, secured an exception to an order of immediate emancipation proclaimed by the Mexican president. By the time Lundy signed his empresario contract in Tamaulipas in 1835, Texas was the only place in Mexico where slavery endured. In-migration by American slaveholders had transformed the demography of the province in just a few years: Texas was populated by roughly 30,000 white expatriate Americans, about 5,000 African American slaves, and fewer than 8,000 native-born Mexicans.[3] For all intents and purposes, Texas was a Mexican slave state, little different from US slave states such as Missouri or Kentucky, where—as in Texas— slaveholders were a minority of the white population yet had an outsized role in state politics.[4] Yet despite Austin's success in keeping emancipation at bay, Texas slaveholders remained skittish. They feared that at any time either the central government in Mexico City or the state government of Coahuila y Tejas—dominated numerically by non-slaveholding Coahuilans—might finally abolish slavery. Seven months after Lundy became an empresario in Tamaulipas, white American-born Texians revolted against the Mexican government. They were motivated at least in part by their anticipation that sooner or later either the state or the federal government would abolish slavery in Texas.

On the surface, Lundy and Austin had much in common: both had spent much of their lives before moving to Mexico in the slave states of the US South. Austin was born in Virginia in 1793, raised in Missouri, and educated in Kentucky. Lundy, born in New Jersey four years before Austin, had been apprenticed to a saddler in Virginia at the age of nine. He later lived in Mount

Pleasant, Ohio, just a few miles from the Virginia border; spent two years in Missouri; moved to Greeneville, Tennessee, in 1821; and moved to Baltimore, Maryland, in 1825. In Missouri, Lundy lived in Herculaneum, a town that Stephen Austin's father, Moses, had founded in 1808; indeed, Lundy and Stephen Austin overlapped there for a time.[5] Yet despite their long residencies in slave states, their positions on slavery diverged markedly. Austin was a slaveholder who, despite expressing occasional misgivings about slavery, was an ardent proslavery advocate.[6] Lundy, by contrast, was a Quaker and a passionate antislavery activist who was at one time the president of his local chapter of the Manumission Society of Tennessee in Greeneville, a town with a large number of Quaker and antislavery residents. Beginning in 1821, he was the editor and publisher of an antislavery monthly, the *Genius of Universal Emancipation*. While Austin settled his colony in Texas with slaveholders, Lundy intended to populate his colony in Tamaulipas with freed slaves.

When historians write about Americans' visions for Texas, they have little to say about Lundy, but the narrative of Austin's colony and the Texas rebellion against Mexico looms large. That emphasis is in many respects appropriate: Austin's colony and the rebellion against Mexico succeeded, while Lundy's scheme failed. Yet neither outcome was inevitable, however much some historians have presented slavery as an irresistibly expansionist institution.[7] At every turn, Austin and other slaveholding expatriate Americans in Texas had to contend with antislavery laws in Mexico and antislavery advocates from the United States such as Lundy. In most histories, Austin's colonization happened in a kind of vacuum; such narratives depict Texas in the early 1820s as a blank slate upon which Austin and other American settlers could inscribe their story. That narrative leaves little room for Lundy, whose antislavery ideals—however much they were compromised by his incessant efforts to make antislavery appealing to slaveholders—were much closer to the policy aims of Mexican authorities and the political leanings of large numbers of white Americans. In a larger sense, the blank-slate narrative—like the manifest destiny narrative of which it is a part—leaves little room for understanding antislavery in the North American borderlands.

On the surface, the story of antislavery in the borderlands seems improbable, if not quixotic. Unlike Austin, who inherited his Texas colony from his father, Lundy's path to northern Mexico was indirect. He was a self-educated saddler who left home at the age of nine and who lived hand-to-mouth throughout his adult life, pouring all his meager resources into his antislavery advocacy. Yet like Austin, Lundy wore his US citizenship lightly: Austin readily gave up his US citizenship to become a Mexican empresario; Lundy was not only ready to do likewise but had long thought of himself as part of a global abolition movement that included antislavery advocates in Britain and Latin America. Like Austin, Lundy had designs on northern Mexico. By the 1830s, just as Austin and his fellow Texas settlers were rebelling against the Mexican government in part to protect the institution of slavery, Lundy and other antislavery advocates had come to believe that they could rely on Mexico's antislavery laws to further their global campaign for abolition.

ANTISLAVERY AND COLONIZATION

Benjamin Lundy was a prominent antislavery activist in the 1820s and early 1830s, a period when no agreed-upon strategy prevailed among the opponents of slavery in the United States. In 1816, George Bourne, an English-born Presbyterian minister in Virginia, had called for immediate abolition without compensation for slaveholders.[8] In 1824, Elizabeth Coltman Heyrick, an English Quaker, likewise called for immediate abolition in the British West Indies.[9] By the eve of the Civil War, immediate abolition had many adherents in the United States; but in the 1820s, in the years before the national evangelical revival of 1831 that inspired antislavery reforms to demand immediate abolition, few antislavery advocates, white or Black, were as radical as Bourne or Heyrick.[10] Rather, in the early years of the American antislavery movement, a variety of proposals, most of which stopped well short of immediate or universal abolition, vied for ideological and popular support. Partial, gradual, and compensated emancipation schemes of varying degrees of feasibility prevailed. An antislavery advocate from St. Louis, for instance, suggested in 1821 that the federal government use a portion of the proceeds from land sales in the West to purchase the freedom of every female slave in the United States. If the US government were to adhere to such a plan, "the children following the condition of the mother, would be free by birth; the existing race of males would be free by death; and slavery itself would be extinguished with the extinction of the present generation."[11] In 1824, the Manumission Society of Tennessee, to which Lundy belonged, proposed a different gradual emancipation plan: no new slave states would be added to the Union, and Congress would mandate that, after a certain date, "there shall be no slave born in this Union."[12] The audience for such gradual emancipation proposals was not fellow members of the antislavery movement, most of whom wished for the immediate emancipation of all slaves. (Indeed, Lundy reprinted Heyrick's call for immediate abolition in the *Genius of Universal Emancipation* in 1826.) Rather, such proposals aimed to win over slaveholders afraid of suddenly losing the labor power they controlled and the capital they had invested in slaves as well as white Americans afraid of the prospect of immediate civil equality for millions of ex-slaves.

Because such fears predominated among white Americans in the 1820s and early 1830s, another scheme vied for the public's attention: colonization. The American Colonization Society, founded in 1817, aimed to settle free African Americans in Liberia on the west coast of Africa. Proponents of colonization presumed that many slaveholders would cheerfully manumit their slaves if only their fears of living as civil equals with former slaves could be assuaged. Nominally, the prospect of colonizing emancipated slaves in Africa removed that putative obstacle to manumission. In practice, however, the American Colonization Society's promise that it would more-or-less immediately put freed slaves on ships bound for Liberia convinced few slaveholders to manumit their slaves. For their part, many of the handful of slaves emancipated on the condition that they emigrate to Liberia resisted expatriation; in July 1836, for instance, 18 of a group of 65 emancipated slaves who had been freed on the condition that they emigrate to Liberia escaped just before their ship left New York.[13] The American Colonization Society thus concentrated on the emigration of African Americans who had long ago become free—and who advocated for freedom and civil equality for all the enslaved. The Black abolitionist David Walker wrote in 1829 that the purpose of colonization was "to get the free people of colour away to Africa, from among the slaves," so that the slaves who would remain in the United States "will be contented to rest in ignorance and wretchedness."[14]

Despite aiming primarily not to rid the United States of slavery, but of African Americans generally and free Blacks particularly, colonization jostled with partial and gradual emancipation schemes under the umbrella of the antislavery movement. White antislavery advocates such as Lundy believed that they could not ignore the extraordinary appeal of the colonization narrative among fellow whites: the prospect of the emigration of all emancipated slaves beyond US borders freed whites from contemplating the possibility of racial equality; encouraged the dream of an all-white republic; allowed whites to congratulate themselves that they were setting free Blacks on a course of pupilage in West Africa or elsewhere that would lead to their betterment; and—because the prospect of settling millions of African Americans abroad was so remote—posed no plausible threat to slavery.[15] Thousands of whites joined local branches of the American Colonization Society in cities and towns in both North and South, and pledged funds to the parent organization to fund emigration.[16] Prominent political leaders, particularly from southern states, joined the organization. One of its notable members was Henry Clay, variously the secretary of state, Speaker of the House, a US senator from Kentucky, and a candidate for president in 1824, 1832, and 1844. In June 1832, Clay borrowed from the antislavery advocates' grab-bag of manumission and colonization ideas and introduced a bill in the Senate that called for proceeds from the sale of public lands in the West to be distributed to the states to use to colonize free Blacks.[17] The American Colonization Society's presidents included Bushrod Washington, an associate justice of the US Supreme Court and the nephew of George Washington, and James Madison, the fourth US president. Politicians in northern free states endorsed the Society as well. In 1829, the Indiana Senate and House of Representatives passed a joint resolution stating that "the true interests of the United States require the removal of this people from amongst us" and pledged their "unqualified" support for the American Colonization Society.[18]

To win the support of colonizationists, white antislavery advocates almost always joined their proposals for emancipation with assurances that free Blacks would be encouraged to emigrate from the United States to West Africa or some other destination. In 1827, the American Convention for Promoting the Abolition of Slavery, to which Lundy belonged, not only endorsed abolishing slavery in the District of Columbia, banning the introduction of slaves into the territories of Arkansas and Florida, and outlawing the interstate sale of slaves but also advocated providing public funding for colonization.[19] In his early years as an antislavery advocate, Lundy, rather than attach himself to any one of the competing antislavery strategies, endorsed all of them, including colonization. In 1821, in one of the first issues of the *Genius of Universal Emancipation*, Lundy called for the abolition of slavery in all federal territories and the District of Columbia; the elimination of all legal impediments on free Blacks; gradual emancipation on a state-by-state basis; the elimination of the three-fifths clause of the US Constitution; and public funding to support the emigration of "all the blacks that may be willing to go to Hayti, or elsewhere."[20]

The ideological and strategic incoherence of Lundy's omnibus antislavery program was emblematic of the 1820s and early 1830s, when antislavery advocates were, individually and as a movement, groping their way toward a strategy that they hoped would have both moral integrity and some measure of popular support. To Lundy, popular support was critical. "The ballot box," Lundy wrote in 1825, "will be the only means . . . by which slavery can be annihilated."[21] Courting popular support, however, meant reaching some kind of accommodation with colonizationists, which meant, in turn, compromising the integrity of the antislavery movement. Black abolitionists never supported colonization; they saw it, correctly, as a sham. Some antislavery activists, such as William Lloyd Garrison, came to renounce popularity in favor of moral principle. In short order, between about 1828 and 1831, Garrison moved from being a supporter of the American Colonization Society and its plan to settle free Black people in Liberia, to a coeditor with Lundy on the *Genius of Universal Emancipation*, to an inveterate foe of colonization and advocate of immediate, universal emancipation. Lundy, who saw himself as more of a pragmatist than Garrison, moved more slowly toward the unpopular notion of immediate emancipation; in many aspects, he never quite reached it. His stance on colonization was even more complex. By the early 1820s, Lundy had come to loathe the American Colonization Society for its cynicism and hypocrisy; nevertheless, he believed that the idea of colonization itself might be salvaged. Yet like Garrison, his thinking evolved: in the early 1820s, like many white Americans, he supported colonization because he believed that slaves were unprepared for freedom and civil equality with whites; but by the early 1830s, he had come to think that colonization might be a way to demonstrate that emancipation posed no threat to white Americans and that emancipated slaves could thrive in the United States or on its borders.

Disagreement among white antislavery advocates such as Garrison and Lundy reflected, in large part, the contradictory beliefs of antislavery activists of the 1820s and early 1830s. One of the fundamental premises of many antislavery advocates was that emancipation—achieved not by slave revolt as in Haiti in 1791 but through a deliberative legislative process or, even better, moral suasion—was an inevitable outcome of the inexorable moral progress of humanity. Emancipation would triumph, Lundy argued in 1833, as it had won victories to that point, "by power of reason, and arguments, and facts, and Christian principles."[22] The international march of moral improvement and the concomitant recession of slavery was the central narrative that guided antislavery activists. Lundy wrote in 1822, "The free states of this Union are on the east, the north, and the west, Hayti and Colombia on the South. The mighty force of Public Opinion, in the former, powerfully aided in its march, shall bear resistless down the majestic Mississippi."[23] Or, as a member of the New York Manumission Society put it in 1824, "As the light of Reason and Religion have advanced, Slavery has receded. . . . As the benefits of education are extended, both among ourselves and the coloured people, the principles of liberty and justice will be more generally recognized and felt; and before their influence, Slavery, with all its attendant evils, will gradually disappear."

He went on that "In most states North and East of Maryland, laws have been enacted for the gradual extinction of Slavery."[24] Indeed, between 1777 and 1804, every northern US state adopted constitutions or enacted laws ending slavery either immediately, or, in most cases, gradually. In 1787, the US federal government barred slavery from the western territories north of the Ohio River; in 1794 the United States forbade American ships to participate in the slave trade; and in 1807 the United States prohibited the importation of slaves. The British Parliament outlawed the slave trade in 1807 and abolished slavery throughout the British Empire in 1833. Lundy celebrated as one state after another in Latin America declared its independence from Spain and shortly thereafter abolished slavery. In Colombia and Venezuela, Lundy wrote in 1821, "*true* and *genuine* republican patriots" had abolished slavery, "notwithstanding the slaves were exceedingly numerous in their country."[25] In 1830, Lundy noted, Mexico banned all commerce in slaves.[26] In 1833, Lundy addressed a letter to a convention of free Black abolitionists in which he reviewed the narrative of the progress of freedom:

> Fifty years ago, the *slave trade*, between Africa and America, was openly tolerated. . . . Now, every government, whose people profess the Christian name, has denounced it, with the severest penalties. Fifty years ago, nearly every state, province, and colony, on this continent, and the adjacent isles, protected and upheld the *system of slavery*, by legal enactments and military force.—now. . . . Every part of the American continent, north and south, except about one-fifth of the area of the United States, and the empire of Brazil, may be considered nearly free from the horrible pollution; and every island of the great West Indian Archipelago, with the single exception of Cuba, is upon the eve of a complete regeneration.[27]

And yet, while antislavery advocates such as Lundy rejoiced at the peaceful abolition of slavery in most of Latin America, it puzzled them that somehow the progress of the antislavery movement seemed to lag in the United States. "Must this great nation," Lundy asked, "be held back in the race of moral improvement by the minions of ambition and cold hearted Avarice? If we permit the people of Hayti and those of the new Republic of Colombia to answer, they will tell us, that if we had the will to do it, we might easily accomplish it."[28] Despite their faith in the expanding jurisdiction of freedom, antislavery advocates had to reconcile their belief in emancipation's inevitability with the incontrovertible evidence that, in mainland North America, slavery was expanding its reach. Between 1792 and 1821, while northern states were gradually dismantling the institution of slavery, the United States admitted six new slave states: Kentucky, Tennessee, Louisiana, Mississippi, Alabama, and Missouri. During that same period, the number of slaves in the United States more than doubled, from fewer than 700,000 to more than 1.5 million.[29] In 1824, at a national meeting of the American Convention for Promoting the Abolition of Slavery, which Lundy attended as a delegate from Tennessee, William Rawle, president of the Pennsylvania Manumission Society, expressed his alarm that slavery might expand into free states in the West. Although the Northwest Ordinance of 1787 had banned slavery from the territory north of the Ohio River, in the first decades of the nineteenth century a large proportion of new settlers in Indiana and Illinois arrived from slave states. "We have seen with astonishment and regret," Rawle wrote, "that the Slave trader, no longer fearful of reproach, has dared to propose to the citizens of Illinois and Indiana, to change their free constitutions, and to become holders of slaves."[30] The prospect that slavery might appear in a place such as a state in the former Northwest Territory where it had once been outlawed outraged antislavery activists because it defied their narrative of the march of emancipation. Lundy, in his capacity as the president of the Greenville, Tennessee, chapter of the Manumission Society of Tennessee, wrote an open letter "To the Citizens of Illinois" in 1824, expressing his concern that "a party has risen up among you, possessed of a considerable degree of wealth and influence, which has for its object the re-establishment of the cruel and anti-republican system of personal slavery in your State." The potential recession of free territory in the United States alarmed Lundy, who lamented, "how degrading would it be to the character of this republic, if the system of slavery should hereafter be extended to one of those states in which it has been hitherto prohibited!"[31]

As early as 1829, Lundy warned that proslavery forces were determined to annex Texas, where, he noted, the Mexican government had sought to bar slavery despite the resistance from slaveholding American colonists such as Austin. Proslavery forces, Lundy proclaimed, wanted to annex Texas "for the avowed purpose of adding five or six more slave holding states to this Union!"[32] As rhetoric, the warning that slavery was reaching into new territory or, worse yet, territory where it had once been banned, stirred Lundy's readership. At the same time, the expansion of the institution of slavery challenged Lundy's ideological narrative of the ever-expanding reach of freedom in ways that he never resolved.

Despite the expansion of slavery, antislavery advocates consoled themselves that the same inexorable moral improvement of humanity that made emancipation inevitable also meant that the condition of slaves was continually improving. At the same national meeting in 1824 where William Rawle, the president of the Pennsylvania Manumission Society, decried the potential expansion of slavery into Illinois and Indiana, a delegate from the New York Manumission Society asserted, "It is believed that the condition of Slaves in the Southern States, is already, in a considerable degree, meliorated." He continued,

> The punishments to which they are now subjected, are less frequent and less severe than those which were formerly inflicted; that a sufficiency of food and clothing is now pretty generally dispensed to them; that there is now more regard paid to the relations of husband and wife, parent and child, than formerly; that the breaking up and separating of families, by sale, has seriously arrested the attention of many Masters; and that some care is taken to prevent occurrence of this kind. There are now not infrequent instances of Slaves being taught to read; and, in some places, they are allowed to assemble for religious worship. Instances of wanton abuse of Slaves, are much less frequent; and the killing of a Slave, has become a very rare occurrence. In some of the Southern States, the killing of a Negro, is, by law, declared to be murder, and made punishable with death. The trade in Slaves, between the different States, has also much diminished. These appearances of improvement in the condition of the coloured population of the Southern States induce us to believe, that the minds of the Slave-holders are more enlightened than formerly, and that a different and better feeling towards their Slaves, now animates the hearts of many of them.[33]

The New York delegate to the 1824 meeting was not alone in his upbeat belief that slaveholders' treatment of slaves was increasingly animated by kindness and humanity. James Jones, the president of the Manumission Society of Tennessee, chimed in that "in East Tennessee, the Slaves, generally speaking, are treated with humanity and tenderness, compared with those of some other sections of the Union."[34] At the 1827 meeting, by which time Lundy had moved from Tennessee to Baltimore and therefore attended as a delegate from Maryland, the Anti-Slavery Society of Maryland announced, "The condition of slavery is considerably ameliorated in Maryland, since the revolution. In general, masters treat their slaves with kindness and humanity."[35]

Yet while white antislavery advocates had faith in the capacity of slaveholders for moral improvement, they were skeptical that slaves had a similar potential. Many antislavery advocates believed that slaves were unlikely to thrive as free people in the United States. Echoing the central premise of colonizationists, they believed that slaves were unprepared for freedom. In 1823, an antislavery advocate from Cambridge, Massachusetts, worried that emancipation might "produce as much evil as it would cure," argued that "the slave must be made to pass through a state of pupilage and minority, to fit him for the enjoyment and exercise of rational liberty." He suggested that ex-slaves be placed "in the same situation in relation to their masters as the peasantry of Russia, in relation to their landlord."[36] The closing report of the 1824 American Convention for Promoting the Abolition of Slavery agreed. "In every age of the world, menial servitude has been a state of ignominy, the lot of ignorance or degradation," the report concluded. "It must be obvious to every friend of African emancipation, that the present condition of many of those among this poor and despised people who have attained their liberty, affords to their enemies the strongest arguments against this freedom. Wretchedness arising from poverty, ignorance, and vice is triumphantly pointed at as an irrefutable argument for the continuance of Slavery." The report called for "giving the children of coloured people literary instruction, and placing them as apprentices in useful trades."[37] Others argued that slaves were adequately prepared for freedom but that nevertheless the prejudices of whites prevented the success of free Blacks. Rawle believed that "our large free coloured population, many of whom become vicious and criminal, through the evils of poverty and want of employment," were "prevented by the prejudices of society from aspiring to honourable and lucrative employments."[38] Lundy shared the view of most antislavery activists of the 1820s and 1830s: that free Blacks could not thrive in the United States. He variously endorsed both white prejudice and Black incapacity as explanations. In 1822, he proposed that free Blacks in the northern states be "admitted to the enjoyment of the rights and immunities of all citizen[s]" except "the elective franchise," adding that "it might be impolitic to grant it to them immediately, as some time must necessarily be allowed for them to acquire the art of exercising it properly."[39] In 1824, he wrote that "the prejudices of white people, against blacks, operate as an almost insurmountable barrier to the progress of emancipation."[40]

Altogether, white antislavery advocates in the 1820s and early 1830s were tentative and inconsistent. Slavery was evil, but slaveholders were becoming more humane and the condition of slaves was improving. Slavery was expanding, but it was also ebbing away. Slaves must be emancipated, but they could not succeed following emancipation. Thus, the Chester County Society for Preventing Kidnapping could call slavery "a disorder in the body politic," much like "a disease in the human body," yet almost in the same breath say that "the policy of immediate emancipation is questionable," because "the opinions of the people generally forbid it altogether." Therefore, they argued, rather than emancipation, antislavery organizations should "initiate the Slaves in habits suited to a state of freedom" so they could "make useful members of society." The Chester County organization recognized that such a program "would be likely to prolong the existence of Slavery"; but, over time, as slaves acquired "the habits of freemen," they would be manumitted. Like the American Colonization Society, the Chester County Society for Preventing Kidnapping suggested that its program was the surest path to a white republic. The organization argued that when released to the "lowest grade of society, on whom the pressure that checks the increase of population falls the heaviest," the population of free Blacks would decrease until "they will cease to exist within our borders."[41] Thus it was that antislavery organizations in the 1820s and early 1830s advocated prolonging the institution of slavery while they yearned for an all-white republic.

COLONISTS, EMIGRANTS, AND REFUGEES

Lundy was keenly aware that many of his white colleagues in the antislavery movement despaired that slaves were prepared for freedom, and that ordinary Americans adhered to that belief even more strongly. He believed, therefore, that colonization needed to remain part of the antislavery program as a way to assure whites that they would not have to endure what they saw as the ignominy of civil equality with ex-slaves. Yet as early as 1821, Lundy had concluded that the popular support the American Colonization Society enjoyed notwithstanding, the organization was not committed to ending slavery in the United States. In that year, Bushrod Washington, the president of the American Colonization Society, sold fifty-four slaves from his Mount Vernon plantation to two buyers from Louisiana. Antislavery activists excoriated Washington for selling his slaves rather than emancipating them in preparation for colonization. Washington strenuously defended his actions in a letter reprinted in the *Federal Republican*, writing that he had the legal right "to dispose of property" in order to recoup the plantation's annual losses of between $500 and $1,000. He added, by way of justification, that his slaves had displayed "insubordination" and "total disregard of all authority." Moreover, he made the sale in anticipation of "the escape of all the laboring men of any value to the northern states." He attributed the breakdown in plantation discipline to "unworthy persons" who had visited Mount Vernon and had given his slaves the impression that "as the nephew of General Washington, or as president of the Colonization Society ... I could not hold them in bondage." He waved away the significance of the sales having separated families, noting that immigrants from Europe and white migrants to the West included "parents who have voluntarily separated themselves from their children" and "children who have left behind them their parents." He added that when two slaves he had once owned escaped to freedom in the North, their parents, who remained at Mount Vernon, never complained about the separation. Washington assured his readers that the slaves he sold "cheerfully consented" to leave Mount Vernon after he treated to them a "short address"—a very different kind of farewell address than the one his uncle had once delivered.[42] Lundy dismissed Washington's explanations as "pitiable sophistry." Despite his criticism of Washington, Lundy also made it clear: "I would not wish it to be thought that I am opposed to the ostensible aims of the American Colonization Society." Yet, he concluded, "I must confess that I have been very much disappointed."[43]

Lundy's disillusionment with the American Colonization Society forced him to reconsider his goals and strategies. He continued to believe that colonization should remain part of a broader antislavery strategy. White animus against the prospect of civil equality with Blacks was, he feared, so powerful that without colonization, no plan for emancipation could succeed. He wrote in 1823 that "until the prejudices of whites are measurably done away ... it will be necessary to colonize a portion of the coloured population to ensure the success of the work of emancipation." Yet if colonization were to succeed, Lundy came to believe, it would have to be accomplished without the American Colonization Society. The distance to West Africa, he complained, "renders it totally impracticable to send a sufficient number there," and the disease-ridden coast had "proved a very grave-yard for Americans without distinction of colour."[44] By 1825, Lundy had dismissed the American Colonization Society entirely. "In the first place, I have ever been aware" he wrote, "that a considerable portion of its members were averse to the abolition of slavery in this country." Second, "although many of them desire the riddance of the whole of the black population," they had chosen a place, Liberia, so remote and inhospitable "that it will be almost impossible to effect the object."[45]

By that time—indeed, by late 1824—Lundy had already arrived at a solution to the dilemma of promoting colonization while remaining a critic of the American Colonization Society's scheme to settle free Blacks in Liberia: Haiti. Two developments spurred his interest in Haiti. First, in

Benjamin Lundy, ca. 1820. Painting by A. Dickenson. Portraits of
Benjamin Lundy, Ohio History Connection, Columbus.

mid-1824, Lundy had placed the *Genius of Universal Emancipation* on hiatus
and relocated from Greenville, Tennessee, to Baltimore, Maryland. Baltimore contained the largest population of free Blacks in the South and, after
Philadelphia, had the second-largest population of free Blacks in the United
States.[46] In Baltimore, Lundy encountered Black poverty and white discrim-
ination against free Blacks that he had not seen in Greenville. After his move
to Baltimore, Lundy despaired that white Americans would in the near future
agree to civil equality with African Americans. "Such are the prejudices we
imbibed in our infancy and have cherished in mature age, and so completely
are they interwoven with our system of thinking and acting, that they prove
a stumbling-block, even to philanthropists as well as others, in the pursuit of

humanity and benevolence," he wrote shortly after arriving in Baltimore. Second, while free Blacks deplored colonization, many in Baltimore supported voluntary emigration to Haiti. A number of prominent African Americans, including Paul Cuffe, Prince Saunders, and James Forten, enthusiastically endorsed Haitian emigration—a project they viewed as distinct from African colonization.[47] Lundy's move to Baltimore coincided with a visit to the United States by the Haitian diplomat Pierre Joseph Marie Granville. The son of a French father and a Haitian mother, Granville was a former officer in Napoléon's army who in 1824 toured several US cities including Baltimore (where he met with the Baltimore Emigration Society) to invite free Blacks to emigrate to Haiti—indeed, the Haitian government, under President Jean-Pierre Boyer, promised to defray the costs of transportation and make land grants to emigrants. For Lundy, Granville offered a solution to all the problems posed by Liberia: Haiti was not only far closer to the United States than Liberia, but Black Haitians had already freed themselves; African American freed people could, of their own free will, join them and demonstrate to white Americans their capacities for self-government. "It is evident," Lundy wrote, "that the degraded condition of our free coloured people might be greatly meliorated by their removal to Hayti, where all would be placed strictly upon an equality."[48]

Lundy had already been an advocate of emigration to Haiti—it had been part of his omnibus antislavery strategy that he proposed in 1821, and he had written a long editorial in favor of it in the *Genius of Universal Emancipation* in 1822.[49] Following Granville's tour of the United States in 1824, and over the next five years, Haiti shifted from being just one part of Lundy's scattershot antislavery program to becoming central to his thinking. Just two months after Granville's visit, Lundy celebrated that roughly 5,000 free Blacks had already departed for Haiti. Taking into account that the average cost of the passage to Haiti was fourteen dollars for an adult and seven dollars for a child, Lundy giddily calculated that if Congress were to appropriate half a million dollars per year and decree "that the future offspring of all slaves should be free at a proper age," then within a decade "the whole of the African race in this country" could be "sent to a clime more congenial to their constitution."[50] In March 1825, Lundy opened a Haitian emigration office in Baltimore.[51]

The American Colonization Society remained unalterably opposed to Haiti. "It is said that President Boyer, on the part of the Republic of Hayti, has offered to take any number of coloured people which the United States may think proper to send there, and even to pay a considerable part of the expense of transporting them, himself," Aaron Coffin, the president of the Manumission Society of North Carolina, wrote in 1824, shortly after Granville's visit. "What more could be asked? But it seems that the Colonization Society, to whom the proposition was made, rejected it, as not being consistent with their plan of colonizing in Africa."[52] Lundy noted the American Colonization Society had spent considerable sums to send just 300 free Blacks to West Africa over the previous six years, compared to the 5,000 who had embarked for Haiti in just the previous six months at a fraction of the cost.[53] And yet both Lundy and Coffin knew that Haiti's proximity to the United States, which they saw as its greatest advantage, was precisely what disqualified it for slaveholders and thus for the American Colonization Society. Since the Haitian Revolution in 1791, slaveholders had lived in terror of a similar slave uprising taking place in the United States.[54] In the years before the War of 1812, Louisiana slaveholders feared that the Spanish would foment a slave uprising.[55] That fear had magnified since the War of 1812, when thousands of slaves had joined the British.[56] "The island of Hayti would be a much more eligible situation" than Liberia, Lundy wrote in 1822, "but some of our southern citizens object to that, because an army could easily be transported from there to our shores, whereby promoting insurrection amongst our slaves."[57]

For a short time, Lundy's hope that the prospect of emigration to Haiti would induce slaveholders to manumit their slaves was rewarded—but only in a limited, costly, and compromised way. Lundy's involvement in Haitian emigration reached its peak in 1825 when, on Lundy's advice, a Virginia slaveholder, David Minge, freed eight-eight slaves and dispatched them to Haiti at his own expense. Following on that success, Lundy traveled to Haiti with another group of eleven freed slaves from North Carolina; Lundy wrote that their owner had "agreed to give them up to me in consideration that I should take them where they could enjoy their rights." Lundy lingered in Haiti for eight weeks, not only settling the eleven free Blacks he had accompanied, but negotiating with Haitian authorities, who in mid-1825 had announced, after paying for the transportation of 6,000 free Blacks to Haiti, that they could afford to pay for no more. In Haiti, Lundy convinced the private Haitian Philanthropic Society to shoulder the expense of transportation—but the private organization required that emigrants indenture themselves to the organization as sharecroppers and turn over one-half of their produce for three years in order to repay the cost of transportation. Apart from these disappointments, the 1825 trip was costly for Lundy personally: when he embarked for Haiti, his wife was seven months pregnant. When he returned, he found that his wife had died in childbirth and his newborn infant twins and his other three children had been dispersed among friends and relatives. Lundy never reunited with his children; to free himself for his antislavery work, he sent the newborn twins to a sister-in-law and the three older children to his father and stepmother. Thus unencumbered, Lundy returned to Haiti in 1828 with twelve emancipated slaves from Maryland.[58]

By 1830, as the Haitian government retreated from welcoming emigrants, another site, Canada, emerged as a possible destination for African Americans. Lundy characteristically gave Canada a full-throated endorsement before fully understanding it. In April 1830, in the first issue of the *Genius of Universal Emancipation* following the departure of Garrison as coeditor, Lundy wrote, "Never, since the spirit of colonizing the people of color first manifested itself in the United States, has a project been revealed, apparently so full of promise, as that of their settlement in Upper Canada." While transporting emigrants to Haiti had ultimately proved to be too expensive, Lundy noted that most of the free Blacks who had removed to Canada had gone there "without assistance."[59] Yet Lundy's account of Black emigration to Canada omitted an important detail: free Black migrants to Canada were not emigrants but refugees from discriminatory laws and pogroms in Ohio. In 1829, Black Ohioans could not vote, serve in the militia, testify in court, or attend public schools. Above all, according to state law, they had to post a $500 bond as a condition of their residency in the state. In Cincinnati, the bond law was only lightly enforced until 1829, when the municipal government informed Black residents that it intended to strictly enforce the law; in effect, because a $500 bond was more than most people could afford, the city authorities ordered Blacks out of the state. White mobs roamed through Black neighborhoods in Cincinnati to make sure of the removal. Between 1,000 and 2,000 Blacks fled, most of them to a settlement in Canada, near the town of London, about 100 miles east of Detroit, Michigan.[60]

The Black flight to Canada in 1829 and 1830 was thus neither the orderly nor, more importantly, the voluntary emigration that Lundy had long advocated; but he could not resist casting it as such in order to contrast it with his bête noire, the American Colonization Society's Liberia project. In 1831, Lundy pronounced, "Two thousand colored persons, from the United States, have settled in Canada, since the date of the Ohio Persecution—more than have gone to Africa in thirteen years!"[61] In early 1832, Lundy visited the settlement in Canada, which the residents and some newfound sponsors—a group of Quakers from Oberlin, Ohio—had named Wilberforce, after the British antislavery advocate, William Wilberforce. Lundy reported that, after some early stumbles because of poor management, the settlement was thriving.

By early 1832, twenty-five families, including "men of known intelligence and public spirit," had "erected tolerably comfortable houses, and cleared a few acres of ground" in Wilberforce.[62]

Yet for Lundy, a familiar problem—white American prejudice—plagued Wilberforce and other Black settlements in Canada. He noted that large numbers of white Americans were settling in London, the nearest town to Wilberforce. He wrote that "the 'yankees' (as they denominate all emigrants from these States) are still actuated by the abominable prejudice toward the colored race."[63] At an inn near Wilberforce where Lundy stayed, long after he went to bed "a fracas occurred" in the "bar-room, among the heterogenous assemblage there." The next morning, "the blame was thrown upon the 'negroes,' by the bar-keeper, who was a 'Yankee' of 'high-pressure' prejudice." In general, Lundy observed, white American emigrants to Canada "retain all the prejudice here, that they formerly held against the colored people in their native country."[64]

SLAVERY AND ANTISLAVERY IN THE US-MEXICO BORDERLANDS

Dissatisfied with both Haiti and Canada as destinations for Black emigrants, Lundy returned to an earlier idea. Long before Haiti or Canada had seized his imagination, Lundy had nurtured the idea that the borderlands of the North American West would be an ideal place for a colony of ex-slaves. As early as 1822 he had published a letter in the *Genius of Universal Emancipation* from "A Carolinian," who wrote that "the most proper plan probably would be to colonize them in our own western territories—say, between the Mississippi and the Missouri." Unlike Haiti, where the government, American slaveholders feared, might launch an invasion and foment a slave rebellion, the West was "distant from any foreign power." Moreover, the Carolinian imagined that racial interaction in the diverse borderlands might erode whites' racism. "The colony might be composed promiscuously of blacks, Indians, and such whites as choose to adopt the colonial life. . . . And if the Indian and negro mind is found to expand, as I confidently believe it would under such regulations, it would very soon cease to be considered a disparagement for the whites to mingle amongst them."[65] Lundy endorsed the notion in the next issue of his journal, writing, "A portion of the blacks might be colonized in some remote part of the Territory of the United States." Not yet ready in 1822 to give up on the American Colonization Society, he added that "some might also be sent to Africa."[66] By the time of the 1824 American Convention for

Promoting the Abolition of Slavery in Philadelphia, Lundy, as the delegate of the Manumission Society of Tennessee, proposed to the convention that it "petition Congress to appropriate a certain parcel of land on the continent of America, to be devoted exclusively to the colonizing of those who may after that time become free." The other delegates, mindful that white American farmers imagined that western lands would someday belong to them and their children, demurred.[67]

Beyond reconsidering the location of a colony, by the late 1820s, Lundy had begun to reconceive the purpose of a colony of ex-slaves. For over a decade, he and other advocates of colonization had proposed various plans designed, in some way or another, to assuage white Americans' fears of living with former slaves as civil equals. As the Carolinian had put it, "If the blacks were liberated and suffered to remain amongst us, the whites would be unwilling to share with them the administration of government, or to admit them as equals in any important particular."[68] Moreover, Lundy realized, colonization was proceeding at a snail's pace; while some 6,000 free Blacks had emigrated to Haiti by the mid-1830s, there remained roughly 2 million slaves in the US South. By then, Lundy had concluded that the project to colonize all American slaves outside the boundaries of the United States was not just unlikely but futile. Yet, Lundy came to believe, colonization might still serve a purpose in the antislavery movement: a small colony on the borders of the United States could demonstrate to white Americans that ex-slaves could thrive as free laborers. Then, Lundy imagined, the very need to colonize all African Americans would be mooted, as whites would shed their fears and welcome Blacks as equals.

For several years Lundy had maintained that slavery was economically unnecessary because planters could profitably employ free laborers rather than use violence to extort the labor of slaves. All that was needed to convince planters to abandon slavery, he believed, was to demonstrate to slaveholders that wage laborers could do the work of slaves at a lower cost. In 1825, Lundy had published a pamphlet, *A Plan for the Gradual Abolition of Slavery in the United States without Danger to the Citizens of the South*, in which he proposed that the US government set aside two sections (1,280 acres) of public land in Tennessee, Alabama, or Mississippi, and settle the land with between fifty and 100 slaves whom the government had purchased. The "experiment farm" would—like utopian communities such as Harmony, Indiana, or Economy, Pennsylvania—operate according to a cooperative system. Teachers would instruct the slaves weekly; their lessons would include "the necessity of hard work." This "school of industry" could also take on the slaves of "kind masters, anxious to manumit their people, but apprehensive of throwing them unprepared into the world." After five years of cooperative labor, the slaves would be freed. Following "one successful experiment," Lundy wrote, "a similar establishment will be placed in each state; and when the advantages of the system become clear, many slaveowners will lease out their property, to be worked in the same way." As plantations shed their slaves, "poor whites" could replace them as wage laborers; redundant African Americans could emigrate to Haiti, "the Mexican territory of Texas, and a fine region beyond the rocky mountains."[69]

Lundy was not alone in thinking that a successful experiment in a free-labor plantation would demonstrate to slaveholding planters the needlessness of slavery. At the 1827 American Convention for Promoting the Abolition of Slavery, the organization finally adopted Lundy's proposal from three years earlier that Congress acquire "an extensive tract, in a great part yet unsettled," in order that "the trial might be made, whether a southern latitude necessarily requires the establishment of domestic slavery, or whether in the Territory of Florida, as well as in other places, the cultivation of land, and the general prosperity of the country, would not be eminently promoted by the use of free labor alone."[70] In 1831, Lundy reprinted a report in the *Genius of Universal Emancipation* explaining how Britain had resettled in Trinidad slaves from the United States who had fought for the British during the War of 1812. According to the report, sugar plantations there had thrived by employing former slaves as wage laborers.[71] Just as importantly, Lundy sought to show that white wage laborers could replace plantation slaves in warm climates. In 1833, Lundy noted that William Wirt, after having served as attorney general in the administrations of James Monroe and John Quincy Adams, had purchased a sugarcane plantation in Florida and employed several hundred Germans immigrants as free laborers.[72]

Where was the likeliest place for an experiment in free Black wage labor to succeed? By the early 1830s, Lundy came to believe that Texas was that place. Northern Mexico, Lundy decided, possessed attributes that Haiti and Canada lacked: it was located close enough to the United States that emigration was affordable, yet it was, he believed, far enough away from the United States to be free of American racial prejudices. Moreover, Lundy could count on Mexico's opposition to slavery. He had long harbored the notion that Mexico was outpacing the United States on the path to universal emancipation. He wrote in 1822 that "unconditional slavery, or involuntary servitude will ere long be completely abolished in the Mexican dominions."[73] Texas,

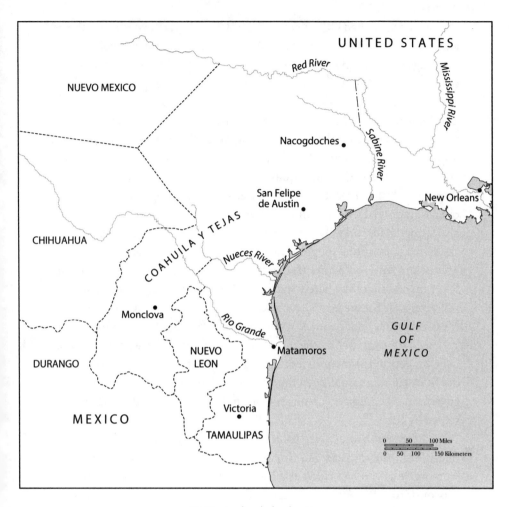

US-Mexico borderlands, 1835.

he predicted in 1831, would become "an asylum for hundreds of thousands of our oppressed colored people."[74] In 1832, he wrote that Texas was the best place "to make experiments relative to the value of free labor." Better yet, the experiment would happen "by the side of our southern slaveholders." The success of free Black laborers in northern Mexico would doom slavery, Lundy argued, "further proving to the people of this nation, that here, in America—the land of his birth and his natural home—he may be fitted for freedom and self-government with perfect ease and safety."[75]

To Lundy, Texas seemed to be an ideal place for his experiment. In the first decades of the nineteenth century, Texas was a lightly settled province over which Spain had little effective control. In 1811, Tejanos, who numbered altogether only about 4,000, had joined in the widespread revolt in New Spain against Spanish rule. Spanish reprisals against the rebels in Texas, beginning in 1812, left the province even weaker and more sparsely populated than before. The Spanish campaign halved the province's population, killing about 1,000 Tejanos and forcing another thousand to flee. In the years that followed, Comanches raided the weakened Tejano settlements with impunity: in 1814, they reduced the ranches surrounding San Antonio to ashes. By 1817, the Spanish were powerless to prevent the pirates Jean and Pierre Lafitte from establishing an extensive smuggling and slave-trading operation on Galveston Island. The remote and ungoverned province was also a magnet for runaway slaves from Louisiana. While most fugitives from Louisiana plantations sought refuge in the swampy areas along the Lower Mississippi River or, before 1821, in the "Neutral Ground" along the Sabine River that neither the United States nor Spain controlled, some made their way across the Sabine into Texas in search of freedom.[76] Little changed when Mexico became independent from Spain in 1821. The Mexican nationalist Tadeo Ortiz warned that "the northern frontier everywhere presents imminent dangers to the integrity of the territory of the Republic."[77] In 1822, in a bid to create some stability in the province, Ortiz proposed to the Mexican government that 10,000 colonists from Ireland and the Canary Islands be settled in Texas.[78]

Spanish authorities were so desperate to populate and stabilize Texas that in 1820 they had agreed to a proposal by Moses Austin, an itinerant entrepreneur who had failed as a lead miner in Virginia and as a banker in Missouri, to settle American expatriates in the province. The empresario agreement Austin made with Spanish authorities endured even after Mexico achieved its independence from Spain and Austin himself died, leaving the leadership of his Texas project to his son, Stephen. The younger Austin almost immediately began appealing to American slaveholders north and east of the Sabine River to migrate to Texas and establish slave labor–based cotton plantations in his colony: he offered American emigrants 177 acres for farming and 4,428 for ranching, with an additional 100 acres for every family member and, most importantly, an additional fifty acres for every slave. By 1830, 20,000 white American settlers and the 1,000 African American slaves they forced to come with them to Texas outnumbered the 5,000 Tejanos in Texas. Mexican authorities knew full well that Austin was settling his colony with slaves and slaveholders. Despite the general ideological opposition to slavery in newly independent Mexico, authorities in Mexico City so craved stability and economic development in Texas that they turned a blind eye to the growing number of slaves in the province.[79]

Lundy imagined that he could provide Mexico with the stability that came with settlement without the taint of slavery. In 1831, even as Texas was quickly emerging as a Mexican slave state, Lundy republished in the *Genius of Universal Emancipation* a letter from "A Free Colored Floridian," originally published in the *New-York Daily Sentinel,* extolling the virtues of Mexico "as a place of safety and permanent refuge" for free Blacks. The Floridian maintained that "the country is boundless in extent, and either entirely uninhabited or thinly settled with people who are mostly colored *and entirely free of all prejudice against complexion. The Constitution and laws of Mexico recognize no difference of merit on account of color,* between the different shades of the human race; and this gives great advantages to a dark complexion over that of a Danish or Saxon origin, which could not long endure the toils of agriculture of a warm climate."[80] To this endorsement of Mexico, Lundy added, "The time has come, when we think it proper to say: That of all the places ever mentioned, as suitable for the emigration of our *southern* colored population, this is the most inviting, and most desirable."[81] The anonymous free African American's endorsement of Mexico was significant to Lundy because, as he frankly acknowledged two years later, "The scheme of planting 'a colony in Texas'—or, rather, of encouraging the emigration of emancipated slaves to Mexico generally, is not of the coloured people's invention. Yet, if they favour the idea of a removal from these States, at all, they will look to that region, in preference to all others."[82] Lundy convinced himself that African Americans would eventually support his Texas emigration plan.

In 1830, Lundy made the first of several visits to Mexico, hoping to secure from the governor of Coahuila y Tejas an empresario contract in order to establish a colony for freed slaves. During his travels in Texas and Tamaulipas, Lundy assembled considerable anecdotal evidence that confirmed his preconception that Mexicans did not harbor the same racial prejudices as most white Americans. He passed through Nacogdoches, Texas, in early July 1832, and was charmed by the racial and ethnic diversity and apparent absence of prejudice of the place. Local Mexican troops celebrated the US Independence Day with "a band of music" and a volley of artillery. Later that day, a "negro slave" prepared a barbecue, attended by Mexicans, white American settlers, "a few Africans" both slave and free, and local Native Americans, who staged a lacrosse game. "Great glee!" Lundy wrote.[83] Passing through Nacogdoches a year later, Lundy encountered an American slaveholder from Louisiana who had emigrated to Texas with "a black female slave, who was in fact his wife."

In Texas, he emancipated his wife and children. "They all live together here in harmony," Lundy wrote. "The Mexican ladies of Nacogdoches are very sociable with them." The farther south into Mexico Lundy traveled, the more he perceived the absence of prejudice. In August 1833, while traveling through Austin's colony, a Mexican from La Bahia, who was traveling with a group of natives Lundy called "Paranamies" (probably Aranama, many of whom resided at the La Bahia mission) invited Lundy to their camp. Lundy "spent several hours of the hottest part of the day" at the camp, where the "Mexican sociability and Indian hospitality rendered me exceedingly comfortable." That October, while in Monclova, the capital of Coahuila y Tejas, Lundy wrote in his journal that "there appears to be no distinction in this place as to freedom, or condition, by reason of color. One complexion is as much respected as another." In Matamoros, a coastal city in Tamaulipas, Lundy was astounded that when local free Blacks complained to the alcalde that an Irish barkeeper had refused to serve them, the alcalde imposed a fine on the owner of the inn.[84] By 1835, Lundy had convinced himself that Mexican society was completely free of the kind of racial prejudice that dominated in the United States. Echoing the language of the Floridian, he wrote,

> Descended from European, African, and original American ancestors, their *color* varies from the Castillian white, to the darkest shades of the torrid climes. Of the creole, or native population, there are very few, if any, of pure European blood.—And there being a complete intermix-ture (and all placed upon a perfect equality,) not a vestige of prejudice against color appears to exist among them. All are, alike, entitled to equal rights, privileges, and immunities; and every one is respected according to merit, without regard to paternal ancestry or the hue of the skin.[85]

However much Lundy wanted to believe in Mexican racial equality, the reality of race in Mexico was more complex. Free Blacks and fugitive slaves who made their way to Mexico in the 1830s had a tenuous legal status that was largely dependent on the good will of local authorities and community members. Like the Ohioans who had driven free Blacks from the state in 1830, many Mexicans opposed both slavery and the presence of free Blacks in their midst.[86]

While Lundy believed that Mexican officials in Texas shared his anti-slavery feelings, Mexican antislavery policies in Texas were complex and contradictory. During the decade of the 1820s, Mexican state and federal authorities made repeated, if sporadic, efforts to abolish slavery in Texas.

Yet in every instance, slaveholders, led by Stephen Austin, found a way to reach an accommodation with them. Austin's colony, and those of other American empresarios in Texas, were important enough to the success of Mexico's northern province that Mexican officials repeatedly compromised their antislavery positions. In 1823, the Mexican federal government forbade the sale or purchase of slaves within Mexico as well as the introduction of slaves into Mexico. It further declared that the children of slaves were to be free at age fourteen. The law tamped down American slaveholders' early enthusiasm for Texas. "The rage for emigrating to Texas is beginning to subside," the *Arkansas Gazette* noted, "in consequence of a late measure adopted by the Mexican Congress, which prohibits the holding of slaves in the Mexican Empire."[87] While the law appeared to be a sweeping blow to slavery, it was in fact a victory for Austin, who spent much of 1822 in Mexico City lobbying legislators. Austin succeeded in convincing Mexican legislators to weaken earlier drafts of the law that would have declared all slaves introduced by American colonists into Mexico free after ten years. In 1826, as legislators in Coahuila y Tejas were drafting a state constitution, Austin leaped into action again when he learned that the draft constitution contained a clause immediately emancipating all slaves. Once again, his lobbying efforts succeeded; in the end, the new constitution allowed slaveholders to retain slaves they already owned, it permitted slaves to be imported into the state until the end of 1827, and it merely freed children of slaves born after publication of the law. In order to evade the laws, Austin counseled slaveholders who wished to emigrate to colonies in Texas to visit a notary in the United States prior to emigration to produce a contract with their slaves in which the slaves would be freed upon emigration to Texas, but simultaneously indentured and contracted to work at a stipulated wage long enough to repay the supposed cost of their transportation to Texas. The wage was set sufficiently low so that the contract could never be fulfilled. The terms of the contract included unborn children of these slaves. Similarly, slaveholders already in Texas could visit a Mexican official and make contracts in which their slaves could free themselves once they had repaid their value; the slaveholder would determine when the repayment was complete. In 1829, by which time there were about 1,000 slaves in Texas, the Mexican president, Vicente Guerrero Saldaña, a liberal mestizo who had come to power through rebellion and was himself overthrown (and later executed) after ruling for less than a year, proclaimed the abolition of slavery in Mexico. Austin and other Texas slaveholders swiftly petitioned the governor of Coahuila y Tejas, José María Viesca y Montes, to exempt Texas from the proclamation. After winning the exemption, Austin wrote to his brother-in-law in late 1829 that he anticipated that "in a few years" Texas would separate from Coahuila and "be a slave state."[88]

Lundy's view of the world scarcely permitted him to understand how Mexico could abolish slavery in 1829 yet then permit it to continue in Texas. His belief in moral progress made no allowance for retrogression on the question of emancipation, even though he was under no illusion about proslavery empresarios such as Austin. "Slavites" in Texas, Lundy predicted in 1832, were determined "to wrest that fine territory from the Mexican Republic" in order to protect slavery.[89] In San Felipe de Austin in July 1833, Lundy was set upon by a mob of American colonists who recognized the well-known antislavery advocate.[90] Yet despite his awareness of the determination of slaveholders, Lundy was confident that emancipation would triumph in Texas.

Lundy was thus ill-adapted to the muddled politics of slavery in Texas. Considering the influence that Austin wielded as a successful empresario, bureaucrats in Coahuila y Tejas gave Lundy's plan for a colony of ex-slaves a cool reception. In the fall of 1833, Lundy met to discuss his plan with both Santiago del Valle, the secretary of state of Coahuila y Tejas, and Juan José de Vidaurri y Villaseñor, the state governor. While the governor was politely encouraging, del Valle expressed concerns, typical of Mexican officials, about the "degradation of the class from which the emigrants were to be selected." Without ever telling Lundy that he would likely never receive an empresario contract, del Valle stymied him with a series of bureaucratic delays and obfuscations. Del Valle began by reminding Lundy that, to discourage further settlement by American slaveholders, the Mexican government had in 1830 prohibited anyone to immigrate from the United States. Yet the law, del Valle assured Lundy, would soon be repealed, and Lundy might have his land grant if he would be patient. Lundy bided his time in Monclova, the capital of Coahuila y Tejas, for a month while awaiting the repeal, supporting himself by selling his possessions piece by piece and making saddle and leather repairs. Hoping perhaps for a higher authority to expedite his empresario contract, Lundy wrote a fawning letter to the Mexican president, Antonio López de Santa Anna, in which he enclosed a portrait of George Washington, called Santa Anna a "genuine patriot," and predicted that Mexico "is destined to rank high among the nations of the earth, at no very distant period."[91] In late 1833, around the time that he wrote to Santa Anna, the Mexican government announced the repeal of the 1830 law banning immigration from the United States to Mexico. However, it stipulated that the repeal would take effect not immediately but in six months. Del Valle told Lundy that he interpreted the law to mean not only that immigration from the United States could not begin for six months, but that the state could not appoint Lundy as an empre-sario until six months had passed. Disappointed, Lundy finally began to grasp that in Mexico, antislavery declarations were not always what they seemed. "It is necessary here," he wrote in his journal, "to oppose slavery, but there is many a wolf in Mexico . . . in the guise of a sheep." Out of money, Lundy returned to the United States. When he returned to Monclova in mid-1834, the six-month waiting period having elapsed, he found that another group of land speculators had secured the land on which he had hoped to plant his colony. "Thus, after all my hardships and perils," Lundy wrote, "I am com-pletely baffled in my attempts to establish colonies in Texas."[92]

Unwilling to return to the United States empty-handed, Lundy resolved to press farther south into Mexico. Despite his frustrations with Mexican officialdom in Texas, Lundy put his trust in another Mexican official, Juan Nepomuceno Almonte, a diplomat, politician, and military officer who was sympathetic to Lundy's plan. Almonte advised him to apply for an empresario contract in Tamaulipas, the Mexican state just south of Coahuila y Tejas, and according to Lundy, Almonte promised to "lend his influence in support of the application." Although Lundy may not have realized it, that influence was considerable: Almonte, the illegitimate son of the popular early nineteenth-century revolutionary priest José María Morelos, was a conspicuous political figure in Mexico City. Over a forty-year political career punctuated by coups and countercoups, Almonte held a variety military commands, diplomatic posts, and cabinet positions. Whether through Almonte's offices or not, within two days of Lundy's arrival in Victoria, he had secured an audience with Francisco Vital Fernández, the Tamaulipas governor. Three weeks later, Lundy had his empresario contract.[93]

Lundy quickly busied himself making plans for the colony. In Tamaulipas, he established a partnership with Richard Pearce, a New Englander who had settled in Matamoros as a sugarcane planter. Pearce agreed to enable Lundy's cherished dream: a plantation staffed by former slaves as wage laborers. "I will take 50 families," Pearce wrote to Lundy in March 1835, only a few weeks after Lundy had secured his empresario contract, "and give them employment on lands of mine, at 6$ a month, and feed them, provided they come provided with tools." The supplies that Pearce considered essential were extensive: two shovels, spades, axes, and hoes in addition to a mattock, wheelbarrow, ox cart, plow, and horse for every adult man who emigrated. To facilitate the transportation of so many people and supplies to Tamaulipas, Pearce advised Lundy to buy a ship "of about 90 or 100 tons."[94] To Lundy, who earlier that same month had found himself (not for the first time) without any funds and had borrowed eight dollars from another American expatriate in Tamaulipas, such an expensive undertaking was inconceivable.[95] Upon returning to the United States to advertise for emigrants, Lundy actively sought partners in his enterprise. The Boston abolitionist couple David Lee Child and Lydia Maria Child became enthusiastic supporters. Through their extensive connections in the antislavery movement, Lundy could anticipate raising considerable sums to finance the colony. Lundy also signed an agreement with a New York merchant, Lyman Spalding, according to which Spalding would share half the cost of transporting and outfitting emigrants and in return receive half of the lands that Lundy was due as an empresario. Moreover, Spalding reserved the right to the lands of any "commercial town" established in the colony. Lundy promised to promote the prospective town's "commercial advantages," and would receive six town lots "in compensation for these services."[96]

Lundy's agreement with Spalding signaled that the colony was quickly becoming less of an asylum for ex-slaves and an experiment meant to demonstrate the feasibility and economy of Black wage labor and more an exercise in land speculation. Despairing that he could bring 250 African American families to Tamaulipas within two years, Lundy opened the colony to white American emigrants as well. "In the admission of settlers, no distinction will be made, in regard to national ancestry or the complexion of the skin," he wrote in a circular advertising the colony in the United States. In that same publication, he appealed directly to white emigrants as any booster of lands in the US West might, comparing settling Tamaulipas to "settling the uninhabited regions of Illinois, Missouri, or Arkansas. It requires the same hardy enterprise—the same courageous fortitude—the same industry and perseverance—the same skill and intelligence, which penetrated those dreary solitudes, laid the foundation of opulent cities, and converted the lonely wilderness deserts into abodes of civilization, wealth, and refinement."[97]

Despite these various economic and ideological compromises, Lundy never settled anyone, white or Black, on his colony. Both to facilitate migration to his colony and to best demonstrate to white Americans the success of free Black agricultural labor, Lundy was determined to locate his colony as close to the United States as possible. Lundy's empresario contract specified that he "remains at liberty to choose the lands which best suit his purposes, anywhere within the limits of the state."[98] Pearce had presciently advised Lundy to establish his colony on the Rio Grande as close as possible to Matamoros. The city would provide a market for the colony's produce; moreover, on the Rio Grande, Pearce wrote, "you enjoy the most perfect security under the protection of the Mexican government." Lundy, however, was determined to plant his colony just south of Texas, in order to demonstrate the feasibility of Black wage labor to Americans as near as he could to the United States. He had his eye on a tract of land in northernmost Tamaulipas, on the southern bank of the Nuéces River, directly on the state border with Coahuila y Tejas. Pearce warned him against the location. writing that "there are spirits in Texas hostile to your enterprise. On the Nuéces, they are among you."[99]

Early in 1836, Lundy was preparing to return to Mexico to prepare for the arrival of the first settlers. He knew, of course, that since October 1835, Texas had been in rebellion against Mexico City, but like many observers, he was confident that the Mexican federal government would suppress the Texians. When the slaveholders' rebellion was crushed, he believed, his position and that of other antislavery advocates in Mexico would be strengthened. "The insurrection in Texas," he wrote in his journal, would not cause him to cancel his journey but only "to defer it a little."[100] His faith in Santa Anna's ability to put down the rebellion was not misplaced. In early 1835, inhabitants in the state of Zacatecas had rebelled against the Mexican government; Santa Anna had personally led a force of several thousand to Zacatecas and swiftly and brutally put down the revolt. In early 1836, Santa Anna marched into Texas with a force of several thousand and won a Pyrrhic victory at the Alamo in March. Yet, in April, as he was pursuing Texian forces under the command of Sam Houston, the Texians counterattacked and, improbably, not only defeated Santa Anna but captured him. As part of the settlement ending the rebellion, Mexican forces withdrew to south of the Rio Grande—well south of the land on the Nuéces River where Lundy planned to make his colony. In theory, Lundy could have forged ahead with his plans to establish his colony on the Nuéces, but with the proslavery Texians holding sway in the region, his colony stood little chance of success. Alternatively, he could have hewed to Pearce's advice and tried to establish his colony farther south, on the Rio Grande, but the successful rebellion in Texas by former American colonists made it unlikely that authorities in Tamaulipas would continue to support an American mission to colonize another Mexican state. In June, Lundy concluded that his project in Tamaulipas was "finished."[101]

After finally abandoning colonization, Lundy no longer felt the need to placate slaveholders. Under the pseudonym "Columbus," he wrote a bitter denunciation of the Texas revolution in the *National Gazette*. Peppering his account with details supplied to him by Almonte and other Mexicans and from his own experiences in Texas, Lundy characterized the revolution as a rebellion of American-born slaveholders against a Mexican government determined to abolish slavery. "The advocates of slavery, in our southern states and elsewhere" he wrote, "want more land on this continent suitable for the culture of sugar and cotton; and if Texas, with the adjoining portions of Tamaulipas, Coahuila, and Santa Fe, east of the Rio Bravo de Norte, can be wrested from the Mexican government, room will be afforded for the redundant slave population in the United States, even to a remote period of time."[102] Lundy was not far off: shortly after declaring its independence in early 1836, Texas requested annexation to the United States as a slave state. Eager to aid the resistance to annexation in whatever way he could, Lundy sent his *National Gazette* articles to John Quincy Adams, whom he had met in Washington in 1831. Adams's long speech in the House of Representatives in May 1836 opposing annexation was based largely on the Columbus essays. Lundy's essays were widely reprinted in northern newspapers; after Adams's speech, Lundy republished the collected essays under his own name as *The War in Texas*. His account stiffened resistance to annexation and contributed to Congress adjourning in July 1836 without having taken any action on annexation—indeed, without even acknowledging Texas's claim to independence.

Delaying annexation was the only reward that Lundy reaped from his efforts in northern Mexico. Had he actually settled his colony with ex-slaves, however, he likely would have done little to hasten the end of slavery in the United States; during the years that Lundy had spent in Texas and Tamaulipas, the antislavery movement had largely moved on from colonization. The core of the abolitionist movement, led by William Lloyd Garrison, had embraced immediatism. Garrison derided his former mentor's scheme in the pages of his new publication, *The Liberator*. The colony would be "too limited, and will be too slow in its results, to aid essentially the antislavery cause, and if it were otherwise, it is not needed to establish either the safety or pecuniary advantages of emancipation," Garrison wrote. "*Cui bono?*" he concluded—Who stands to benefit?[103] The question was appropriate not only for Lundy's plan but for all colonization schemes. For a decade and a half, Lundy, like other colonizationists, had essentially aimed his appeal to slaveholders and other racists. In appealing to racists, Lundy, consciously or not, had endorsed their racism: you need not fear to emancipate your slaves, he told them, for I will whisk them out of the country; neither need you fear that free Blacks will degrade American society, for I will show you that they can thrive as free laborers—but I shall do so outside the borders of the United States. Garrison's brand of abolitionism, which made no such effort to appeal to slaveholders, was on the rise—he founded the immediatist American Anti-Slavery Society in December 1833, while Lundy was in Texas.

Had he lived a few years longer, Lundy might have evolved to become an immediatist like his former protégé. However, in failing health, Lundy moved to Illinois in 1838 to live with his children, who had grown to adulthood while he was abroad in Haiti, Canada, and Mexico. He died a year later. Although he had been wrong about many things, in his last years, he learned at least one thing that proved to be right: American slaveholders would not hesitate to destroy a national political union to protect slavery. As a consequence of the foiling of his colonization scheme by the revolution in Texas, Lundy had come to believe that American slaveholders were irredeemable. He wrote to Adams in June 1836 that if slaveholders were willing to use violence to detach themselves from Mexico in order to protect the institution of slavery, there was little that would prevent them from seceding from the United States. "Unless the Despots of the Slave States can establish their authority over the Union, safely and permanently, they will, ere long, endeavor to set up for themselves," he warned. "Depend on it, we are upon the eve of an important crisis. The plans for a Southern Confederacy are maturing."[104]

CHAPTER FIVE

Converts

By the spring of 1838, the Presbyterian missionary Gideon Pond was in deep despair. After two years at Lac qui Parle, a Dakota village on the Minnesota River (then known as the St. Peter's River), he had become fluent in the Dakota language. Yet he lamented that he did not understand the Dakota worldview. In an effort to gain that understanding, Pond accompanied a group of Dakota on an extended duck hunting excursion. A fellow missionary at Lac qui Parle, Stephen Riggs, wrote, "Mr. Pond had been yearning to see inside of an Indian. He had been wanting to be an Indian, if only for half an hour, so that he might know how an Indian felt, and by what motives they could be moved." From the perspective of the Dakota, the hunting expedition proved to be a spectacular failure. A cold spell discouraged the return of ducks to the north. Other game was similarly scarce. The hunting party, including Pond, went hungry most of the time. "But Mr. Pond was seeing inside of Indians," Riggs wrote, "and was quite willing to starve a good deal in the process."[1]

Riggs and the other missionaries at Lac qui Parle shared Pond's eagerness to experience the Dakota world, including its privations, as the Dakota did, if in so doing they might gain an understanding that would help them to persuade more Dakota to convert. The missionaries steeped themselves in the Dakota language, culture, and experience because the success of their mission to convert the Dakota demanded it: in the 1830s, the Dakota were an autonomous and regionally powerful nation; the missionaries were able to live and proselytize in Lac qui Parle only because the Dakota permitted them to be there. Like Benjamin Lundy, who put himself under the protection of the Mexican state government of Tamaulipas in his effort to establish a colony of freed slaves, the missionaries effectively put themselves under the protection of the Dakota. Unlike Lundy, whose colony never materialized, Pond, Riggs, and other missionaries proselytized among the Dakota for decades. Yet the missionaries' willingness to embrace Dakota culture and experience to the point of suffering was not merely a practical part of their missionary work. It sprang from an even deeper religious source; it was a manifestation of the religious asceticism that had originally brought them to Lac qui Parle. After a few years in the borderlands, the missionaries expressed and understood that asceticism in terms of the culture and environment of the Dakota.

Few historians who study Indigenous people north of Mexico have portrayed missionaries as motivated to understand, much less share, the cultures of Indigenous people. Indeed, among such historians, the opposition of Christian missionaries and native cultures is nearly an article of faith. Since the publication of Robert F. Berkhofer's *Salvation and the Savage* in 1962, most historians have portrayed the interaction between Indigenous people and missionaries as a contest between native cultural persistence and American cultural imperialism.[2] Since the beginning of the twenty-first century, scholars who adhere to the paradigm of settler colonialism have similarly interpreted missions in North America and throughout European empires as instruments of Indigenous cultural erasure.[3]

On the surface, the Lac qui Parle missionaries resemble the type that such historians have described: ethnocentric agents of assimilation. Like Marcus Whitman, a Presbyterian evangelist so odious to the Cayuse of Oregon that they killed him and his household in 1847, the Lac qui Parle evangelists were devout Presbyterians. Like Whitman, they established their mission in the mid-1830s, under the auspices of the American Board of Commissioners for Foreign Missions, as Americans began to settle in the trans-Mississippi borderlands in large numbers. Like the Cayuse, who in 1847 tried to drive American settlers out of Oregon, the Dakota rose up against Minnesota settlers in 1862. For decades, historians of encounters between the Dakota and Americans have categorized the Lac qui Parle missionaries together with Whitman, seeing them as threats to the Dakota's precontact cultural integrity. Roy W. Meyer and Gary C. Anderson, the leading historians to study the nineteenth-century Dakota, have argued that the Lac qui Parle missionaries were, at best, culturally insensitive to the Dakota and, at worst, bent on the eradication of Dakota culture.[4]

Curiously, when reconstructing nineteenth-century Dakota culture and history on its own terms, these scholars relied heavily on the writings of the missionaries they excoriated. Particularly helpful were Stephen Riggs's *Dakota Grammar, Texts, and Ethnography*, a work so authoritative that John Wesley Powell published it in a Bureau of American Ethnology series; and Samuel Pond's detailed study, *The Dakota or Sioux in Minnesota as They Were in 1834*, a model of ethnographic description. In his study of the Dakota, Pond separated his heartfelt desire to convert the Dakota to Christianity from his description of their beliefs and traditions. "It may be thought strange that the writer, who was so many years a missionary among the Dakotas, has said nothing about the way in which they received or rejected Christianity," he wrote somewhat apologetically in his introduction to the study. He explained that his "main object has been to show what manner of people the Dakotas were as savages, while they still maintained the customs of their ancestors."[5] Pond, like the other Lac qui Parle missionaries, sometimes misunderstood the Dakota and resented the Dakota religious leaders who preached against them. But unlike Whitman, they were usually sensitive and scholarly observers of the Indigenous people around them. Unlike the fate that befell Whitman and his family in Oregon, when some Dakota rose up against white settlers in 1862, several Dakota, both converts and non-converts, spirited the missionaries and their families to safety.

A close look at Lac qui Parle reveals that the missionaries fit poorly into the role of cultural imperialists, while the Dakota are miscast as exemplars of precontact cultural persistence. With a few exceptions, notably their insistence that male Dakota converts cut their hair and don American-style clothing, the missionaries did not insist upon acculturation to American norms. Rather, the missionaries were themselves alienated from many aspects of secular American culture: they were Sabbatarians; early adherents of abolitionism; and teetotalers in a society in which heavy drinking was common. The Dakota community was not in pristine cultural isolation when the missionaries arrived but had been transformed by nearly two centuries of cultural and economic change resulting from the presence of French and British fur traders in the western Great Lakes and eastern Great Plains regions. By the time the missionaries came to Lac qui Parle, the Dakota had incorporated firearms, alcohol, woven cloth, and metal utensils into their material culture. To provide more furs for trade with the French, they had migrated southwest to the Minnesota River, away from their homeland on the Upper Mississippi

River. Numerous French fur traders had married Dakota women. Until the 1850s, the Dakota in Lac qui Parle retained their political autonomy from the United States. Like Indigenous people who could choose to accept to reject the US offer of vaccine, the Dakota were free to accept or reject the message of Christian missionaries—indeed, the Dakota of Lac qui Parle could have expelled the missionaries from the community at any point in the 1830s and 1840s. As anthropologists would put it, any acculturation that happened at Lac qui Parle was not "directed" but "permissive."[6]

Accordingly, Lac qui Parle in the 1830s and 1840s was not the scene of a simple conflict between monolithic cultures in which whites held power but rather a culturally eclectic community. Missionaries accommodated to some aspects of Dakota culture. Some segments of the Dakota community found it to their advantage to adopt some of the customs of the missionaries; and other Dakota, while they had no real interest in converting to Christianity, saw an advantage in having the missionaries live among them. The Dakota and the missionaries compromised in order to achieve a common goal: both groups sought to preserve Lac qui Parle's relative autonomy from the United States. The Dakota wanted to maintain their economic and political independence. The missionaries sought to isolate both themselves and their Dakota converts from an American society they regarded as thoroughly sinful. Like an arranged marriage, missionary-Dakota accommodation was by no means perfectly harmonious. Rather, as in the tense, contested French-Anishinaabeg "middle ground" that Richard White described in the eighteenth-century Great Lakes region, the Dakota and missionaries periodically struggled with cultural differences, misinterpreted each other, become frustrated, and vowed to quit their endeavor. Rather than simply evidence of an irreconcilable conflict, however, those conflicts and misunderstandings were part of the creation of their common mission.[7]

O MAN OF GOD, FLEE THESE THINGS AND FOLLOW AFTER RIGHTEOUSNESS

The missionaries who traveled to Lac qui Parle had two objectives. Their first purpose, of course, was to convert the Dakota to their version of evangelical Protestantism. Their second and equally important goal, however, was to remove themselves from secular American society. Much like the members of utopian or cooperative communities, nearly 100 of which were founded in the United States before the Civil War, the Lac qui Parle missionaries embarked upon an experiment to isolate themselves from American society and find in the Lac qui Parle community a rarefied moral atmosphere. Although the missionaries resembled utopian communitarians in their desire to live among like-minded people in a closed community, in important respects Lac qui Parle was yet more radical than most utopian communities. Most utopian communities, whether secular or religious, located themselves near one another because they saw themselves as engaged in separate yet parallel endeavors; their proximity allowed them to compare and learn from other communities' experiences. Most communities also located themselves not far from established towns and settlements, in large part because most communitarians, while they wanted to achieve some separation from American society, nonetheless imagined that they needed to be close enough to ordinary Americans that their examples might spark a larger transformation of society.[8]

Yet the Lac qui Parle missionaries—Thomas, Margaret, and Jane Williamson; Alexander, Lydia, and Frances Huggins; Stephen and Mary Riggs; and Samuel, Gideon, and Sarah Pond—had little interest in transforming American society. In their view, drunkenness, carnality, profanity, slavery, and other sins were so pervasive that American society was probably irredeemable. This view put them at odds with the beliefs of the preachers who led the Second Great Awakening, the evangelical movement for revival and reform that inflamed the United States in the 1820s and 1830s and inspired some religious utopian communities and many evangelical missions. The charismatic itinerant revivalist Charles Grandison Finney, for instance, the most important preacher to lead the Second Great Awakening, rejected the Calvinist ideas that human beings were innately sinful and that there was nothing people could do to save their souls from damnation—or to put society on a course of righteousness. Rejecting the old Calvinist theology that salvation was a gift from God bestowed on the wholly undeserving, Finney maintained, "Religion is the work of man." Converts could, of their own free will, choose obedience to God, Finney believed. To make such a choice was not a miracle, not a "Divine interference," not something "beyond the ordinary powers of nature." Sin was a choice, according to Finney, and in his revival meetings, he encouraged people to believe that they could choose an earthly life without sin.[9] By extension, if *everyone* chose to be born again in sinlessness, society might be completely reformed. Almost everywhere he traveled, Finney's message had a profound effect. After Finney preached in the town of Andover, Massachusetts, in 1831, a total of 200 people—close to 10 percent of Andover's population—joined one of the town's two churches in just one year.[10] In western New York, where Finney preached frequently, he and other evangelical preachers staged seventy-eight protracted meetings (well-planned religious services stretching over several days) and another forty-six spontaneous "awakenings" in the years between 1831 and 1850: an average of one major religious event every other month for nearly twenty years. In the late 1830s, nearly half of all baptisms in western New York occurred at protracted meetings.[11]

Revivalism thrived especially in New England, western New York, and the northern tier of the trans-Appalachian West because the combination of the market revolution and westward migration had unsettled these regions.[12] The commercialization of agriculture prompted the migration of thousands from the overcrowded New England countryside to the "Yankee West" of Ohio, Michigan, and northern Indiana and Illinois. The rise of commercial agriculture buoyed the fortunes of some migrants to this region. The father of Margaret Williamson and Sarah Pond, for instance, owned a thriving farm in Brown County, Ohio. Economic changes buffeted the opportunities of others, however. In the 1810s, the father of Samuel and Gideon Pond emigrated from Connecticut to New York but was unable to establish himself there as a farmer. The family returned to Connecticut in failure; by the early 1830s, the downwardly mobile Pond brothers found themselves, like many young men in antebellum New England, working as hired farmhands.[13] Whether they profited from the market revolution or not, the men and women of the Yankee diaspora felt themselves to be spiritually rootless in an increasingly commercialized and mobile society. In this environment, religious revivalism thrived.

On the surface, therefore, the Lac qui Parle missionaries appear to be exactly the sort of antebellum Americans that social historians have identified as acutely susceptible to Finney's style of religious revivalism. Before their emigration to Lac qui Parle, they inhabited the most fertile soil for revivalism in the United States: New England and the Yankee West. Yet the Second Great Awakening provides little guidance to the nature of nineteenth-century missions, because it was a disparate movement in time, space, and faith. Because Finney's notion that converts could choose a life without sin propped up the emerging Whig ideology of hard work, sobriety, and social mobility as well as social reform movements such as temperance and abolitionism, historians have paid him considerable attention.[14] Yet not all evangelical Protestants joined the temperance movement or the Whig Party. Some, such as the Lac qui Parle missionaries, preferred to retreat from American society rather than try to reform it. The Lac qui Parle missionaries were what the sociologist Max Weber called "other-worldly asceticists." Instead of concentrating on the improvement of society, the focus of the "worldly asceticists" who dominated the Second Great Awakening reform movements, the Lac qui Parle missionaries sought spiritual solace in a withdrawal from earthly entanglements.[15]

Rather than reforming American society, the Lac qui Parle missionaries, impelled in many cases by grief and thwarted ambition, sought to remove themselves from it. Gideon and Samuel Pond were the first to go. Samuel was born in 1808 and Gideon in 1810, the fifth and sixth children of Sarah Pond and Elnathan Pond. Beginning in 1812, as the revolution in commercial agriculture was beginning, Elnathan tried farming in New York; after four years, however, he returned in failure to his home in Washington, Connecticut. In Washington, Samuel was apprenticed to a clothier and Gideon to a carpenter. Both boys gave up their apprenticeships after a short time, however, to become hired hands on farms near Washington. In Washington, as elsewhere in the United States, the market revolution had transformed the countryside. Successful commercial farmers bought up the land of their less fortunate neighbors and hired men to work the fields. Already by 1800 in the Northeast and Middle Atlantic states, one-third of the men under the age of thirty-five had no land of their own and worked as agricultural laborers. A farmhand in the 1820s earned only about ten dollars a month—at that rate, it would have taken the Pond brothers years to have enough capital to buy farms of their own.[16] The young men's lives changed dramatically in 1831, however, when a months-long religious revival swept through Washington, part of a national evangelical revival that year. Every morning at sunrise during the course of the revival, crowds of farm workers from around Washington met for prayer meetings. The brothers were among the 100 residents of Washington who announced themselves to have been born again.[17] The Pond brothers were so affected by the revival that they left New England for the Upper Mississippi River the next year. "I want to be God's servant," Gideon wrote to his sister, explaining his decision. His conversion liberated him from struggling for material gain in a world in which the odds were stacked against him. As he told his sister, "I strive not to desire a treasure in this world but I want to be 'rich in faith'—an heir to the kingdom of Heaven."[18]

Thomas Williamson, by contrast, never struggled for wealth. He was born in South Carolina in 1800. His father, a well-to-do Presbyterian minister, registered his disapproval of slavery by moving the family north of the Ohio River in 1805. As a young man, Williamson progressed steadily upward toward professional respectability. In 1820, he graduated from Jefferson College, a Presbyterian institution in western Pennsylvania; in 1824, he took a degree in medicine from Yale Medical College. He set up a medical practice in Ripley, Ohio, a town on the Ohio River upriver from Cincinnati, and three years later married Margaret Poage, the daughter of a wealthy Ripley land speculator who, like Williamson's father, had moved north to Ohio from Kentucky in order to live in a free state. Thomas and Margaret seemed destined for a life of material and spiritual comfort: his medical practice prospered; both he and Margaret, without having made sacrifices of their own, enjoyed a life of piety in which they could congratulate themselves that they were the heirs of men who had distanced themselves from the evil of slavery. In the first six years of their marriage, however, all three of Thomas and Margaret's children died. In their grief, the Williamsons changed the course of their lives. Williamson abandoned his medical practice and was one of the first students to enroll at Lane Theological Seminary in Cincinnati, a redoubt of Presbyterian revivalism and abolitionism, where the early community included the abolitionist Theodore Dwight Weld and the temperance advocate and anti-Catholic nativist Lyman Beecher. In 1834, Williamson was licensed to preach. Rather than accept a call to a congregation in the settled East, he and Margaret chose to go to a place that would not remind them of what they had lost: he was appointed by the American Board of Commissioners for Foreign Missions to seek to convert the Indigenous people of the Upper Mississippi.[19] Margaret Williamson's sister, Sarah, also joined them on their mission into the borderlands. Eventually, Thomas Williamson's sister Jane joined them as well. Before embarking, Williamson recruited Alexander and Lydia Huggins, a couple he knew from the Presbyterian community near Ripley who were active in helping to shuttle fugitive slaves north. Alexander Huggins's sister Frances, who taught at a school for fugitives and later joined her brother in Lac qui Parle, suggested why so many family and friends joined the missionary movement together: "We all had enough missionary Spirit to be glad to have our friends go as missionaries but it was dreadful hard to part with them."[20]

Unexpected family deaths also impelled Stephen Riggs into the Presbyterian ministry. Riggs was born in Steubenville, Ohio, about forty miles west of Pittsburgh, in 1812. The son of a blacksmith, as a teen he had planned to apprentice himself to his older sister's husband and become a harness maker. Riggs's younger brother, whom Riggs's father intended to educate for the ministry, was the favored son. In quick succession, however, Riggs's sister and younger brother died; the first death put an end to his plans to apprentice himself to his brother-in-law, the second impelled Riggs to assume the burden of fulfilling his brother's calling. He attended Williamson's alma mater, Jefferson College, followed by Western Theological Seminary in

Pennsylvania. Before finishing his studies, Riggs resolved, like Williamson, to do something other than serve a congregation in the settled part of the United States. He wrote that "early in my course of education, I had considered the claims of the heathen upon us Christians, and upon myself personally as a believer in Christ," and resolved that "I would go somewhere among the unevangelized," perhaps in East Asia or among the Indigenous people of North America.[21] As a missionary, he would exceed the expectations placed on him by his family to fulfill his brother's ambitions—and he would also distance himself from their scrutiny.

Like Stephen Riggs, Mary Longley chafed against the expectations placed on her. Her parents dispatched her and her older sister to a series of schools for girls and young women in Massachusetts: first Mary Lyon's Female Seminary in Buckland, then to the Amherst Female Seminary, and finally to the Ipswich Female Seminary. At these places, Mary and her sister were expected to imbibe the virtues to which the daughters of the New England middle class of the 1830s were consigned: chastity, duty, domesticity, and devotion to their future husbands and children.[22] Mary's letters to her brother attest to her irritation with the stultifying curriculum. Upon arriving at Ipswich in 1833, she wrote to her brother that she and her classmates had been invited to the schoolmistress's home. "Last evening I spent an hour at Miss Grant's house, given for the young ladies, to cultivate their social affections & improve the manners I suppose," she wrote acidly. After a year at Ipswich, Mary resolved to escape the role assigned to her by embracing its tenets: she volunteered to go to the West, to improve "the destitute & ignorant state of females in Illinois" with the gospel of the New England female seminaries. Such a mission, she believed, would be worthy of her "talents of a superior order, devoted to a high & noble purpose." After spending a year in Bethlehem, Indiana, a town about 100 miles down the Ohio River from Cincinnati, she accepted an invitation from Dyer Burgess, a Cincinnati abolitionist, to meet Stephen Riggs, "a man of promising talents now a member of the Western Theological Seminary preparing for a mission to China." Riggs was seeking a wife to accompany him on his missionary work, and Burgess straightforwardly asked Mary "whether [she] was under any particular engagement." Seizing the chance for missionary work in an exotic place, she "provided [she] was not."[23]

Apart from these personal motivations, the impetus to withdraw from American society and migrate west was also rooted in the missionaries' dour emphasis on moral iniquity. They scoffed at Finney's notion that people could choose a life without sin. Instead, they maintained that believing

Christians must acknowledge their own sinfulness and trust that a merciful God would forgive them and grant them salvation. Anticipation of that hoped-for salvation was the central narrative of their lives. Rather than the spiritual perfection toward which social reformers strived, the Lac qui Parle missionaries were obsessed with their moral shortcomings. After Samuel Pond attended the revivals in Washington, he did not experience the heady enthusiasm typical of some Second Great Awakening revivals. Rather, he felt the moral despair reminiscent of early Calvinists who agonized over whether they would be among the elect who would be granted salvation. "Soon after I joined the church I lost all hope that I was, or ever could be a Christian, and for many months my mental sufferings were intense."[24] Two years later he confessed, "My salvation never appeared more difficult. . . . If I am ever saved it will be an astonishing act of free grace & sovereign mercy."[25] The feeling of moral inadequacy continued to plague the missionaries after they had migrated to Lac qui Parle. Gideon Pond recorded in his diary in 1837 that he was "entangled in the snare of the devil," and that "my heart is filth and pollution and my life but corruption." He pleaded, "I might see my innate hatefulness before God and repent and be humble"; and he prayed, "O Lord be merciful to me a Sinner." On his twenty-eighth birthday he remarked on the swift passage of the past year and lamented, "I find myself the same vile and hateful sinner I was when it commenced."[26] Similarly, Thomas Williamson confessed to Gideon Pond in 1840 that "The Wicked One" had "assailed" him during the past winter. "I have not for twenty years been so much tempted to anger and fretfulness."[27]

Obsessed with their own moral frailties, the missionaries were similarly sensitive to the moral shortcomings of others. Traveling to Lac qui Parle in 1833, Samuel Pond described Galena, Illinois, as "one of the strongholds of the prince of darkness," because Sabbath-breaking, drunkenness, gambling, profanity, Catholicism ("that religion is worse than no religion") and poor church attendance prevailed.[28] On their way to Lac qui Parle in 1837, Stephen and Mary Riggs stopped to observe the Sabbath in Davenport, Iowa. Mary was horrified by the "frequent volleys of dreadful oaths" that emanated from a grocery near her hotel, "a devil's den indeed." The young couple found the environment so unbearable that their consciences "did not chide for removing, even on the Sabbath," to more Christian accommodations.[29] After their brief sojourns in these frontier towns—which appear in their descriptions as Sodom and Gomorrah on the Mississippi—the missionaries moved on to Lac qui Parle, out of reach of the corruption of civilized society. The Riggses' decision to retreat from Davenport was indicative of their spiritual character;

to remain in American society, even as advocates of abolition, temperance, and Sabbatarianism, might have distracted them from the contemplation of their own sins and may, indeed, have imperiled their salvation by tempting them into moral compromise and complacency.[30] Scripture—particularly the letters of Paul—encouraged them to distance themselves from a sinful society that was replete with temptation. In Paul's first letter to the Corinthians (1 Corinthians 10:13–14) they read—in the King James version of the Bible that was ubiquitous in nineteenth-century America—that God "will not suffer you to be tempted above that ye are able, but will with the temptation also make a way to escape. . . . Wherefore, my dearly beloved, flee from idolatry." In Paul's first letter to Timothy (1 Timothy 6:4–11), they read of how to respond to pride, envy, strife, and "the love of money": "from such withdraw thyself." The letter continued, "O man of God, flee these things, and follow after righteousness, godliness, faith, love, patience, meekness."

Convinced of their own proclivity toward wickedness, the Lac qui Parle missionaries had no confidence in their ability to resist the vices that surrounded them in the United States. Accordingly, even before their emigration, they associated only with other Protestant religious radicals, ministers, seminary students, and their families. They found spouses within this clique: Dyer Burgess, an antislavery and anti-Masonic advocate, arranged the marriage of Stephen and Mary Riggs.[31] After a few years, most of the Lac qui Parle missionaries not already related by blood were related by marriage: Gideon Pond married Margaret Williamson's sister, Sarah Poage, in November 1837, which for a time put a stop to his condemnations of his sinfulness in his diary.[32] To remove themselves from the reaches of temptation, these likeminded Protestants, who had isolated themselves within American society, found an even more profound isolation in Lac qui Parle, a place that, according to one of the missionaries, was "farther from civilization than any . . . village of Indians south of Alaska."[33] Indeed, Lac qui Parle in the early 1830s was perched on the western edge of what was then called Michigan Territory, making it the westernmost outpost of any organized territory in the United States. The nearest American settlement was Cassville, a town on the Upper Mississippi River more than 300 miles to the southeast.[34] The missionaries welcomed the isolation that Lac qui Parle afforded them. They were not so much apostles of nineteenth-century American culture as apostates.

A mission in the western borderlands, the missionaries believed, would place them closer to primitive purity and away from commerce and corruption. Alexander Huggins, Thomas Williamson, Margaret Williamson, and Sarah Pond followed the examples of their fathers who had migrated to

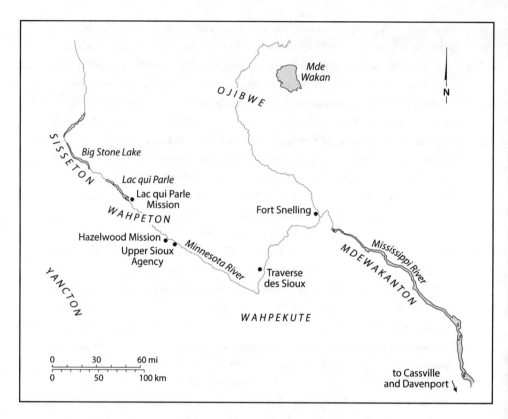

Dakota country, 1830s–1840s.

southern Ohio from South Carolina and Kentucky to escape what Williamson called "the wrong of slavery."[35] The missionaries' ideological rejection
of secular society became actual when they exiled themselves to Lac qui
Parle. "A resurrection to new life had just taken place," Stephen Riggs wrote
upon reaching Lac qui Parle in 1837.[36] Once established, the missionaries
considered the relative isolation of Lac qui Parle from American society an
advantage. They idealized the Dakota as noble savages: heathens, to be sure,
but still uncorrupted by secular American culture. In December 1833, Samuel
Pond complained to his brother that they needed to proselytize among the
Dakota before traders were able to sell alcohol to them, writing, "It is found
by experience that if onc[e] the Indians are in a situation to obtain Spirits
there is but little prospect of doing them any good. The main body of the
Sioux are not now in that condition but ere long they will be, then help will
be too late."[37] The next year, he further urged that every effort be made to
convert the Dakota before "white men and whiskey are among them."[38] By

1840, only three years after he had come to Lac qui Parle, Stephen Riggs was already considering moving farther west. After a visit to the Lakota near Fort Pierre on the Missouri River, he wrote, "Those Indians seem more favorably disposed to receive the gospel than most of the tribe in the vicinity of Lac-qui-Parle and especially Fort Snelling. As yet they have not formed a prejudice against it."[39] In 1840, Thomas Williamson likewise warned Samuel Pond that the Dakota would be irredeemable once they had been fully exposed to the vices of American secular culture. "As a general thing," he wrote, "there can be little doubt that the more remote mission stations are from white settlements the fairer will be the prospect of conferring saving benefits on those for whom we labor." Their mission could succeed, he concluded, only among Indigenous people who were "out of the reach of white influence."[40] Williamson and his fellow missionaries were, of course, also white, but neither he nor his fellow missionaries considered themselves emissaries of a white American society they had rejected. Williamson's warning reflected the central tenet of the missionaries' beliefs: by coming to Lac qui Parle, they had renounced an irreligious American society and insulated themselves from its temptations. Given their own moral weaknesses, they believed that if they had stayed in the settled East, they might have been tempted to tolerate sinfulness in their fellow Americans, or, worse yet, in themselves. Thus, they isolated themselves from American society not merely to save the souls of the Dakota. Their own salvations depended upon it as well.

KINSPEOPLE

As they isolated themselves from American society, the missionaries integrated themselves into the community of the 400 Dakota at Lac qui Parle. While Lac qui Parle seemed remote to the missionaries, the region around the Dakota village had been a busy scene of complex cultural interactions since the mid-seventeenth century. The Upper Minnesota River and Red River valleys were for two centuries zones of cultural and economic mediation and accommodation. The region was a borderland in the political sense: it was one of the contested places where imperial rivals and Indigenous nations met. Ecologically, the region was a border zone between the grasslands to the west and the woodlands to the east.[41] Economically, the Dakota were intermediaries in an intertribal trade between the woodland nations to the east and their kinspeople, the Lakota, in the Great Plains.[42] Beginning in the seventeenth century, fur traders widened the scope of trade, creating a highly fluid hybridization of native and European cultures. By the early nineteenth century, the region was a mélange of Siouan, Anishinaabe, French, British, and American cultures.

When the missionaries arrived, the Dakota had inhabited the prairies and forests of the Upper Mississippi for more than a thousand years. Their early settlements centered for centuries not near Lac qui Parle on the Upper Minnesota River, however, but on the shores of what they called Mde Wakan, or Spirit Lake, a large, shallow lake about seventy-five miles north of the juncture of the Mississippi and Minnesota Rivers. The Mde Wakan region was rich in both animal life and wild plant foods. Jonathan Carver, an American who explored the Upper Mississippi in 1766, called the region "a most delightful country, abounding with all the necessaries of life, that grow spontaneously. . . . Wild rice grows here in great abundance; and every part is filled with trees bending under their loads of fruits, such as plums, grapes, and apples."[43] Archaeologists who have excavated settlements near Mde Wakan dating to the early fourteenth century have found that the Dakota, living in houses built of poles and bark, relied primarily on wild rice, which as Carver attested grew in the many shallow lakes in the region; Dakota women harvested the rice with relative ease by bending the stalks of the plant over their canoes and then, using their paddles, beating the seeds from the stalk directly into the vessels. Archaeological remains also show that for centuries the Dakota cultivated both corn and squash. Cultivated crops were so important to Dakota subsistence in this early period that they called May *Wozupiwi* (planting moon), and October *Wayuksapiwi* (corn-harvest moon). They supplemented rice, corn, and squash with fishing and the hunting of deer, elk, ducks, and turtles.[44]

By about 1300, the Dakota (which means "kin" or "ally") had coalesced as the Oceti Sakowin Oyate, or People of the Seven Council Fires. By the eighteenth century, the seven divisions of the Oceti Sakowin overspread a region from the Upper Mississippi to the Upper Missouri River. Four divisions, collectively known as the Isanti (dwells at the place of knife flint), inhabited the woodlands and prairies of the Upper Mississippi: the Sisseton (people of the swamps), the Wahpeton (people of the leaves), the Wahpekute (people who shoot among the leaves), and the Mdewakanton (people of Mde Wakan). Two divisions, the Yancton and Yanctonai (both of which mean "people of the end village," a reference to the former location of their villages near Mde Wakan), had by the eighteenth century migrated to the prairies west of the Minnesota River. The seventh division, the Tetonwan, or dwellers of the prairie, migrated still farther west, to the shortgrass plains and the Black Hills, where, by the late eighteenth century, they had abandoned agriculture entirely and became horse-mounted, nomadic bison hunters. The Oceti Sakowin held sway over an extensive territory, and their confederacy was populous; by the mid-seventeenth century, it numbered about 38,000.[45] In practice, the divisions were autonomous. By the end of the eighteenth century, while the several leaders of the four Isanti (or Santee) woodland divisions met every spring, they and the Tetonwan were too distant from one another to be able to meet regularly—indeed, the Tetonwan developed a dialect that differed from that of the Dakota who remained in the woodlands and eventually called themselves the Lakota.[46] Nevertheless, many Dakota traveled from the woodlands to the Great Plains every summer to hunt bison; there, they met, feasted, and intermarried with their Lakota kinspeople. When Thomas Jefferson wrote to the secretary of war in 1804 that the "the Sioux are great" north of the Missouri River, and that the United States was, by comparison, "miserably weak" in their territory, he was probably thinking of the overarching confederation that extended from the Tetonwan on the Upper Missouri to the Mdewakanton on the Upper Mississippi.[47]

Like the Osages on the Lower Missouri, the Dakota leveraged themselves to a position of preeminence on the Upper Mississippi by exploiting the fur-bearing game in their territory for trade. Adapting themselves to the fur trade meant incorporating large numbers of French voyageurs into their villages. The transition began in the second half of the seventeenth century, as French fur traders diffused into the Great Lakes region and the woodlands and prairies to the west of the Great Lakes. The Dakota, seeking firearms to keep pace with neighboring Indigenous nations, initiated a commerce with the French and, later, with the British and the Americans, that lasted more than a century. The Dakota had an abundance of furs, deerskins, and pelts to trade: Zebulon Pike, who ascended the Mississippi River in 1805, reported that the region around Mde Wakan "is considered as one of the best fur hunting grounds for some hundreds of miles."[48] The trade brought the Dakota into intimate contact with French traders. By the middle of the eighteenth century, numerous French voyageurs resided in Dakota villages in order to prosecute the fur trade. Virtually all French traders in the seventeenth and eighteenth centuries found themselves adopted into the villages in which they were resident; they were given Dakota names and thereafter addressed as "brother." For the Dakota, the trade that then ensued with their French brothers was not a commercial exchange but a giving of gifts between kinspeople. To further earn the trust of the Dakota and thus facilitate their trade, most French traders married Dakota women. Many of the mixed-ancestry or Métis children of these *mariages à la façon du pays* became bilingual second-generation traders themselves.[49]

The fur trade brought more than French trade goods, culture, and genes into Dakota villages. As the Dakota were drawn into the fur trade by degrees, they devoted more time to hunting, sometimes traveling great distances in search of game. They planted fewer crops and, apart from the products of the hunt, came to depend increasingly on gathering wild rice. As they came to rely on hunting not only for trade but for their subsistence, many Dakota villages migrated southwest away from the Mde Wakan and toward the Upper Minnesota River and the prairies that surrounded it—the region to which Lac qui Parle belonged. There was less wild rice to be gathered there, but prairie turnips were abundant. More importantly, the Upper Minnesota River region still abounded with wildlife, while the Mde Wakan region no longer supported significant numbers of fur-bearing animals. George Monk, a North West Company trader, wrote from his post on the Upper Mississippi in 1806 that "Beaver formerly abounded here, but is now very scarce."[50] In the meandering rivers of the northern Great Plains, however, there were still beaver to exploit. By the late eighteenth century, the Dakota concentrated on trapping beaver in the northern prairies—or they served as conduits in a trade in beaver pelts between their Lakota kinspeople in the plains and traders in Québec. The voyageur Jean Baptiste Trudeau wrote in 1796, "The Sioux tribes are those who hunt most for the beaver and other peltries of the Upper Missouri. They scour all the rivers and the streams without fearing anyone. They carry away, every springtime, from out of our territory, a great number of them, which they exchange for merchandise with the other Sioux, situated on the St. Peter's and Des Moines rivers, frequented by the traders of Canada."[51] Moreover, in the prairies on both banks of the Minnesota River, the Dakota found large numbers of bison. Abandoning their permanent pole-and-bark houses for tepees made of bison hides, most Dakota established a seasonal subsistence routine of hunting bison in the summer in the prairies before returning to the woodlands in the fall to harvest wild rice and hunt deer.[52]

The Dakota commercial hunting economy in the prairies did not endure long. By the first decades of the nineteenth century, the Dakota fur trade economy was collapsing. In 1806, the Dakota produced about 8,000 beaver pelts a year. In 1820, however, the American Fur Company collected only 760 beaver pelts from its posts on the Upper Mississippi; by 1827, that number had fallen to 321. To make up for the decline in beaver pelts, the trade shifted to the less profitable muskrat. In 1827, muskrat made up 85 percent of the pelts that the fur trader Joseph Rolette collected. Rolette's returns that year were

Medicine Dance of the Dahcotah or Sioux Indians, 1848. Painting by
Seth Eastman. Peabody Museum of Archeology and Ethnology,
Harvard University, Cambridge, Massachusetts.

$25,000, down from $75,000 in 1805.[53] Traveling on the Minnesota River
in 1823 at the behest of the War Department, William Keating, a professor
of minerology and chemistry at the University of Pennsylvania, wrote that
"game seems to be disappearing very rapidly from the face of the country."[54]

In the face of these changes—migration and the rise and impending collapse of the fur trade—many Dakota found solace in their faith. The central
religious ceremony of the Isanti Dakota, the *Wakan Wacipi*, or Sacred Dance,
reinforced Dakota social cohesion in the face of the changes. The ritual was
open only to members of the Wakan Wacipi society, although every member
of the community participated in the Sacred Feast that accompanied the ceremony. The members of the Wakan Wacipi society adhered to a set of principles that emphasized peace, service, and community: do not quarrel; do not
refuse a friend's invitation; love and respect one another; be kind; treat other
members of the Wakan Wacipi as equals; comfort and be generous to the
relatives of the deceased. The Wakan Wacipi itself was a days-long ceremony
performed perhaps two or three times a year in virtually every Dakota village.
The ceremony took place in an arbor constructed by the members of the
Wakan Wacipi society: a brush enclosure, about four feet high and ten feet

wide, with a tepee at the west end to house the leaders of the Wakan Wacipi, and another tepee at the east end to serve both as an entrance to the arbor and as a place to house the members of the *akicita*, the men's warrior society that policed behavior in the village during the ceremony. On the central day of the ceremony, the members of the Wakan Wacipi society, lining the walls of the arbor and facing one another, danced to a drumbeat and sang a series of sacred songs. The proper order of the songs was recorded on a *dowánpi* (song stick)—a flat board no more than two feet long inscribed with glyphs representing the songs. The songs—sung, for instance, for women recovering from sickness and for success in hunting deer—consumed a day. The dance itself was a life renewal ceremony in which dancers symbolically died and were resurrected. In the course of the dance, dancers would touch their medicine bag to the chest of another dancer, symbolically shooting them; those touched by a medicine bag would symbolically die by falling to the ground; after a certain time had passed, they would revive and cough up a small shell or pebble as a sign of their rebirth. As they performed this ritual death and rebirth, the dancers sang:

> Tuwa niye he?
> Cehpi pejihuta niye he?
> Yani kta ce.

> Who are you?
> Is your flesh medicine?
> You will live.

According to Samuel Pond, the Wakan Wacipi arbor "was always surrounded by a host of spectators, who, aware of the solemnity of the occasion, observed the strictest decorum." Although Pond deplored the Wakan Wacipi as an elaborate superstition, he conceded that many of the "wakan men" who led the Wakan Wacipi were "kind to their families and staunch friends, with as much magnanimity and generosity as we could reasonably expect to find among savage pagans."[55]

Lac qui Parle in the 1830s, when the missionaries first arrived, reflected all the recent changes in Dakota culture and economy: migration to the Minnesota River from the Mde Wakan homeland, the cultural influence of the French fur trade, the abandonment of agriculture in favor of bison hunting, and the decline of fur-bearing game. Lac qui Parle was not a long-standing Dakota village; the settlement took shape around a fur trade post established there in 1826 by the fur trader Joseph Renville, the son of a French fur trader,

Joseph de Rainville, and a Mdewakanton woman, Miniyuha. At Lac qui Parle, Renville built two log structures—one a house for himself and his family and the other a store—and surrounded the buildings with a stockade. Beginning around 1830, about 350 Wahpetons from Little Rapids, a site on the Lower Minnesota River near its juncture with the Mississippi, migrated west and resettled near Renville's post at Lac qui Parle.[56] In all likelihood, the Wahpetons migrated to Lac qui Parle because by 1830 the Upper Minnesota River region sustained more game than the area near the Mississippi River. For the same reason, a number of Mdewakantons, including kinspeople of Miniyuha, migrated to Lac qui Parle.[57]

Renville, born in 1779 in the Dakota village of Kaposia on the east bank of the Mississippi River, exemplified the multicultural character of the Dakota borderlands of the early nineteenth century. As a fluent speaker of both French and Dakota, he was hired as an interpreter for Zebulon Pike's Upper Mississippi exploration in 1805. At the end of the expedition, Pike recommended Renville to James B. Wilkinson, writing, "He is a man respected by the Indians, and I believe and honest one."[58] Pike's endorsement notwithstanding, Renville fought with the British against the United States in the War of 1812. He followed his father into the fur trade after the war, first as an employee of the Hudson's Bay Company, and then, beginning in 1822, as one of the founding partners of the Columbia Fur Company. With several posts on the Upper Mississippi, the Columbia Fur Company siphoned away enough profits from John Jacob Astor's American Fur Company that Astor bought out Renville and his partners in 1827.[59] Renville continued in the trade as Astor's employee, centering his commerce at his post near Lac qui Parle. Within his stockade, according to Samuel Pond, Renville "lived in barbaric splendor quite like an African king," maintaining a retinue of thirty to forty young men "formed into a sort of society, which he often feasted and harangued. . . . Their adherence to him and devotion to his interests added greatly for a time to his importance."[60]

Renville's largesse toward his followers was an example of reciprocal giving among biological or fictive kin, a Dakota cultural tradition that cushioned the impact of change in the borderlands. Since the seventeenth century, in response to the influx of strangers such as Renville's father, the Dakota had incorporated important visitors into their network of "social kinship," enveloping the strangers in bonds of reciprocal obligation. Marriage between a fur trader and a Dakota woman, for instance, helped to solidify the outsider's social obligations to the community. Renville's generosity certainly added to his prestige in Lac qui Parle, but as one of the wealthiest persons in the Lac qui Parle community, any other course of action would have been an egregious social breach. As a Métis culturally fluent in Dakota and French mores, Renville used his prestige to mediate change. Renville was what cultural historians have termed a "cultural broker": an individual who bridged gaps between cultures.[61]

While the Dakota could integrate the commercialism of the fur trade into the culture of reciprocal obligations and social kinship, they could not mitigate the fur trade's demand for wildlife. By the late 1820s, game was so scarce that the trade in furs had shifted away from the Minnesota and Upper Mississippi Rivers. Few furs from the Great Plains passed through Lac qui Parle to Canada—as they once had when the French and the British had dominated the fur trade of the Great Lakes and northern Great Plains— instead, they went to American traders in St. Louis via the Missouri River.[62] In 1832, an American Fur Company steamboat ascended the Missouri River as far as the mouth of the Yellowstone River, inaugurating a trade in bison robes along the Missouri that bypassed the old trade route through Lac qui Parle.[63] By the 1830s, faced with a waning fur trade and depleted populations of game near Lac qui Parle, many Dakota confronted a crisis of subsistence. Some died each year in dangerous winter hunting expeditions. Shortly after his arrival in Lac qui Parle, Alexander Huggins noted, "Some days ago one woman came to the Dr.'s, said they were starving; one man, she said, was past sitting up; the Dr. gave the woman some turnips and potatoes and went to see the man; he was far gone."[64] Gideon Pond recorded that the Dakota were "poor and needy—many of them absolutely suffering from want, naked and hungry."[65] While Renville was wealthy by Lac qui Parle standards, as the trade declined in the 1830s he slipped steadily into a sort of genteel poverty. By 1843, he owed $4,200 to his corporate superiors, the American Fur Company.[66] By that time, his fur trading operation had become a means to support his social obligations to the Dakota community.

TO SEE INSIDE OF AN INDIAN

The Dakota subsistence crisis brought the missionaries to Lac qui Parle. The Dakota subsistence economy was strictly divided by gender; women were primarily responsible for planting and gathering; men for hunting. As hunters were increasingly unable to find game, the contributions of women to the subsistence of the Dakota community assumed critical importance. Renville encouraged the women of Lac qui Parle to intensify their cultivation of corn, and he invited the missionaries to the village in the hope that they could help to make the Dakota community agriculturally self-sufficient. Beginning in 1834, the missionaries brought, along with their religious message, livestock, seeds, implements, and methods of intensive agriculture. Indeed, Alexander Huggins and the Pond brothers initially came to the Dakota mission not as ministers but as farmers. "From the beginning," wrote Stephen Riggs, "it had been part of our work to make more than two stalks of corn grow where one grew before."[67] By 1837, the Lac qui Parle missionaries had a small horse-powered grinding mill, and they farmed five acres of corn, potatoes, wheat, peas, and turnips. The Dakota women, who tilled their corn fields with digging sticks, envied the missionaries' plot. "Plowing," Samuel Pond's son later noted, "was one of the arts of civilization which Indians, and especially Indian women, could appreciate."[68] By 1839, Huggins plowed fifty acres each spring for the Dakota women to plant corn. In the late 1830s, owing to the missionaries' advice and assistance to Dakota women, forty Lac qui Parle families could store enough corn each winter to forgo the dangerous winter hunts.[69]

The missionaries' agricultural prowess helped them to convert some Dakota, especially women. One of the obstacles to conversion was the mobility of the Dakota; expeditions to hunt and gather food interrupted the missionaries' lessons. Greater yields of corn, however, contributed to the number of Dakota who remained in Lac qui Parle throughout the year. Just as importantly, their advice and assistance on agricultural matters facilitated contact between the missionaries and Dakota women and helped to raise the missionaries' stature. For their part, the missionaries were favorably disposed toward Dakota women, praising them for their chastity and industry. For these reasons, forty of the fifty Dakota converts between 1835 and 1842 were women. Some were the daughters or former wives of French fur traders, marginalized socially and economically in the Dakota village when the fur trade had declined and their French husbands and fathers had abandoned the Dakota country.[70] Others, such as Toteedootawin, or Her Scarlet House, one of the first Dakota women to convert to Christianity, had felt marginalized as second wives in polygamous households.

Like their strict gender division of labor, many Dakota rituals assigned specific roles based on gender. The missionaries' success in converting women caused a number of Dakota to regard the mission church as "an assembly of women." The first Dakota man to join the church, Simon Anawanymane, in 1841, was accused by his peers of having "made himself a woman." In a ritual sense, this is exactly what Anawanymane had done: for a Dakota man, gender identity was bound up in religious rituals; according to

Stephen Riggs, Anawanymane "had been inducted into manhood through the ceremonies of his religion."[71] Moreover, the missionaries insisted that male converts adopt American dress and cut their hair—the latter a sign of mourning among the Dakota. If Riggs was insensitive to Dakota notions of masculinity, at least he was no hypocrite; he cheerfully defied white American gender roles by attending to certain household chores, such as milking, that in nineteenth-century rural America were quintessential women's work.[72] The stiffest resistance to the mission church came from the all-male warrior societies that were periodically empowered to police community behavior. In the village, the societies sometimes took it upon themselves to keep children from attending the mission school and women from visiting the church.[73] On one occasion, some Dakota men surreptitiously killed one of the missionaries' cows—a direct assault on the new food sources that the missionaries had introduced to the Dakota community.[74]

Yet these spasms of resistance were relatively rare. Even the most irreconcilable Dakota men understood that the missionaries contributed to the subsistence and independence of the community. Stephen Riggs wrote that Ishtahba, or Sleepy Eyes, one of the leading men of the Dakota community, "appreciated the temporal benefits which have attended missionary efforts" and was "always kind and friendly to missionaries" despite being "firmly attached to the religion of his fathers."[75] Gideon Pond noted in his diary in January 1840 that some Dakota men would endure a sermon and even sing "two or three hymns in their language" in return for "a good supper."[76] Williamson's medical skills were also in great demand. Williamson wrote to Samuel Pond that the "Great part of my time is taken up in giving medicine" to the Dakota, and that he spent "four-fifths of my time" working for the Dakota's material rather than spiritual welfare. Similarly, Samuel Pond complained that much of his time was spent in improving the material lives of the Dakota rather than in missionary work. Williamson counseled patience, advising Pond that the good will that the missionaries earned among the Dakota by "labouring for the temporal benefit of the Indians" would eventually lead to conversions: "We have spent more labour in preparing the ground than is usually spent in raising a crop in the States. . . . The same may be the case in Spiritual as well as temporal things. We well know that God alone can prepare the hearts of this people to receive his word. . . . [If] God is pleased to make use of human instrumentality in making known his truth perhaps he does the same in preparing the minds of men to hear it."[77]

Recognizing the missionaries' contribution to the community, some Dakota incorporated the missionaries into Lac qui Parle's social kinship network. One of the Dakota's first steps was to give the missionaries names in the Dakota language—as they had done with fur traders for over a century. When Stephen and Mary Riggs's son, Alfred, was born in 1837, the Dakota named him Zitkadan Washtay, or Good Bird. "In those days," Riggs wrote, "it was a habit with them to give names to the white people who came among them."[78] Riggs apparently viewed the Dakota's naming of his son as no more than a colorful custom. Among the Dakota, however, naming was an act of ritual importance that implied social kinship. More than a mere formality, it represented incorporation into the community and the Dakota network of reciprocal obligations. Other aspects of the Dakota religion likewise emphasized social integration. Pledges of comradeship and membership in various dancing societies such as the Wakan Wacipi, for instance, were mediated by and expressed in religious terms. These ceremonies and others bound the Dakota together: elder relatives with children, comrades with one another, society members toward their common purpose. By tightening the social ligaments that connected individuals and small groups within Lac qui Parle, these religious practices aimed at preserving the autonomy and strengthening the cohesion of Dakota society.[79]

Whether or not they understood the social importance of naming, the missionaries certainly were drawn into the Dakota social network. Mary was, at first, unable to breastfeed Alfred/Zitkadan Washtay, and relied on Dakota women both to nurse her son and to attend to her health.[80] On Alfred/Zitkadan Washtay's first birthday, his only present, according to Stephen Riggs, was "a very small bow and arrow, from an Indian man who is a frequent visitor."[81] Although Riggs may not have recognized the importance of the gift, older male relatives among the Dakota were responsible for instructing and disciplining boys. As Alfred/Zitkadan Washtay grew, the Dakota man might be expected to provide him with larger weapons and teach him something of their manufacture and use. In their own manner, the missionaries reciprocated: in 1839, Stephen and Mary Riggs took an orphaned ten-year-old Dakota girl, An-paye-too-o-kee-tan In-win, or Appearing Day, into their household.[82]

The missionaries' study of the Dakota language further integrated them into the Lac qui Parle community. Thomas Williamson believed that Indigenous people "can only be instructed in religion in a language in which they think." He criticized other missions to Native Americans where "the money and labor have been chiefly expended in trying to instruct them in the English language, instead of preaching the gospel to them in their own language."[83] The missionaries, therefore, applied themselves to learning Dakota and conducted their lessons and services in the Dakota language. A fur trader who visited Lac qui Parle in 1837 was struck by the novelty of the bicultural mission church: "Nothing could be more interesting than to see the Savage of the wilderness assemble with the sons and daughters of the Lord in the place appointed for prayer; to hear the wild and rude sons of the forest sing the praises of their Maker and Savior, in their own uncultivated and barbarous tongue."[84] The use of the Dakota language at the mission was more than a novelty, however. Language is an important part—perhaps the most import-ant part—of cultural identity. By translating their message into Dakota the missionaries invited Indigenous people to convert without abandoning this crucial aspect of Dakota culture.

Because the success of their mission depended on their mastery of the language, the missionaries were eager to learn Dakota. "From the time of our arrival we considered the acquisition of the Dakota language of paramount importance," Samuel Pond recalled. Upon his arrival in Minnesota in 1834, Samuel Pond learned from a fur trader how to ask the name of a thing in Da-kota. "He told me and I wrote it down, and then, approaching a Dakota who was standing by a pile of iron, I asked its name. He promptly replied *maza* and then dipped a little water in his hand from the river and said *mini*—then took up a handful of sand and said *wiyaka*." No other discovery, Pond wrote, "ever afforded me so much pleasure as it did to be able to say in Dakota 'What do you call this?' . . . We began the study of the language there on the banks of the Mississippi." From that moment on, the Pond brothers "were ever on the alert to catch some new word or phrase from the mouths of the Indians."[85] In order to further his knowledge of the Dakota language, Samuel Pond, like his brother Gideon, accompanied some Dakota on a hunting trip. "The language was the game I went to hunt, and I was as eager in pursuit of that as the Indians were in pursuit of deer."[86] Stephen Riggs and Alexander Huggins did likewise, accompanying a group of Dakota on a bison-hunting expedition to the Missouri River in the fall of 1840.[87] Riggs and the Pond brothers were able to able to hold conversations with the Dakota within a year.

Samuel Pond mastered Dakota more quickly than the others. To facilitate transcribing the Dakota words that he and his brother were learning, Pond created a "suitable alphabet" for Dakota. Although Dakota vowel sounds are "common to the English," Pond found that "with the consonants it is differ-ent, for there are sounds in the language which no English letter or combi-nation of letters can be made to express. To meet this difficulty we took such letters from the English alphabet as are not needed in Dakota and gave them new names and new powers, and we also made the single characters c and x represent the English sounds of *ch* and *sh*." When Thomas Williamson arrived in the Dakota country in 1835, a year after the Ponds, he told them, according to Samuel, that he and the other missionaries would use the Ponds' Dakota alphabet "for the present till they could have time to discover what alterations were required, for it was not to be supposed that untutored laymen could perform a literary work so well that a college graduate could not mend it." Despite his initial confidence, Williamson struggled to learn Dakota. After a year in Lac qui Parle, Williamson asked one of the Ponds to join him there to help him learn the language. Two years after Gideon Pond had relocated to Lac qui Parle, Williamson had acquired enough facility in writing Dakota that he was able to translate Scripture, but he was still unwilling to speak Dakota in public—instead, he preached in French, and relied on Joseph Renville to translate his message into Dakota.[88]

Williamson's struggles notwithstanding, mastering the Dakota language became the chief intellectual activity of the Lac qui Parle missionaries. With the assistance of Renville, the missionaries busied themselves translating portions of the Bible into Dakota: Williamson read a verse aloud from a French Bible, Renville repeated the verse in Dakota, and Williamson, Riggs, and Gideon Pond transcribed Renville's words.[89] They peppered their correspondence with Dakota terms, and competed in the effort to compile the most complete lexicon.[90] In 1836, Samuel Pond issued a Dakota spelling book, and in 1839 the Pond brothers published a Dakota translation of the *History of Joseph*, from Genesis 37–47. Also in 1839, Gideon Pond and Riggs collaborated on a *Dakota First Reading Book*. Samuel Pond wrote to his sister in 1840, "I spend most of my time in writing Sioux. I have lately finished a Dictionary containing about three thousand words. I have written a small Grammar."[91] In 1842, Samuel Pond wrote a *Second Dakota Reading Book*, which consisted of Hebrew Bible stories, and in 1844 he published a Dakota *Catechism*. When Stephen Riggs went to Boston in 1842 to publish the portions of the Bible that the missionaries had translated to Dakota, he found it difficult to remember some English words. "We had been forgetting our mother tongue somewhat in the effort made to learn Dakota."[92] The Dakota language had become, by the early 1840s, the medium of the missionaries' isolation from American society.

It was also the medium of evangelization. To preach, the missionaries had to render ideas and metaphors into symbols that were meaningful to the Dakota. Like all clerics, the missionaries chose to preach from scriptural narratives that they hoped would resonate with their listeners. The story of Joseph, one of the first stories that the missionaries translated, told of people saved from famine by divine guidance—a narrative the missionaries believed would strike a chord with the Dakota.[93] Similarly, one of the first portions of the Bible that Gideon Pond sough to translate into Dakota was the Thirty-first Psalm, which speaks of God as a refuge from adversities—much the same way that the missionaries thought of Lac qui Parle.[94] The missionaries also seized on Dakota idioms. To translate the term "to pray," the missionaries adopted the Dakota term *chakiya*, "to cry to." Riggs wrote that when one Dakota woman was "troubled to know how prayer could reach God. . . . I told her in this we were all little children. . . . He made the ear, and shall He not hear? He made, in a large sense, all languages, and shall he not be able to understand Dakota words? . . . Prayer was now, as through all ages it had been, the child's cry in the ear of the great Father."[95]

Religious practice at Lac qui Parle was an ongoing negotiation between doctrine and popular understanding, between Presbyterian clergy and Dakota laity. Particularly, the Dakota pressed the missionaries to emphasize Christian practices that resembled Dakota traditions of reciprocal social obligations. In August 1837, Gideon Pond recorded in his diary that Wamdi Okiye, or Eagle Help, the principal chief at Lac qui Parle, reproached the missionaries "not in anger but with savage mildness because we teach that we should love others as ourselves and do not share with them what we ourselves possess."[96] In 1838, Joseph Renville, whose family was the first to join the mission church, successfully encouraged the Dakota converts to boycott a service at the church. Renville called for the boycott because the missionaries had refused to lend their spinning wheel to his daughters. "If you can do without me I can do without you," Renville told the missionaries.[97] An apology from Riggs settled the matter, but the Dakota converts continued to press the missionaries to share their resources, particularly the corn, potatoes, and turnips from their gardens. The significant aspect of these exchanges was not, as the missionaries sometimes complained, that the Dakota were improvident and inveterate beggars, but that they perceived the similarity between the Dakota obligation to share and the missionaries' claims to be devout believers in the principle of Christian charity.

Dakota listeners interpreted the Christian message, such as the parable of the prodigal son (Luke 15: 11–32), according to their traditions of social kinship and reciprocity. In the parable, a father splits his inheritance between his two sons. The elder son abides by his father but the younger leaves home and squanders his wealth. Utterly impoverished and hungry, the son returns to his father, who welcomes him by clothing him and slaughtering a fatted calf for a feast. The reunion between forgiving father and repentant son, the killing of the calf, and the celebration that follows reflects the core of the Christian message. The prodigal son represents all sinners, and his father the forgiving God. The slaughtered calf, in this sense, is the crucified Christ. The feast represents the prodigal son's redemption. In recognition of the importance of this part of the parable, the missionaries plainly tried to render it in Dakota idioms. The father clothes his repentant son not in a robe and shoes but in a *sina* (blanket) and *hanpa* (moccasins). The elder son, who complains that despite his steadfastness his father had never sacrificed even a kid for him, complains in the Dakota version that his father has not given him even a *tacincadan* (fawn). A still more compelling challenge for the missionaries was translating "calf" in a way that both maintained the narrative integrity of the parable and the symbolic importance of the calf as representative of the crucified Savior. In Dakota, *pte* referred to both bison and domesticated cows. The term for "calf" that the missionaries employed in the parable, *ptezicadan*, could mean either a bison or domesticated calf.[98] This story of hunger and feast, of the sacrifice of a calf to celebrate a reunion of kin must have resonated among the Dakota. The bison was more than just an important material resource for the Dakota. During the course of the summer bison hunts, the Dakota consumed bison meat in communal feasts that, while contributing to subsistence, more importantly reaffirmed kinship and social solidarity. In the communal hunts, the Dakota set upon the bison together at an agreed-upon time; the rare hunter who violated this rule and hunted alone—thus scattering the herd—was ostracized. The spoils of the hunt were widely distributed among the members of the community.[99] In short, the missionaries told a narrative of faithlessness, repentance, and forgiveness; a parable of otherworldly salvation. The Dakota heard a story of faithlessness, repentance, and forgiveness; a tale of the obligations of kinship and community.

The missionaries struggled to maintain their interpretation of doctrine against the Dakota efforts to interpret it to their liking. When Renville's son journeyed from Traverse des Sioux to Lac qui Parle on a Sunday, Williamson asked him, if it had been his intention to travel on the Sabbath. "Yes, I did intend to travel," the young man replied, "but I expected to repent of it when I got home." The missionaries saw such behavior as laxity. They attributed such moral lapses to the influence of Renville, "whose ideas of religion were derived chiefly from Catholics," according to Samuel Pond (for whom "Catholic" had only a pejorative meaning). In 1838, Pond refused to admit to the church several members of Renville's retinue on the grounds of their inadequate knowledge of the gospel. Renville threatened, "I have prepared these persons for admission to the church and if you do not admit them they will never attend your meeting again." A compromise was reached: the men were admitted after a period of catechizing.[100] Renville did not desist in his efforts to loosen the strictures for conversion; in the spring of 1839, he attempted to replace the Presbyterians with a Catholic mission, which he hoped would be less doctrinaire. Unable to bring a priest to Lac qui Parle, he and his family returned to services after a few months' nonattendance.[101]

The missionaries tuned their message to the ears of the Dakota, but accepted the conversions only of those Dakota who met their stringent requirements. The missionaries' brand of Christianity was not open to all. Just as the missionaries had chosen to associate only with a small number of like-minded ascetics, they selected for church membership only the most committed converts from the ranks of the Dakota: three people in 1836, four in 1837, nine in 1838, ten in 1839, five in 1840, and nine in 1841.[102] At Lac qui Parle, unprepared applicants were rejected. In 1838, Gideon Pond wrote, "Five or six women have offered themselves as candidates for admission but were not received on account of their ignorance of the doctrines of the gospel."[103] Perhaps because of the missionaries' efforts to instruct converts, backsliding was rare in Lac qui Parle. Of the fifty Dakota who converted to Christianity between 1835 and 1842, only two were later expelled from the church.[104]

Some Dakota religious ideas could be reconciled with Christianity. One of the first Dakota converts, Toteedootawin, had been a leading member of the Wakan Wacipi. Like the mission church, membership in the Wakan Wacipi society was open only to those who had undergone a rigorous initiation. While Stephen Riggs was repulsed by the heathenism that the Wakan Wacipi represented to him, the celebration of a resurrection to new life were central to both the Sacred Dance and the mission church. The principles of the Wakan Wacipi—peace, harmony, kindness, generosity, equality, respect, and love—would have been easy for the missionaries to recognize, if they could have seen past the ritual's paganism. Upon Toteedootawin's conversion (and her baptism as "Catherine"—the missionaries, like the Dakota, welcomed people into their community by renaming them), Riggs praised her as giving "as good evidence of being a christian as any that have been received" at the time of her admission to the mission church.[105]

As long as the Dakota community remained autonomous, individuals such as Toteedootawin or Ishtahba were able freely to accept or reject the missionaries' message. Yet the autonomy and isolation at Lac qui Parle was short-lived. The decline of the community had two causes. First, a late frost in the spring of 1842 caused the Lac qui Parle corn crop to fail. Many of the Dakota women who had joined the mission church migrated elsewhere, either to the plains to join the bison hunters, or east to receive federal stipends like the Mdewakantons. Some never returned.[106] By 1846, while Riggs remained at Lac qui Parle, most of the missionaries had dispersed among other Dakota communities: the Williamsons went to Kaposia; Samuel Pond to Shakopee; Gideon and Sarah Pond and the Hugginses to Traverse des Sioux. In 1854, after most of the mission buildings at Lac qui Parle were consumed in a fire, Riggs and most of the members of the mission church moved down the Minnesota River to Hazelwood, near the Upper Sioux Agency, a Dakota reservation.[107] Second, and more importantly, the enormous influx of set-tlers to the Dakota's country—which became the Minnesota Territory in 1849—destroyed the isolation from white American society that both the missionaries and the Dakota coveted. In 1835, the missionaries had been, except for a few fur traders, nearly the only white Americans in what would become Minnesota Territory. By 1850, the territory had an American popu-lation of 20,000. Between 1855 and 1856 the population rose from 40,000 to 100,000. In 1857, one year before Minnesota was admitted to the Union, the territory had a population of over 150,000.[108]

Far from welcoming this influx of white settlers, the Lac qui Parle mission-aries resented it. As a result of "the filling up of this new land by white settlers," Stephen Riggs wrote that "all over the country were seen the same selfishness, the same speculation, the same jumping of claims. Hence the state of society in a new country is very undesirable."[109] While Marcus Whitman had seen his facilitation of US expansion in Oregon as his "greatest work," the Lac qui Parle missionaries more resembled the Presbyterian missionaries to the Cherokees and Choctaws in the 1820s and 1830s who galvanized resistance to removal. Some of these missionaries helped the Cherokees draw up a consti-tution and claim sovereignty in the effort to avoid removal from Georgia.[110] Likewise, in 1856, after Stephen Riggs and most of the members of the Lac qui Parle mission church had relocated to Hazelwood, he drew up a consti-tution for the "Hazelwood Republic," in the hope of achieving a measure of Dakota political autonomy for the community. Seventeen men, including Simon Anawanymane, signed the document, in which they professed their faith in the Christian God and swore obedience to the United States. They elected a Dakota convert, Paul Wa-za-ku-te-ma-ni, or Paul Shoots His Gun Walking, to a two-year term as president, and others to offices as secretary and judge.[111] Rather than a capitulation to US authority, the Hazelwood Republic reflected a recognition that, surrounded by tens of thousands of white settlers, to remain autonomous the Dakota must adopt the form of a local elected government.

In the borderlands, not all missionaries were cut from the same cloth. The Lac qui Parle missionaries' religious rejection of mainstream American culture and their appetite for ascetic deprivation impelled them into the Dakota country. There, their religious asceticism acquired the character of the borderlands. "In order to prosecute their work successfully," Samuel Pond's son later wrote, the missionaries "deemed it essential that they should fully understand the language, habits, customs, hopes, and fears of an Indian; that they should be able to talk like a native, and, as far as might be, live like one—on Indian fare, in an Indian tent, with Indians if need be."[112] The missionaries' ascetic zeal for the rejection of secular American society became an ascetic zeal to share the culture of the Dakota community.

Accordingly, the Lac qui Parle mission station was far from being an outpost of acculturation to American mores. The missionaries' essentialist interpretation of Christianity—the belief that the true nature of the faith transcended all secular human cultures—not only made possible their estrangement from American culture but permitted them to view Dakota culture with an anthropological detachment. For the Lac qui Parle missionaries, the idea of replicating all aspects of secular American culture among the Dakota was unthinkable. The salvation that the Lac qui Parle missionaries offered the Dakota did not depend on their assimilation. Just as the missionaries' faith had taken them outside of their own society, they delivered to the Dakota the message that Christianity superseded secular culture, whether American or Dakota. They won a few adherents—mostly Métis and women whose marriage to fur traders or whose status as second wives had partly estranged them from the Dakota community. For these outliers of Dakota society, the mission church offered the comfort of social integration.

Whether they recognized it or not, the Lac qui Parle missionaries joined in the ongoing negotiation between cultures in the borderlands. Like the fur traders before them, the missionaries found themselves enveloped in obligations to the Dakota community. It was an envelopment that the missionaries—seeking refuge from the temptations of secular American culture—welcomed. The Dakota welcomed the missionaries because their presence in Lac qui Parle contributed to the community's autonomy. For a few years, the Dakota and the missionaries found a common mission: maintaining the autonomy of Lac qui Parle. It was by no means a perfect arrangement, but both the Dakota and the missionaries knew it to be better than incorporation into American society.

Conclusion

In the first decades of the nineteenth century, slaves fled to a provisional freedom in borderlands Florida; the United States subsidized trade and offered vaccine to many Indigenous nations to try to win their allegiance against European imperial competitors (while those Indigenous nations played the United States against its imperial competitors to try to extract the best terms); antislavery advocates tried to create a colony of freed slaves in the borderlands between the United States and Mexico; Protestant missionaries tried to preserve the autonomy of an Indigenous community on the Minnesota River to protect both their converts and themselves from white American settlers they saw as sinful. The central argument of this book is that these things happened because North American borderlands were places where the power of the United States and its imperial competitors was at its weakest. Acknowledging such weaknesses renders these experiments in the borderlands legible; it reveals narrative visions for the borderlands that offer alternatives to manifest destiny. Fears—of Indigenous people, disease, European imperial competitors, slave revolt, damnation, both the expansion of slavery and the end of slavery, and the prospect of American empire, among other things—were the catalysts for these experiments.

By contrast, stories of American ambition and one-sided conquest cannot adequately account for these experiments, except to suggest that they were merely exceptions to the rule of inexorable white, slaveholding American expansion. Rather than conceiving of manifest destiny as an explanation for US territorial expansion, this book understands manifest destiny as a historical problem: a partisan idea that, in the first half of the nineteenth century, had purchase among some Americans, but which was contested, only partly realized, and which fails to explain much of what happened in the borderlands.

That is all well and good for the first half of the nineteenth century, one might think. By midcentury, however, what did any of it matter? By the 1840s, the United States had driven the Florida maroons and their Seminole allies either into exile in the Indian Territory or into the swamps at the southern extreme of the Florida peninsula; the United States had abandoned its efforts to win the good will of Indigenous people through subsidized trade and vaccination in favor of relying on military power to force them into submission; Texas, far from becoming a colony of freed slaves, had by the end of the 1840s a population of nearly 60,000 African American slaves; and the autonomy of the handful of Dakota to whom Protestant missionaries ministered hung by a thread: in 1851, the Dakota would submit to a treaty that forced them to cede most of the southern half of what became the state of Minnesota to the United States. Nationally, the 1844 presidential election elevated the determined expansionist James K. Polk to the White House; a few months later, the US Congress resolved to offer Texas admission to the Union. Both the election of Polk and the vote to annex Texas were closely contested, reflecting the divisions and uncertainties about expansion that had characterized American society for decades. Nevertheless, once the votes had been taken, such uncertainties seemingly vanished: in rapid succession between 1845 (the year that John O'Sullivan's "manifest destiny" editorial appeared) and 1848, the United States annexed Texas, secured Oregon by treaty with Britain, provoked war with Mexico, and annexed most of northern Mexico west of Texas. As if to confirm that the period of US tentativeness and weaknesses was over and a new age of expansion and empire had begun, in the 1850s and 1860s the United States consolidated its earlier conquests and added more territory, carving off another piece of northern Mexico in 1854 and acquiring Alaska in 1867.

The Civil War, while leading to the emancipation of slaves in the South, was a war for empire in the western borderlands. During the Civil War, white Americans in some parts of the western borderlands seized the opportunity that the conflict presented to form military units to settle grievances against Indigenous people and take territory from them. In 1863, for instance, Kit

Carson, with 700 New Mexico volunteers and a large number of Ute auxiliaries, starved the Navajo into submission by systematically destroying their agricultural plots and extensive flocks of sheep. In 1864, in an effort to drive Indigenous people from Colorado and speed the territory's admission to statehood, John Chivington led two companies of Colorado volunteer militia in a murderous attack on noncombatant Southern Cheyenne in their winter camp near Sand Creek.[1]

Following the Civil War, the United States—led by a federal government made more powerful by war—steadily consolidated its empire. In the last decades of the nineteenth century, US dominion in North America was startlingly different from the tentative, compromised, and contested US presence in its borderlands in the first years of the century. That newfound authority in the borderlands reflected not only a more powerful federal government but changes in the American economy and society: in the first half of the nineteenth century, the United States was sparsely populated and agrarian; in 1820, there were fewer than 10 million Americans, making the US population one-third that of France and one-fifth that of Russia. The United States emerged in the last years of the century, however, as a densely populated industrial nation. The US population in 1900 was 78 million—third in the world behind China and Russia. Whereas as late as 1860 the United States' relative share of world manufacturing output was a mere 7 percent (ranking the United States behind Britain, France, China, and India), by 1880 its share had risen to 14 percent (making the United States second only to Britain), and by 1900, at 24 percent, the United States was the world leader.[2] In these last decades of the nineteenth century, as the United States became an industrial power, industrialists replaced slaveholders at the vanguard of US expansion. The United States then lurched into its borderlands in the North American West in a series of rapid industrial spasms. In 1852, there were only six miles of rail west of the Mississippi River—a short stretch west of St. Louis of the ambitiously-titled Pacific Railroad. By 1900, the United States possessed over 180,000 miles of rail—over a third of the railroad mileage in the world. Much of that mileage was in the West. Railroads facilitated the industrial exploitation of the natural resources (many of which were found in the West) critical to industrial growth: coal, copper, iron ore, timber, and grain. To consolidate the control over natural resources in the West, beginning in the 1870s the US Army followed in the wake of railroads, miners, loggers, ranchers, and farmers, prosecuting wars against the Lakota, Blackfeet, Cheyenne, Modoc, Nez Perce, and other Indigenous nations and forcing them to submit to the reservation system. American industrialists crossed international borders to exploit resources as well. By the early twentieth century, foreign investors, mostly American, controlled virtually all of Mexico's underground minerals. In the same period, the United States extended its imperial reach overseas into the Caribbean and the Pacific. In short, in the last decades of the nineteenth century, an industrial United States imposed its sovereignty in North America and beyond in a way that had largely eluded the agrarian United States of the first half of the nineteenth century.[3]

Over twenty years ago, a pair of historians argued that this trajectory— from borderlands, characterized by imperial weakness and Indigenous autonomy, to bordered lands, characterized by powerful nation-states able to impose their sovereignty fully—was the likely fate of all border regions.[4] The field of borderlands studies has largely adhered to this way of ordering borderlands history: many historians have depicted borderlands before the nineteenth century as places of political accommodation and cultural malleability, where autonomous Indigenous nations maintained their control of territory through a diplomacy that pitted competing empires against each other; by contrast, when historians have examined twentieth-century borderlands, they have tended to see them as places of ethnic cleansing and state violence.[5] Other historians, particularly those who advance the idea that the United States was and remains a settler colonial state, depict border regions as *always* having been characterized by conquest and ethnic violence.[6] Neither historians who adhere to the paradigm of borderlands-to-borders nor those who are partisans of settler colonialism see border regions from the mid-nineteenth century onward as places where the expansionist state has remained at its weakest.

Yet, in the 1850s and 1860s, despite the United States' consolidation of its conquests and acquisition of new territories in North America and beyond, legacies of the early nineteenth-century borderlands endured, albeit sometimes in tentative, episodic, and limited ways. Border regions remained contested places where US sovereignty was at its weakest and where marginalized people therefore were able to carve out small measures of autonomy. Despite its new wealth, power, and population, the United States was not able simply to impose its will everywhere; as in the first half of the nineteenth century, the reach of the United States often exceeded its grasp. Such limitations were apparent at the conclusion of the war with Mexico in 1848, seemingly the moment of the expansionists' greatest triumph, when US officials could not agree among themselves how much of Mexico they should annex. Nicholas Trist, the US negotiator in Mexico, reached an agreement with Mexico that acquired for the United States New Mexico, Alta California, and the disputed region south of the Nuéces River. He did so despite Polk's urgent efforts to recall him to Washington and replace him with a negotiating team that would press Mexico also to cede Baja California and a right-of-way through the Isthmus of Tehuantepec. Trist's Mexican negotiating partners exploited the disagreements among the Americans to retain as much of their territory as they could.[7]

Even in the reduced territory that the United States took from Mexico, the United States struggled through the 1850s to impose its sovereignty. In 1859, Senator Jefferson Davis of Mississippi, meditating on the prospect of secession two years before he became president of the Confederacy, predicted that because much of the territory the United States had acquired was desert, California would eventually detach itself from the rest of the United States. "Shall the United States commence her downward step by losing the rich possessions she now holds on the Pacific as the inevitable consequence of that separation which mountains and deserts command?" he asked his Senate colleagues.[8] A few years earlier, as secretary of war in the administration of Franklin Pierce, Davis had made one of the last—and most quixotic—experiments in the North American borderlands in an effort to achieve US sovereignty in the desert: he had dispatched two US Navy ships to Smyrna in the Ottoman Empire, bought seventy-six camels, and shipped them to Galveston, Texas. The camels, Davis envisioned, would provide the US military with the means to impose US control over the desert environment. George Perkins Marsh, the foremost naturalist in the United States, agreed with Davis that camels would enable the United States to assert its sovereignty in its newly acquired desert. "A body of armed men, advancing under the quick pace of trained dromedary," Marsh wrote, "would strike with a salutary terror the Comanches, Lipans, and other savage tribes upon our borders."[9] In 1856, Davis ordered the camels to be part of an expedition from Galveston to California, and he ruled the experiment a success by the time the camels had reached San Antonio: "These tests fully realize the anticipations entertained of their usefulness in the transportation of military supplies."[10] Davis's successor as secretary of war, John Floyd, like Davis constructed a narrative of success around the camel experiment, writing fulsomely, "The entire adaptation of camels to military operations on the plains may now be taken as demonstrated." He requested that Congress authorize the purchase of an additional 1,000 camels.[11] Yet the United States acquired no further camels, and many of those that Davis had bought died in droughts that struck Southern California in the mid-1860s; the survivors found their way into circuses and menageries.[12]

Other US imperial ventures in the 1850s and 1860s likewise came to naught. In 1854, for instance, the initiative of the Pierce administration to annex Cuba fizzled. The American filibuster William Walker's efforts to detach Sonora and Baja California from Mexico in 1854, and his subsequent effort to rule Nicaragua in 1855 were ignominious failures. The US Guano Islands Act of 1856, under which the United States asserted its sovereignty over several small islands in the Pacific and Caribbean, had almost no practical effect in the years after its passage. In 1868, the United States conceded defeat to the Lakota following a two-year war and, according to the terms of the peace, abandoned three forts in the territory it ceded to them. In 1870, a US effort to annex the Dominican Republic ended in failure.[13] Even in the last years of the nineteenth century, in the face of policies intended to break up reservations into individual allotments and assimilate Indigenous people into white American culture, Indigenous people continued to resist the power of the US state in regions where US settlement bordered on Indigenous homelands. The Crees and Ojibwe, for instance, evaded US authority by crossing the border into Canada. Indigenous people had nowhere near the power they had possessed in the first part of the nineteenth century, but neither were they powerless. The Ghost Dance, an intertribal religious revival movement preaching both Indigenous cultural persistence and accommodation to whites, swept through the West beginning in 1889. The United States thought it had eradicated the movement in 1890 when it killed 300 Ghost Dancers at Wounded Knee in South Dakota, but the movement persisted well into the twentieth century.[14] For its part, the United States in the closing decades of the nineteenth century was more powerful than it had been at the outset of the century, but its authority was not limitless. Nor had white Americans in the second half of the nineteenth century come to a consensus about expansion.[15] Thus, despite the vastly increased power of the United States, territorial expansion proceeded fitfully and was beset by setbacks, while experiments and improvisations endured in the US borderlands.

Most late nineteenth-century historians and pundits waved away the defeat at the hands of the Lakota in 1868 and the failed annexations of Cuba and the Dominican Republic much as they had forgotten, or had chosen not to remember, the camel experiment, the autonomy of Florida maroons, the US policies of subsidizing trade and offering smallpox vaccine to Indigenous people, the vision of Texas as an experiment in free Black labor, and the efforts of a few Presbyterian missionaries to protect Dakota autonomy. For Americans at the end of the nineteenth century, and to a considerable extent for Americans in recent years, it was and is tempting to dismiss such things as nothing more than feeble and doomed efforts by a few outliers to resist the manifest destiny of the United States to extend its dominion across North America and beyond. Leaving aside the teleology of such views—the assumption that the way things turned out was the *only* way it could have turned out—we might ask, did the experiments of the first half of the nineteenth century yield any legacies?

What became of the descendants of the slaves who fled to Florida? In 1832, the United States negotiated with a group of Seminole leaders who represented only some of the Seminole villages and obtained those leaders' assent to a treaty that called not only for the removal of the Seminoles to the Indian Territory but for the reabsorption of the Seminoles back into the Creek confederacy and, in all probability, the reenslavement of Black Seminoles by white and Creek slaveholders. Black Seminoles such as Abraham had no intention of returning to slavery. Together with the Red Stick Creeks, who had migrated south to join the Seminoles in 1814 after their defeat in the Creek civil war, Abraham and other Black Seminoles violently resisted removal. The resulting conflict—the Second Seminole War—continued until 1842 and resulted in the deaths of roughly 1,600 US soldiers. (This was the struggling campaign "against a miserable band of five or six hundred invisible Seminole Indians" to which John Quincy Adams referred in 1836 in the House of Representatives.)[16] Unable to defeat the Seminoles on their own, the United States hired Creek auxiliaries—from the same Creek villages and factions that had fought alongside Andrew Jackson in the Creek civil war in the 1810s, that had joined Jackson in his invasion of Spanish Florida in 1818, and that had agreed, in the 1830s, against the wishes of other Creeks, to a removal treaty with Jackson's administration. Abraham and other Black Seminoles such as John Horse knew that they could not defeat the combined forces of the United States and what remained of the Creek confederacy—but they could make the war costly enough that the United States would change the terms of removal. In 1838, the commanding officer of the US forces arrayed against the Seminoles, General Thomas Jessup, who two years earlier had concluded that the conflict "is a negro, not an Indian war," offered the concession that Abraham and other Black Seminoles sought: the United States would formally acknowledge the freedom of Black Seminoles who agreed to removal.[17]

Like Abraham, John Horse, who in the 1840s effectively succeeded Abraham as the leader of the Black Seminoles, submitted to removal to the Indian Territory in return for his emancipation. Apart from a brief return to Florida to help the United States try to complete its war against remaining Seminoles, he abided in the Indian Territory until 1849, when, fearing reenslavement at the hands of local Creeks and white Americans, he organized the exodus of roughly 300 Black Seminoles to Mexico. Pursued by Creeks and harassed by white Texans, the group reached the Rio Grande in July 1850. Mexican authorities welcomed the Black Seminoles as settlers who would help secure the northern border against Comanches. Much as in the mid-eighteenth century when the first Cowkeeper had migrated with his followers to the Florida borderlands and settled in a place outside of the control of Spain, Britain, or the Creek confederacy, Horse had found a place where the Creeks, Mexicans, and Americans could not effectively reach him. For the most part, in the second half of the nineteenth century, neither the United States nor Mexico was able to exercise much control over the border region: migrants crossed freely; bandits and Indigenous groups such as the Comanches and Apaches had more sway in much of the region than either the United States or Mexico. In short, the Black Seminoles sought out a place—the US border with Mexico—where, at midcentury, state control remained most elusive.[18]

The US-Mexico border was not the only midcentury North American borderland where non-white actors were able to challenge existing hierarchies. The Civil War created new borderlands that led, ultimately, to the end of slavery in the United States. The existence of free territory on the borders of some slave states had been a threat to the institution of slavery since the eighteenth century—as the 1789 flight of Patty, Daniel, and Abram from the Bewlie plantation in Georgia to Florida exemplified. Since 1821, when the US acquisition of Florida had eliminated it as a place to which slaves might flee to freedom, most fugitives had looked north. Between Nat Turner's rebellion in Virginia in 1831 and the outbreak of the Civil War in 1861, roughly 1,000 slaves escaped to the North every year. Aiding them in their flight—and usually offering them sanctuary—were communities of free Blacks in northern cities, which one historian has called "maroon societies." When the Civil War began in 1861, the Union Army, advancing into the Confederacy, steadily brought the border between freedom and slavery ever closer to dense populations of slaves in the Deep South. Hundreds of thousands of slaves seized the opportunity to free themselves by fleeing to one of hundreds of Union camps. There, Union soldiers gathered the escapees into improvised "contraband camps." In effect, the contraband camps were maroon communities, and the Union had stumbled into a policy of supporting marronage. The Emancipation Proclamation, which Abraham Lincoln announced in September 1862—promising to free all slaves in areas still held by the Confederacy on January 1, 1863—was in part meant to encourage slaves to continue to escape from slavery and thus undermine the Confederacy from within. By 1865, at least half a million slaves had fled to Union lines. Much as the Spanish in Florida had enrolled escaped slaves into the colonial militia, in time, significant numbers of escaped slaves joined the Union war effort. By the end of the Civil War, the Union Army had enlisted 179,000 Black soldiers, roughly one-half of whom had been slaves at the start of the war; the Navy enlisted 10,000 Black sailors.[19] The flight of hundreds of thousands of slaves to freedom during the Civil War was the culmination of North American slaves' centuries-long strategy of emancipating themselves by seeking out the border between slavery and freedom.

Just as importantly, during the war, white Americans' support for immediate, unconditional emancipation finally eclipsed support for colonization— the scheme to settle freed slaves outside the borders of the United States that Benjamin Lundy had pursued so single-mindedly in the 1820s and 1830s. That the war undercut support for colonization was a somewhat unexpected development: Lincoln had been a public proponent of colonization since at least 1858; like Lundy, he imagined that a long-term, gradual abolition program that included colonization would be more palatable than immediate and unconditional abolition to white Americans who feared the prospect of civil equality with Blacks. In March 1861, one of Lincoln's first acts as president was to dispatch an envoy to Guatemala to investigate the possibility of establishing a colony of freed slaves either there or in Honduras. The Guatemalans and Hondurans, however, firmly declined the proposal. The emergence of emancipation as a Union war aim—a shift made clear in the Second Confiscation Act in July 1862 (which freed slaves belonging to those who had engaged in insurrection against the United States) and the preliminary Emancipation Proclamation a month later (which declared free all slaves in territories held by the Confederacy on January 1, 1863), together with the formation in February 1863 of the first Black Union regiment (the Fifty-Fourth Massachusetts) effectively mooted colonization as a policy of the Lincoln administration. Like Lundy, Lincoln eventually abandoned colonization; he did not mention colonization publicly after the Emancipation Proclamation took effect.[20]

Yet for the rest of the nineteenth century, many Americans—some white and some Black—continued to imagine that the solution to the problem of race in the United States lay beyond US borders. Colonization thus persisted in US politics: some white Americans saw it as a way to achieve an all-white republic; some Black Americans, frustrated by oppression and segregation in the post–Civil War United States, saw it as a chance to achieve the promises of freedom. In 1869, the administration of Ulysses S. Grant sought to annex the Dominican Republic and transform it into a colony for Black Americans; the Senate, however, rejected the annexation treaty in 1870. Grant had imagined, as he explained in a message to Congress in 1876, that "the emancipated race of the South would have found there a congenial home.... In many cases of great oppression and cruelty, such as have been practiced upon them in many places within the last eleven years, whole communities would have sought refuge in Santo Domingo. . . . The possession of this territory would have left the negro 'master of the situation' by enabling him to demand his rights at home on pain of finding them elsewhere."[21] In 1889, William Ellis, who had been born a slave in South Texas in 1859 but, capitalizing on his fluency in Spanish, had reinvented himself as Guillermo Eliseo, a Mexican businessman, received a contract from the Mexican government to colonize as many as 20,000 Americans in Mexico. Ellis's Mexican colonization project was no more successful than Lundy's—Ellis and his partners were unable to raise funds for the colony, and two years after granting the contract, the Mexican government canceled it. In early 1895, however, Ellis settled roughly 800 African Americans on a hacienda in Tlahualilo, on the border of the states of Coahuila and Durango.[22] The largest migration of African Americans in the postwar period was not beyond the borders of the United States but merely beyond the borders of the former Confederacy. In 1879, Henry Adams, a former slave and a veteran of the Union Army, organized 4,000 African Americans to take advantage of the 1862 Homestead Act and migrate from Mississippi and Louisiana to homesteads in Kansas. Adams was not the only person advocating that African Americans leave the former Confederacy for lands in the West. Altogether, more than 26,000 African Americans moved to Kansas in the 1870s.[23]

For Indigenous people, migration to the west was by no means the movement toward freedom that it was for some African Americans, yet neither was it the end of their autonomy. By 1842, the United States had forced the removal of 3,000 Seminoles to the Indian Territory; yet a few hundred Seminoles remained in the swamplands of central and southern Florida under the leadership of Holata Micco, or Alligator Chief. Holata Micco was a descendant of both the first Cowkeeper, who in the eighteenth century had separated from the Creek confederacy and led his followers to Cuscowilla, and of Bolek, who had fought against Andrew Jackson's invasion of Florida in 1818 and subsequently migrated with his followers from Cuscowilla to the remote wetlands of central Florida. In 1854, Jefferson Davis, the secretary of war, resolved to force the removal of the remaining Seminoles from the peninsula. By early 1856, the United States had mustered over 1,400 troops

Conclusion

in the region; US forces outnumbered male Seminoles of fighting age by a ratio of 14–1. In the ensuing war—the Third Seminole War—however, the United States discovered what the Spanish, British, and earlier Americans had learned in previous conflicts in the Florida borderlands: they had less effective power than they imagined. The Seminoles raided nearby white settlements, forcing the settlers to flee the area; the United States could not force the Seminoles into a decisive battle; the Seminoles instead routinely eluded the US troops. After two years of conflict, however, the United States seemed to have prevailed: Holata Micco and his followers agreed to removal to the Indian Territory. Yet when he embarked for the West, he was accompanied by only thirty-eight men and eighty-five women and children. A larger number of Seminoles remained ensconced in the Great Cypress Swamp in southern Florida; US authorities decided to pretend they were not there and simply declared a victorious end to the protracted and indecisive conflict.[24]

When Holata Micco and his few followers arrived in the Indian Territory in 1858, they were not obliged to share a reservation with the more numerous Creeks as the first Seminoles to be removed had been. As early as 1851, the Seminoles in the Indian Territory had suggested to US officials that the Seminoles who remained in Florida might be more easily induced to submit to removal if they knew they were bound for their own reservation rather than for subordination to the Creeks in the Indian Territory, who numbered more than 20,000. In 1856, when US progress against the Seminoles in Florida was flagging, the western Seminoles seized the opportunity to renew their call for a separate reservation under their own tribal government. US officials, as part of their effort to find a face-saving way out of the conflict in Florida, agreed.[25] In 1856, then, the Seminoles in the Indian Territory achieved what Cowkeeper, William Bowles, and other Seminole leaders had sought to achieve since the eighteenth century: acknowledgment of the Seminoles' independence from the Creeks. What the Seminoles had achieved, to borrow a phrase from an eminent scholar of Indigenous history, was to transform a reservation meant to be little more than a prison into a homeland.[26]

Like the Seminoles, the Osages used what bargaining power remained to them at midcentury to negotiate for a reservation in part of their homeland that provided them with as much autonomy as they could extract from US authorities. They had to do so in the context of fewer natural resources on which to rely. The disestablishment of the factory system in 1822 and the arrival of steamboats to the Missouri River in 1832 had opened the Great Plains to the fur trade. In the middle decades of the nineteenth century, horse-mounted hunters, including the Lakota, Blackfeet, and the Osages themselves, collectively provided traders on the Missouri with roughly 100,000 bison robes annually. By the mid-1850s, Indian agents in the Great Plains reported that the number of bison and other game was noticeably diminished. The competition for resources among Indigenous nations was particularly acute for the Osages. In 1825, with the resources that had been the foundation of their autonomy depleted, the United States bullied the Osages into ceding 45 million acres in the Arkansas River valley. All that remained to the Osages was a strip of land north of the Indian Territory. Part of the funds they received for the land went to discharge debts the Osages had incurred to private traders since the disestablishment of the factory system.

Despite the loss of land (losses that continued in 1870, when the United States forced the Osages to cede their reservation in Kansas in exchange for a smaller reservation in the Indian Territory), the Osages remained influential in the region. Until the 1850s, they were commercial emissaries between white merchants in Arkansas and Missouri and the Comanches to their southwest, exchanging manufactured goods for horses and mules the Comanches had stolen in Mexico.[27] Not least, the Osages pursued a strategy that borderlands nations, including the Dakota, Seminoles, Creeks, Cherokees, and others had employed since the eighteenth century: drawing outsiders, including whites, Blacks, and natives from other Indigenous nations into their society through adoption and marriage. The practice, part of a larger process that one Indigenous historian has called "Intertribalism," not only bolstered the Osage population but asserted that, despite the newfound ability of the United States to more effectively assert its sovereignty in Indigenous territory, the United States was the not the only nation to grant citizenship.[28]

While the Osages negotiated, sought out a commercial role, and integrated whites and other natives into Osage culture to retain part of their homeland, the Dakota went to war with the United States to try to reclaim theirs. In 1862, four years after the United States negotiated an end to its conflict with the Seminoles, the Dakota attacked US forces and white settlers in Minnesota. Hunger was the primary cause of the violence. Even before the arrival of the Lac qui Parle missionaries to Dakota country in the mid-1830s, game populations in the region had been gradually diminishing. In 1851, the Dakota had agreed to a treaty with the United States in which they ceded most of southern Minnesota; all they retained was a strip of land along the Minnesota River. In 1858, they ceded their land on the northern bank of the river to the United States—the strip they retained contained both Lac qui Parle and Stephen Riggs's Hazelwood Republic. In return for these extensive cessions, the United States promised the Dakota provisions and thousands of dollars in yearly annuity payments. Yet, the United States diverted most of the funds to fur traders and other merchants to whom the Dakota owed debts and rarely delivered the promised provisions. In 1861, Dakota crops failed, and by the summer of 1862 many Dakota were starving. In July 1862, several thousand hungry Dakota gathered at the Upper Sioux Agency on the Minnesota River, not far from the Hazelwood mission, to demand food. In August, a group of four Dakota hunters, frustrated and hungry because of their inability to find any game and refused in their attempt to buy alcohol on credit, approached a farmstead near Acton, located about seventy-five miles east of Lac qui Parle, where they killed the uncooperative whiskey dealer and four other settlers. In the ensuing violence, the Dakota—led by a Mdewakanton, Little Crow, killed 700 settlers and forced thousands to flee.

Little Crow was well-known to the Lac qui Parle missionaries. A kinsman of Joseph Renville's wife, he had settled in Lac qui Parle in 1837 and studied with both Gideon Pond and Stephen Riggs, learning enough English to be able to write his name. Although he was never interested in converting to Christianity, many of the converts in Lac qui Parle were his relatives, including the Renvilles and two of Little Crow's four wives. He occasionally attended the mission church with his convert wives.[29] Perhaps because Little Crow and other Dakota knew them, the Lac qui Parle missionaries and their families largely escaped the violence. Only one member of the missionaries' large extended families—Amos Huggins, the son of Alexander and Lydia Huggins and a teacher at a government school at Lac qui Parle in 1862—was killed in the war. The killing happened while the leader of the Lac qui Parle community, Wakanmane, or Walking Spirit, was not present. Huggins was unknown to his killers: they were not Dakota from Lac qui Parle but from a community near the Lower Sioux Agency. Though Wakanmane was not a Christian convert, when he returned to Lac qui Parle, he shielded Huggins's wife and children from harm and saw to it that they were delivered safely to US forces. The Riggs, Williamson, and Pond families escaped to safety in St. Paul shortly after the violence began. Stephen Riggs maintained, "We could trust our own Indians that we should not be personally injured," but if they had encountered Dakota who were unknown to them, they might have suffered the same fate as Amos Huggins.[30] Two Dakota men who were members of the Hazelwood church, Simon Anawanymane and Lorenzo Lawrence, escorted several other white families to safety.[31]

In the reprisals that followed, the United States executed the leaders or suspected leaders of the uprising; imprisoned hundreds of Dakota men; and exiled virtually all the Dakota to reservations in Nebraska or the Dakota

Territory. The war permanently altered the character of the Dakota mission. The violence shattered Dakota communities, making it impossible to reestablish a mission among an existing Dakota village. Stephen Riggs, Thomas Williamson, and Gideon Pond devoted three years to ministering to the hundreds of Dakota men imprisoned first at Fort Snelling and later at Davenport, Iowa (near the place where the use of foul language had offended Stephen and Mary Riggs fifteen years earlier). Judged by the number of converts, the missionaries experienced their greatest success during these years, converting 450 Dakota, mostly men, in the prisons.[32] The prison mission, however, marked the beginning of the end of the "permissive" acculturation of Lac qui Parle, where the Dakota had been at liberty to accept or reject the missionaries' message, and the onset of "directed" acculturation.

The transition to a directed acculturation was seemingly completed by John Williamson and Alfred Riggs, who succeeded their parents to mission work among the Dakota. Beginning in the 1870s, they administered reservation boarding schools for the Dakota and Yancton in their exile in Nebraska and South Dakota. While they followed in their parents' footsteps as missionaries to the Dakota, they did not share their parents' abhorrence for white American society. When John Williamson decided, in 1860, to exchange his pulpit in Indiana for the Dakota mission, he rued losing the comforts of his life in the settled East.[33] What they shared with their parents was a commitment to preach to the Dakota in the Dakota language. They were ideally prepared to do so: as boys, they had been playmates of Dakota children at Lac qui Parle and had learned to speak Dakota with native fluency.

Typically, boarding schools were notorious for their efforts to repress native cultures. Col. Richard Pratt, who headed the Carlisle Indian School in Pennsylvania, summed up the philosophy of such places in 1892: "A great general has said that the only good Indian is a dead one. . . . In a sense, I agree with the sentiment, but only in this: that all the Indian there is in the race should be dead. Kill the Indian in him, and save the man."[34] The schools that Williamson and Riggs administered were different, however—unlike virtually every other boarding school, they did not forbid pupils to speak their native language—indeed, Riggs and Williamson instructed pupils in both Dakota and English and, like their parents, held worship services in Dakota. Somewhat unintentionally, Riggs, the director of the Santee Normal Training School in Santee, Nebraska, emerged an advocate for the preservation of the Dakota language. When a sixteen-year-old Dakota boy named Ohiyesa encountered Alfred Riggs at Santee in 1874 as a new and uncertain student who spoke little English, he was surprised that Riggs "spoke the Sioux language very well." On Ohiyesa's first day in the school, Riggs presented him not only with an English primer but with two books in Dakota: translations of the Psalms and *Pilgrim's Progress*. Throughout the 1870s and 1880s, the federal government repeatedly threatened to cut off funding for the Santee school if Riggs and his staff persisted in teaching in both Dakota and English. Ultimately, Riggs decided to decline federal funding and continue to teach and worship in Dakota.[35] Ohiyesa, as Charles Eastman, went from Santee to Dartmouth to medical school at Boston University and had a long career as a physician, social reformer, and advocate for Indigenous rights and cultures. His advocacy for Indigenous people was made possible, in part, by the welcome that Alfred Riggs gave him at Santee in 1874 and by Riggs's rejection of the assimilationist ideology of other boarding schools. Riggs's protection of the Dakota language was a consequence of the kinship that the Dakota had extended to the missionaries at Lac qui Parle half a century earlier.

The welcome that the Dakota at Lac qui Parle had extended to Alfred Riggs in the 1830s was not exceptional. Through intermarriage, adoption, and alliance, Indigenous people and African American fugitives incorporated outsiders such as Riggs into their communities. Some white Americans, in turn, who believed in the corrupting influence of commerce, the efficacy of vaccination, the power of Christian faith, or the gradual moral improvement of humanity sought to incorporate Indigenous people and slaves into the parts of the fragmented American society that they represented. The vehicles of incorporation that white Americans used were particular to the nineteenth century: establishing a colony of freed slaves, regulating trade, vaccinating against smallpox in the interest of public health, and seeking converts to Christianity. These visions for an inclusive society are no longer our models for inclusivity insofar as they reflected the racism and sectarianism of the nineteenth century, but they demonstrate that nineteenth-century Americans were hardly united around the eliminationist, expansionist ideals of manifest destiny. Instead, visions of inclusion and of conquest existed in tension with each other in the nineteenth century.

Because of those tensions, the experiences of people such as Charles Eastman and John Horse were certainly not universal. In the second half of the nineteenth century, a powerful US state pushed most African Americans and Indigenous people to the poorest margins of American society. Segregation, debt peonage, and white supremacist violence kept most African Americans as second-class citizens. Indigenous people suffered from the impoverishing effect of having their reserves divided into individual allotments; few parents could avoid having their children vacuumed up into boarding schools which, unlike Santee, were determined to quash Indigenous cultures. And yet, at the height of its imperial power at the end of the nineteenth century, American society was not united in these efforts, just as it had been at odds about expansion earlier in the century. A single, unified American culture—unified around territorial expansion, slaveholding, market capitalism, or cultural assimilation, for instance—never existed. American cultures of the nineteenth century were diverse, complex, and contradictory—something that was readily apparent in the borderlands. The Dakota-language primers at the Santee school, the contraband camps of the Civil War, the resistance of the Seminoles in the swamps of southern Florida, the emigration of freedmen and freedwomen to Mexico and the West, and the absorption of white, Black, and Indigenous outsiders into Indigenous societies are the enduring legacies of the age of the borderlands.

NOTES

ABBREVIATIONS

GCSP George Champlin Sibley Papers, Missouri Historical Society, St. Louis

GMSS George and Mary Sibley Series, Mary Ambler Archives, Lindenwood University, St. Charles, MO

MHS Minnesota Historical Society, St. Paul

NARA National Archives and Records Administration, Washington, DC

OHS Ohio Historical Society, Columbus

INTRODUCTION

1. "Speech of Hon. John Q. Adams," 447; "More Bloodshed in Georgia," *Boston Observer and Religious Intelligencer*, February 26, 1835, 71.

2. "Speech of Hon. John Q. Adams," 447–51.

3. John Quincy Adams, diary and miscellaneous entries, May 25, 1836, John Quincy Adams Diary 48, Massachusetts Historical Society, Boston.

4. See Morrison, "Westward the Curse of Empire," 221–49; Morrison, "'New Territory versus No Territory,'" 25–51.

5. Lewis Cass, Detroit, to Henry Rowe Schoolcraft, Sault Ste. Marie, April 7, 1822, Henry Rowe Schoolcraft Papers, Huntington Library, San Marino, CA.

6. For American anxieties about the Louisiana Purchase, see Kastor, *Nation's Crucible*; Kastor, "'What Are the Advantages of Acquisition?,'" 1003–35. For powerful Indigenous nations, see Covington, *Seminoles of Florida*; Hämäläinen, *Comanche Empire*; Witgen, *Infinity of Nations*. For the fears of slave revolt, see Alan Taylor, *Internal Enemy*; Herschthal, "Slaves, Spaniards, and Subversion," 283–311; Audain, "Scheme to Desert," 40–56.

7. For sugar plantations in the Caribbean, see R. Dunn, *Sugar and Slaves*; Mintz, *Sweetness and Power*; Roberts, *Slavery and Enlightenment*. For the silver mines of New Spain and Peru,

see Brading, *Miners and Merchants in Bourbon Mexico*; Brading and Cross, "Colonial Silver Mining," 545–79; Tutino, *Making a New World*.

8. Erbig, *Where Caciques and Mapmakers Met*; Aron, *American Confluence*; Van Zandt, *Brothers among Nations*; Barr, *Peace Came in the Form of a Woman*; Duval, *Native Ground*; Gallay, *Indian Slave Trade*; Hinderaker, *Elusive Empires*; Usner, *Indians, Settlers, and Slaves*; R. White, *Middle Ground*.

9. According to the historian Christopher Bayly, between 1780 and 1830, the British Empire transformed from one in which Britain's "relationships with its dependencies was largely mediated through groups of complaisant mercantile elites and creoles" to one in which "the colonial state began seriously to discipline and control marginal groups and to create wider spheres for the exercise of state power." Bayly, *Imperial Meridian*, 4–6. The historian Steven Pincas has argued that these distinct forms of empire represented longstanding partisan differences in Britain between Tories, who preferred a commercial system, and Whigs, who preferred a territorial one. See Pincas, "Addison's Empire," 99–117.

10. Erbig, *Where Caciques and Mapmakers Met*, 1–15.

11. R. White, "Frederick Jackson Turner," 4.

12. Zebulon Pike, "Journal of a voyage to the source of the Mississippi in the years 1805 and 1806," January 3, 1806, in D. Jackson, *Journals of Zebulon Montgomery Pike*, 76.

13. See Schlesinger, *Age of Jackson*; Horsman, *Race and Manifest Destiny*; Drinnon, *Facing West*; Wallace, *Long, Bitter Trail*; Stephanson, *Manifest Destiny*; Hitela, *Manifest Design*; Greenberg, *Manifest Destiny and American Territorial Expansion*; Frymer, *Building an American Empire*; Dahl, *Empire of the People*; Grandin, *End of the Myth*.

14. Aron, *How the West Was Lost*, 130.

15. Rothman, *Slave Country*.

16. See Schlesinger, *Age of Jackson*, 427–28; Wilentz, *Rise of American Democracy*, esp. 562–63.

17. Watson, "Andrew Jackson's Populism," 218–39; Morrison, "Westward the Curse of Empire," 221–49; Morrison, "'New Territory versus No Territory,'" 25–51. For the Whigs, see Holt, *Rise and Fall of the American Whig Party*. For the agrarian program of the anti-expansionists, see Stoll, *Larding the Lean Earth*.

18. See Novak, *People's Welfare*; Novak, "Myth of the 'Weak' American State," 752–72; Witt, "Law and War in American History," 768–78; Gerstle, "State Both Strong and Weak," 779–85; J. Adams, "Puzzle of the American State," 786–91; Novak, "Long Live the Myth of the Weak State?," 792–800. An early form of this argument can be found in Hartz, *Liberal Tradition in America*. One historian who has argued that the federal government exercised a powerful interest in the early nineteenth-century West focused his attention on Ohio—the part of the West closest to the settled East. See Bergmann, *American National State*. Another conceded that in the West in the first half of the nineteenth century, the United States possessed "vague" powers that allowed some Americans to "imagine" a "prospect of expansion" and a "developmental vision" of the West. See Balogh, *Government Out of Sight*, 70, 75. 128, 167–205.

19. Stephen Long, "A General Description of the Country Traversed by the Exploring Expedition," in E. James, *Account of an Expedition*, 147–48.

20. Keating, *Narrative of an Expedition*, 238.

21. Newell, *Regular Army before the Civil War*, 7–8.

22. Tejada, "Unfree Soil."

23. US Congress, House, *Defence of Western Frontier*, 1–14. See also "On the Establishment of a Line of Posts and Military Roads for the Defence of the Western Frontiers Against the Indians," March 3, 1836, in *American State Papers: Military Affairs*, 6:149–55.

24. George C. Sibley, "Notes of an Official Excursion," box 1, GCSP.

25. For the importance of acknowledging the power of Indigenous nations in North American borderlands history, see Witgen, *Infinity of Nations*; and Wunder and Hämäläinen, "Of Lethal Places and Lethal Essays," 1229–34, a critique of Adelman and Aron, "From Borderlands to Borders," 814–41. See also Hämäläinen and Truett, "On Borderlands," 338–61. For the Comanche, see Hämäläinen, *Comanche Empire*; for the Osages, see Din and Nasatir, *Imperial Osages*; for the Navajo, see DeLay, *War of a Thousand Deserts*; for the Lakota and the Navajo, see A. C. Isenberg, "Between Mexico and the United States," 85–109.

26. See Sahlins, *Boundaries*, 276; Baud and Van Schendel, "Toward a Comparative History of Borderlands," 215.

27. The classic statement of how slaves lacked historical agency is Elkins, *Slavery*. More thoughtful considerations of the problem of agency are W. Johnson, "On Agency," 113–24; and Nash, "Agency of Nature," 67–69. See also Mintz, "Slave Life on Caribbean Sugar Plantations," 13. For settler colonialism, see Wolfe, "Land, Labor, and Difference," 866–905; Wolfe, "Settler Colonialism and the Elimination of the Native," 387–409; Veracini, "'Settler Colonialism,'" 313–33. For efforts to apply settler colonialism to North America, see Ostler, "'To Extirpate the Indians,'" 587–622; Ostler, *Surviving Genocide*; Madley, *American Genocide*. For a critique of settler colonialism from the perspective of environmental history, see A. C. Isenberg and Kessler, "Settler Colonialism and the Environmental History of the North American West," 57–66.

28. Oakes, *Ruling Race*, esp. 130–36; Oakes, *Slavery and Freedom*, esp. 130–34; Saxton, *Rise and Fall of the White Republic*; Slaughter, *Bloody Dawn*; Roediger, *Wages of Whiteness*; Ignatiev, *How the Irish Became White*; W. Johnson, *Soul by Soul*.

29. Mulroy, *Freedom on the Border*, 36–58.

30. See Hahn, *Nation under Our Feet*; Hoxie, "From Prison to Homeland," 1–24.

31. See Horsman, *Race and Manifest Destiny*; Drinnon, *Facing West*; Hitela, *Manifest Design*; Frymer, *Building an American Empire*; Grandin, *End of the Myth*.

32. See Judson, "Marking National Space on the Habsburg Austrian Borderlands," 122–35.

33. See Vickery, "'Herrenvolk' Democracy and Egalitarianism," 309–28; Fredrickson, *White Supremacy*, xi–xii. For Harrison, see Jortner, *Gods of Prophetstown*.

34. See Axtell, "White Indians of Colonial America," 55–88; Blu, *Lumbee Problem*; Demos, *Unredeemed Captive*; W. Hart, "Black 'Go-Betweens' and the Mutability of 'Race,'" 88–113; Blansett, "Intertribalism in the Ozarks," 475–97; Graybill, *Red and the White*; Jacoby, *Strange Career of William Ellis*.

35. For the Creeks and slavery, see Saunt, *New Order of Things*. Some Cherokees, Choctaws, and Chickasaws were also slaveholders. See Krauthamer, *Black Slaves, Indian Masters*.

36. See J. W. Hall, *Uncommon Defense*.

37. Strang, "Violence, Ethnicity, and Human Remains," 973–94.

38. See Hixson, *American Settler Colonialism*; Ostler, *Surviving Genocide*.

39. For removal, see Green, *Politics of Indian Removal*; Wallace, *Long, Bitter Trail*.

40. On borderlands as sites of projects and experiments, see K. Brown, *Biography of No Place*, 18–51; and Bartov and Weitz, *Shatterzone of Empires*, 1.

41. For an overview of the period, see Sellers, *Market Revolution*; Appleby, *Inheriting the Revolution*; Masur, *1831*; Howe, *What Hath God Wrought*. For changes in the economy, see Pessen, "Egalitarian Myth," 989–1034; Dublin, *Women at Work*; Prude, *Coming of Industrial Order*; Wilentz, *Chants Democratic*; Steinberg, *Nature Incorporated*; Sheriff, *Artificial River*; Bruegel, *Farm, Shop, Landing*; Stoll, *Larding the Lean Earth*; Mihm, *Nation of Counterfeiters*; Rockman, *Scraping By*. For the law, see Hurst, *Law and the Conditions of Freedom*; Horwitz, *Transformation of American Law*. For slavery, see G. Wright, *Political Economy*; W. Johnson, *Soul by Soul*. For mobility, see Thernstrom, *Poverty and Progress*; Oberly, "Westward Who?," 431–40. For women, gender, and the family, see Cott, *Bonds of Womanhood*; Ryan, *Cradle of the Middle Class*; Halttunen, *Confidence Men and Painted Women*; Stansell, *City of Women*; Ulrich, *Midwife's Tale*. For religious revivals, reform movements, and utopianism, see P. Johnson, *Shopkeeper's Millennium*; Rorabaugh, *Alcoholic Republic*; Nissenbaum, *Sex, Diet, and Debility*; N. O. Hatch, *Democratization of American Christianity*; P. Johnson and S. Wilentz, *Kingdom of Matthias*. For politics, see Ashworth, *"Agrarians" and "Aristocrats"*; N. Isenberg, *Sex and Citizenship*; Altschuler and Blumin, *Rude Republic*; Holt, *Rise and Fall of the American Whig Party*; Diemer, *Politics of Black Citizenship*.

42. See Horsman, *Race and Manifest Destiny*; Drinnon, *Facing Wes*; Stephanson, *Manifest Destiny*; Hitela, *Manifest Design*; Frymer, *Building an American Empire*; Grandin, *End of the Myth*.

43. O'Sullivan, "Annexation," 5–10.

44. Hudson, *Mistress of Manifest Destiny*.

45. Greenberg, *Manifest Destiny and American Territorial Expansion*, 1–2.

46. Greenberg, *Manifest Destiny and American Territorial Expansion*, 2. Greenberg's definition of manifest destiny as an American consensus is little changed from the way historians have understood the concept for a half-century. In 1980, the historian William Appleman Williams wrote in *Empire as a Way of Life* that Americans "liked empire," because it "provided them with renewable opportunities, wealth, and other benefits and satisfactions including a psychological sense of well-being and power." There were no dissenters, according to Williams: the whole US "citizenry was involved in the development, consolidation, and entrenchment of one particular outlook." W. A. Williams, *Empire as a Way of Life*, 10, 13. In recent decades, some historians have expanded the paradigm of manifest destiny from the 1840s into the first decades of the nineteenth century and even back to the pre-Revolutionary period. See Greene, "Colonial History and National History," 247–48; Owsley and Smith, *Filibusters and Expansionists*.

47. Richards, *Breakaway Americas*; Rodriguez, "'Greatest Nation on Earth,'" 50–83; Schlereth, "Privileges of Locomotion," 995–1020; Reséndéz, *Changing National Identities*.

48. For nineteenth-century Americans' contradictory and sometimes confused ideas about divine providence and the destiny of the nation, see Guyatt, *Providence and the Invention of the United States*.

49. See Sampson, *John L. O'Sullivan*.

50. Willson, *American History*, 497; Swinton, *First Lessons in Our Country's History*, 153–54; Ellis, *Epochs in American History*. See also Eggleston, *First Book in American History*, 190–200.

51. "More 'Manifest Destiny,'" *New York Times*, November 24, 1875, 4; "Manifest Destiny," *New York Times*, February 1, 1882, 4. See also "The Manifest Destiny Debate," *New York Times*, January 15, 1869, 4; "'Manifest Destiny' in the South Pacific," *New York Times*, July 16, 1875, 4.

Notes to Introduction

For a critique of Ottoman belligerence toward Russia using the term "manifest destiny," see "The Impending War," *Chicago Daily Tribune*, April 10, 1877, 4. For a critique of the United States, Japan, Great Britain, and other imperial powers in China, see "Manifest Destiny of China," *New York Tribune*, June 28, 1900, 3; for a critique of Russian imperialism in China using the term, see "'Manifest Destiny' in Russia," *New York Tribune*, January 2, 1901, 8. For inventive uses of the term, see "Resurrexit!," *Chicago Daily Tribune*, October 9, 1881, 17; "Our Suburban Neighbors," *New York Times*, November 23, 1874, 4; "Bridges and Tunnels," *New York Times*, May 13, 1883, 8; "Manifest Destiny," *Los Angeles Times*, January 1, 1887, 20; "Manifest Destiny—The Star of Empire—Territorial Expansion," *Los Angeles Times*, December 14, 1888, 4; "The Anti-Saloon Republicans," *Washington Post*, May 3, 1888, 4.

52. Roosevelt, *Winning of the West*, 4:262.

53. Roosevelt, *Winning of the West*, 1:vii, x. For similar sentiments, see W. Wilson, *History of the American People*, 4:256–58; Dunning et al., *English Race and America's Making*. See also Slotkin, "Nostalgia and Progress," 608–37.

54. Turner, "Significance of the Frontier," 199–227.

55. See E. D. Adams, *Power of Ideals in American History*; McElroy, *Winning of the Far West*; Fuess, *Life of Caleb Cushing*; Weinberg, *Manifest Destiny*.

56. Pratt, "Origin of 'Manifest Destiny,'" 795–98.

57. See Butler, "Enthusiasm Described and Decried," 305–25; Rodgers, "In Search of Progressivism," 113–32.

58. For the fear of slave revolts, see Sharples, *World That Fear Made*. For narratives that emphasized the victimhood of white Americans who died at the hands of Indigenous people—and thus rationalized further US expansion—see R. White, "Frederick Jackson Turner," 7–66.

59. On narratives, see Cronon, "Place for Stories," 1347–76.

CHAPTER 1

1. *Georgia Gazette* (Savannah), May 21, 1789, in Windley, *Runaway Slave Advertisements*, 4:166. For the Morels, see Groves, "Beaulieu Plantation," 204. For the plantations of coastal Georgia, see Stewart, *"What Nature Suffers to Groe."*

2. See, for instance, Foner, *Gateway to Freedom*. Blight, *Passages to Freedom*, devotes only one of its fifteen chapters to Florida.

3. Spitzer, "Spanish Cimarron," 145–47. See also Schwaller, *African Maroons*, 21. William Simmons, a South Carolina physician who toured Florida in 1822, wrote in his memoir of his journey that "the term *Seminole*, when strictly translated, means, a 'Wild People,' or *Outsettlers*; the ancestors of the tribe having detached themselves from the main body of the Creeks, and dwelt remotely, wherever the inducements of more abundant game, or greater scope for freedom of action, might casually lead them; pursuing, in this respect, a course of life, analogous to the habits of many of our western borderers, at the present day. They were thus, in fact, *Emigrants* from the Creeks." Simmons, *Notices of East Florida*, 54–55. Thomas Woodward, who also dwelled among the Creek in the first decades of the nineteenth century, wrote in 1858 that "'Siminole,' in the Creek language, signifies wild, or runaway, or outlaw." T. S. Woodward, *Woodland Reminiscences of the Creek*, 25.

4. For *grand marronage*—flight to permanent freedom—see Price, *Maroon Societies*; M. C. Campbell, *Maroons of Jamaica*; Usner, *Indians, Settlers, and Slaves*, 58–59, 107–8; Jane G. Landers, "*Cimarron* and Citizen," in Landers and Robinson, *Slaves, Subjects, and Subversives*, 111–45; Schwaller, "Contested Conquests," 609–38; Schwaller, *African Maroons*. For *petit marronage*—taking flight as intermittent respite from slavery—see Nevius, *City of Refuge*.

5. Grandin, *End of the Myth*, 55; Greenberg, *Manifest Destiny and American Territorial Expansion*, 8; Remini, *Andrew Jackson and His Indian Wars*, 165–66; Owsley and Smith, *Filibusters and Expansionists*, 16.

6. For the Spanish effort to trade Florida for Gibraltar in 1720, see D. J. Weber, *Spanish Frontier in North America*, 176–77. For the Spanish desire to acquire Gibraltar from Britain in 1783 rather than Florida, see José Moñino y Redondo, Count of Floridablanca, to Pedro Pablo Abarcca de Bolea, Count of Aranda, January 2, 1783, in Lockey, *East Florida*, 41–44. In the 1810s, Florida was peripheral to the centers of Spanish power in the New World; Texas, however, was a buffer that protected the economic center of New Spain: the silver-mining region of Bajío. See Tutino, "Globalizing the Comanche Empire," 67–74.

7. In seventeenth- and eighteenth-century Spanish America, *ladinos*—Spanish-speaking, Catholic slaves who tended to be urban domestic workers or artisans—had access to the cash economy and could often earn enough to purchase their freedom. Spanish American colonies thus typically came to possess a combination of both slaves and free Blacks. See Landers, "Africans in Spanish Colonies," 84–103. For the brutality of the work regime on plantations in the British Caribbean and the US South, see Roberts, "Whip and the Hoe," 108–30.

8. "The Case of a Negro Named Frank," September 11, 1784; and Francis Philip Fatio and John Leslie to Vicente Manuel de Zéspedes, October 5, 1784, in Lockey, *East Florida*, 270–71, 284–85.

9. See Fede, "Legitimized Violent Slave Abuse in the American South," 93–150.

10. Simmons, *Notices of East Florida*, 42.

11. Landers, "Spanish Sanctuary," 296–313.

12. Giddings, *Exiles of Florida*, 2–3.

13. Jane G. Landers, "Southern Passage: The Forgotten Route to Freedom in Florida," in Blight, *Passages to Freedom*, 117–31; Landers, "Transforming Bondsmen into Vassals," 126.

14. The enslaved people who led the largest slave uprising in South Carolina—the Stono Rebellion in 1739—were marching toward Florida when the South Carolina militia overtook them and defeated them. See P. Wood, *Black Majority*, 308–23.

15. TePaske, "Fugitive Slave," 1–12; Riordan, "Finding Freedom in Florida," 24–43; Mulroy, *Freedom on the Border*, 8–9.

16. Spain's overriding ambition was to reclaim from Britain not Florida but Gibraltar. See Moñino y Redondo to Abarcca de Bolea, January 2, 1783, in Lockey, *East Florida*, 41–44.

17. Giddings, *Exiles of Florida*, 20–21.

18. Antonio Fernández to Vicente Manuel de Zéspedes, August 2, 1784, in Lockey, *East Florida*, 339. See also J. L. Wright, "Blacks in British East Florida," 440.

19. Clavin, *Aiming for Pensacola*, 25. See also Vicente Manuel de Zéspedes to José de Ezpeleta, January 28, 1785, in Lockey, *East Florida*, 451.

20. Fernández to Zéspedes, August 2, 1784, in Lockey, *East Florida*, 339.

21. Giddings, *Exiles of Florida*, 12–13.

22. Landers, "Spanish Sanctuary," 311–12.

23. "Royal Order," November 4, 1784; James Hume to Patrick Tonyn, July 26, 1784; "Memorial of Samuel Farley," September 24, 1784; Patrick Tonyn to Vicente Manuel de Zéspedes, October 11, 1784, in Lockey, *East Florida*, 304, 329, 366–67, 375.

24. *Gazette of the State of Georgia* (Savannah), June 19, 1783; *Georgia State Gazette or Independent Register* (Augusta), October 21, 1786; *Gazette of the State of Georgia* (Savannah), October 16, 1788; and *Georgia Gazette* (Savannah), December 10, 1789, in Windley, *Runaway Slave Advertisements*, 4:106, 160, 173, 182.

25. For a comparison of the West African slave trade and the North American fur trade (which functioned similarly to the North American slave trade), see Wolf, *Europe and the People without History*.

26. Covington, *Seminoles of Florida*, 3.

27. Gallay, *Indian Slave Trade*, 200, 294–99.

28. Kelton, *Epidemics and Enslavement*, 143–49, 184–85.

29. Thornton, *American Indian Holocaust and Survival*, 79.

30. Ramsey, *Yamasee War*; Kelton, *Epidemics and Enslavement*, 202–20.

31. P. Wood, *Black Majority*, 142–55.

32. Saunt, *New Order of Things*, 12; Covington, *Seminoles of Florida*, 5.

33. Saunt, *New Order of Things*, 13.

34. Swanson, *Indian Tribes of North America*, 111.

35. Knight, "Formation of the Creeks," 374.

36. Ethridge, *Creek Country*, 32.

37. Porter, "Founder of the 'Seminole Nation,'" 362–84; Porter, "Cowkeeper Dynasty," 341–49.

38. Silver, *New Face on the Countryside*, 92–93.

39. R. White, *Roots of Dependency*, 99.

40. Thomas Forbes to Bernardo del Campo, September 28, 1783, in Lockey, *East Florida*, 161–63.

41. Richter, *Facing East from Indian Country*, 174. For the eighteenth-century commercial revolution in North America, see Breen, *Marketplace of Revolution*; E. A. Perkins, "Consumer Frontier," 486–510.

42. There were over 100,000 head of cattle in South Carolina by 1750. See Saunt, *New Order of Things*, 47; Carson, "Native Americans, the Market Revolution, and Culture Change," 1–18. There were 20,000 cattle in Spanish Florida by 1700. See Jordan, *North American Cattle-Ranching Frontiers*, 103, 106. For Indigenous people's adaptation to cattle-raising, see R. White, *Roots of Dependency*, 99–101; Silver, *New Face on the Countryside*, 196. For livestock in colonial North America, see V. Anderson, *Creatures of Empire*.

43. Simmons, *Notices of East Florida*, 51.

44. Mulroy, *Freedom on the Border*, 6–7; Covington, *Seminoles of Florida*, 5, 26.

45. W. Bartram, *Travels*, 188–92.

46. W. Bartram, *Travels*, 210, 253–58, 436.

47. John Devereux DeLacy to Thomas Jefferson, December 18, 1801, in *Papers of Thomas Jefferson*, 36:135–57.

48. W. Bartram, *Travels*, 183–84.

49. Giddings, *Exiles of Florida*, 97.

50. Simmons, *Notices of East Florida*, 49–50.

51. Giddings, *Exiles of Florida*, 79, 97.

52. McCall, *Letters from the Frontier*, 160.

53. W. Bartram, *Travels*,184.

54. Simmons, *Notices of East Florida*, 76.

55. W. Bartram, *Travels*, 162.

56. Vicente Manuel de Zéspedes to Bernardo de Gálvez, August 16, 1784, in Lockey, *East Florida*, 255; Baynton, *Authentic Memoirs of William Augustus Bowles*, 22; Giddings, *Exiles of Florida*, 97–98.

57. J. Bartram, "Diary of a Journey through the Carolinas, Georgia, and Florida," 54–55.

58. Stork, *Description of East-Florida*, i.

59. Proclamation of James Grant, October 7, 1763, quoted in Stork, *Description of East-Florida*, v.

60. Stork, *Description of East-Florida*, 8, 14, 23–24, 26.

61. W. Bartram, *Travels*, 60, 206, 209, 251.

62. Le Conte, "Observations on the Soil and Climate of East Florida," 30.

63. Schoepf, *Travels in the Confederation*, 239.

64. McAlister, "William Augustus Bowles and the State of Muskogee," 317–18. For "English mestizo," see Vicente Manuel de Zéspedes to Bernardo de Galvez, June 12, 1785, in Lockey, *East Florida*, 557.

65. Alexander McGillivray to Vicente Manuel de Zéspedes, August 22, 1785, in Lockey, *East Florida*, 682–83.

66. Vicente Manuel de Zéspedes to Bernardo de Gálvez, August 16, 1784, in Lockey, *East Florida*, 254. See also Thomas Forbes to Bernardo del Campo, September 28, 1783; Vicente Manuel de Zéspedes to Bernardo de Gálvez, March 22, 1784; Bernardo de Gálvez to José de Gálvez, May 22, 1784; Vicente Manuel de Zéspedes to Bernardo de Gálvez, June 12, 1785; and Vicente Manuel de Zéspedes to José de Gálvez, September 16, 1785, in Lockey, *East Florida*, 161–63, 188–89, 194–95, 556–58, 724–26.

67. "Address of the Principal Inhabitants to Governor Tonyn," June 6, 1783, in Lockey, *East Florida*, 114–15.

68. "Memorial of Panton, Leslie, and Company," July 31, 1784, in Lockey, *East Florida*, 257–60. In 1784, Zéspedes was aware that McGillivray was an "associate" of Panton, Leslie, and Company. See Vicente Manuel de Zéspedes to Arturo O'Neill, September 12, 1784, in Lockey, *East Florida*, 274.

69. "Extract of a Letter to Captain Bissett in London," May 20, 1783, in Lockey, *East Florida*, 173.

70. Francis Philip Fatio to Bernardo de Gálvez, March 18, 1783, in Lockey, *East Florida*, 480–82.

71. Schoepf, *Travels in the Confederation*, 2:231.

72. Vicente Manuel de Zéspedes to Bernardo de Gálvez, August 9, 1784; Patrick Tonyn to Thomas Townshend, May 15, 1783; "Memorial of Grey Elliott," July 5, 1783; Patrick Tonyn to Evan Nepean, October 1, 1783; Patrick Tonyn to Lord North, November 1, 1783; and Patrick Tonyn to Vicente Manuel de Zéspedes, July 5, 1784, in Lockey, *East Florida*, 96–99, 135–36, 167–68, 174–76, 214–16, 249.

73. Patrick Tonyn to Archibald McArthur, May 21, 1784, in Lockey, *East Florida*, 288–89.

74. "To Thomas Jefferson from John Devereux DeLacy, 18 December 1801," *Papers of Thomas Jefferson*, 36:135–57.

75. For Bowles's life, see Baynton, *Authentic Memoirs of William Augustus Bowles*; J. L. Wright, *William Augustus Bowles*.

76. The historian Eliga Gould has called Bowles's State of Muskogee a "postcolonial" state. See Gould, "Independence and Interdependence," 729–52.

77. McAlister, "Marine Forces of William Augustus Bowles," 4–5.

78. *Record in the Case of Colin Mitchell and Others, versus the United States*, 19, 24.

79. McAlister, "Marine Forces," 5; J. L. Wright, *William Augustus Bowles*, 62–108.

80. McAlister, "William Augustus Bowles and the State of Muskogee," 322–23; J. L. Wright, *William Augustus Bowles*, 121. For the 1790 Treaty of New York between the Creek and the United States, see J. L. Wright, "Creek-American Treaty of 1790," 379–400.

81. "Bowles' Proclamation of War," April 5, 1800, in McAlister, "Marine Forces," 6.

82. Benjamin Hawkins to Henry Dearborn, July 18, 1801, in C. L. Grant, *Letters, Journals, and Writings of Benjamin Hawkins*, 2:361.

83. "Conditions in the 'State of Muskogee,'" in McAlister, "Marine Forces," 11.

84. Saunt, *New Order of Things*, 207–13.

85. Din, "William Augustus Bowles on the Georgia Frontier," 305–32.

86. In a letter to the *Nassau Gazette*, Bowles made clear that when the Muskogee navy captured a ship, "the Cargoes &c are sold for the benefit of the Captors and the state. The Captain & Crew drawing two-thirds of all Prize Money & the State one." See "Conditions in the 'State of Muskogee,'" in McAlister, "Marine Forces," 10–11. The US Navy continued to award prize money to sailors through the Spanish-American War; the British Navy continued to do so through World War I.

87. For the seizure of Bowles, see Braund and Braund, "Journal of John Forbes" 514–16. See also J. L. Wright, *William Augustus Bowles*, 153–71; Pound, *Benjamin Hawkins*, 191–96.

88. Benjamin Hawkins to James Madison, July 11, 1803, in C. L. Grant, *Letters, Journals, and Writings of Benjamin Hawkins*, 2:458.

89. J. B. Miller, "Rebellion in East Florida," 173–86; O'Riordan, "1795 Rebellion in East Florida."

90. McMichael, *Atlantic Loyalties*.

91. Cusick, *Other War of 1812*. See also Cusick, "Some Thoughts on Spanish East and West Florida as Borderlands," 133–56.

92. James Innerarity to Alexander Gordon, July 27, 1812, in Innerarity, "Letters of James Innerarity," 136–37. For James and John Innerarity, see T. C. Kennedy, "Sibling Stewards of a Commercial Empire," 259–89.

93. For the War of 1812, see Pratt, *Expansionists of 1812*; Horsman, *Causes of the War of 1812*; Edmunds, *Shawnee Prophet*; Stagg, *Mr. Madison's War*; Dowd, *Spirted Resistance*; Remini, *Andrew Jackson and His Indian Wars*; Alan Taylor, *Civil War of 1812*; Cleves et al., "Interchange: The War of 1812," 520–55; Maass, "'Difficult to Relinquish Territory Which Had Been Conquered,'" 70–97. For impressment, see Brunsman, *Evil Necessity*; Gilje, *Free Trade and Sailors' Rights in the War of 1812*.

94. Alan Taylor, *Civil War of 1812*, 166–73, 187–95, 208–33, 240–67, 387–407.

95. Saunt, *New Order of Things*, 249–72.

96. Remini, *Andrew Jackson and His Indian Wars*, 62–79.

97. See Simmons, *Notices of East Florida*, 41–42.

98. See Andrew Jackson to James Monroe, November 14, 1814, in Bassett, *Correspondence of Andrew Jackson*, 2:99.

99. John Innerarity, Narrative of British Operations in the Floridas, 1815, Helen H. Cruzat Collection, P.K. Yonge Library of Florida History, University of Florida, Gainesville. See also "Pensacola," *Niles Weekly Register* (Baltimore, MD), January 7, 1815, 303.

100. See Clavin, *Battle of Negro Fort.*

101. Benjamin Hawkins to Andrew Jackson, August 12, 1815, in C. L. Grant, *Letters, Journals, and Writings of Benjamin Hawkins*, 2:748.

102. Such fears were common in the US South. See Sharples, *World That Fear Made.*

103. David Holmes to Jackson, June 19, 1814, in Bassett, *Correspondence of Andrew Jackson*, 2:8.

104. "Milledgeville," *Niles Weekly Register* (Baltimore, MD), January 7, 1815, 303.

105. For runaways to Prospect Bluff, see Clavin, *Battle of Negro Fort*, 90–92; Clavin, "Runaway Slave Advertisements in Antebellum Florida," 426–43.

106. Edmund Pendleton Gaines to Andrew Jackson, May 14, 1816; Ferdinand Louis Amelung to Andrew Jackson, June 4, 1816, in Moser et al., *Papers of Andrew Jackson*, 4:30–31, 39–40.

107. Ferdinand Louis Amelung to Andrew Jackson, June 4, 1816, in Bassett, *Correspondence of Andrew Jackson*, 2:242–43.

108. Benjamin Hawkins to William H. Crawford, February 16, 1816, in C. L. Grant, *Letters, Journals, and Writings of Benjamin Hawkins*, 2:773–74.

109. William H. Crawford to Andrew Jackson. March 15, 1816, in Moser et al., *Papers of Andrew Jackson*, 4:15–16.

110. Andrew Jackson to Mauricio de Zuñiga, April 23, 1816, in Moser et al., *Papers of Andrew Jackson*, 4:22–23.

111. Mauricio de Zuñiga to Andrew Jackson. May 26, 1816, in Moser et al., *Papers of Andrew Jackson*, 4:42.

112. Andrew Jackson to Edmund P. Gaines, April 8, 1816, in Bassett, *Correspondence of Andrew Jackson*, 2:238–39.

113. Benjamin Hawkins to William H. Crawford, April 2, 1816, in C. L. Grant, *Letters, Journals, and Writings of Benjamin Hawkins*, 2:779.

114. Benjamin Hawkins to Tustunnuggee Hopoie, April 30, 1816, in C. L. Grant, *Letters, Journals, and Writings of Benjamin Hawkins*, 2:784.

115. Benjamin Hawkins to Andrew Jackson, March 21, 1816, in C. L. Grant, *Letters, Journals, and Writings of Benjamin Hawkins*, 2:778. The Seminoles swiftly rejected that delegation, which included Tustunnuggee Hopoie; he fled back to Hawkins.

116. Benjamin Hawkins to Mauricio de Zuñiga, May 24, 1816, in C. L. Grant, *Letters, Journals, and Writings of Benjamin Hawkins*, 2:789.

117. For a survey of the dispute over the number killed, see Clavin, *Battle of Negro Fort*, 123, 227. Clavin considers the higher estimates more reliable than Dumont and Innerarity, whom he calls "Spanish sources," as "the Spanish acquired their information second-hand."

118. Edmund Pendleton Gaines to "the Seminole Chiefs," August 1817, in *American State Papers: Foreign Relations*, 4:585–86.

119. See Benjamin Hawkins to John Houston McIntosh, November 26, 1814; Benjamin Hawkins to Jackson, May 5, 1815; Benjamin Hawkins to Thomas Pinckney, May 12, 1815;

and Edward Nicolls to Benjamin Hawkins, April 28, 1815, in C. L. Grant, *Letters, Journals, and Writings of Benjamin Hawkins*, 2:706–7, 725–26, 729–30. See also Bolek to José Maria Coppinger, c. 1817, in *American State Papers: Military Affairs*, 1:727.

120. Report of the Senate Committee, February 24, 1819, in *American State Papers: Military Affairs*, 1:739.

121. Edmund Pendleton Gaines to Andrew Jackson, November 21, 1817; and Edmund Pendleton Gaines to Crawford, November 26, 1817, in *American State Papers: Indian Affairs*, 2:160.

122. Andrew Jackson to William H. Crawford, September 7, 1816, in Moser et al., *Papers of Andrew Jackson*, 4:60–61.

123. John C. Calhoun to Andrew Jackson, December 26, 1817; and Andrew Jackson to James Monroe, January 6, 1818, in Bassett, *Correspondence of Andrew Jackson*, 2:341–42, 345–46.

124. James Monroe to Andrew Jackson, July 19, 1818, in Moser et al., *Papers of Andrew Jackson*, 4:226. While US officials contended that they were justified in their invasion of Florida because Spain was too weak to police the Seminoles, a letter that Kinache and Bolek wrote to Charles Cameron, the British governor of the Bahamas, following the attack on Fowltown was closer to the truth. The Seminole leaders had appealed without success to the Spanish to protect them from American attacks, or at least to provide them with arms and ammunition to defend themselves. "We have applied to the Spanish officer at the fort of St. Marks, but his small supply prevented his being able to assist us." Kinache and Bolek to Charles Cameron, undated, in *American State Papers: Military Affairs*, 1:724.

125. M. L. Woodward, "Spanish Army," 586–607.

126. James Monroe to Andrew Jackson, July 19, 1818, in Moser et al., *Papers of Andrew Jackson*, 4:226. Moreover, Calhoun warned Jackson that the United States could defeat Spain, "but such a war would not continue long without involving other parties; and it certainly would in a few years be an English war." John C. Calhoun to Andrew Jackson, September 8, 1818, in Bassett, *Correspondence of Andrew Jackson*, 2:393.

127. James Monroe, "Spain and the Seminole Indians," March 25, 1818, in *American State Papers: Foreign Relations*, 4:183.

128. Young, "Topographical Memoir," 140–44.

129. Report of the Senate Committee, February 24, 1819, in *American State Papers: Military Affairs*, 1:741.

130. Andrew Jackson to John C. Calhoun, April 8, 1818, in Moser et al., *Papers of Andrew Jackson*, 4:189–90.

131. Andrew Jackson to Francisco Caso y Luengo, April 6, 1818; and Caso y Luengo to Andrew Jackson, April 7, 1818, in Moser et al., *Papers of Andrew Jackson*, 4:186–89.

132. Andrew Jackson to John C. Calhoun, April 8, 1818, in Moser et al., *Papers of Andrew Jackson*, 4:190.

133. Andrew Jackson to John C. Calhoun, April 20, 1818, in Moser et al., *Papers of Andrew Jackson*, 4:193–95.

134. For the trial, see "Minutes of the proceedings of a special court," April 26, 1818, in *American State Papers: Military Affairs*, 1:721–22, 728–35.

135. Andrew Jackson to John C. Calhoun, May 5, 1818, in Moser et al., *Papers of Andrew Jackson*, 4:197–99.

136. Andrew Jackson to José Masot, May 23, 1818, in Moser et al., *Papers of Andrew Jackson*, 4:208. Jackson had to have known that the accusation that 500 Indigenous people were in Pensacola was false. On November 9, 1817, Gaines had written to Jackson that the number of Indigenous people at Pensacola was about 35. Edmund Pendleton Gaines to Andrew Jackson, November 9, 1817, in *American State Papers: Military Affairs*, 1:686.

137. Andrew Jackson to Edmund Pendleton Gaines, August 7, 1818, in "Report of the Senate Committee," February 24, 1819, in *American State Papers: Military Affairs*, 1:744; Jackson to Calhoun, November 28, 1818, in *American State Papers: Military Affairs*, 1:752.

138. John C. Calhoun to Edmund Pendleton Gaines, August 14, 1818, in *American State Papers: Military Affairs*, 1:696.

139. Luis de Onís to James Monroe, December 30, 1815; Onís to Monroe, January 2, 1816; Onís to Monroe, January 19, 1816; Onís to Monroe, February 22, 1816; Monroe to Onís, June 10, 1816; Monroe to Onís January 14, 1817; Onís to Monroe, January 16, 1817; Onís to Monroe, February 10, 1817; Adams to Onís, January 16, 1818; Onís to Adams, January 24, 1818; Onís to Adams, June 17, 1818; Onís to Adams, June 24, 1818; Onís to Adams, July 8, 1818; Onís to Adams July 21, 1818; Adams to Onís, July 23, 1818; Onís to Adams, August 5, 1818; Onís to Adams October 24, 1818; and Adams to Onís, October 31, 1818, in *American State Papers: Foreign Affairs*, 4:422–24, 426–31, 437–41; 463–68, 495–98, 504–6, 529–30.

140. S. Perkins, *General Jackson's Conduct in the Seminole War*, 22–23.

141. Giddings, *Exiles of Florida*, 68–70.

142. Horatio Dexter, "Observations on the Seminole Indians," 1823, RG 75, M 271, roll 4, Letters Received, Office of Indian Affairs, NARA.

143. Weik, "Role of Ethnogenesis," 206–38.

144. Report from the Committee on Military Affairs, January 12, 1819; and Report of the Senate Committee, February 24, 1819, in *American State Papers: Military Affairs*, 1:735, 740–41.

145. Grandin, *End of the Myth*, 55.

146. Harris, "Cession of Florida," 223–38.

147. Giddings, *Exiles of Florida*, 83. The Army officer James McCall, who met Abraham in Florida in 1826, claimed in 1836 that Abraham "was once a slave of Dr. Sierra of Pensacola." McCall, *Letters from the Frontiers*, 302. This seems unlikely, as Abraham spoke no Spanish but only English and one of the Seminole languages. See Porter, "Negro Abraham," 2–3.

148. See Anthony Rutant, sworn statement July 7, 1835, in *American State Papers: Military Affairs*, 4:498.

149. McCall, *Letters from the Frontier*, 160.

150. Giddings, *Exiles of Florida*, 83. See also Porter, "Abraham," 102–16.

CHAPTER 2

1. Faragher et al., *Out of Many*, 186; Foner, *Give Me Liberty!*, 262. See also Balogh, *Government Out of Sight*, 168–69.

2. For a synopsis of the negotiations to buy Louisiana, see McCoy, *Elusive Republic*, 196–99; Baptist, *Half Has Never Been Told*, 44–49. For Spain's disputation of the borders, see D. J. Weber, *Spanish Frontier in North America*, 292–93.

3. Sibley, "Account of Louisiana," 89.

4. Murrin, "Great Inversion," 409; North, *Economic Growth of the United States*, 34, 49; D. R. Meyer, *Roots of American Industrialization*, 94–95; Larkin, *Reshaping of Everyday Life*, 8; M. Williams, *Americans and Their Forests*, 101–2.

5. Madison, "First Annual Message," 462.

6. Sellers, *Market Revolution*; Stokes and Conway, *Market Revolution in America*; Gilje, "Rise of Capitalism in the Early Republic," 159–81; Larson, *Market Revolution in America*.

7. Bushman, "Markets and Composite Farms in Early America," 351–74; Breen, "Empire of Goods," 467–99; Breen, "'Baubles of Britain,'" 73–104; Breen, *Marketplace of Revolution*; E. A. Perkins, "Consumer Frontier," 486–510.

8. Albert Gallatin, "Roads and Canals," April 4, 1808, in *American State Papers: Miscellaneous*, 1:724–41.

9. Burlingame, "Buffalo in Trade and Commerce," 266; Haeger, "Business Strategy and Practice in the Early Republic," 183–202; Clayton, "Growth and Economic Significance of the Fur Trade," 214.

10. Thomas Jefferson to William Henry Harrison, February 27, 1803; Thomas Jefferson to Andrew Jackson, February 16, 1803, in Lipscomb and Bergh, *Writings of Thomas Jefferson*, 10:357–60, 369–70.

11. Wallace, "Obtaining Lands," 25–41.

12. English speakers have used the term *factor* to mean a business agent as early as the fifteenth century. By the early seventeenth century, the East India Company used the term to refer to employees who managed trading posts. In the late seventeenth century, Royal African Company posts on the West African coast that traded in enslaved people were known as *factories*. By the late eighteenth century, when the US factory system began, the term *factor* had a common usage as the manager of a trading house.

13. For the factory system, see Coman, "Government Factories," 368–88; Way, "United States Factory System," 220–35; Plaisance, "Chickasaw Bluffs Factory," 41–56; Peake, *History of the United States Indian Factory System*; Craig, "Fur Trade around Ft. Wayne."

14. See Din and Nasatir, *Imperial Osages*; Rollings, *Osage*; Edwards, *Osage Women and Empire*; DuVal, *Native Ground*, 110. For the Pawnees, see R. White, *Roots of Dependency*, 147–211.

15. Vehik, "Dhegiha Origins and Plains Archaeology," 231–52; DuVal, *Native Ground*, 3.

16. For the Lower Missouri as a meeting point in the eighteenth and nineteenth centuries, see Aron, *American Confluence*.

17. Auguste Chouteau, December 8, 1816, GCSP.

18. For the Pueblo Revolt, see Spicer, *Cycles of Conquest*, 162; John, *Storms Brewed in Other Men's Worlds*, 98–103.

19. Hilliard, "Equestrian Pictograph in Western Arkansas," 327–30. For the diffusion of horses from New Mexico into the Great Plains, see A. C. Isenberg, *Destruction of the Bison*, 39–41.

20. Lettre de du Tisné à M. de Bienville, Datée des Kascakias, le 22 Novembre 1719, in Margry, *Découvertes et établissements des Français dans l'ouest*, 313–15.

21. George C. Sibley, "Notes of an Official Excursion," box 1, GCSP.

22. Zebulon Pike, "Journal of the Western Expedition," September 14, 1806, in D. Jackson, *Journals of Zebulon Montgomery Pike*, 1:317. The cabrie is *Antilocapra americana*, the pronghorn antelope. For Pike see Orsi, *Citizen Explorer*.

23. George C. Sibley, "Notes of an Official Excursion."

24. Zénon Trudeau to Manuel Gayoso de Lemos y Amorin, January 15, 1798, in Nasatir, *Before Lewis and Clark*, 2:539. See also "Distribution of Missouri Trading Posts, May 1–3, 1794," in Nasatir, *Before Lewis and Clark*, 1:209–11; Zénon Trudeau to Gayoso de Lemos, December 20, 1797, in Nasatir, *Before Lewis and Clark*, 2:529–32. For an 1803 estimate of the scale of the Osage trade in furs that is almost the same as that of Trudeau, see de Finiels, *Account of Upper Louisiana*, 90.

25. "Literary News: Illinois, August 1, 1790," in Nasatir, *Before Lewis and Clark*, 1:133–34.

26. Manuel Pérez to Esteban Rodriguez Miró, November 8, 1791, in Nasatir, *Before Lewis and Clark*, 1:149–50.

27. Esteban Rodriguez Miró to the Ministerio de Hacienda de Indias, August 7, 1792, in Nasatir, *Before Lewis and Clark*, 1:159. For the English control of trade on the Upper Mississippi, see Zénon Trudeau to Gayoso de Lemos, December 20, 1797, in Nasatir, *Before Lewis and Clark*, 2:528.

28. Manuel Pérez to Esteban Rodriguez Miró, April 5, 1791, in Nasatir, *Before Lewis and Clark*, 1:145.

29. Hammon, *My Father, Daniel Boone*, 120, 122. For Boone, see Faragher, *Daniel Boone*.

30. Wiegers, "Proposal for Indian Slave Trading," 187–202.

31. Ekberg, *Stealing Indian Women*, 13–59. See also Rushforth, "'A Little Flesh We Offer You,'" 777–808.

32. Zénon Trudeau to Gayoso de Lemos, December 20, 1797, in Nasatir, *Before Lewis and Clark*, 2:526.

33. Zénon Trudeau to Francisco Luis Héctor de Carondelet, May 6, 1793, in Nasatir, *Before Lewis and Clark*, 1:172–73.

34. Luis Héctor de Carondelet to Zénon Trudeau, May 11, 1796, in Nasatir, *Before Lewis and Clark*, 2:426.

35. De Finiels, *Account of Upper Louisiana*, 90.

36. Thomas Jefferson to Henry Dearborn, July 13, 1804, in D. Jackson, *Letters of the Lewis and Clark Expedition*, 1:199–202.

37. Thwaites, *Original Journals of the Lewis and Clark Expedition*, 1:36–37.

38. Rollings, *Osage*, 183–84; A. C. Isenberg, *Destruction of the Bison*, 60.

39. Thwaites, *Original Journals of the Lewis and Clark Expedition*, 1:109–10.

40. Charles de Hault de Lassus to Casa Calvo, April 3, 1801, in Nasatir, *Before Lewis and Clark*, 2:631.

41. See Rushforth, *Bonds of Alliance*.

42. Pike, "Journal of the Western Expedition," August 15, 1806, in D. Jackson, *Journals of Zebulon Montgomery Pike*, 1:304. Pike's "Dissertation on Louisiana," 1810; James Wilkinson to Henry Dearborn, August 2, 1806; and Deposition of William T. Lamme, in D. Jackson, *Journals of Zebulon Montgomery Pike*, 2:33, 128, 163.

43. Zénon Trudeau to Luis Héctor de Carondelet, April 18, 1795, in Nasatir, *Before Lewis and Clark*, 1:320–21.

44. Summary by Charles de Hault de Lassus of Trade Licenses Issued at St. Louis, 1799–1804; Charles de Hault de Lassus to Gayoso de Lemos, October 28, 1799; Manuel Lisa and Others to Manuel de Salcedo, June 4, 1802; and Concession by Manuel de Salcedo to

Manuel Lisa and Others, June 12, 1802, in Nasatir, *Before Lewis and Clark*, 2:590–92, 605–6, 577–680, 687–89.

45. Charles de Hault De Lassus to Manuel de Salcedo, August 28, 1802, in Nasatir, *Before Lewis and Clark*, 2:705.

46. James B. Wilkinson's "Report," April 6, 1807; and Pike's "Dissertation on Louisiana," 1810, in D. Jackson, *Journals of Zebulon Montgomery Pike*, 2:12, 16–17, 32. For the Osage leadership system, see Rollings, *Osage*, 22, 46–49, 164–66,196–98.

47. Louis Vilemont to minister, Sedan, France, July 3, 1802, in Nasatir, *Before Lewis and Clark*, 2:694.

48. Auguste Chouteau to Albert Gallatin, November 7, 1804, in Nasatir, *Before Lewis and Clark*, 2:759.

49. Thomas Jefferson to the Osages, July 16, 1804, in D. Jackson, *Letters of the Lewis and Clark Expedition*, 1:199–202.

50. Meriwether Lewis to William Henry Harrison, July 26, 1808, in D. Jackson, *Letters of the Lewis and Clark Expedition*, 2:625–26.

51. Thomas Jefferson to Meriwether Lewis, August 21, 1808, Jefferson Papers, *Founders Online*, NARA, https://founders.archives.gov/documents/Jefferson/99-01-02-8555.

52. Coues, *History of the Lewis and Clark Expedition*, 1:30. For the site of Fort Osage, see George C. Sibley to Samuel H. Sibley, September 16, 1808, GCSP.

53. See Eccles, "Fur Trade and Eighteenth-Century Imperialism," 341–62; R. White, *Middle Ground*, 94–141.

54. Coman, "Government Factories."

55. For the role of alcohol in commerce between Indians and Euro-Americans, see Mancall, *Deadly Medicine*.

56. John Mason to William H. Crawford, March 6, 1816, vol. C, 485–88, Letters Sent, 1807–1823, Superintendent of Indian Trade, NARA.

57. John Calhoun, "Alteration of the System for Trading with the Indians," December 8, 1818, in *American State Papers: Indian Affairs*, 2:181–85.

58. Thomas Jefferson, "Trade," January 18, 1803, in *American State Papers: Indian Affairs*, 1:684.

59. Thomas Jefferson, "Trade," January 18, 1803, in *American State Papers: Indian Affairs*, 1:684. See also Sheehan, *Seeds of Extinction*, 119–23.

60. Jefferson, *Notes on the State of Virginia*, 51.

61. Kappler, *Indian Affairs*, 2:95–96.

62. See Thomas McKenney to all factors, June 18, 1816, vol. D, 63, Letters Sent, 1807–1823, Superintendent of Indian Trade, NARA.

63. Thomas McKenney to George C. Sibley, October 21, 1816; and McKenney to Sibley, February 22, 1817, vol. D, 152, 245–48, Letters Sent, 1807–1823, Superintendent of Indian Trade, NARA.

64. John Calhoun, "Alteration of the System for Trading with the Indians," December 8, 1818, in *American State Papers: Indian Affairs*, 2:183.

65. For republicanism, see Bailyn, *Ideological Origins of the American Revolution*; G. Wood, *Creation of the American Republic*; Banning, *Jeffersonian Persuasion*; McCoy, *Elusive Republic*; Breen, *Tobacco Culture*. For an interpretation of late eighteenth-century political economy

that emphasized liberalism rather than republicanism, see Appleby, *Capitalism and a New Social Order*. For a cogent analysis of the differences between Federalist and republican ideologies, see Merrill, "Anticapitalist Origins of the United States," 465–97; Merrill, "Putting 'Capitalism' in Its Place," 315–26.

66. Kloppenberg, "Virtues of Liberalism," 20.

67. See McCoy, *Elusive Republic*, 166–259; Appleby, *Capitalism and a New Social Order*, 79–105.

68. See Christian, *Before Lewis and Clark*, 115.

69. Rohrbaugh, "'A Freehold Estate Therein,'" 46–59; P. W. Gates, "Role of Land Speculators in Western Development," 314–33; Herbert, "Methods and Operations," 502–15; S. B. Adams, "Yazoo Fraud," 155–65; Heath, "Yazoo Land Fraud," 274–91; Elsmere, "Notorious Yazoo Land Fraud Case," 425–42.

70. Haeger, *John Jacob Astor*, 51.

71. John Mason to all factors, April 16, 1811, vol. B, 288, Letters Sent, 1807–1823, Superintendent of Indian Trade, NARA; George C. Sibley to Samuel H. Sibley, January 18, 1809; George C. Sibley, "Notes of an Official Excursion." See also John Calhoun, "Alteration of the System for Trading with the Indians," December 8, 1818, in *American State Papers: Indian Affairs*, 2:181–85.

72. For Sibley's appointment, see Henry Dearborn to George C. Sibley, May 17, 1808, GCSP.

73. For Hopkins, see Ahlstrom, *Religious History of the American People*, 407–9; C. T. Jones, *George Champlin Sibley*, 3–4.

74. John Sibley, memorandum book, January 1, 1800–December 29, 1800, GMSS.

75. John Sibley, Memorandum, May 1, 1809, GMSS.

76. George C. Sibley to Samuel H. Sibley, September 15, 1813, GMSS.

77. George C. Sibley to Samuel H. Sibley, January 21, 1815, GMSS.

78. By 1805, John Sibley was corresponding with Jefferson. See Thomas Jefferson to John Sibley, May 27, 1805, in Lipscomb and Bergh, *Writings of Thomas Jefferson*, 11:79–81.

79. George C. Sibley to Samuel H. Sibley. October 25, 1806. Sibley owed the $500 debt to John Winslow, a Fayetteville, North Carolina, merchant, for whom Sibley had worked as a clerk and bookkeeper from 1800 to 1805. For Sibley's debt to Winslow, see George C. Sibley to Samuel H. Sibley, September 16, 1808; and George C. Sibley Diary, May 20, 1808, and August 10, 1809, GMSS.

80. For his debt of $14,000, see John Sibley to J. S. Johnston, January 4, 1825; John Sibley to J. S. Johnston, July 25, 1825; John Sibley to Edward Bates, January 29, 1827; John Sibley to A. Leonard, May 18, 1827; and J. S. Johnston to John Sibley, March 13, 1828, GCSP.

81. George C. Sibley to Samuel H. Sibley, September 25, 1813, GMSS.

82. Christian, *Before Lewis and Clark*, 51.

83. George C. Sibley to Samuel H. Sibley, September 16, 1808; and George C. Sibley to Samuel H. Sibley, February 12, 1811, GMSS.

84. *Lorr v. Sibley*, Superior Court Files, 1816, box 38, folder 13, Supreme Court of Missouri Collection, Missouri State Archives. Copies in GMSS. See also Winn, "Frown of Fortune," 35–61.

85. John Mason to George C. Sibley, May 24, 1808, vol. A, 144–47, Letters Sent, 1807–1823, Superintendent of Indian Trade, NARA.

86. George C. Sibley Diary, September 25, 1808, GCSP.

87. See Rollings, *Osages*, 224–26.

88. George C. Sibley Diary, November 7, 1808, and March 9, 1811, GCSP. Lt. Louis Lorimer, an 1806 graduate of West Point, was the son of Pierre-Louis de Lorimier, a French fur trader and his French-Shawnee wife.

89. George C. Sibley to William Clark, February 21, 1811, GCSP.

90. George C. Sibley to Samuel H. Sibley, January 18, 1809, GCSP.

91. George C. Sibley, "Notes of an Official Excursion."

92. George C. Sibley, "Notes of an Official Excursion."

93. For the volume of trade before the War of 1812, see "Amount of Merchandise Furnished Each Trading House, November 1807–September 1811," RG 75, M 234, roll 750, doc. 157, Letters Received, Office of Indian Affairs, NARA. Following the war, see Thomas McKenney to John C. Calhoun, March 17, 1818, vol. E, 7–10, Letters Sent, 1807–1823, Superintendent of Indian Trade, NARA. For the volume of trade after the war, see "Statement showing the amount and costs (including transportation and other charges) of the goods furnished annually to each factory or Indian trading-house since the peace of 1815," April 12, 1820, in *American State Papers: Indian Affairs*, 2:208.

94. George C. Sibley, "The Factory System," *National Intelligencer* (Washington, DC), April 18, 1822.

95. George C. Sibley, "Notes of an Official Excursion."

96. George C. Sibley, "Notes of an Official Excursion."

97. George C. Sibley, "Notes of an Official Excursion."

98. D. K. Weber, *Spanish Frontier in North America*, 292–93.

99. The Spanish captured Pike in New Mexico, imprisoned him as a spy, and returned him to the United States by a different route. For the custom of distributing medals, see Ewers, "Symbols of Chiefly Authority," 272–86.

100. Sibley was careful to bring flags and medals with him. See George C. Sibley to William Clark, May 4, 1811, GCSP.

101. George C. Sibley, "Notes of an Official Excursion."

102. George C. Sibley, "Notes of an Official Excursion."

103. Lee, "'Better View of the Country,'" 89–120.

104. See Dowd, *Spirited Resistance*, 194–96; Edmunds, *Shawnee Prophet*, 161–83; Sheehan, *Seeds of Extinction*, 243–75.

105. Violette, *History of Missouri*, 74–75.

106. George C. Sibley to Samuel H. Sibley, September 25, 1813; and George C. Sibley to Samuel H. Sibley, September 9, 1816, GCSP.

107. *Lorr v. Sibley* (1816).

108. Chambers, *Old Bullion Benton*, 81–100; Winn, "Frown of Fortune," 44–51.

109. *Lorr v. Sibley* (1816).

110. George C. Sibley to Samuel H. Sibley, August 20, 1815, GCSP.

111. Rorabaugh, "Political Duel in the Early Republic," 1–23; Etcheson, "Manliness and the Political Culture of the Old Northwest," 59–77; Freeman, "Dueling as Politics," 289–318.

112. Winn, "Frown of Fortune," 51–52.

113. Chambers, *Old Bullion Benton*, 81–100.

114. See George Sibley to Thomas L. McKenney, April 16, 1819, in *American State Papers: Indian Affairs*, 2:362.

115. "The Osages," in *American State Papers: Indian Affairs*, 1:763.

116. Coman, "Government Factories," 378–84; "Operations of the Factory System," in *American State Papers: Indian Affairs*, 2:326–64. For government relations with the fur trading companies, see Trennert, "Fur Trader as Indian Administrator," 1–19; Rowe, "Government Relations with the Fur Trappers of the Upper Missouri," 481–505.

117. Thomas McKenney to George C. Sibley, June 21, 1821, Territorial Papers of the United States, vol. 15, The Territory of Louisiana-Missouri Territory, 1815–1821. Copy in GMSS.

118. Downs, "American Merchants and the China Opium Trade," 418–42.

119. Wishart, *Fur Trade of the American West*.

120. George C. Sibley, in E. James, *Account of an Expedition*, 274–78.

121. George C. Sibley, "Factory System."

122. George C. Sibley to Samuel H. Sibley, September 9, 1813; George C. Sibley to Samuel H. Sibley, May 6, 1815; George C. Sibley to Samuel H. Sibley, January 14, 1816; George C. Sibley to Samuel H. Sibley, July 10, 1817; and George C. Sibley to Samuel H. Sibley, July 10, 1819, GCSP.

123. George C. Sibley to John O'Fallon, December 19, 1818, GCSP.

124. George C. Sibley to Jeremiah W., June 1, 1823; and Sibley to George Graham, October 6, 1823, GCSP.

125. George C. Sibley to J. S. Johnston, January 4, 1825, GCSP.

126. James Barbour to Benjamin Reeves, George Sibley, and Pierre Menard, March 16, 1825, GMSS.

127. Sellers, *Market Revolution*, 76–82, 97–100; G. R. Taylor, *Transportation Revolution*, 17–28.

128. Benton, *Thirty Years' View*, 41–44.

129. Gregg, *Road to Santa Fe*, 57–59.

130. Gregg, *Road to Santa Fe*, 157–58.

131. George C. Sibley to the "Principal Alcalde" of Taos, August 19, 1826, William Gillet Ritch Papers, Huntington Library, San Marino, CA.

132. Hämäläinen, *Comanche Empire*; A. C. Isenberg, *Destruction of the Bison*, 34, 100.

133. T. D. Hall, *Social Change in the Southwest, 1350–1880*, 134–66; D. J. Weber, *Mexican Frontier*, 122–46; Moorhead, *New Mexico's Royal Road*, 28–75.

134. T. James, *Three Years among the Indians and Mexicans*, 115, 118.

135. Hämäläinen, *Comanche Empire*, 158–60. The Bents were the sons of Silas Bent, a prominent Anglophone member of the Missouri junto. For the Bents, see Beyreis, *Blood in the Borderlands*.

136. Torget, *Seeds of Empire*, 36–37.

137. Thomas Jefferson to Horatio G. Spofford, March 17, 1814, *Papers of Thomas Jefferson, Retirement Series*, 7:248–49.

CHAPTER 3

1. Meriwether Martin to Lewis Cass, November 28, 1832, RG 75, M 234, roll 750, Letters Received, Office of Indian Affairs, NARA.

2. Tabeau, *Narrative of Loisel's Expedition*, 130–31. For the rise of the Lakota, see Holder, *Hoe and the Horse on the Plains*; R. White, "Winning of the West," 319–43; A. C. Isenberg. *Destruction of the Bison*, 35–36, 41; Hämäläinen, *Lakota America*.

3. See Crosby, *Ecological Imperialism*.

4. Mallery, "Pictographs of the North American Indians," 89–146; Mallery, "Picture Writing of the American Indians," 266–328, esp. 308, 313, 317. Mallery relied on the winter counts of Lone Dog, a Yanctonai, and Battiste Good, a Brulé Lakota. See also Sundstrom, "Smallpox Used Them Up," 305–43.

5. A. C. Isenberg, *Destruction of the Bison*, 53–61.

6. For the outbreak among the Pawnees, see US Congress, House, *Small Pox among the Indians*, 1–2. For outbreaks in the early nineteenth-century Great Plains, see Thornton, *American Indian Holocaust and Survival*, 91–94, 130; Stearn and Stearn, *Effect of Smallpox on the Destiny of the Amerindian*, 72–94; G. R. Campbell, "Plains Indian Historical Demography and Health," v–xiii.

7. For Indigenous people's adaptations and cultural borrowing, see G. Anderson, *Kinsmen of Another Kind*; Merrell, *Indians' New World*; R. White, *Middle Ground*; Usner, *Indians, Settlers, and Slaves*; Hinderaker, *Elusive Empires*; A. C. Isenberg, *Destruction of the Bison*; Richter, *Facing East from Indian Country*.

8. Thornton, *American Indian Holocaust and Survival*, 43, 109, 133, estimated that there were 600,000 Indigenous people living in the United States (including the territories that would be added to the United States) in 1800. That number declined to 250,000 by 1890. In the 1830s, the United States did not yet include Texas, New Mexico, or California. These places were home to dense native populations; California alone, according to Thornton, had a native population of 210,000 in 1834. For the native population of California, see also Hurtado, *Indian Survival on the California Frontier*. Conservatively, there were perhaps another 50,000 natives in Texas and New Mexico. See G. Anderson, *Conquest of Texas*, 4. Native population decline between 1800 and 1890 was not consistent—much of it likely took place after 1837, beginning with the smallpox epidemic of 1837–40. The highest Indigenous population in the smaller United States of 1832 was roughly 340,000. Pearson, "Lewis Cass and the Politics of Disease," 14–17, estimates that the number of Indigenous people vaccinated was between 39,000 and 54,000; if the number vaccinated was at the low end, it was 11 percent of the total native population; at the high end, between 15 and 16 percent. Estimates of Native American population prior to 1492, and of the extent of population decline up until the end of the nineteenth century, have been subject to longstanding scholarly debate. In the early twentieth century, the ethnologist James Mooney put the native population of North America in 1492 at just over 1 million. See Mooney, *Aboriginal Population of America*. Estimates have crept upward since then, peaking at 18 million in Dobyns, *Their Number Become Thinned*; other high estimates include Thornton, *American Indian Holocaust and Survival*; Stannard, *American Holocaust*. The most notable critic of the newer, higher estimates is Henige, "On the Contact Population of Hispaniola," 217–37; Henige, "Their Numbers Become Thick," 169–91. For a survey of the historians' debate, see Daniels, "Indian Population of North America," 298–320.

9. S. F. Cook, "Smallpox in Spanish and Mexican California," 29–43; Hackett, "Averting Disaster," 575–609; Sköld, "Escape from Catastrophe," 1–25; Walker, "Early Modern Japanese State," 121–60.

10. See Green, *Politics of Indian Removal*; Green and Perdue, *Cherokee Nation and the Trail of Tears*; G. Anderson, *Conquest of Texas*; Faragher, "'More Motley than Mackinaw,'" 304–26. For the Ainu, see Walker, *Conquest of Ainu Lands*; for the Saami, see Broadbent, *Lapps and Labyrinths*.

11. *United States Statutes at Large*, 4:514–15.

12. See, for instance, Pearce, *Savagism and Civilization*; Drinnon, *Facing West*; Horsman, *Race and Manifest Destiny*; Wallace, *Long, Bitter Trail*; Stephanson, *Manifest Destiny*; Hitela, *Manifest Design*; Nugent, *Habits of Empire*; Greenberg, *Manifest Destiny and American Territorial Expansion*; Frymer, *Building an American Empire*; Grandin, *End of the Myth*. For settler colonialism, see Wolfe, "Land, Labor, and Difference," 866–905; Wolfe, "Settler Colonialism and the Elimination of the Native," 387–409; Veracini, "'Settler Colonialism,'" 313–33. For efforts to apply settler colonialism to North America, see Ostler, "'To Extirpate the Indians,'" 587–622; Ostler, *Surviving Genocide*; Madley, *American Genocide*. For a critique of settler colonialism from the perspective of environmental history, see A. C. Isenberg and Kessler, "Settler Colonialism and the Environmental History of the North American West," 57–66.

13. John Winthrop to Nathaniel Rich, May 22, 1634, in A. B. Forbes, *Winthrop Papers*, 3:166–68. Those who argued that Winthrop's view represented colonists generally included Pearce, *Savagism and Civilization*; Crosby, *Columbian Exchange*, 41; Thornton, *American Indian Holocaust and Survival*, 71; Drinnon, *Facing West*; Horsman, *Race and Manifest Destiny*. For more recent versions, see Stannard, *American Holocaust*; Wallace, *Long, Bitter Trail*; Wallace, *Jefferson and the Indians*. By the end of the nineteenth century, American physicians and scientists explained the depopulation of Indigenous people owing to disease as an unavoidable example of the survival of the fittest. See D. S. Jones, *Rationalizing Epidemics*, 2.

14. Barber and Barber, *Historical, Political, and Pictorial American Scenes*, 123–24. For providentialism in colonial, revolutionary, and antebellum American thought and culture, see Guyatt, *Providence and the Invention of the United States*. It was, in fact, European colonists who routinely enslaved natives in the seventeenth and eighteenth centuries. See Gallay, *Indian Slave Trade*. For Indigenous slavery in New England, see Hardesty, *Black Lives, Native Lands, White Worlds*.

15. Thornton, *American Indian Holocaust and Survival*.

16. A. T. Thompson, "To Save the Children," 439–40.

17. For a discussion of the concept of "herd immunity," see J. R. McNeill, *Mosquito Empires*, 44. For the effects of the vaccination program in preventing higher mortality during an outbreak of smallpox in North American in 1837–40, see Trimble, "1832 Inoculation Program," 257–64.

18. See Pearson, "Lewis Cass and the Politics of Disease," 14–17. Historians who have followed Pearson's argument include D. S. Jones, *Rationalizing Epidemics*, 114–17; Mann, *Tainted Gift*, 25; and Fenn, *Encounters at the Heart of the World*, 324. For the full document that Pearson quotes, see Lewis Cass to John Dougherty, May 9, 1832, RG 75, M 21, roll 8, Letters Sent, Office of Indian Affairs, NARA. In January 1833, Elbert Herring, the Commissioner of Indian Affairs, likewise indicated that the program would be resumed in order to vaccinate Indians it had not reached in its first season. See US Congress, House, *Vaccination-Indians*, 1–3.

19. See Kelton, "Cherokee Medicine and the Smallpox Outbreak of 1824," 151–70.

20. For medical hybridization, see Marsland, "Modern Traditional Healer," 751–65. For hybridity, see Kraidy, *Hybridity*.

21. Kelton, "Avoiding the Smallpox Spirits," 45–71.

22. Chardon, *Chardon's Journal at Fort Clark*, 133.

23. "To be understood," according to the historian Joanne Bourke, "individuals communicating their fears need to conform to certain narrative structures, including genre, syntax, form, order, and vocabulary." Bourke, "Fear and Anxiety," 120. The historian Jill Lepore has argued that New England colonists and their descendants made sense of the terrors they experienced during King Philip's War—a conflict between natives and colonists in which roughly five thousand of the latter died—through the manipulation of language and narrative. Lepore, *Name of War*. Likewise, the historian Alan Taylor has argued that settlers in frontier New York in the early nineteenth century carried with them stories that emphasized the dangers of the wilderness; these stories encouraged settlers to destroy forests and wildlife. Alan Taylor, "'Wasty Ways,'" 291–310.

24. Shuttleton, *Smallpox and the Literary Imagination*, 28–31, 42–66.

25. "We shall divert through our own Country a branch of commerce which the European States have thought worthy of the most important struggles and sacrifices, and in the event of peace on terms which have been contemplated by some powers we shall form to the American union a barrier against the dangerous extension of the British Province of Canada and add to the Empire of liberty an extensive and fertile Country thereby converting dangerous Enemies into valuable friends." Thomas Jefferson to George Rogers Clark, December 25, 1780, *Papers of Thomas Jefferson*, 4:327–38. Jefferson used the phrase again some thirty years later, writing, "We should have such an empire for liberty as she has never surveyed since the creation & I am persuaded no constitution was ever before so well calculated as ours for extensive empire & self government." Thomas Jefferson to James Madison, April 27,1809, *Papers of Thomas Jefferson, Retirement Series*, 160.

26. See Lindemann, *Medicine and Society in Early Modern Europe*; Shurkin, *Invisible Fire*, 25–27; Glynn and Glynn, *Life and Death of Smallpox*. For immunity amnesia, see Mina et al., "Measles Virus Infection," 599–606.

27. For native depopulation, see Crosby, *Ecological Imperialism*; N. D. Cook, *Born to Die*; Dobyns, *Their Number Become Thinned*.

28. For smallpox during the American Revolution, see Fenn, *Pox Americana*, 259–77. See also S. F. Cook, "Smallpox Epidemic of 1779," 940.

29. W. H. McNeill, *Plagues and Peoples*, 221–22.

30. Boylston, "Origins of Inoculation," 309–13.

31. Heberden and Franklin, *Some Account of the Success of Inoculation*.

32. Of the 10,670 inhabitants of Boston in 1721, 6,006 contracted the disease and 850 died. The influential minister Cotton Mather advised inoculation, but Boston physicians disagreed about the efficacy of the procedure. Grob, *Deadly Truth*, 73; P. Miller, *New England Mind*, 345–66. See also Minardi, "Boston Inoculation Controversy," 47–76.

33. Marsden, *Jonathan Edwards*, 491–96. For the inoculation procedure, see Rothstein, *American Physicians in the Nineteenth Century*, 29–32.

34. Jenner, *Inquiry into the Causes and Effects*.

35. R. White, *Middle Ground*, 11, 146, 422; Gibson, *Kickapoos*, 3–40; J. Herring, *Kenekuk the Kickapoo Prophet*, 7–12.

36. Hunter, *Narrative of the Captivity and Suffering of Isaac Knight*, 18.

37. For the Métis, see Peterson, "Many Roads to Red River," 63. For a notable tale of resistance to repatriation, see Demos, *Unredeemed Captive*.

38. See Strong, *Captive Selves, Captivating Others*; Colley, *Captives*.

39. Hunter, *Captivity and Suffering of Isaac Knight*, 15.

40. Hunter, *Captivity and Suffering of Isaac Knight*, 16.

41. Horn, *Narrative of the Captivity and Suffering of Mrs. Horn*, 130.

42. Fenn, "Biological Warfare in Eighteenth-Century North America," 1552–80.

43. Hunter, *Captivity and Suffering of Isaac Knight*, 34.

44. Fenn, *Pox Americana*, 28. For Bouquet, see Ranlet, "British, the Indians, and Smallpox," 427–41.

45. Thomas Jefferson to Benjamin Waterhouse, December 25, 1800, in Martin, "Jefferson as a Vaccinator," 19.

46. Waterhouse, *Prospect of Exterminating the Small Pox*, 5, 37.

47. Thomas Jefferson to John Vaughan, November 5, 1821, in Coxe, *Practical Observations on Vaccination*, 120–21.

48. William A. Trimble to John C. Calhoun, August 7, 1818, in Hemphill, *Papers of John C. Calhoun*, 3:16.

49. "An Act to Encourage Vaccination," February 27, 1813, in *Laws of the United States from the 4th of March, 1789, to the 4th of March, 1815*, 4:508–9; US Congress, House, *Memorial of Josiah Meigs*, 1–8. See also US Congress, Senate, *Memorial of Sylvanus Fansher*, 1–12. For Washington's inoculation order during the American Revolution, see Fenn, *Pox Americana*, 93–95; Becker, "Smallpox in Washington's Army," 381–430.

50. Pickard and Buley, *Midwest Pioneer*, 23.

51. John Dougherty to William Clark, October 29, 1831; and James Jackson to Lewis Cass, March 16, 1832, H.doc. 190, 22nd Cong., 1st Sess.

52. William Trimble to John C. Calhoun, August 7, 1818, in Hemphill, *Papers of John C. Calhoun*, 3:16.

53. Douglas Houghton to Henry Schoolcraft, September 21, 1832, in Mason, *Schoolcraft's Expedition to Lake Itasca*, 303.

54. Isaac McCoy to Lewis Cass, March 23, 1832, H.doc. 190, 22nd Cong., 1st Sess.

55. Halttunen, "Humanitarianism and the Pornography of Pain," 303–34.

56. See Lewis Cass to John Dougherty, May 9, 1832; Lewis Cass, Circular, Department of War, May 10, 1832; Lewis Cass to John Dougherty, May 11, 1832; Lewis Cass to Meriwether Martin, May 12, 1832; and Lewis Cass to William Marshall, May 15, 1832, RG 75, M 21, roll 8, Letters Sent, Office of Indian Affairs, NARA.

57. See Berkhofer, "Protestants, Pagans, and Sequences," 201.

58. Lewis Cass to John Dougherty, May 9, 1832, RG 75, M 21, roll 8, Letters Sent, Office of Indian Affairs, NARA.

59. Meriwether Martin to Lewis Cass, November 28, 1832, RG 75, M 234, roll 750, Letters Received, Office of Indian Affairs, NARA.

60. Rusnock, "Catching Cowpox," 17–36; and Bennett, "Smallpox and Cowpox under the Southern Cross," 37–62.

61. Coxe, *Practical Observations on Vaccination*, 18–94.

62. Elbert Herring, "Report from the Office of Indian Affairs," November 22, 1832, H.doc. 2, 22nd Cong., 2nd Sess., 175. See also US Congress, House, *Vaccination-Indians*, 2.

63. See Huerkamp, "History of Smallpox Vaccination," 617–35. This interpretation of vaccination remains among European historians, particularly those who focus on the resistance to compulsory vaccination in late nineteenth-century Britain. See S. Williamson, *Vaccination Controversy*; Durbach, *Bodily Matters*.

64. Bhattacharya and Brimnes, "Simultaneously Global and Local," 1–16.

65. Schwarze, *History of the Moravian Missions*, 174–75; McLoughlin, *Cherokee Renascence in the New Republic*, 380, 385; Kelton, "Cherokee Medicine and the Smallpox Outbreak of 1824," 151–70.

66. Pfeiffer, *Art and Practice of Western Medicine*; C. E. Rosenberg, *Cholera Years*, 40–81; C. E. Rosenberg, *Explaining Epidemics*; Valencius, *Health of the Country*.

67. Thomas Jefferson to Meriwether Lewis, June 20, 1803, in D. Jackson, *Letters of the Lewis and Clark Expedition*, 61–66.

68. E. James, *Account of an Expedition*, 202. See also Lewis Edwards to Maj. Stephen H. Long, May 27, 1819, in Hemphill, *Papers of John C. Calhoun*, 4:80. The vaccine was drenched en route to James and proved useless.

69. Warrick, "American Indian Policy in the Upper Old Northwest," 109–25; Fixico, "Alliance of the Three Fires," 1–23; B. M. White, "'Give Us a Little Milk,'" 60–71. For the extent of the Ojibwe trade with the Hudson's Bay Company, see Journal of Lieutenant James Allen, July 17, 1832, in Mason, *Schoolcraft's Expedition*, 209.

70. See Witgen, *Infinity of Nations*; W. W. Warren, *History of the Ojibway People*.

71. McKenney, *Sketches of a Tour to the Lakes*, 265.

72. Journal of Douglas Houghton, July 2, July 10, July 14, 1832, in Mason, *Schoolcraft's Expedition*, 247–57.

73. Douglas Houghton to Richard Houghton, June 24, 1832, in Mason, *Schoolcraft's Expedition*, 298.

74. Journal of Douglas Houghton, July 17, 1832; and Journal of Lieutenant James Allen, July 17, 1832, in Mason, *Schoolcraft's Expedition*, 206–10, 259–60.

75. Hackett, "Averting Disaster," 575–609.

76. Walker, "Early Modern Japanese State," 121–60.

77. For Missouri's trade with New Mexico, see D. J. Weber, *Mexican Frontier*, 122–46.

78. For Flint's treatment of Boone, see Slotkin, *Regeneration through Violence*, 418–27.

79. See Batman, *American Ecclesiastes*, 14.

80. Pattie, *Personal Narrative of James O. Pattie*, 12–33, 64, 86–87, 130–39, 146–47, 227.

81. Pattie, *Personal Narrative of James O. Pattie*, 64–66, 98, 168, 296.

82. For the California missions, see D. J. Weber, *Spanish Frontier in North America*; Hackel, *Children of Coyote, Missionaries of Saint Francis*.

83. Pattie, *Personal Narrative of James O. Pattie*, 344–59.

84. S. F. Cook, "Smallpox in Spanish and Mexican California," 173–83; Valle, "James Ohio Pattie and the 1827–1828 Alta California Measles Epidemic," 28–36.

85. Pattie, *Personal Narrative of James O. Pattie*, 347–48.

86. See Reséndez, *Changing National Identities at the Frontier*; Torget, *Seeds of Empire*.

87. Rigau-Pérez, "Introduction of Smallpox Vaccine," 393–423; A. T. Thompson, "To Save the Children," 431–55; S. F. Cook, "Smallpox in Spanish and Mexican California," 29–43.

Danish physicians had also acquired the vaccine and begun to vaccinate both the free and slave populations of the Danish West Indies—the islands of St. Thomas, St. John, and St. Croix. See Jensen, "Safeguarding Slaves," 95–124.

88. Fenn, "Biological Warfare in Eighteenth-Century North America," 1552.

CHAPTER 4

1. Francisco Vital Fernández and Benjamin Lundy, Documento de contrata para una empresa de colonización, March 10, 1835; and, State of Tamaulipas, circular, November 17, 1833, Benjamin Lundy Papers, OHS. See also Lundy's journal in Earle, *Life, Travels, and Opinions*, 167.

2. On the attractiveness of Mexican Texas to Americans and the facility with which Americans became Mexican citizens, see Reséndez, *Changing National Identities at the Frontier*; Schlereth, "Privileges of Locomotion," 995–1020; Rodriguez, "'Greatest Nation on Earth,'" 50–83. For Indigenous peoples' raids in northern Mexico, see Hämäläinen, *Comanche Empire*; DeLay, *War of a Thousand Deserts*.

3. Baptist, *Half Has Never Been Told*, 266; Manchaca, *Recovering History*, 172.

4. See Aron, *How the West Was Lost*.

5. Dillon, *Benjamin Lundy and the Struggle*, 179.

6. E. C. Barker, "Influence of Slavery," 3–36.

7. See, for instance, Rothman, *Slave Country*; Johnson, *River of Dark Dreams*; Beckert, *Empire of Cotton*.

8. Bourne, *Book and Slavery Irreconcilable*, 3–16.

9. Heyrick, *Immediate, Not Gradual Abolition*.

10. P. Johnson, *Shopkeeper's Millennium*, 5; Barnes, *Anti-slavery Impulse*.

11. *St. Louis Enquirer*, reprinted in *Genius of Universal Emancipation* 1 (September 1821): 41–42.

12. James Jones, in *Minutes of the Eighteenth Session of the American Convention for Promoting the Abolition of Slavery*, 18.

13. Earle, *Life, Travels, and Opinions*, 288.

14. Walker, *Walker's Appeal*, 52. For African Americans' resistance to colonization, see Mills, *World Colonization Made*.

15. For the popularity of colonization, see Guyatt, "'The Outskirts of Our Happiness,'" 986–1011; D. B. Davis, *Problem of Slavery*, 83–87. For the early critique of colonization, see McDaniel, *Problem of Democracy*, 37–40.

16. See, for instance, the founding charter of the Piqua Colonization Society, Piqua, Ohio, October 21, 1826, Forest Wilson Papers, OHS. Article 2 of the charter reads, "The object to which [the Piqua Colonization Society's] views shall be exclusively directed is the colonization, on the coast of Africa, with their own consent, of the free people of colour of the United States; and this Society will contribute its funds and effort to the attainment of that object, in aid of the Am. C. Soc."

17. Clay, speaking on June 20, 1832, 22nd Cong., 1st Sess., *Register of Debates in Congress*, 8:1116–17.

18. Joint Resolution of the Legislature of the State of Indiana, in Favor of Colonizing Free People of Color, February 16, 1829, Huntington Library, San Marino, CA. For the support for colonization in the states of the Old Northwest, see S. M. Davis, "'Here They Are in the Lowest State.'"

19. *Minutes of the Twentieth Session of the American Convention for Promoting the Abolition of Slavery*, 6–21.

20. Lundy, in *Genius of Universal Emancipation* 1 (September 1821): 33.

21. Lundy, in *Baltimore (MD) Courier*, September 24, 1825. See also Lundy, in *Genius of Universal Emancipation* 3 (November 1823): 70.

22. Lundy, "Immediate Emancipation," *Genius of Universal Emancipation*, 3rd ser., 3 (September 1833): 161.

23. Lundy, in *Genius of Universal Emancipation* 2 (July 1822): 4.

24. "Address from the New York Manumission Society," in *Minutes of the Eighteenth Session of the American Convention for Promoting the Abolition of Slavery*, 7.

25. Lundy, in *Genius of Universal Emancipation* 1 (December 1821): 87.

26. Lundy, "Mexican Decree," *Genius of Universal Emancipation* 3rd ser., 1 (May 1830): 87.

27. Lundy, in *Genius of Universal Emancipation* 3rd ser., 3 (June 1833): 117–18.

28. Lundy, in *Genius of Universal Emancipation* 2 (September 1822): 5.

29. Hammond, "Slavery, Settlement, and Empire," 175–206.

30. William Rawle (president of the Pennsylvania Manumission Society), in *Minutes of the Eighteenth Session of the American Convention for Promoting the Abolition of Slavery*, 11.

31. Lundy, "Address from the Greenville Branch of the Manumission Society of Tennessee to the Citizens of Illinois," *Genius of Universal Emancipation* 3 (May 1824): 161–63.

32. Lundy, *War in Texas*, 27. Lundy first asserted that proslavery forces sought to annex Texas and create five or six slave states in *Genius of Universal Emancipation* (September 1829). See also Lundy, "Mexico and the United States," *Genius of Universal Emancipation*, 3rd ser., 2 (December 1831): 102.

33. "Address from the New York Manumission Society," in *Minutes of the Eighteenth Session of the American Convention for Promoting the Abolition of Slavery*, 5–6.

34. James Jones (president of the Manumission Society of Tennessee), in *Minutes of the Eighteenth Session of the American Convention for Promoting the Abolition of Slavery*, 16–17.

35. *Minutes of the Twentieth Session of the American Convention for Promoting the Abolition of Slavery*, 49.

36. "A Plan for the General Emancipation of Slaves," *Genius of Universal Emancipation* 3 (December 1823): 88.

37. *Minutes of the Eighteenth Session of the American Convention for Promoting the Abolition of Slavery*, 39–40.

38. Rawle, in *Minutes of the Eighteenth Session of the American Convention for Promoting the Abolition of Slavery*, 12–13.

39. Lundy, in *Genius of Universal Emancipation* 1 (February 1822): 117.

40. Lundy, "Emigration to Hayti," *Genius of Universal Emancipation* 4 (November 1824): 19.

41. Chester County Society for Preventing Kidnapping, in *Minutes of the Eighteenth Session of the American Convention for Promoting the Abolition of Slavery*, 20–22.

42. Bushrod Washington to Frederick G. Schaeffer, September 18, 1821, in the *Federal Republican*, reprinted in *Genius of Universal Emancipation* 1 (September 1821): 52–55.

43. Lundy, "American Colonization Society," *Genius of Universal Emancipation* 1 (September 1821): 55.

44. Lundy, "Colonization," *Genius of Universal Emancipation* 3 (September 1823): 33.

45. Lundy, in *Genius of Universal Emancipation* 4 (February 1825): 72.

46. For free blacks in Baltimore and Philadelphia, see Diemer, *Politics of Black Citizenship*. For Black and white workers in Baltimore, see Rockman, *Scraping By*.

47. See Fanning, *Caribbean Crossing*; Power-Greene, *Against Wind and Tide*, 17–45.

48. Lundy, "Migration to Hayti"; and Lundy, "Baltimore Emigration Society," *Genius of Universal Emancipation* 4 (October 1824): 2, 27.

49. Lundy, in *Genius of Universal Emancipation* 1 (February 1822): 119.

50. Lundy, "Emigration to Haiti," *Genius of Universal Emancipation* 4 (November 1824): 17–18.

51. Earle, *Life, Travels, and Opinions*, 194.

52. Aaron Coffin, "President's Address to the Manumission Society of North Carolina," September 27, 1824, reprinted in *Genius of Universal Emancipation* 4 (October 1824): 40–42.

53. Lundy, in *Genius of Universal Emancipation* 4 (February 1825): 72.

54. Paulus, *Slaveholding Crisis*.

55. Herschthal, "Slaves, Spaniards, and Subversion in Early Louisiana," 283–311.

56. Alan Taylor, *Internal Enemy*.

57. Lundy, in *Genius of Universal Emancipation* 1 (January 1822): 111. See also S. Perkins, *World As It Is*, 483. Perkins wrote that emigration to Haiti "did not meet the approbation of the South, because it was too near the southern portion of the United States."

58. Earle, *Life, Travels, and Opinions*, 23–24, 29; Dillon, *Benjamin Lundy*, 95–103, 142. For the eleven freed slaves from North Carolina Lundy transported to Haiti in 1825, see the testimonial of P. E. Thomas, May 1, 1825, Manumission and Colonization Society of North Carolina Papers, OHS.

59. Lundy, "The Canada Colony," *Genius of Universal Emancipation*, 3rd ser., 1 (April 1830): 1. For Canada as a destination for fugitive slaves in the early nineteenth century, see Wigmore, "Before the Railroad," 437–54.

60. Litwack, *North of Slavery*, 72–73; Middleton, *Black Laws*; S. M. Davis, "'Here They Are in the Lowest State.'" Lundy editorialized against the discriminatory laws in Ohio in 1822. Lundy, "To the General Assembly of the State of Ohio," *Genius of Universal Emancipation* 2 (December 1822): 93–94.

61. Lundy, "Canada Colored Settlement," *Genius of Universal Emancipation*, 3rd ser., 2 (July 1831): 34.

62. Lundy, "Wilberforce Settlement," *Genius of Universal Emancipation*, 3rd ser., 2 (March 1832): 153–54. For the earlier stumbles, see Lundy, "Colony in Canada," *Genius of Universal Emancipation*, 3rd ser., 1 (August 1830): 69.

63. Lundy, "Wilberforce Settlement," 154.

64. Lundy, "Tour in Upper Canada," *Genius of Universal Emancipation*, 3rd ser., 2 (April 1832): 171.

65. "Letter from 'A Carolinian,'" *Genius of Universal Emancipation* 1 (January 1822): 111.

66. Lundy, in *Genius of Universal Emancipation* 1 (February 1822): 120.

67. Manumission Society of Tennessee, in *Minutes of the Eighteenth Session of the American Convention for Promoting the Abolition of Slavery*, 18, 25, 28.

68. "Letter from 'A Carolinian,'" 110.

69. Lundy, *Plan for the Gradual Abolition of Slavery*, 1–12.

70. *Minutes of the Twentieth Session of the American Convention for Promoting the Abolition of Slavery*, 31.

71. "Free Labour in Trinidad," *Genius of Universal Emancipation*, 3rd ser., 1 (October 1830): 159–60.

72. Lundy, "Culture of Sugar Cane by Free Laborers," *Genius of Universal Emancipation*, 3rd ser., 3 (April 1833): 81.

73. Lundy, in *Genius of Universal Emancipation* 2 (August 1822): 17.

74. Lundy, "Geographical Description of Texas," *Genius of Universal Emancipation*, 3rd ser., 2 (December 1831, suppl.): 114.

75. Lundy, in *Genius of Universal Emancipation*, 3rd ser., 3 (November 1832): 8.

76. See Torget, *Seeds of Empire*, 1–3, 30–52; Hämäläinen, *Comanche Empire*, 184–90; Haggard, "Neutral Ground," 1001–28; Audain, "Scheme to Desert," 40–56.

77. Tadeo Ortiz to Lucas Alamán, October 31, 1830; Kelley and Hatcher, "Tadeo Ortiz de Ayala, II," 153.

78. "Report of the Secretary of State on the Petition, May 17, 1822," Kelley and Hatcher, "Tadeo Ortiz de Ayala, I," 78.

79. Torget, *Seeds of Empire*, 62, 69–72.

80. A Free Colored Floridian, "Prejudice against Color," *Genius of Universal Emancipation*, 3rd ser., 2 (October 1831): 87.

81. Lundy, "The Mexicans," *Genius of Universal Emancipation*, 3rd ser., 2 (October 1831): 87.

82. Lundy. "Mexican Colonization," *Genius of Universal Emancipation*, 3rd ser., 3 (June 1833), 114.

83. Lundy, Journal of Journey to Texas, July 2–6, 1832, Benjamin Lundy Papers, OHS.

84. Earle, *Life, Travels, and Opinions*, 42, 63, 116, 149.

85. Lundy, *Circular*, 14.

86. Cornell, "Citizens of Nowhere," 351–74.

87. "Texas," *Arkansas Gazette* (Little Rock), June 25, 1822. The *Arkansas Gazette* was reliably opposed to American settlements in Texas—its editors viewed Texas as a competitor to the development of Arkansas.

88. Stephen Austin to James F. Perry, December 31, 1829, in E. C. Barker, *Austin Papers*, 2:309.

89. Lundy, "The Texas Country," *Genius of Universal Emancipation*, 3rd ser., 2 (May 1832): 193.

90. Earle, *Life, Travels, and Opinions*, 39–40.

91. Benjamin Lundy to Antonio López de Santa Anna, December 30, 1833, Benjamin Lundy Papers, OHS. Santa Anna wrote a polite reply on February 24, 1834. See Earle, *Life, Travels, and Opinions*, 128.

92. Earle, *Life, Travels, and Opinions*, 63, 65, 68, 78–81, 89–90, 127–28.

93. Earle, *Life, Travels, and Opinions*, 130, 162, 167–68.

94. Richard Pearce to Benjamin Lundy, March 31, 1835, Benjamin Lundy Papers, OHS.

95. Earle, *Life, Travels, and Opinions*, 166.

96. Articles of Agreement between Benjamin Lundy and Lyman A. Spalding, January 28, 1836, Benjamin Lundy Papers, OHS.

97. Lundy, *Circular*, 4–5.

98. Vital Fernández and Lundy, Documento de contrata, March 10, 1835.

99. Richard Pearce to Benjamin Lundy, March 31, 1835, Benjamin Lundy Papers, OHS. For Lundy's interest in the land on the Nuéces, see Earle, *Life, Travels, and Opinions*, 151–52.

100. Earle, *Life, Travels, and Opinions*, 188.

101. Benjamin Lundy to John Quincy Adams, June 9, 1836, quoted in Dillon, *Benjamin Lundy*, 219.

102. Lundy, *War in Texas*, 39.

103. Garrison, "Benjamin Lundy," *The Liberator* (Boston), May 2, 1835, 71.

104. Benjamin Lundy to John Quincy Adams, June 9, 1836, quoted in Dillon, *Benjamin Lundy*, 219.

CHAPTER 5

1. S. R. Riggs, *Mary and I*, 15.

2. See Berkhofer, *Salvation and the Savage*; Vogel, "Missionary as Acculturation Agent," 185–201. Berkhofer drew heavily on G. G. Brown, "Missions and Cultural Diffusion," 214–19. See also Bowden, *American Indians and Christian Missions*; R. H. Jackson and E. Castillo, *Indians, Franciscans, and Colonization*; Daggar, "Mission Complex," 467–91. There is a small counterinterpretation emphasizing Indigenous people's cultural adaptability and the open-mindedness of certain missionary groups, particularly Jesuits and Pietists, who are depicted as exceptions to the rule. These studies are typified by Ronda, "Generations of Faith," 369–94; Axtell, "Were Indian Conversions *Bona Fide*?," 100–124; McLoughlin, *Champions of the Cherokees*; Merritt, "Dreaming of the Savior's Blood," 723–46; Cassidy, "'More Noise They Make,'" 1–34. For the complexities of Indigenous identity and religious conversion, see Bruchac, "Hill Town Touchstone," 712–48.

3. See Hixson, *American Settler Colonialism*, 39, 63, 123, 148, 150; Ostler, *Surviving Genocide*, 341.

4. R. W. Meyer, *History of the Santee Sioux*, 53; G. Anderson, *Kinsmen of Another Kind*; B. Forbes, "Evangelization and Acculturation among the Santee Dakota Indians," 1.

5. S. W. Pond, *Dakota or Sioux in Minnesota*. Pond wrote this study between 1865 and 1875. S. R. Riggs, *Dakota Grammar, Texts, and Ethnography*. Riggs completed a draft of the study before his death in 1883. For a definition of ethnohistory, see Axtell, *European and the Indian*, 3–15.

6. See Berkhofer, "Protestants, Pagans, and Sequences," 201.

7. R. White, *Middle Ground*, 51–93. Gideon Pond was ready to quit in 1838. See Gideon Pond to Rebecca Hines, September 27, 1838; and Gideon Pond to Ruth Pond, October 21, 1838, Pond Brothers Papers, MHS. For an overview of the Lac qui Parle community, see C. M. Gates, "Lac qui Parle Indian Mission," 133–51; Willand, *Lac qui Parle and the Dakota Mission*; Parker, *Lac qui Parle*; Blegen, "Pond Brothers," 273–81; Ackermann, "Joseph Renville of Lac qui Parle," 231–46.

8. Guarneri, "Reconstructing the Antebellum Communitarian Movement," 463–88. See also Holloway, *Utopian Communities in America*; Curtis, *Season in Utopia*; Carden, *Oneida*; Spann, *Brotherly Tomorrows*; Spann, *Hopedale*; Clark, *Communitarian Movement*.

9. Finney, *Lectures on Revivals of Religion*, 9, 12.

10. Shiels, "Scope of the Second Great Awakening," 223–46.

11. C. D. Johnson, "Protracted Meeting Myth," 349–83.

12. P. Johnson, *Shopkeeper's Millenium*, 9. For migration from New England, see Alan Taylor, *William Cooper's Town*; S. E. Gray, *Yankee West*, 119–38.

13. Eli Lundy Huggins, "Boyhood Reminiscences of General Huggins," Alexander G. Huggins Papers, MHS; M. L. Riggs, *Small Bit of Bread and Butter*, iii–v. S. R. Riggs, *Mary and I*, 4; S. W. Pond, *Two Volunteer Missionaries*, 13.

14. See, for instance, P. Johnson, *Shopkeeper's Millennium*.

15. Max Weber defined other-worldly asceticism as "a radical ethico-religious critique of the relationship to society. . . . Not only do the simple, 'natural' virtues within the world not guarantee salvation, but they actually place salvation in hazard. . . . The 'world' in a religious sense . . . is a realm of temptations. . . . Concentration upon the actual pursuit of salvation may entail a formal withdrawal from the 'world': from social and psychological ties with family, from the possession of worldly goods, and from political, social, and erotic activities." M. Weber, *Economy and Society*, 2:528.

16. Stoll, *Larding the Lean Earth*, 91; P. W. Gates, *Farmer's Age*; Schob, *Hired Hands and Plowboys*.

17. Samuel Pond's Narrative, Pond Brothers Papers, MHS; S. W. Pond, *Two Volunteer Missionaries*, 7–18.

18. Gideon Pond to Ruth Pond, October 21, 1838, Pond Brothers Papers, MHS.

19. S. R. Riggs, "In Memory of Rev. Thos. S. Williamson, M.D.," 372–73. For Lane Seminary, see Lesick, *Lane Rebels*. For Beecher, see Harding, *Certain Magnificence*. For Weld, see Abzug, *Passionate Liberator*.

20. Frances Huggins Pettijohn, "A Family History," Alexander G. Huggins Papers, MHS.

21. S. R. Riggs, *Mary and I*, 23–27.

22. See Cott, *Bonds of Womanhood*; Ryan, *Cradle of the Middle Class*.

23. Mary Riggs to Alfred Longley, July 23, 1832; Mary Riggs to Alfred Longley, Thanksgiving eve, 1833; Mary Riggs to Alfred Longley, November 24, 1834; and Mary Riggs to Alfred Longley, February 2, 1836, in M. L. Riggs, *Small Bit of Bread and Butter*, 5–7, 11.

24. Samuel Pond's Narrative.

25. Samuel Pond, Galena, Illinois, to Gideon Pond, Washington, Connecticut, October 6, 1833, Pond Brothers Papers, MHS.

26. Gideon Pond Diary, July 1, 1837, July 9, 1837, July 18, 1837, July 27, 1837, and June 30, 1838, Pond Brothers Papers, MHS.

27. Thomas Williamson to Gideon Pond, February 24, 1840, Pond Brothers Papers, MHS.

28. Samuel Pond to Gideon Pond, October 6, 1833, Pond Brothers Papers, MHS.

29. S. R. Riggs, *Mary and I*, 12–13. Mary Riggs likewise called St. Louis a "depot of iniquity." Mary Riggs to Martha Longley, May 10, 1837, in M. L. Riggs, *Small Bit of Bread and Butter*, 27–28.

30. M. Weber, *Economy and Society*, 2:528.

31. S. R. Riggs, *Mary and I*, 27; Mary Riggs to Alfred Longley, February 2, 1836; Mary Riggs to Alfred Longley, April 26, 1836; and Mary Riggs to Martha Longley, May 17, 1836, in M. L. Riggs, *Small Bit of Bread and Butter*.

32. Gideon Pond Diary, November 1, 1837.

33. Williamson, "Planting the Gospel in Minnesota among the Dakotas," Thomas Smith Williamson and Family Papers, MHS.

34. S. R. Riggs, *Tah-koo Wah-kan*, 4.

35. S. R. Riggs, "In Memory of Rev. Thomas S. Williamson, M.D.," New York *Evangelist* (July 17, 1879).

36. S. R. Riggs, *Mary and I*, 15.

37. Samuel Pond to Gideon Pond, December 3, 1833, Pond Brothers Papers, MHS.

38. Samuel Pond to Dr. Fowler, May 1834, Pond Brothers Papers, MHS.

39. S. R. Riggs, "Journal of a Tour from Lac-qui-Parle to the Missouri River."

40. Thomas Williamson to Samuel Pond, September 23, 1840, Pond Brothers Papers, MHS. See also T. Williamson, "Indian Tribes," 593.

41. Spector and Johnson, *Archeology, Ecology, and Ethnohistory*.

42. W. R. Wood, "Plains Trade in Prehistoric and Protohistoric Intertribal Relations," 98–109.

43. Carver, *Three Years Travels*, 62. The apple trees Carver saw were probably Prairie Crabapple (*Malus ioensis*), a native North American species found where woodlands and tallgrass prairies meet.

44. Gibbon, *Sioux*, 18, 27–29; Howard, *Dakota or Sioux Indians*; Whelan, "Dakota Indian Economics and the Nineteenth-Century Fur Trade," 250.

45. G. C. Anderson, *Kinsmen of Another Kind*, 18.

46. For the migration of the Lakota to the Great Plains and their transition to horse-mounted bison hunting, see R. White, "Winning of the West," 319–43; A. C. Isenberg, *Destruction of the Bison*, 35–36. The Assiniboine, who call themselves the Nakota, and the Stoney (or Nakoda), separated from the Dakota and migrated to the northern Great Plains before the seventeenth century. For Dakota, Nakota, and Lakota dialects, see Parks and DeMallie, "Sioux, Assiniboine, and Stoney Dialects," 233–55.

47. Thomas Jefferson to Henry Dearborn, July 13, 1804, in D. Jackson, *Letters of the Lewis and Clark Expedition*, 199–202.

48. Zebulon Pike, "Observations on the Country and the Indians," in D. Jackson, *Journals of Zebulon Montgomery Pike*, 202.

49. G. C. Anderson, *Kinsmen of Another Kind*, 52–53. By the late 1820s, the Great Lakes region—which included the lands of the Dakota on its western periphery—had a Métis population of ten to fifteen thousand. Peterson, "Many Roads to Red River," 63.

50. Monk, "Some Account of the Department of Fond du Lac or Mississippi," 28–39.

51. "Trudeau's Description of the Upper Missouri," 1796, in Nasatir, *Before Lewis and Clark*, 2:382.

52. G. C. Anderson, "Early Dakota Migration and Intertribal War," 17–36; S. W. Pond, *Dakota or Sioux in Minnesota*, 26–31; R. W. Meyer, *History of the Santee Sioux*, 20–23; G. C. Anderson, *Kinsmen of Another Kind*, 2–7.

53. G. C. Anderson, *Kinsmen of Another Kind*, 108–9. The Hudson's Bay Company experienced a similar decline in the export of beaver pelts and filled that deficit with muskrats. See Carlos and Hoffman, "North American Fur Trade," 979.

54. Keating, *Narrative of an Expedition to the Source of St. Peter's*, 302–3.

55. S. W. Pond, *Dakota or Sioux in Minnesota*, 93–96; Skinner, *Medicine Ceremony of the Menomini, Iowa, and Wahpeton Dakota*, 281–83; Mniyo and Goodvoice, *Red Road and Other Narratives*, 32–33, 42, 230; Howard, *Canadian Sioux*, 120–28.

56. Stephen Riggs to S. L. Babcock, November 19, 1850, Stephen R. Riggs and Family Papers, MHS.

57. See G. Anderson, *Little Crow*, 40–43.

58. Zebulon Pike to James Wilkinson, September 23, 1805, in D. Jackson, *Journals of Zebulon Montgomery Pike*, 1:239.

59. J. S. Gray, "Honore Picotte, Fur Trader," 186–202.

60. S. W. Pond, *Dakota or Sioux in Minnesota*, 17–18.

61. See Richter, "Cultural Brokers and Intercultural Politics," 40–67. For the woodland fur trade and "social kinship," see G. C. Anderson, *Kinsmen of Another Kind*, x–xii, 51, 58–76, 95. For "social kinship," Anderson drew on Deloria, *Speaking of Indians*, 24–26. For women in the fur trade, see Van Kirk, "Role of Native Women," 53–62.

62. R. White, "Winning of the West," 319–43.

63. A. C. Isenberg, *Destruction of the Bison*, 93.

64. Alexander Huggins Journal, January 18, 1838, Alexander G. Huggins Papers, MHS.

65. Gideon Pond to Ruth Pond, October 21, 1838, Pond Brothers Papers, MHS.

66. Ackermann, "Joseph Renville of Lac qui Parle," 238.

67. S. R. Riggs, "Dakota Mission," 119.

68. S. W. Pond, *Two Volunteer Missionaries*, 37. For a discussion of the missionaries and agriculture, see C. M. Gates, "Lac qui Parle Indian Mission," 138.

69. US Congress, Senate, *Report of the Commissioner of Indian Affairs*, 486–87.

70. S. W. Pond, *Dakota or Sioux in Minnesota*, 140–53.

71. S. R. Riggs, *Tah-koo Wah-kan*, 176–77.

72. For Stephen Riggs's domestic labors, see Mary Riggs to Martha Longley, July 31, 1837, in M. L. Riggs, *Small Bit of Bread and Butter*, 43. According to John Mack Faragher, a man who milked a cow in nineteenth-century rural America was held in "supreme contempt." See Faragher, *Women and Men on the Overland Trail*, 51.

73. S. R. Riggs, "Dakota Mission," 118–22.

74. Thomas Williamson to Gideon Pond, February 24, 1840, Pond Brothers Papers, MHS.

75. Stephen Riggs, "Sleepy Eyes," *Minnesota Free Press* (St. Peter), January 27, 1858.

76. Gideon Pond Diary, January 13, 1840.

77. Thomas Williamson to Samuel Pond, September 23, 1840, and October 22, 1840, Pond Brothers Papers, MHS.

78. S. R. Riggs, *Mary and I*, 51.

79. See Deloria, *Speaking of Indians*.

80. Mary Riggs to Thomas and Martha Longley, December 15, 1837, in M. L. Riggs, *Small Bit of Bread and Butter*, 58.

81. S. R. Riggs, *Mary and I*, 51.

82. Mary Riggs to Thomas and Martha Longley, March 22, 1839; and Mary Riggs to Moses Longley, July 10, 1851, in M. L. Riggs, *Small Bit of Bread and Butter*, 92, 205.

83. T. Williamson, "Indian Question," 613, 619. In this respect, the Lac qui Parle mission resembled Evan and John Jones's work among the Cherokee; they, too, labored to translate

their message into the Indians' native language. See McLoughlin, *Champions of the Cherokees*, 35–40.

84. Peter Garrioch Diary, September 3, 1837, MHS.

85. Samuel Pond's Narrative.

86. S. W. Pond, "Two Missionaries in the Sioux Country," 28.

87. S. R. Riggs, "Journal of a Tour from Lac-qui-Parle to the Missouri River," 330.

88. Samuel Pond's Narrative; Gideon Pond to Rebecca Hine, September 27, 1838, Pond Brothers Papers, MHS.

89. S. R. Riggs, *Tah-koo Wah-Kan*, 160–65.

90. Stephen Riggs to Samuel Pond, December 28, 1839, Pond Brothers Papers, MHS.

91. Samuel Pond to Ruth Pond, January 7, 1840; and Thomas Williamson to Samuel Pond, May 28, 1840, Pond Brothers Papers, MHS.

92. S. R. Riggs, *Mary and I*, 75.

93. Samuel Pond's Narrative.

94. Gideon Pond Diary, July 17, 1837.

95. S. R. Riggs, *Mary and I*, 50–51.

96. Gideon Pond Diary, August 14, 1837.

97. Samuel Pond's Narrative.

98. S. R. Riggs, *Dakota Grammar, Texts, and Ethnography*, 150–51.

99. A. C. Isenberg, *Destruction of the Bison*, 85–86.

100. Samuel Pond's Narrative.

101. See Mary Riggs to Thomas and Martha Longley, March 22, 1839; and Mary Riggs to Martha Longley, April 22, 1939, in M. L. Riggs, *Small Bit of Bread and Butter*, 92, 97.

102. S. R. Riggs, *Tah-koo Wah-kan*, 143–44.

103. Gideon Pond to Rebecca Hines, September 27, 1838, Alexander G. Huggins Papers, MHS.

104. Williamson, "Planting the Gospel in Minnesota," Thomas Smith Williamson and Family Papers, MHS.

105. For Stephen Riggs's endorsement of Toteedootawin's faith, see Stephen Riggs to Samuel and Gideon Pond, December 28, 1838, Pond Brothers Papers, MHS. See also Stephen Riggs, "Dakota Portraits," 481–568. For a description of the Sacred Dance, see S. W. Pond, *Dakota or Sioux in Minnesota*, 93–96; G. Pond, "Dakota Superstitions," 222–28; S. R. Riggs, *Dakota Grammar, Texts, and Ethnology*, 227–29.

106. Williamson, "Planting the Gospel in Minnesota," Thomas Smith Williamson and Family Papers, MHS.

107. S. R. Riggs, *Tah-koo Wah-kan*, 147–48, 261.

108. Blegen, *Minnesota*, 173.

109. S. R. Riggs, *Tah-koo Wah-kan*, 256.

110. For Whitman, see Limerick, *Legacy of Conquest*, 40. For the Cherokee mission, see McLoughlin, *Champions of the Cherokees*; for the Choctaws, see Baird, "Cyrus Byington and the Presbyterian Choctaw Mission," 19–40.

111. "The Hazelwood Republic," Thomas L. Riggs Papers, Center for Western Studies, Augustana University, Sioux Falls, SD. For the Hazelwood Republic, see Sweet, "Native Suffrage," 99–110.

112. S. W. Pond Jr., *Two Volunteer Missionaries*, 58.

CONCLUSION

1. For the purchase of Alaska, see Hill, "Myth of Seward's Folly," 43–64. For Carson's campaign against the Navajo, see A. C. Isenberg, "Between Mexico and the United States," 85–109. For Sand Creek and the US war against the Lakota, see Kelman, *Misplaced Massacre*, 5–17; Kopaczewski, "Seed of Robbery," 8–39.

2. P. Kennedy, *Rise and Fall of the Great Powers*, 149.

3. For the industrial West in the last decades of the nineteenth century, see Cronon, *Nature's Metropolis*; Igler, "Industrial Far West," 159–92; Igler, *Industrial Cowboys*; Truett, *Fugitive Landscapes*; A. C. Isenberg, *Mining California*; A. C. Isenberg, *Destruction of the Bison*, 123–63; A. C. Isenberg, "Industrial Empire," 333–45. For the US empire, see LaFeber, *New Empire*; E. S. Rosenberg, *Spreading the American Dream*.

4. Adelman and Aron, "From Borderlands to Borders," 814–41. For an elaboration of the "borderlands to borders" argument, see Aron, *American Confluence*. For an earlier view that in many ways anticipated Adelman and Aron's argument, see Faragher, "'More Motley Than Mackinaw,'" 304–26.

5. For early borderlands as places of cultural and political accommodation, see R. White, *Middle Ground*; Usner, *Indians, Settlers*; Hinderaker, *Elusive Empires*; DuVal, *Native Ground*; Barr, *Peace Came in the Form of a Woman*. For modern borderlands as places of ethnic cleansing and state violence, see K. Brown, *Biography of No Place*; Hernandez, *Migra!*; R. L. Nelson, "Baltics as Colonial Playground," 9–19; Delgada, "Border Control and Sexual Policing," 157–78; Bartov and Weitz, *Shatterzone of Empires*; Glassheim, *Cleansing the Czechoslovak Borderlands*.

6. For settler colonialism, see Wolfe, "Settler Colonialism and the Elimination of the Native," 387–409; Veracini, "Introducing Settler Colonial Studies," 1–12. An early statement of this interpretation of the borderlands as places of conquest W. A. Williams, *Empire as a Way of Life*; a recent one is Grandin, *End of the Myth*.

7. See del Castillo, *Treaty of Guadalupe Hidalgo*; Ohrt, *Defiant Peacemaker*.

8. "Remarks on the Pacific Railroad Bill," January 20, 1859, in Rowland, *Jefferson Davis, Constitutionalist*, 416.

9. Marsh, *Camel*, 5, 93, 100, 170, 181, 188.

10. US Congress, Senate, *Report of the Secretary of War*, December 1, 1856, 23.

11. US Congress, Senate, *Report of the Secretary of War*, December 6, 1858, 14.

12. A. C. Isenberg, "'Land of Hardship and Distress,'" 84–101.

13. For the Caribbean, see May, *Southern Dream*. For US efforts to assert its sovereignty in the Pacific in the 1850s, see A. C. Isenberg, "Environment, the United States," 371–77. For the Lakota war, see A. C. Isenberg, *Destruction of the Bison*, 123–56.

14. See Rensink, *Native but Foreign*; Hurtado, *Indian Survival on the California Frontier*; Iverson, *When Indians Became Cowboys*; Harring, *Crow Dog's Case*; L. S. Warren, *God's Red Son*; E. M. Nelson, "Mni Luzahan and 'Our Beautiful City,'" 167–97.

15. See Burge, *Failed Vision of Empire*; Tyrell and Sexton, *Empire's Twin*; Osborne, *"Empire Can Wait"*; Beisner, *Twelve against Empire*.

16. "Speech of Hon. John Q. Adams," 447–51.

17. Porter, *Black Seminoles*, 32–34, 66–95.

18. For the lack of either US or Mexican effective control of the border region before 1900, see Graybill, *Policing the Great Plains*; J. Thompson, *Cortina*; Cool, *Salt Warriors*; Ball, *United States Marshals*; Vanderwood, *Disorder and Progress*; St. John, *Line in the Sand*; B. H. Johnson, *Revolution in Texas*.

19. For "maroon societies," see Hahn, *Nation under Our Feet*, 62–115. See also Berlin et al., *Slaves No More*, 1–76; McPherson, *Ordeal by Fire*, 377–84; Manning, *Troubled Refuge*; Amy Taylor, *Embattled Freedom*.

20. C. A. Barker, *Memoirs of Elisha Oscar Crosby*, 76, 87–91; Foner, *Fiery Trial*, 127, 184–85, 221–24, 258–61.

21. U. S. Grant, Eighth Annual Message to Congress, December 5, 1876.

22. Jacoby, *Strange Career of William Ellis*, 74–97.

23. Painter, *Exodusters*.

24. For the Third Seminole War, see Covington. *Seminoles of Florida*, 128–44.

25. See Lancaster, *Removal Aftershock*, 96–115.

26. Hoxie, "From Prison to Homeland," 1–24.

27. Baird, *Osage People*, 30–66; T. P. Wilson, *Underground Reservation*, 1–23. For the fur trade in the Great Plains, see A. C. Isenberg, *Destruction of the Bison*, 93–122.

28. See Blansett, "Intertribalism in the Ozarks," 475–97.

29. G. Anderson, *Massacre in Minnesota*; G. Anderson, *Little Crow*; R. W. Meyer, *History of the Santee Sioux*, 109–32; Kopaczewski, "Seed of Robbery," 100–154.

30. S. R. Riggs, *Mary and I*, 180.

31. S. R. Riggs, *Tah-koo Wah-kan*, 307–9.

32. Williamson, "Planting the Gospel in Minnesota," Thomas Smith Williamson and Family Papers, MHS.

33. Barton, *John P. Williamson*, 44–45.

34. Pratt, "Advantages of Mingling Indians with Whites," 46.

35. Eastman, *From the Deep Woods to Civilization*, 40–48; R. W. Meyer, *History of the Santee Sioux*, 187–90.

BIBLIOGRAPHY

PRIMARY SOURCES

Archival and Manuscript Collections

Boston, Massachusetts
  Massachusetts Historical Society
    John Quincy Adams Diary 48
Columbus, Ohio
  Ohio Historical Society
    Benjamin Lundy Papers
    Manumission and Colonization Society of North Carolina Papers
    Forest Wilson Papers
Gainesville, Florida
  P.K. Yonge Library of Florida History, University of Florida
    Narrative of the Operations of the British in Florida, 1815, Helen H. Cruzat Collection
San Marino, California
  Huntington Library
    William Gillet Ritch Papers
    Joint Resolution of the Legislature of the State of Indiana, in Favor of Colonizing
      Free People of Color, February 16, 1829
    Henry Rowe Schoolcraft Papers
Sioux Falls, South Dakota
  Center for Western Studies, Augustana University
    Thomas L. Riggs Papers
St. Charles, Missouri
  Mary Ambler Archives, Lindenwood University
    George and Mary Sibley Series

St. Louis, Missouri
  Missouri Historical Society
    George Champlin Sibley Papers
St. Paul, Minnesota
  Minnesota Historical Society
    Peter Garrioch Diary, 1837
    Alexander G. Huggins Papers
    Pond Brothers Papers
    Stephen R. Riggs and Family Papers.
    Thomas Smith Williamson and Family Papers
Washington, DC
  National Archives and Records Administration
    Jefferson Papers (*Founders Online*, founders.archives.gov)
    Office of Indian Affairs, Letters Received, Record Group 75
    Office of Indian Affairs, Letters Sent, Record Group 75
    Superintendent of Indian Trade, Letters Sent, 1807–1823

Government Publications

American State Papers: Foreign Relations. Vol. 4, *1815–1822.* Washington, DC: Gales and Seaton, 1834.
American State Papers: Indian Affairs. Vol. 1, *1789–1814.* Washington, DC: Gales and Seaton, 1834.
American State Papers: Indian Affairs. Vol. 2, *1815–1827.* Washington, DC: Gales and Seaton, 1834.
American State Papers: Military Affairs. Vol. 1, *1789–1819.* Washington, DC: Gales and Seaton, 1832.
American State Papers: Military Affairs. Vol. 6, *1836–1837.* Washington, DC: Gales and Seaton, 1861.
American State Papers: Miscellaneous. Vol. 1, *1789–1809.* Washington, DC: Gales and Seaton, 1834.
Kappler, Charles J., ed. *Indian Affairs: Laws and Treaties.* Vol. 2. Washington, DC: Government Printing Office, 1904.
Laws of the United States from the 4th of March, 1789, to the 4th of March, 1815. Vol. 4. Philadelphia: John Birent and W. John Dunae, 1815–45.
Record in the Case of Colin Mitchell and Others, versus the United States. Supreme Court of the United States, January Term, 1831. Washington, DC: Duff Green, 1831.
"Speech of Hon. John Q. Adams." Appendix to the *Congressional Globe,* 447–51, 24th Cong., 1st Sess., May 25, 1836.
United States Statutes at Large, Vol. 4, *1824–1835.* 22nd Cong., 1st Sess., May 5, 1832, ch. 75, 514–15, www.loc.gov/resource/llsalvol.llsal_004/?sp=562&r=-0.107,0.544,1.14,0.747,0.
US Congress. House. *Defence of Western Frontier.* 26th Cong., 1st Sess., April 1, 1840, H.doc.161.

US Congress. House. *Small Pox among the Indians. Letter from the Secretary of War upon the Subject of the Small Pox among the Indian Tribes.* 22nd Cong., 1st Sess., March 30, 1832, H.doc.190.

US Congress. House. *Memorial of Josiah Meigs.* 16th Cong., 1st Sess., January 5, 1820, H.doc.29.

US Congress. House. *Message from the President of the United States to the Two Houses of Congress.* 22nd Cong., 2nd Sess., December 7, 1830, H.doc.2.

US Congress. House. *Papers Relating to the Foreign Relations of the United States.* 44th Cong., 2nd Sess. December 4, 1876, H.ex.doc.1.

US Congress. House. *Vaccination-Indians.* 22nd Cong., 2nd Sess., January 31, 1833, H.doc.82.

US Congress. *Register of Debates in Congress.* 22nd Cong., 1st Sess., vol 8, 1832.

US Congress. Senate. *Memorial of Sylvanus Fansher.* 25th Cong., 2nd Sess., April 18, 1838, S.doc.385.

US Congress. Senate. *Report of the Commissioner of Indian Affairs.* 27th Cong., 3rd Sess., November 16, 1842, S.doc.1.

US Congress. Senate. *Report of the Secretary of War.* 34th Cong., 3rd Sess., December 1, 1856, S.ex.doc.5.

US Congress. Senate. *Report of the Secretary of War.* 35th Cong., 2nd Sess., December 6, 1858, S.ex.doc.1.

Newspapers and Periodicals

Arkansas Gazette (Little Rock)
Baltimore (MD) Courier
Boston Observer and Religious Intelligencer
Chicago Daily Tribune
Genius of Universal Emancipation
   (Mount Pleasant, OH, 1821;
   Greeneville, TN, 1821–24;
   Baltimore, MD, 1824–35)

The Liberator (Boston)
Los Angeles Times
Minnesota Free Press (St. Peter)
National Intelligencer (Washington, DC)
New York Times
New York Tribune
Niles Weekly Register (Baltimore, MD)
Washington Post

Published Sources

Barber, John Warner, and Elizabeth G. Barber. *Historical, Political, and Pictorial American Scenes.* Cincinnati: J. H. Jackson, 1851.

Barker, Charles Albro, ed. *Memoirs of Elisha Oscar Crosby: Reminiscences of California and Guatemala from 1849 to 1864.* San Marino, CA: Huntington Library, 1945.

Barker, Eugene C. ed. *The Austin Papers.* Vol. 2, *Annual Report of the American Historical Association for the Year 1922.* Washington, DC: Government Printing Office, 1928.

Bartram, John. "Diary of a Journey through the Carolinas, Georgia, and Florida from July 1, 1765, to April 10, 1766." *Transactions of the American Philosophical Society* 33 (December 1942): 1–120.

Bartram, William. *Travels through North and South Carolina, Georgia, East and West Florida, the Cherokee Country, the Extensive Territories of the Muscogulges or Creek Confederacy, and the Country of the Chactaws. Containing an Account of the Soil and Natural Productions of those Regions, together with Observations on the Manners of the Indians.* Dublin: J. Moore, 1793.

Bassett, John Spencer, ed. *Correspondence of Andrew Jackson.* Vol. 2, *May 1, 1814 to December 31, 1819.* Washington, DC: Carnegie Institute of Washington, 1927.

Baynton, Benjamin. *Authentic Memoirs of William Augustus Bowles, Esquire, Ambassador from the United Nations of Creeks and Cherokees to the Court of London.* London: R. Faulder, 1791.

Benton, Thomas Hart. *Thirty Years' View.* New York: Appleton, 1861.

Bourne, George. *The Book and Slavery Irreconcilable, with Animadversions upon Dr. Smith's Philosophy.* Philadelphia, 1816.

Braund, Kathryn H., and Kathleen H. Braund, eds., "A Journal of John Forbes, Part 2: The Continuation of a Journal of Talks with the Four Nations Assembled at Hickory Ground May and June 1803." *Florida Historical Quarterly* 94 (Winter 2016): 514–16.

Carver, Jonathan. *Three Years Travels through the Interior Parts of North America.* Philadelphia: Key and Simpson, 1796.

Chardon. Francis A. *Chardon's Journal at Fort Clark, 1834–1839.* Edited by Annie Heloise Abel. Pierre, SD, 1932.

Coues, Elliott, ed. *The History of the Lewis and Clark Expedition.* Vol. 1. New York: Harper, 1893.

Coxe, John Redman. *Practical Observations on Vaccination: Or, Inoculation for the Cow-Pock.* Philadelphia: James Humphreys, 1802.

de Finiels, Nicolas. *An Account of Upper Louisiana.* Edited by Carl J. Ekberg and William E. Foley. Columbia: University of Missouri Press, 1989.

Earle, Thomas, ed. *The Life, Travels, and Opinions of Benjamin Lundy, Including His Journeys to Texas and Mexico; with a Sketch of Contemporary Events, and a Notice of the Revolution in Hayti.* Philadelphia: William D. Parrish, 1847.

Eastman, Charles A. *From the Deep Woods to Civilization: Chapters in the Autobiography of an Indian.* Boston: Little, Brown, 1916.

Eggleston, Edward. *A First Book in American History.* New York: American Book Company, 1899.

Ellis, Edward. *Epochs in American History.* Chicago: A. Flanagan, 1896.

Finney, Charles G. *Lectures on Revivals of Religion.* Oberlin, OH: E. J. Goodrich, 1868.

Giddings, Joshua. *The Exiles of Florida, or, The Crimes Committed by Our Government Against the Maroons, Who Fled from South Carolina and Other Slave States, Seeking Protection under Spanish Laws.* Columbus, OH: Follett, Foster, 1858.

Grant, C. L., ed. *Letters, Journals, and Writings of Benjamin Hawkins.* Vol. 2, *1802–1816.* Savannah, GA: Beehive Press, 1980.

Gregg, Kate L., ed. *The Road to Santa Fe: The Journal and Diaries of George Champlin Sibley and Others Pertaining to the Surveying and Marking of a Road from the Missouri Frontier to the Settlements of New Mexico.* Albuquerque: University of New Mexico Press, 1952.

Hammon, Neal O., ed. *My Father, Daniel Boone: The Draper Interviews with Nathan Boone.* Lexington: University Press of Kentucky, 1999.

Heberden, William, and Benjamin Franklin. *Some Account of the Success of Inoculation for the Small-pox in England and America Together with Plain Instructions, by Which Any Person May Be Enabled to Perform the Operation and Conduct the Patient through the Distemper.* London: W. Strahan, 1759.

Hemphill, W. Edwin, ed. *The Papers of John C. Calhoun.* Vol. 3, *1818–1819.* Columbia: University of South Carolina Press, 1967.

———. *The Papers of John C. Calhoun.* Vol. 4, *1819–1820.* Columbia: University of South Carolina Press, 1969.

Heyrick, Elizabeth Coltman. *Immediate, Not Gradual Abolition; or, an Inquiry into the Shortest, Safest, and Most Effectual Means of Getting Rid of West Indian Slavery.* London, 1824.

Horn, Sarah Ann. *A Narrative of the Captivity and Suffering of Mrs. Horn.* St. Louis: Kremle, 1839. Reprinted in *Comanche Bondage: Beale's Settlement and Sarah Ann Horn's Narrative,* edited by Carl C. Rister, 95–198. Glendale: Clark, 1955.

Hunter, Hiram A. *A Narrative of the Captivity and Suffering of Isaac Knight from Indian Barbarity.* Evansville, 1839.

Innerarity, James. "Letters of James Innerarity: The War of 1812." *Florida Historical Society Quarterly* 10 (January 1932): 134–38.

Jackson, Donald, ed. *The Journals of Zebulon Montgomery Pike, with Letters and Related Documents.* 2 vols. Norman: University of Oklahoma Press, 1966.

———, ed. *Letters of the Lewis and Clark Expedition, with Related Documents, 1783–1854.* 2 vols. 2nd ed. Urbana: University of Illinois Press, 1978.

James, Edwin. *Account of an Expedition from Pittsburgh to the Rocky Mountains, Performed in the Years 1819, 1820.* London: Longman, Hurst, Rees, Orme, and Brown, 1823. Reprinted in *Early Western Travels, 1748–1846,* vol. 17, edited by Reuben Gold Twaites. Cleveland: Clark, 1904.

James, Thomas. *Three Years among the Indians and Mexicans.* Edited by Walter B. Douglas. St. Louis: State Historical Society of Missouri, 1916.

Jefferson, Thomas. *Notes on the State of Virginia.* Edited by William Peden. New York: Norton, 1982.

———. *The Papers of Thomas Jefferson.* Vol. 4, *October 1780 to February 1781,* edited by Barbara B. Oberg. Princeton, NJ: Princeton University Press, 2004.

———. *The Papers of Thomas Jefferson.* Vol. 36, *1 December 1801–3 March 1802,* edited by Barbara B. Oberg. Princeton, NJ: Princeton University Press, 2009.

———. *The Papers of Thomas Jefferson: Retirement Series.* 1809–26. www.monticello.org /research-education/for-scholars/papers-of-thomas-jefferson/.

Jenner, Edward. *An Inquiry into the Causes and Effects of Variolae Vaccinae, or Cow-Pox.* London: Sampson Low, 1798.

Keating, William H. *Narrative of an Expedition to the Source of St. Peter's River.* Philadelphia: Carey and Lea, 1824.

Kelley, Edith Louise, and Mattie Austin Hatcher, eds. "Tadeo Ortiz de Ayala and the Colonization of Texas, 1822–1833, I." *Southwestern Historical Quarterly* 32 (July 1928): 74–86.

———. "Tadeo Ortiz de Ayala and the Colonization of Texas, 1822–1833, II." *Southwestern Historical Quarterly* 32 (October 1928): 152–64.

Le Conte, John. "Observations on the Soil and Climate of East Florida." In *Le Conte's Report on East Florida,* edited by Richard Adicks. Orlando: University Presses of Florida, 1978.

Lipscomb, Andrew A., and Albert E. Bergh, eds. *The Writings of Thomas Jefferson*. Vol. 10. Washington, DC, 1905.

Lockey, Joseph Byrne, ed. and trans. *East Florida, 1783–1785: A File of Documents*. Berkeley: University of California Press, 1949.

Looney, J. Jefferson, ed. *The Papers of Thomas Jefferson, Retirement Series*. Vol. 7. Princeton, NJ: Princeton University Press, 2010.

Lundy, Benjamin. *A Circular, Addressed to Agriculturalists, Manufacturers, Mechanics, &c. on the Subject of Mexican Colonization, with a General Statement Respecting Lundy's Grant, in the State of Tamaulipas, Accompanied by a Geographical Description, &c. of That Interesting Portion of the Mexican Republic*. Philadelphia: J. Richards, 1835.

———. *A Plan for the Gradual Abolition of Slavery in the United States without Danger to the Citizens of the South*. Baltimore, MD: Benjamin Lundy, 1825.

———. *The War in Texas; A Review of Facts and Circumstances, Showing That This Contest Is the Result of a Long Premeditated Crusade against the Government, Set on Foot by Slaveholders, Land Speculators, &c. with the View of Re-establishing, Extending, and Perpetuating the System of Slavery and the Slave Trade in the Republic of Mexico*. Philadelphia: Merrihew and Gunn, 1836.

Madison, James. "First Annual Message (November 29, 1809)." In *A Compilation of the Messages and Papers of the Presidents*, vol. 1, edited by James D. Richardson, 466–68. New York: Bureau of National Literature, 1897.

Mallery, Garrick. "Pictographs of the North American Indians." In *Fourth Annual Report of the Bureau of American Ethnology, 1882–83*, 89–146. Washington, DC: Government Printing Office, 1886.

———. "Picture Writing of the American Indians." In *Tenth Annual Report of the Bureau of American Ethnology, 1888–89*, 266–328. Washington, DC: Smithsonian Institution, 1893.

Mann, Barbara Alice. *The Tainted Gift: The Disease Method of Frontier Expansion*. Santa Barbara, CA: ABC-CLIO, 2009.

Margry, Pierre, ed. *Découvertes et établissements des Français dans l'ouest et dans le sud de l'Amérique septentrionale, 1614-1754. Sixième partie: Exploration des affluents du Mississippi et découverte des montagnes Rocheuses*. Paris: Maisonneuve et Ch. Leclerc, 1888.

Marsh, George Perkins. *The Camel: His Organization, Habits, and Uses*. Boston: Ould and Lincoln, 1856.

Mason, Philip P., ed. *Schoolcraft's Expedition to Lake Itasca: The Discovery of the Source of the Mississippi*. Lansing: Michigan State University Press, 1958.

McCall, James A. *Letters from the Frontier*. Philadelphia: J. B. Lippincott, 1868.

McKenney, Thomas L. *Sketches of a Tour to the Lakes, of the Character and Customs of the Chippeway Indians*. Baltimore, 1827.

Minutes of the Eighteenth Session of the American Convention for Promoting the Abolition of Slavery and Improving the Condition of the African Race, Convened at Philadelphia, On the Seventh Day of October, 1823. Philadelphia: B. Wright, 1825.

Minutes of the Twentieth Session of the American Convention for Promoting the Abolition of Slavery and Improving the Condition of the African Race, Convened at Philadelphia, on the Second of October, 1827. Baltimore, MD: Benjamin Lundy, 1827.

Monk, George Henry. "Some Account of the Department of Fond du Lac or Mississippi." In "A Description of Northern Minnesota by a Fur-Trader in 1807," edited by Grace Lee Nute. *Minnesota History Bulletin* 5, no. 1 (February 1923): 28–39.

Moser, Harold D., David R. Roth, and George H. Hoemann, eds. *The Papers of Andrew Jackson*. Vol. 4, *1816–1820*. Knoxville: University of Tennessee Press, 1994.

Nasatir, A. P., ed. *Before Lewis and Clark: Documents Illustrating the History of the Missouri, 1785–1804*. 2 vols. Lincoln: University of Nebraska Press, 1990.

O'Sullivan, John L. "Annexation." *Democratic Review* 17 (July–August 1845): 5–10.

Pattie, James O. *The Personal Narrative of James O. Pattie of Kentucky*. Edited by Timothy Flint. Cincinnati: John H. Wood, 1831. Reprint, Chicago: Lakeside, 1930.

Perkins, Samuel. *General Jackson's Conduct in the Seminole War, Deliniated in a History of That Period, Affording Conclusive Reasons Why He Should Not Be the Next President*. Brooklyn, CT: John Gray, Jr., 1828.

———. *The World As It Is: Containing a View of the Present Condition of Its Principal Nations*. New Haven, CT: Thomas Belknap, 1841.

Pond, Gideon. "Dakota Superstitions." *Collections of the Minnesota Historical Society* 2 (1860–1867): 222–28.

———. "Paganism a Demon-Worship." *Presbyterian Quarterly Review* 9 (January 1861): 353–80.

Pond, Samuel W. *The Dakota or Sioux in Minnesota as They Were in 1834*. St. Paul: Minnesota Historical Society Press, 1986.

———. "Two Missionaries in the Sioux Country," edited by Theodore C. Blegen. *Minnesota History* 21 (March 1940): 15–32.

Pond, Samuel W., Jr. *Two Volunteer Missionaries among the Dakotas*. Boston: Congregational Sunday School and Publishing Society, 1893.

Pratt, Richard H. "The Advantages of Mingling Indians with Whites." *Proceedings of the National Conference of Charities and Correction*. Denver, 1892.

Riggs, Maida Leonard, ed., *A Small Bit of Bread and Butter: Letters from the Dakota Territory, 1832–1869*. South Deerfield, MA: Ash Grove Press, 1996.

Riggs, Stephen R. *Dakota Grammar, Texts, and Ethnography*. Contributions to North American Ethnology, vol. 9, edited by James Owen Dorsey. Washington, DC: Government Printing Office, 1893.

———. "The Dakota Mission." *Collections of the Minnesota Historical Society* 3 (1870–80): 114–28.

———. "Dakota Portraits." *Minnesota History* 2 (1918): 481–568.

———. "In Memory of Rev. Thos. S. Williamson, M.D." *Collections of the Minnesota Historical Society* 3 (1870–80): 372–73.

———. "Journal of a Tour from Lac-qui-Parle to the Missouri River." *Missionary Herald* 37 (April 1841).

———. *Mary and I: Forty Years with the Sioux*. Chicago: W. G. Holmes, 1880.

———. *Tah-koo Wah-kan, or, The Gospel among the Dakotas*. Boston: Congregational Publishing Society, 1869.

Rowland, Dunbar, ed. *Jefferson Davis, Constitutionalist: His Letters, Papers, and Speeches*. Vol. 3. Jackson: Mississippi Department of Archives and History, 1923.

Schoepf, Johann David. *Travels in the Confederation, 1783–1784*. Vol. 2, trans. and ed. Alfred J. Morrison. Philadelphia: William J. Campbell, 1911.

Sibley, John. "An Account of Louisiana, 1803." In *Old South Leaflets*, vol. 5. Boston: Old South Meeting House, 1902.

Simmons, William Hayne. *Notices of East Florida, with an Account of the Seminole Nation of Indians*. Charleston, SC: A. E. Miller, 1822.

Stork, William. *A Description of East-Florida, with a journal kept by John Bartram of Philadelphia, botanist to His Majesty for the Floridas, upon a journey from St. Augustine up the River St. John's, as far as the lakes*. London: W. Nicoll, 1769.

Swinton, William. *First Lessons in Our Country's History: Bringing Out Its Salient Points, and Aiming to Combine Simplicity with Sense*. New York: Ivison, Blakeman, Taylor, 1872.

Tabeau, Pierre-Antoine. *Narrative of Loisel's Expedition to the Upper Missouri*. Edited by Annie Heloise Abel. Norman: University of Oklahoma Press, 1939.

Thwaites, Reuben Gold, ed. *Original Journals of the Lewis and Clark Expedition, 1804–1806*. 8 vols. New York: Dodd, Mead, 1904.

Walker, David. *Walker's Appeal, in Four Articles: Together with a Preamble, to the Coloured Citizens of the World, but in Particular, and Very Expressly, to Those of the United States of America*. 1829; Chapel Hill: University of North Carolina Press, 2011.

Waterhouse, Benjamin. *A Prospect of Exterminating the Small Pox, Part II*. Cambridge, MA: University Press, 1802.

Williamson, Thomas. "The Indian Question." *Presbyterian Quarterly and Princeton Review*, n.s., 5, no. 20 (October 1876): 608–24.

———. "The Indian Tribes, and the Duty of the Government to Them." *American Presbyterian and Theological Review* 13 (1864): 587–611.

Willson, Marcius. *American History: Comprising historical sketches of the Indian tribes, a description of American antiquities. With an inquiry into their origin and the origin of the Indian tribes, history of the United States, with appendices showing its connection with European history: History of the present British provinces; history of Mexico; and history of Texas, brought down to the time of its admission into the American Union*. New York: Ivison and Phinney, 1856.

Windley, Lathan A., ed. *Runaway Slave Advertisements: A Documentary History from the 1730s to 1790*. Vol. 4, *Georgia*. Westport, CT: Greenwood Press, 1983.

Woodward, Margaret L. "The Spanish Army and the Loss of America, 1810–1824." *Hispanic American Historical Review* 48 (November 1968): 586–607.

Woodward, Thomas S. *Woodland Reminiscences of the Creek, or Muscogee Indians*. Montgomery: Barrett and Wimbish, 1859.

Young, Hugh. "A Topographical Memoir on East and West Florida with Itineraries of General Jackson's Army, 1818." *Florida Historical Quarterly* 13 (January 1935): 140–44.

SECONDARY SOURCES

Abzug, Robert H. *Passionate Liberator: Theodore Dwight Weld and the Dilemma of Reform*. New York: Oxford University Press, 1980.

Ackermann, Gertrude. "Joseph Renville of Lac qui Parle." *Minnesota History* 12, no. 3 (September 1931): 231–46.

Adams, Ephraim Douglass. *The Power of Ideals in American History*. New Haven, CT: Yale University Press, 1913.

Adams, Julia. "The Puzzle of the American State . . . and Its Historians." *American Historical Review* 115, no. 3 (June 2010): 786–91.

Adams, Samuel B. "The Yazoo Fraud." *Georgia Historical Quarterly* 7, no. 2 (June 1923): 155–65.

Adelman, Jeremy, and Stephen Aron. "From Borderlands to Borders: Empires, Nation-States and the People in between in North American History." *American Historical Review* 104, no. 3 (June 1999): 814–41.

Ahlstrom, Sydney E. *A Religious History of the American People.* New Haven, CT: Yale University Press, 1972.

Altschuler, Glenn, and Stuart Blumin. *Rude Republic: Americans and Their Politics in the Nineteenth Century.* Princeton, NJ: Princeton University Press, 2001.

Anderson, Gary C. *The Conquest of Texas: Ethnic Cleansing in the Promised Land, 1820–1875.* Norman: University of Oklahoma Press, 2005.

———. "Early Dakota Migration and Intertribal War: A Revision." *Western Historical Quarterly* 11, no. 1 (January 1980): 17–36.

———. *Kinsmen of Another Kind: Dakota-White Relations in the Upper Mississippi Valley, 1650–1862.* Lincoln: University of Nebraska Press, 1984.

———. *Little Crow: Spokesman for the Sioux.* St. Paul: Minnesota Historical Society Press, 1986.

———. *Massacre in Minnesota: The Dakota War of 1862, the Most Violent Ethnic Conflict in American History.* Norman: University of Oklahoma Press, 2019.

Anderson, Virginia DeJohn. *Creatures of Empire: How Domestic Animals Transformed Early America.* New York: Oxford University Press, 2004.

Appleby, Joyce. *Capitalism and a New Social Order: The Republican Vision of the 1790s.* New York: New York University Press, 1984.

———. *Inheriting the Revolution: The First Generation of Americans.* Cambridge, MA: Harvard University Press, 2000.

Aron, Stephen. *American Confluence: The Missouri Frontier from Borderland to Border State.* Bloomington: Indiana University Press, 2009.

———. *How the West Was Lost: The Transformation of Kentucky from Daniel Boone to Henry Clay.* Baltimore, MD: Johns Hopkins University Press, 1996.

Ashworth, John. *"Agrarians" and "Aristocrats": Party Political Ideology in the United States, 1837–1846.* New York: Cambridge University Press, 1983.

Audain, Mekala. "A Scheme to Desert: The Louisiana Purchase and Freedom Seekers in the Louisiana-Texas Borderlands, 1804–1806." In *In Search of Liberty: African American Internationalism in the Nineteenth-Century Atlantic World,* edited by Ronald Johnson and Ousmane K. Powers-Greene, 40–56. Athens: University of Georgia Press, 2021.

Axtell, James. *The European and the Indian: Essays in the Ethnohistory of Colonial North America.* New York: Oxford University Press, 1981.

———. "Were Indian Conversions *Bona Fide?*" In *After Columbus: Essays in the Ethnohistory of Colonial North America,* 100–124. New York: Oxford University Press, 1989.

———. "The White Indians of Colonial America." *William and Mary Quarterly* 32 (January 1975): 55–88.

Bailyn, Bernard. *The Ideological Origins of the American Revolution.* Cambridge, MA: Belknap Press, 1967.

Baird, W. David. "Cyrus Byington and the Presbyterian Choctaw Mission." In *Churchmen and the Western Indians, 1820–1920,* edited by Clyde Milner and Floyd O'Neil, 19–40. Norman: University of Oklahoma Press, 1985.

————. *The Osage People*. Phoenix: Indian Tribal Series, 1972.

Ball, Larry D. *The United States Marshals of New Mexico and Arizona Territories, 1846–1912*. Albuquerque: University of New Mexico Press, 1978.

Balogh, Brian. *A Government Out of Sight: The Mystery of National Authority in Nineteenth-Century America*. New York: Cambridge University Press, 2009.

Banning, Lance. *The Jeffersonian Persuasion: Evolution of a Party Ideology*. Ithaca, NY: Cornell University Press, 1978.

Baptist, Edward E. *The Half Has Never Been Told: Slavery and the Making of American Capitalism*. New York: Basic Books, 2014.

Barker, Eugene C. "The Influence of Slavery in the Colonization of Texas." *Mississippi Valley Historical Review* 11, no. 1 (June 1924): 3–36.

Barnes, Gilbert Hobbs. *The Anti-slavery Impulse, 1830–1844*. New York: Harcourt, Brace, 1964.

Barr, Juliana. *Peace Came in the Form of a Woman: Indians and Spaniards in the Texas Borderlands*. Chapel Hill: University of North Carolina Press, 2007.

Barton, Winifred W. *John P. Williamson: A Brother to the Sioux*. New York: Fleming H. Revell, 1919.

Bartov, Omer, and Eric D. Weitz, eds. *Shatterzone of Empires: Coexistence and Violence in the German, Habsburg, Russian, and Ottoman Borderlands*. Bloomington: Indiana University Press, 2013.

Batman, Richard. *American Ecclesiastes: The Stories of James Pattie*. New York: Harcourt Brace Jovanovich, 1984.

Baud, Michiel, and Willem Van Schendel. "Toward a Comparative History of Borderlands." *Journal of World History* 8, no. 2 (Fall 1997): 211–42.

Bayly, C. A. *Imperial Meridian: The British Empire and the World, 1780–1830*. Harlow: Longman, 1989.

Becker, Ann M. "Smallpox in Washington's Army: Strategic Implications of Disease during the American Revolutionary War." *Journal of Military History* 68, no. 2 (2004): 381–430.

Beckert, Sven. *Empire of Cotton: A Global History*. New York: Vintage, 2015.

Beisner, Robert L. *Twelve against Empire: The Anti-imperialists, 1898–1900*. New York: McGraw-Hill, 1968.

Bennett, Michael J. "Smallpox and Cowpox under the Southern Cross: The Smallpox Epidemic of 1789 and the Advent of Vaccination in Colonial Australia." *Bulletin of the History of Medicine* 83, no. 1 (Spring 2009): 37–62.

Bergmann, William H. *The American National State and the Early West*. New York: Cambridge University Press, 2012.

Berkhofer, Robert F. "Protestants, Pagans, and Sequences among North American Indians, 1760–1860." *Ethnohistory* 10, no. 3 (Summer 1963): 201–32.

————. *Salvation and the Savage: An Analysis of Protestant Missions and American Indian Response, 1787–1862*. Louisville: University of Kentucky Press, 1962.

Berlin, Ira, Barbara J. Fields, Stever F. Miller, Joseph P. Reidy, and Leslie S. Rowland. *Slaves No More: Three Essays on Emancipation and the Civil War*. New York: Cambridge University Press, 1992.

Beyreis, David C. *Blood in the Borderlands: Conflict, Kinship, and the Bent Family, 1821–1920*. Lincoln: University of Nebraska Press, 2020.

Bhattacharya, Sanjoy, and Niels Brimnes. "Simultaneously Global and Local: Reassessing Smallpox Vaccination and Its Spread, 1789–1900." *Bulletin of the History of Medicine* 83 (Spring 2009): 1–16.

Blansett, Kent. "Intertribalism in the Ozarks, 1800–1865." *American Indian Quarterly* 34, no. 4 (Fall 2010): 475–97.

Blegen, Theodore C. *Minnesota: A History of the State.* Minneapolis: University of Minnesota Press, 1963.

———. "The Pond Brothers." *Minnesota History* 15 (September 1934): 273–81.

Blight, David W., ed. *Passages to Freedom: The Underground Railroad in History and Memory.* Washington. DC: Smithsonian Books, 2004.

Blu, Karen I. *The Lumbee Problem: The Making of an American Indian People.* New York: Cambridge University Press, 1980.

Bourke, Joanna. "Fear and Anxiety: Writing about Emotion in Modern History." *History Workshop Journal* 55, no. 1(Spring 2003): 111–33.

Bowden, Henry Warner. *American Indians and Christian Missions: Studies in Cultural Conflict.* Chicago: University of Chicago Press, 1981.

Boylston, Arthur. "The Origins of Inoculation." *Journal of the Royal Society of Medicine* 105, no. 7 (July 2012): 309–13.

Brading, David A. *Miners and Merchants in Bourbon Mexico, 1763–1810.* Cambridge: Cambridge University Press, 1971.

Brading, David A., and Harry E. Cross. "Colonial Silver Mining: Mexico and Peru." *Hispanic American Historical Review* 52, no. 4 (November 1972): 545–79.

Breen, T. H. "'Baubles of Britain': The American and Consumer Revolutions of the Eighteenth Century." *Past and Present* 119 (May 1988): 73–104.

———. "An Empire of Goods: The Anglicization of Colonial America, 1690–1776." *Journal of British Studies* 25, no. 4 (October 1986): 467–99.

———. *The Marketplace of Revolution: How Consumer Politics Shaped American Independence.* New York: Oxford University Press, 2005.

———. *Tobacco Culture: The Mentality of the Great Tidewater Planters on the Eve of Revolution.* Princeton, NJ: Princeton University Press, 1985.

Broadbent, Noel. *Lapps and Labyrinths: Saami Prehistory, Colonization, and Cultural Resilience.* Washington, DC: Smithsonian Institution Press, 2010.

Brown, G. Gordon. "Missions and Cultural Diffusion." *American Journal of Sociology* 50, no. 3 (November 1944): 214–19.

Brown, Kate. *A Biography of No Place: From Ethnic Borderland to Soviet Heartland.* Cambridge, MA: Harvard University Press, 2005.

Bruchac, Margaret M. "Hill Town Touchstone: Reconsidering William Apess and Colrain, Massachusetts." *Early American Studies* 14, no. 4 (Fall 2016): 712–48.

Bruegel, Martin. *Farm, Shop, Landing: The Rise of a Market Society in the Hudson River Valley, 1780–1860.* Durham, NC: Duke University Press, 2002.

Brunsman, Denver. *The Evil Necessity: British Naval Impressment in the Eighteenth-Century Atlantic World.* Charlottesville: University of Virginia Press, 2013.

Burge, Daniel J. *A Failed Vision of Empire: The Collapse of Manifest Destiny, 1845–1872.* Lincoln: University of Nebraska Press, 2022.

Burlingame, Merrill G. "The Buffalo in Trade and Commerce." *North Dakota Historical Quarterly* 3 (July 1929): 262–91.

Bushman, Richard L. "Markets and Composite Farms in Early America." *William and Mary Quarterly* 55, no. 3 (July 1998): 351–74.

Butler, Jon. "Enthusiasm Described and Decried: The Great Awakening as Interpretive Fiction." *Journal of American History* 69, no. 2 (September 1982): 305–25.

Campbell, Gregory R. "Plains Indian Historical Demography and Health." *Plains Anthropologist* 34, no. 124 (May 1989): v–xiii.

Campbell, Mavis C. *The Maroons of Jamaica, 1655–1796: A History of Resistance, Collaboration, and Betrayal*. Granby, MA: Bergen and Garvey, 1988.

Carden, Maren Lockwood. *Oneida: Utopian Community to Modern Corporation*. Baltimore, MD: Johns Hopkins University Press, 1969.

Carlos, Ann M., and Elizabeth Hoffman, "The North American Fur Trade: Bargaining to a Joint Profit Maximum under Incomplete Information, 1804–1821." *Journal of Economic History* 46, no. 4 (December 1986): 967–86.

Carson, James Taylor. "Native Americans, the Market Revolution, and Culture Change: The Choctaw Cattle Economy, 1690–1830." *Agricultural History* 71, no. 1 (Winter 1997): 1–18.

Cassidy, Michelle. "'The More Noise They Make': Odawa and Ojibwe Encounters with American Missionaries in Northern Michigan, 1837–1871." *Michigan Historical Review* 38, no. 2 (Fall 2021): 1–34.

Cayton, Andrew R. L., and Frederika J. Teute, eds. *Contact Points: American Frontiers from the Mohawk Valley to the Mississippi, 1750–1830*. Chapel Hill: University of North Carolina Press, 1998.

Chambers, William Nisbet. *Old Bullion Benton: Senator from the New West*. Boston: Little, Brown, 1956.

Christian, Shirley. *Before Lewis and Clark: The Story of the Chouteaus, the French Dynasty That Ruled America's Frontier*. New York: Farrar, Straus and Giroux, 2004.

Clark, Christopher. *The Communitarian Movement: The Radical Challenge of the Northampton Association*. Ithaca, NY: Cornell University Press, 1996.

Clavin, Matthew J. *Aiming for Pensacola: Fugitive Slaves on the Atlantic and Southern Frontiers*. Cambridge, MA: Harvard University Press, 2015.

———. *The Battle of Negro Fort: The Rise and Fall of a Fugitive Slave Community*. New York: New York University Press, 2019.

———. "Runaway Slave Advertisements in Antebellum Florida: A Retrospective." *Florida Historical Quarterly* 94, no. 3 (Winter 2016): 426–43.

Clayton, James L. "The Growth and Economic Significance of the Fur Trade, 1790–1890." *Minnesota History* 40, no. 4 (Winter 1966): 210–20.

Cleves, Rachel Hope, Nicole Eustace, Paul Gilje, Matthew Rainbow Hale, Cecilia Morgan, Jason M. Opal, Lawrence A. Peskin, and Alan Taylor. "Interchange: The War of 1812." *Journal of American History* 99, no. 2 (September 2012): 520–55.

Colley, Linda. *Captives: Britain, Empire, and the World*. New York: Anchor, 2004.

Coman, Katherine. "Government Factories: An Attempt to Control Competition in the Fur Trade." *Bulletin of the American Economic Association* 1, no. 2 (April 1911): 368–88.

Cook, Noble David. *Born to Die: Disease and New World Conquest, 1492–1650*. New York: Cambridge University Press, 1998.

Cook, Sherburne F. "The Smallpox Epidemic of 1779 in Mexico." *Bulletin of the History of Medicine* 7 (July 1939): 937–69.

———. "Smallpox in Spanish and Mexican California, 1770–1845." *Bulletin of the History of Medicine* 7 (February 1939): 29–43.

Cool, Paul. *Salt Warriors: Insurgency on the Rio Grande.* College Station: Texas A&M University Press, 2008.

Cornell, Sarah E. "Citizens of Nowhere: Fugitive Slaves and Free African Americans in Mexico, 1833–1857." *Journal of American History* 100, no. 2 (September 2013): 351–74.

Cott, Nancy. *The Bonds of Womanhood: "Woman's Sphere" in New England, 1780–1835.* New Haven, CT: Yale University Press, 1977.

Covington, James W. *The Seminoles of Florida.* Gainesville: University Press of Florida, 1993.

Craig, Winifred Campbell. "The Fur Trade around Ft. Wayne." MA thesis, Butler University, 1929.

Cronon, William. *Nature's Metropolis: Chicago and the Great West.* New York: Knopf, 1991.

———. "A Place for Stories." *Journal of American History* 78, no. 4 (March 1992): 1347–76.

Crosby, Alfred W., Jr. *The Columbian Exchange: Biological and Cultural Consequences of 1492.* Westport, CT: Greenwood Press, 1972.

———. *Ecological Imperialism: The Biological Expansion of Europe, 900–1900.* New York: Cambridge University Press, 1986.

———. "Virgin Soil Epidemics as a Factor in the Aboriginal Depopulation of America." *William and Mary Quarterly* 33, no. 2 (April 1976): 289–99.

Curtis, Edith. *A Season in Utopia: The Story of Brook Farm.* New York: Thomas Nelson and Sons, 1961.

Cusick, James G. *The Other War of 1812: The Patriot War and the American Invasion of Spanish East Florida.* Gainesville: University Press of Florida, 2003.

———. "Some Thoughts on Spanish East and West Florida as Borderlands." *Florida Historical Quarterly* 90, no. 2 (Fall 2011): 133–56.

Daggar, Lori J. "The Mission Complex: Economic Development, 'Civilization,' and Empire in the Early Republic." *Journal of the Early Republic* 36, no. 3 (Fall 2016): 467–91.

Dahl, Adam. *Empire of the People: Settler Colonialism and the Foundations of Modern Democratic Thought.* Lawrence: University Press of Kansas, 2018.

Daniels, John D. "The Indian Population of North America in 1492." *William and Mary Quarterly* 49 (April 1992): 298–320.

Davis, David Brion. *The Problem of Slavery in the Age of Emancipation.* New York: Knopf, 2014.

Davis, Samuel M. "'Here they are in the lowest state of social gradation—aliens—political— moral—social aliens, strangers, though natives': Removal and Colonization in the Old Northwest, 1815–1870." PhD diss., Temple University, 2019.

DeLay, Brian. *War of a Thousand Deserts: Indian Raids and the U.S.-Mexican War.* New Haven, CT: Yale University Press, 2008.

del Castillo, Richard Griswold. *The Treaty of Guadalupe Hidalgo: A Legacy of Conflict.* Norman: University of Oklahoma Press, 1990.

Delgada, Grace Peña. "Border Control and Sexual Policing: White Slavery and Prostitution along the U.S.-Mexico Borderlands, 1903–1930." *Western Historical Quarterly* 43, no. 2 (Summer 2012): 157–78.

Deloria, Ella C. *Speaking of Indians.* New York: Friendship Press, 1944.

Demos, John. *The Unredeemed Captive: A Family Story from Early America*. New York: Vintage, 1995.

Diemer, Andrew K. *The Politics of Black Citizenship: Free African Americans in the Mid-Atlantic Borderland, 1817–1863*. Athens: University of Georgia Press, 2016.

Dillon, Merton L. *Benjamin Lundy and the Struggle for Negro Freedom*. Urbana: University of Illinois Press, 1966.

Din, Gilbert C. "William Augustus Bowles on the Georgia Frontier: A Reexamination of the Spanish Surrender of Fort San Marcos de Apalache." *Georgia Historical Quarterly* 88, no. 3 (Fall 2004): 305–32.

Din, Gilbert C., and A. P. Nasatir. *The Imperial Osages: Spanish-Indian Diplomacy in the Mississippi Valley*. Norman: University of Oklahoma Press, 1983.

Dobyns, Henry F. *Their Number Become Thinned: Native American Population Dynamics in Eastern North America*. Knoxville: University of Tennessee Press, 1983.

Dowd, Gregory Evans. *A Spirited Resistance: The North American Indian Struggle for Unity, 1745–1815*. Baltimore, MD: Johns Hopkins University Press, 1993.

Downs, Jacques M. "American Merchants and the China Opium Trade, 1800–1840." *Business History Review* 42, no. 4 (Winter 1968): 418–42.

Drinnon, Richard. *Facing West: The Metaphysics of Indian Hating and Empire Building*. New York: Schoken, 1990.

Dublin, Thomas. *Women at Work: The Transformation of Work and Community in Lowell, Massachusetts, 1826–1860*. New York: Columbia University Press, 1981.

Dunn, Richard S. *Sugar and Slaves: The Rise of the Planter Class in the English West Indies, 1624–1713*. Chapel Hill: University of North Carolina Press, 1972.

Dunning, William A., David S. Muzzey, and Robert Livingston Schuyler, ed. *The English Race and America's Making*. New York: Columbia University, ca. 1921.

Durbach, Nadia. *Bodily Matters: The Anti-vaccination Movement in England, 1853–1907*. Durham, NC: Duke University Press, 2005.

DuVal, Kathleen. *The Native Ground: Indians and Colonists in the Heart of the Continent*. Philadelphia: University of Pennsylvania Press, 2006.

Eccles, W. J. "The Fur Trade and Eighteenth-Century Imperialism." *William and Mary Quarterly* 40 (July 1983): 341–62.

Edmunds, R. David. *The Shawnee Prophet*. Lincoln: University of Nebraska Press, 1983.

Edwards, Tai S. *Osage Women and Empire: Gender and Power*. Lawrence: University Press of Kansas, 2018.

Ekberg, Carl J. *Stealing Indian Women: Native Slavery in the Illinois Country*. Urbana: University of Illinois Press, 2007.

Elkins, Stanley. *Slavery: A Problem in American Institutional and Intellectual Life*. Chicago: University of Chicago Press, 1959.

Elsmere, Jane. "The Notorious Yazoo Land Fraud Case." *Georgia Historical Quarterly* 51, no. 4 (December 1967): 425–42.

Erbig, Jeffrey Alan, Jr. *Where Caciques and Mapmakers Met: Border Making in Eighteenth-Century South America*. Chapel Hill: University of North Carolina Press, 2020.

Etcheson, Nicole. "Manliness and the Political Culture of the Old Northwest, 1790–1860." *Journal of the Early Republic* 15, no. 1 (Spring 1995): 59–77.

Ethridge, Robbie. *Creek Country: The Creek Indians and Their World*. Chapel Hill: University of North Carolina Press, 2003.

Ewers, John C. "Symbols of Chiefly Authority." In *The Spanish in the Mississippi Valley, 1762–1804*, edited by John F. McDermott, 272–86. Urbana: University of Illinois Press, 1974.

Fanning, Sara. *Caribbean Crossing: African Americans and the Haitian Emigration Movement*. New York: New York University Press, 2015.

Faragher, John M. *Daniel Boone: The Life and Legend of an American Pioneer*. New York: Holt, 1982.

————. "'More Motley Than Mackinaw': From Ethnic Mixing to Ethnic Cleansing on the Frontier of Lower Missouri, 1783–1833." In *Contact Points: American Frontiers from the Mohawk Valley to the Mississippi, 1750–1830*, edited by Andrew R. L. Cayton and Frederika Teute, 304–26. Chapel Hill: University of North Carolina Press, 1998.

————. *Women and Men on the Overland Trail*. New Haven, CT: Yale University Press, 1979.

Faragher, John M., Maji Jo Buhle, Daniel H. Czitron, and Susan H. Armitage. *Out of Many: A History of the American People*. Vol. 1, *To 1877*, 9th ed. Hoboken, NJ: Pearson, 2020.

Fede, Andrew. "Legitimized Violent Slave Abuse in the American South, 1619–1865: A Case Study of Law and Social Change in Six Southern States." *American Journal of Legal History* 29 (April 1985): 93–150.

Fenn, Elizabeth. "Biological Warfare in Eighteenth-Century North America: Beyond Jeffery Amherst." *Journal of American History* 86, no. 4 (March 2000): 1552–80.

————. *Encounters at the Heart of the World: A History of the Mandan People*. New York: Hill and Wang, 2014.

————. *Pox Americana: The Great Smallpox Epidemic of 1775–82*. New York: Hill and Wang, 2001.

Fixico, Donald L. "The Alliance of the Three Fires in Trade and War, 1630–1812." *Michigan Historical Review* 20, no. 2 (Fall 1994): 1–23.

Foner, Eric. *The Fiery Trial: Abraham Lincoln and American Slavery*. New York: Norton, 2010.

————. *Gateway to Freedom: The Hidden History of the Underground Railroad*. New York: Norton, 2016.

————. *Give Me Liberty! An American History*. Vol. 1, *To 1877*. New York: Norton, 2006.

Forbes, Allyn Bailey, ed. *Winthrop Papers*. Vol. 3, *1631–1637*. Boston: Massachusetts Historical Society, 1943.

Forbes, Bruce. "Evangelization and Acculturation among the Santee Dakota Indians, 1834–1864." PhD diss., Princeton University, 1977.

Fredrickson, George M. *White Supremacy: A Comparative Study in American and South African History*. New York: Oxford University Press, 1981.

Freeman, Joanne B. "Dueling as Politics: Reinterpreting the Burr-Hamilton Duel." *William and Mary Quarterly* 53, no. 2 (April 1996): 289–318.

Frymer, Paul. *Building an American Empire: The Era of Territorial and Political Expansion*. Princeton, NJ: Princeton University Press, 2017.

Fuess, Claude M. *The Life of Caleb Cushing*. 2 vols. New York: Harcourt, Brace and Co., 1923.

Gallay, Alan. *The Indian Slave Trade: The Rise of the English Empire in the American South*. New Haven, CT: Yale University Press, 2002.

Gates, Charles M. "The Lac qui Parle Indian Mission." *Minnesota History* 16 (June 1935): 133–51.

Gates, Paul Wallace. *The Farmer's Age: Agriculture, 1815–1860*. New York: Holt, Rinehart and Winston, 1960.

———. "The Role of Land Speculators in Western Development." *Pennsylvania Magazine of History and Biography* 66 (July 1942): 314–33.

Gerstle, Gary. "A State Both Strong and Weak." *American Historical Review* 115, no. 3 (June 2010): 779–85.

Gibson, Arrell M. *The Kickapoos: Lords of the Middle Border*. Norman: University of Oklahoma Press, 1963.

Gilje, Paul. *Free Trade and Sailors' Rights in the War of 1812*. New York: Cambridge University Press, 2013.

———. "The Rise of Capitalism in the Early Republic." *Journal of the Early Republic* 16, no. 2 (Summer 1996): 159–81.

Glassheim, Eagle. *Cleansing the Czechoslovak Borderlands: Migration, Environment, and Health in the Former Sudetenland*. Pittsburgh, PA: University of Pittsburgh Press, 2018.

Glynn, Ian, and Jennifer Glynn. *The Life and Death of Smallpox*. New York: Cambridge University Press, 2004.

Gibbon, Guy. *The Sioux: The Dakota and Lakota Nations*. Malden, MA: Blackwell, 2003.

Gould, Eliga. "Independence and Interdependence: The American Revolution and the Problem of Postcolonial Nationhood, circa 1802." *William and Mary Quarterly* 74, no. 4 (October 2017): 729–52.

Grandin, Greg. *The End of the Myth: From the Frontier to the Border Wall in the Mind of America*. New York: Metropolitan Books, 2019.

Gray, John S. "Honore Picotte, Fur Trader." *South Dakota History* 6, no. 2 (March 1976): 186–202.

Gray, Susan E. *The Yankee West: Community Life on the Michigan Frontier*. Chapel Hill: University of North Carolina Press, 1996.

Graybill, Andrew. *Policing the Great Plains: Rangers, Mounties, and the North American Frontier, 1875–1910*. Lincoln: University of Nebraska Press, 2007.

———. *The Red and the White: A Family Saga of the American West*. New York: Norton, 2013.

Green, Michael D. *The Politics of Indian Removal: Creek Government and Society in Crisis*. Lincoln: University of Nebraska Press, 1982.

Green, Michael D., and Theda Perdue. *The Cherokee Nation and the Trail of Tears*. New York: Penguin, 2007.

Greenberg, Amy S. *Manifest Destiny and American Territorial Expansion: A Brief History with Documents*. Boston: Bedford, 2012.

Greene, Jack. "Colonial History and National History: Reflections on a Continuing Problem." *William and Mary Quarterly* 64, no. 2 (April 2007): 235–50.

Grob, Gerald N. *The Deadly Truth: A History of Disease in America*. Cambridge, MA: Harvard University Press, 2002.

Groves, Robert Walker. "Beaulieu Plantation." *Georgia Historical Quarterly* 37, no. 3 (September 1953): 200–209.

Guarneri, Carl J. "Reconstructing the Antebellum Communitarian Movement: Oneida and Fourierism." *Journal of the Early Republic* 16, no. 3 (Autumn 1996): 463–88.

Guyatt, Nicholas. "'The Outskirts of Our Happiness': Race and the Lure of Colonization in the Early Republic." *Journal of American History* 95, no. 4 (March 2009): 986–1011.

————. *Providence and the Invention of the United States, 1607–1876*. Cambridge: Cambridge University Press, 2007.

Hackel, Steven W. *Children of Coyote, Missionaries of Saint Francis: Indian-Spanish Relations in Colonial California, 1769–1850*. Chapel Hill: University of North Carolina Press, 2005.

Hackett, Paul. "Averting Disaster: The Hudson's Bay Company and Smallpox in Western Canada during the Late Eighteenth and Early Nineteenth Centuries." *Bulletin of the History of Medicine* 78, no. 3 (2004): 575–609.

Haeger, John D. "Business Strategy and Practice in the Early Republic: John Jacob Astor and the American Fur Trade." *Western Historical Quarterly* 19, no. 2 (May 1988): 183–202.

————. *John Jacob Astor: Business and Finance in the Early Republic*. Detroit: Wayne State University Press, 2017.

Haggard, J. Villasana. "The Neutral Ground between Louisiana and Texas, 1806–1821." *Louisiana Historical Quarterly* 28 (October 1945): 1001–128.

Hahn, Steven. *A Nation under Our Feet: Black Political Struggles in the Rural South from Slavery to the Great Migration*. Cambridge, MA: Harvard University Press, 2003.

Hall, John W. *Uncommon Defense: Indian Allies in the Black Hawk War*. Cambridge, MA: Harvard University Press, 2009.

Hall, Thomas D. *Social Change in the Southwest, 1350–1880*. Lawrence: University Press of Kansas, 1989.

Halttunen, Karen. *Confidence Men and Painted Women: A Study of Middle-Class Culture in America, 1830–1870*. New Haven, CT: Yale University Press, 1982.

————. "Humanitarianism and the Pornography of Pain in Anglo-American Culture." *American Historical Review* 100, no. 2 (April 1995): 303–34.

Hämäläinen, Pekka. *The Comanche Empire*. New Haven, CT: Yale University Press, 2008.

————. *Lakota America: A New History of Indigenous Power*. New Haven, CT: Yale University Press, 2019.

Hämäläinen, Pekka, and Samuel Truett. "On Borderlands." *Journal of American History* 98, no. 2 (September 2011): 338–61.

Hammond, John Craig. "Slavery, Settlement, and Empire: The Expansion and Growth of Slavery in the Interior of the North American Continent, 1770–1820." *Journal of the Early Republic* 32, no. 2 (Summer 2012): 175–206.

Hardesty, Jared. *Black Lives, Native Lands, White Worlds: A History of Slavery in New England*. Amherst: Bright Leaf, 2019.

Harding, Vincent. *A Certain Magnificence: Lyman Beecher and the Transformation of American Protestantism, 1775–1863*. Brooklyn: Carlson, 1991.

Harring, Sidney L. *Crow Dog's Case: American Indian Sovereignty, Tribal Law, and United States Law in the Nineteenth Century*. New York: Cambridge University Press, 1994.

Harris, Lester. "The Cession of Florida and John Quincy Adams, Secretary of State, U.S.A." *Florida Historical Quarterly* 36 (January 1958): 223–38.

Hart, William B. "Black 'Go-Betweens' and the Mutability of 'Race,' Status, and Identity on New York's Pre-revolutionary Frontier." In *Contact Points: American Frontiers from the Mohawk Valley to the Mississippi, 1750–1830*, edited by Andrew R. L. Cayton and Frederika J. Teute, 88–113. Chapel Hill: University of North Carolina Press, 1998.

Hartz, Louis. *The Liberal Tradition in America*. New York: Harcourt, Brace, 1955.

Hatch, Nathan O. *The Democratization of American Christianity*. New Haven, CT: Yale University Press, 1989.

Heath, William Estill. "The Yazoo Land Fraud." *Georgia Historical Quarterly* 16 (December 1932): 274–91.

Henige, David. "On the Contact Population of Hispaniola: History as Higher Mathematics." *Hispanic American Historical Review* 58, no. 2 (May 1978): 217–37.

———. "Their Numbers Become Thick: Native American Historical Demography as Expiation." In *The Invented Indian: Cultural Fictions and Government Policies*, edited by James Clifton, 169–91. New Brunswick: Transaction Publishers, 1990.

Herbert, Archer Butler. "The Methods and Operations of the Scioto Group of Speculators." *Mississippi Valley Historical Review* 1 (March 1915): 502–15.

Hernandez, Kelly Lytle. *Migra! A History of the U.S. Border Patrol*. Berkeley: University of California Press, 2010.

Herring, Joseph B. *Kenekuk the Kickapoo Prophet*. Lawrence: University Press of Kansas, 2019.

Herschthal, Eric. "Slaves, Spaniards, and Subversion in Early Louisiana: The Persistent Fears of Black Revolt and Spanish Collusion in Territorial Louisiana." *Journal of the Early Republic* 36, no. 2 (Summer 2016): 283–311.

Hill, Michael A. "The Myth of Seward's Folly." *Western Historical Quarterly* 50, no. 1 (Spring 2019): 43–64.

Hilliard, Jerry. "An Equestrian Pictograph in Western Arkansas." *Plains Anthropologist* 34, no. 126 (November 1989): 327–30.

Hinderaker, Eric. *Elusive Empires: Constructing Colonialism in the Ohio Valley, 1673–1800*. New York: Cambridge University Press, 1997.

Hitela, Thomas. *Manifest Design: American Exceptionalism and Empire*. Ithaca, NY: Cornell University Press, 2003.

Hixson, Walter L. *American Settler Colonialism: A History*. New York: Palgrave Macmillan, 2013.

Holder, Preston. *The Hoe and the Horse on the Plains: A Study of Cultural Development among North American Indians*. Lincoln: University of Nebraska Press, 1970.

Holloway, Mark. *Utopian Communities in America, 1680–1880*. Mineola, NY: Dover, 2011.

Holt, Michael F. *The Rise and Fall of the American Whig Party: Jacksonian Politics and the Onset of the Civil War*. New York: Oxford University Press, 2003.

Horsman, Reginald. *The Causes of the War of 1812*. Philadelphia: University of Pennsylvania Press, 1962.

———. *Race and Manifest Destiny: The Origins of American Racial Anglo-Saxonism*. Cambridge, MA: Harvard University Press, 1981.

Horwitz, Morton. *The Transformation of American Law, 1780–1860*. Cambridge, MA: Harvard University Press, 1976.

Howard, James H. *The Canadian Sioux*. 2nd ed. Lincoln: University of Nebraska Press, 2014.

———. *The Dakota or Sioux Indians: A Study in Human Ecology*. Lincoln, NE: J & L Reprint Company, 1980.

Howe, Daniel Walker. *What Hath God Wrought: The Transformation of America, 1815–1848*. New York: Oxford University Press, 2009.

Hoxie, Frederick E. "From Prison to Homeland: The Cheyenne River Indian Reservation before World War I." *South Dakota History* 10 (Winter 1979): 1–24.

Hudson, Linda. *Mistress of Manifest Destiny: A Biography of Jane McManus Storm Cazneau, 1807–1878.* Austin: Texas State Historical Association, 2001.

Huerkamp, Claudia. "The History of Smallpox Vaccination in Germany: A First Step in the Medicalization of the General Public." *Journal of Contemporary History* 20, no. 4 (October 1985): 617–35.

Hurst, James Willard. *Law and the Conditions of Freedom in the Nineteenth-Century United States.* Madison: University of Wisconsin Press, 1956.

Hurtado, Albert L. *Indian Survival on the California Frontier.* New Haven, CT: Yale University Press, 1988.

Igler, David. *Industrial Cowboys: Miller and Lux and the Transformation of the Far West, 1850– 1920.* Berkeley: University of California Press, 2005.

————. "The Industrial Far West: Region and Nation in the Late Nineteenth Century." *Pacific Historical Review* 69 (May 2000): 159–92.

Ignatiev, Noel. *How the Irish Became White.* New York: Routledge, 1995.

Isenberg, Andrew C. "Between Mexico and the United States: From *Indios* to Vaqueros in the Pastoral Borderlands." In *Mexico and Mexicans in the Making of the United States,* edited by John Tutino, 85–109. Austin: University of Texas Press, 2012.

————. *The Destruction of the Bison: An Environmental History, 1750–1920.* 2nd ed. New York: Cambridge University Press, 2020.

————. "Empire and Borderlands." *Great Plains Quarterly* 41 (Summer–Fall 2021): 301–8.

————. "An Empire of Remedy: Vaccination, Natives, and Narratives in the North American West." *Pacific Historical Review* 86, no. 1 (February 2017): 84–113.

————. "The Environment, the United States, and the World in the Nineteenth Century." In *The Cambridge History of America and the World.* Vol. 2, *1820–1900,* edited by Kristin Hoganson and Jay Sexto, 361–83. New York: Cambridge University Press, 2021.

————. "Industrial Empire: The American Conquest of the West, 1845–1900." In *The Routledge History of Nineteenth-Century America,* edited by Jonathan D. Wells, 333–45. New York: Routledge, 2018.

————. "'A land of hardship and distress': Camels, North American Deserts, and the Limits of Conquest." *Global Environment* 12 (March 2019): 84–101.

————. "The Market Revolution in the Borderlands: George Champlin Sibley in Missouri and New Mexico, 1808–1826." *Journal of the Early Republic* 21, no. 3 (Fall 2001): 445–65.

————. *Mining California: An Ecological History.* New York: Hill and Wang, 2005.

————. "'To See inside of an Indian': Missionaries and Dakotas in the Minnesota Borderlands." In *Conversion: Old Worlds and New,* edited by Kenneth Mills and Anthony Grafton, 218–40. Rochester, NY: University of Rochester Press, 2003.

Isenberg, Andrew C., and Lawrence H. Kessler, "Settler Colonialism and the Environmental History of the North American West." *Journal of the West* 56, no. 4 (Fall 2017): 57–66.

Isenberg, Andrew C., and Thomas Richards Jr. "Alternative Wests: Rethinking Manifest Destiny." *Pacific Historical Review* 86, no. 1 (February 2017): 4–17.

Isenberg, Nancy. *Sex and Citizenship in Antebellum America.* Chapel Hill: University of North Carolina Press, 1998.

Iverson, Peter. *When Indians Became Cowboys: Native Peoples and Cattle Ranching in the American West.* Norman: University of Oklahoma Press, 1994.

Jackson, Robert H., and Edward Castillo. *Indians, Franciscans, and Colonization: The Impact of the Mission System on California Indians.* Albuquerque: University of New Mexico Press, 1995.

Jacoby, Karl. *The Strange Career of William Ellis: The Texas Slave Who Became a Mexican Millionaire.* New York: Norton, 2016.

Jensen, Niklas Thode. "Safeguarding Slaves: Smallpox, Vaccination, and Governmental Health Policies among the Enslaved Population in the Danish West Indies, 1803–1848." *Bulletin of the History of Medicine* 83, no. 1 (Spring 2009): 95–124.

John, Elizabeth A. H. *Storms Brewed in Other Men's Worlds: The Confrontation of Indian, Spanish, and French in the Southwest, 1540–1795.* College Station: Texas A&M Press, 1975.

Johnson, Benjamin Heber. *Revolution in Texas: How a Forgotten Rebellion and Its Blood Suppression Turned Mexicans into Americans.* New Haven, CT: Yale University Press, 2003.

Johnson, Curtis D. "The Protracted Meeting Myth: Awakenings, Revivals, and New York State Baptists, 1789–1850." *Journal of the Early Republic* 34, no. 3 (Fall 2014): 349–83.

Johnson, Paul. *A Shopkeeper's Millennium: Society and Revivals in Rochester, New York, 1815–1837.* New York: Hill and Wang, 1978.

Johnson, Paul, and Sean Wilentz. *The Kingdom of Matthias: A Story of Sex and Salvation in 19th-Century America.* New York: Oxford University Press, 1995.

Johnson, Walter. "On Agency." *Journal of Social History* 37, no. 1 (Autumn 2003): 113–24.

———. *River of Dark Dreams: Slavery and Empire in the Cotton Kingdom.* Cambridge, MA: Harvard University Press, 2017.

———. *Soul by Soul: Life Inside the Antebellum Slave Market.* Cambridge, MA: Harvard University Press, 2001.

Jones, Charles T. *George Champlin Sibley: The Prairie Puritan.* Independence, MO: Jackson County Historical Society, 1970.

Jones, David S. *Rationalizing Epidemics: Meanings and Uses of American Indian Mortality since 1600.* Cambridge, MA: Harvard University Press, 2004.

Jordan, Terry G. *North American Cattle-Ranching Frontiers: Origins, Diffusion, and Differentiation.* Albuquerque: University of New Mexico Press, 1993.

Jortner, Adam. *The Gods of Prophetstown: The Battle of Tippecanoe and the Holy War for the American Frontier.* New York: Oxford University Press, 2011.

Judson, Pieter M. "Marking National Space on the Habsburg Austrian Borderlands, 1880–1918." In *Shatterzone of Empires: Coexistence and Violence in the German, Habsburg, Russian, and Ottoman Borderlands,* edited by Omer Bartov and Eric D. Weitz, 122–35. Bloomington: Indiana University Press, 2013.

Kastor, Peter J. *The Nation's Crucible: The Louisiana Purchase and the Creation of America.* New Haven, CT: Yale University Press, 2004.

———. "'What Are the Advantages of Acquisition?': Inventing Expansion in the Early American Republic." *American Quarterly* 60, no. 4 (December 2008): 1003–35.

Kelman, Ari. *A Misplaced Massacre: Struggling over the Memory of Sand Creek.* Cambridge, MA: Harvard University Press, 2013.

Kelton, Paul. "Avoiding the Smallpox Spirits: Colonial Epidemics and Southeastern Indian Survival." *Ethnohistory* 51, no. 1 (Winter 2004): 45–71.

―――. "Cherokee Medicine and the Smallpox Outbreak of 1824." In *Indigenous Knowledge and the Environment in Africa and North America*, edited by David Gordon and Shepard Krech III, 151–70. Athens: Ohio University Press, 2012.

―――. *Epidemics and Enslavement: Biological Catastrophe in the Native Southeast, 1492–1715.* Lincoln: University of Nebraska Press, 2007.

Kennedy, Paul. *The Rise and Fall of the Great Powers: Economic Change and Military Conflict, 1500 to 2000.* New York: Vintage, 1987.

Kennedy, Thomas C. "Sibling Stewards of a Commercial Empire: The Innerarity Brothers in the Floridas." *Florida Historical Quarterly* 67, no. 3 (January 1989): 259–89.

Key, Joseph Patrick. "Indians and Ecological Conflict in Territorial Arkansas." *Arkansas Historical Quarterly* 59, no. 2 (Summer 2000): 127–46.

Kloppenberg, James T. "The Virtues of Liberalism: Christianity, Republicanism, and Ethics in Early American Political Discourse." *Journal of American History* 74, no. 1 (June 1987): 9–33.

Knight, Vernon James, Jr. "The Formation of the Creeks." In *The Forgotten Centuries: Indians and Europeans in the American South, 1521–1704*, edited by Charles Hudson and Carmen Chaves Tesser, 373–92. Athens: University of Georgia Press, 1994.

Kopaczewski, James G., Jr. "The Seed of Robbery: Contraband and Borderland Policies in the United States Civil War Era." PhD diss., Temple University, 2022.

Kraidy, Marwan M. *Hybridity, or the Cultural Logic of Globalization.* Philadelphia: Temple University Press, 2005.

Krauthamer, Barbara. *Black Slaves, Indian Masters: Slavery, Emancipation, and Citizenship in the Native American South.* Chapel Hill: University of North Carolina Press, 2013.

LaFeber, Walter. *The New Empire: An Interpretation of American Expansion, 1860–1898.* Ithaca, NY: Cornell University Press, 1963.

Lancaster, Jane J. *Removal Aftershock: The Seminoles' Struggles to Survive in the West, 1836–1866.* Knoxville: University of Tennessee Press, 1994.

Landers, Jane G. "Africans in Spanish Colonies." *Historical Archeology* 31 (1997): 84–103.

―――. "Spanish Sanctuary: Fugitives in Florida, 1687–1790." *Florida Historical Quarterly* 62 (January 1984): 296–313.

―――. "Transforming Bondsmen into Vassals: Arming Slaves in Colonial Spanish America." In *Arming Slaves: From Classical Times to the Modern Age*, edited by Christopher Leslie Brown and Philip D. Morgan, 120–45. New Haven, CT: Yale University Press, 2006.

Landers, Jane G., and Barry M. Robinson, eds. *Slaves, Subjects, and Subversives: Blacks in Colonial Latin America.* Albuquerque: University of New Mexico Press, 2006.

Larkin, Jack. *The Reshaping of Everyday Life, 1790–1840.* New York: Harper and Row, 1988.

Larson, John Lauritz. *The Market Revolution in America: Liberty, Ambition, and the Eclipse of the Common Good.* New York: Cambridge University Press, 2009.

Lee, Robert. "'A Better View of the Country': A Missouri Settlement Map by William Clark." *William and Mary Quarterly* 79, no. 1 (January 2022): 89–120.

Lepore, Jill. *The Name of War: King Philip's War and the Origins of American Identity.* New York: Knopf, 1998.

Lesick, Lawrence Thomas. *The Lane Rebels: Evangelicalism and Antislavery in Antebellum America.* Metuchen, NJ: Scarecrow Press, 1980.

Limerick, Patricia Nelson. *Legacy of Conquest: The Unbroken Past of the American West.* New York: Norton, 1987.

Lindemann, Mary. *Medicine and Society in Early Modern Europe.* Cambridge: Cambridge University Press, 1999.

Litwack, Leon. *North of Slavery: The Negro in the Free States, 1790–1860.* Chicago: University of Chicago Press, 1965.

Maass, Richard W. "'Difficult to Relinquish Territory Which Had Been Conquered': Expansionism and the War of 1812." *Diplomatic History* 39, no. 1 (January 2015): 70–97.

Madley, Benjamin. *An American Genocide: The United States and the California Indian Catastrophe, 1846–1873.* New Haven, CT: Yale University Press, 2016.

Mancall, Peter C. *Deadly Medicine: Indians and Alcohol in Early America.* Ithaca, NY: Cornell University Press, 1995.

Manchaca, Martha. *Recovering History, Constructing Race: The Indian, Black, and White Roots of Mexican Americans.* Austin: University of Texas Press, 2001.

Mann, Barbara Alice. *The Tainted Gift: The Disease Method of Frontier Expansion.* Santa Barbara, CA: ABC-CLIO, 2009.

Manning, Chandra. *Troubled Refuge: Struggling for Freedom in the Civil War.* New York: Knopf, 2016.

Marsden, George M. *Jonathan Edwards: A Life.* New Haven, CT: Yale University Press, 2004.

Marsland, Rebecca. "The Modern Traditional Healer: Locating 'Hybridity' in Modern Traditional Medicine, Southern Tanzania." *Journal of Southern African Studies* 33, no. 4 (December 2007): 751–65.

Martin, Henry A. "Jefferson as a Vaccinator." *North Carolina Medical Journal* 7 (January 1881): 2–34.

Masur, Louis P. *1831: Year of Eclipse.* New York: Hill and Wang, 2001.

May, Robert E. *The Southern Dream of a Caribbean Empire, 1854–1861.* Baton Rouge: Louisiana State University Press, 1973.

McAlister, Lyle N. "The Marine Forces of William Augustus Bowles and His 'State of Muskogee.'" *Florida Historical Quarterly* 32 (July 1953): 3–27.

———. "William Augustus Bowles and the State of Muskogee." *Florida Historical Quarterly* 40 (April 1962): 317–28.

McCoy, Drew. *The Elusive Republic: Political Economy in Jeffersonian America.* Chapel Hill: University of North Carolina Press, 1980.

McDaniel, W. Caleb. *The Problem of Democracy in the Age of Slavery: Garrisonian Abolitionists and Transatlantic Reform.* Baton Rouge: Louisiana State University Press, 2013.

McElroy, Robert McNutt. *The Winning of the Far West: A History of Regaining Texas, of the Mexican War, and the Oregon Question; and of Successive Additions to the Territory of the United States, within the Continent of America: 1829–1867.* New York: G. P. Putnam's Sons, 1914.

McLoughlin, William G. *Champions of the Cherokees: Evan and John B. Jones.* Princeton, NJ: Princeton University Press, 1990.

———. *Cherokee Renascence in the New Republic.* Princeton, NJ: Princeton University Press, 1986.

McMichael, Andrew. *Atlantic Loyalties: Americans in Spanish West Florida, 1785–1810.* Athens: University of Georgia Press, 2008.

McNeill, J. R. *Mosquito Empires: Ecology and War in the Greater Caribbean, 1620–1914*. New York: Cambridge University Press, 2010.

McNeill, William H. *Plagues and Peoples*. New York: Vintage, 1976.

McPherson, James M. *Ordeal by Fire: The Civil War and Reconstruction*. 3rd ed. Boston: McGraw-Hill, 2001.

Merrell, James. *The Indians' New World: Catawbas and Their Neighbors from European Contact through the Era of Removal*. Chapel Hill: University of North Carolina Press, 1989.

Merrill, Michael. "The Anticapitalist Origins of the United States." *Review: Journal of the Fernand Braudel Center* 13 (Fall 1990): 465–97.

———. "Putting 'Capitalism' in Its Place: A Review of Recent Literature." *William and Mary Quarterly* 52 (April 1995): 315–26.

Merritt, Jane T. "Dreaming of the Savior's Blood: Moravians and the Indian Great Awakening in Pennsylvania." *William and Mary Quarterly* 54, no. 4 (October 1997): 723–46.

Meyer, David R. *The Roots of American Industrialization*. Baltimore, MD: Johns Hopkins University Press, 2003.

Meyer, Roy W. *History of the Santee Sioux: United States Indian Policy on Trial*. Lincoln: University of Nebraska Press, 1967.

Middleton, Stephen. *The Black Laws: Race and the Legal Process in Early Ohio*. Athens: Ohio University Press, 2005.

Mihm, Stephen. *A Nation of Counterfeiters: Capitalists, Con Men, and the Making of the United States*. Cambridge, MA: Harvard University Press, 2007.

Miller, Janice Borton. "The Rebellion in East Florida in 1795." *Florida Historical Quarterly* 57, no. 2 (October 1978): 173–86.

Miller, Perry. *The New England Mind: From Colony to Province*. Cambridge, MA: Harvard University Press, 1953.

Mills, Brandon. *The World Colonization Made: The Racial Geography of Early American Empire*. Philadelphia: University of Pennsylvania Press, 2020.

Mina, Michael J., Tomasz Kula, Yumei Leng, Mamie Li, Rory D. de Vries, Mikael Knif, Heli Siljander, et al. "Measles Virus Infection Diminishes Preexisting Antibodies That Offer Protection against Other Pathogens." *Science* 366, no. 6465 (November 2019): 599–606.

Minardi, Margot. "The Boston Inoculation Controversy of 1721: An Incident in the History of Race." *William and Mary Quarterly* 61, no. 1 (January 2004): 47–76.

Mintz, Sidney W. "Slave Life on Caribbean Sugar Plantations: Some Unanswered Questions." In *Slave Cultures and the Cultures of Slavery*, edited by Stephen Palmie, 12–22. Knoxville: University of Tennessee Press, 1995.

———. *Sweetness and Power: The Place of Sugar in Modern History*. New York: Viking, 1985.

Mniyo, Samuel, and Robert Goodvoice. *The Red Road and Other Narratives of the Dakota Sioux*, edited by Daniel M. Beveridge. Lincoln: University of Nebraska Press, 2020.

Mooney, James. *The Aboriginal Population of America North of Mexico*. Washington, DC: Smithsonian Institution, 1928.

Moorhead, Max L. *New Mexico's Royal Road: Trade and Travel on the Chihuahua Trail*. Norman: University of Oklahoma Press, 1954.

Morrison, Michael A. "'New Territory versus No Territory': The Whig Party and the Politics of Western Expansion, 1846–1848." *Western Historical Quarterly* 23 (February 1992): 25–51.

————. "Westward the Curse of Empire: Texas Annexation and the American Whig Party." *Journal of the Early Republic* 10, no. 2 (Summer 1990): 221–49.

Mulroy, Kevin. *Freedom on the Border: The Seminole Maroons in Florida, the Indian Territory, Coahuila, and Texas*. Lubbock: Texas Tech University Press, 2003.

Murrin, John M. "The Great Inversion, or Court versus Country: A Comparison of the Revolutionary Settlements in England (1688–1721) and America (1776–1816)." In *Three British Revolutions: 1641, 1688, 1776*, edited by J. G. A. Pocock, 368–454. Princeton, NJ: Princeton University Press, 1980.

Nash, Linda. "The Agency of Nature or the Nature of Agency?" *Environmental History* 10, no. 1 (January 2005): 67–69.

Nelson, Elaine Marie. "Mni Luzahan and 'Our Beautiful City': Indigenous Resistance in the Black Hills up to 1937." In *Indian Cities: Histories of Indigenous Urbanization*, edited by Kent Blansett, Cathleen Cahill, and Andrew Needham, 167–97. Norman: University of Oklahoma Press, 2022.

Nelson, Robert L. "The Baltics as Colonial Playground: Germany in the East, 1914–1918." *Journal of Baltic Studies* 42, no. 1 (March 2011): 9–19.

Nevius, Marcus P. *City of Refuge: Slavery and Petit Marronage in the Great Dismal Swamp, 1765–1856*. Athens: University of Georgia Press, 2020.

Newell, Clayton R. *The Regular Army before the Civil War, 1845–1860*. Washington, DC: Center of Military History, 2014.

Nissenbaum, Stephen. *Sex, Diet, and Debility in Jacksonian America: Sylvester Graham and Health Reform*. Chicago: Dorsey Press, 1988.

North, Douglas C. *The Economic Growth of the United States, 1790–1860*. New York: Norton, 1966.

Novak, William A. "Long Live the Myth of the Weak State? A Response to Adams, Gerstle, and Witt." *American Historical Review* 115, no. 3 (June 2010): 792–800.

————. "The Myth of the 'Weak' American State." *American Historical Review* 113, no. 3 (June 2008): 752–72.

————. *The People's Welfare: Law and Regulation in Nineteenth-Century America*. Chapel Hill: University of North Carolina Press, 1996.

Nugent, Walter. *Habits of Empire: A History of American Expansion*. New York: Alfred A. Knopf, 2008.

Oakes, James. *The Ruling Race: A History of American Slaveholders*. New York: Knopf, 1982.
————. *Slavery and Freedom: An Interpretation of the Old South*. New York: Knopf, 1990.

Oberly, James W. "Westward Who? Estimates of Native White Interstate Migration after the War of 1812." *Journal of Economic History* 46, no. 2 (June 1986): 431–40.

Ohrt, Wallace. *Defiant Peacemaker: Nicholas Trist in the Mexican War*. College Station: Texas A&M University Press, 1997.

O'Riordan, Cormac. "The 1795 Rebellion in East Florida." MA thesis, University of North Florida, 1995.

Orsi, Jared. *Citizen Explorer: The Life of Zebulon Pike*. New York: Oxford University Press, 2014.

Osborne, Thomas J. *"Empire Can Wait": American Opposition to Hawaiian Annexation, 1893–1898*. Kent, OH: Kent State University Press, 1981.

Ostler, Jeffrey. *Surviving Genocide: Native Nations and the United States from the American Revolution to Bleeding Kansas*. New Haven, CT: Yale University Press, 2019.

———. "'To Extirpate the Indians': An Indigenous Consciousness of Genocide in the Ohio Valley and Lower Great Lakes, 1750s–1810." *William and Mary Quarterly* 72, no. 4 (October 2015): 587–622.

Owsley Frank L., and Gene A. Smith. *Filibusters and Expansionists: Jeffersonian Manifest Destiny, 1800–1821*. Tuscaloosa: University of Alabama Press, 1997.

Painter, Nell Irvin. *Exodusters: Black Migration to Kansas after Reconstruction*. New York: Knopf, 1976.

Parker, Donald Dean. *Lac qui Parle: Its Missionaries, Traders, and Indians*. Brookings: South Dakota State College, 1964.

Parks, Douglas R., and Raymond J. DeMallie. "Sioux, Assiniboine, and Stoney Dialects: A Classification." *Anthropological Linguistics* 34, no. 1–4 (Spring–Winter, 1992): 233–55.

Paulus, Carl Lawrence. *The Slaveholding Crisis: Fear of Insurrection and the Coming of the Civil War*. Baton Rouge: Louisiana State University Press, 2017.

Peake, Ora Brooks. *A History of the United States Indian Factory System, 1795–1822*. Denver, CO: Sage, 1954.

Pearce, Roy Harvey. *Savagism and Civilization: A Study of the Indian and the American Mind*. Baltimore, MD: Johns Hopkins University Press, 1965.

Pearson, J. Diane. "Lewis Cass and the Politics of Disease: The Indian Vaccination Act of 1832." *Wicazo Sa Review* 18, no. 2 (Fall 2003): 9–35.

———. "Medical Diplomacy and the American Indian: Thomas Jefferson, the Lewis and Clark Expedition, and the Subsequent Effects on American Indian Health and Public Policy." *Wicazo Sa Review* 19, no. 1 (Spring 2004): 105–30.

Perkins, Elizabeth A. "The Consumer Frontier: Household Consumption in Early Kentucky." *Journal of American History* 78, no. 2 (September 1991): 486–510.

Pessen, Edward. "The Egalitarian Myth and American Social Reality: Wealth, Mobility, and Equality in the 'Era of the Common Man.'" *American Historical Review* 76, no. 4 (October 1971): 989–1034.

Peterson, Jacqueline. "Many Roads to Red River: Métis Genesis on the Great Lakes Region, 1680–1815." In *The New Peoples: Being and Becoming Métis in North America*, edited by Jacqueline Peterson and Jennifer S. H. Brown, 37–72. Lincoln: University of Nebraska Press, 1985.

Pfeiffer, Carl J. *The Art and Practice of Western Medicine in the Early Nineteenth Century*. Jefferson, NC: McFarland, 1971.

Pickard, Madge E., and R. Carlyle Buley. *The Midwest Pioneer: His Ills, Cures, and Doctors*. New York: Henry Schuman, 1946.

Pincas, Steven. "Addison's Empire: Whig Conceptions of Empire in the Early Eighteenth Century." *Parliamentary History* 31, no. 1 (February 2012): 99–117.

Plaisance, Aloysius. "The Chickasaw Bluffs Factory and Its Removal to the Arkansas River, 1818–1822." *Tennessee Historical Quarterly* 11, no. 1 (March 1952): 41–56.

Porter, Kenneth W. "Abraham." *Phylon* 2 (1941): 102–16.

———. "The Cowkeeper Dynasty of the Seminole Nation." *Florida Historical Quarterly* 30 (April 1952): 341–49.

———. "The Founder of the 'Seminole Nation' Secoffee or Cowkeeper." *Florida Historical Quarterly* 27 (April 1949): 362–84.

———. "The Negro Abraham." *Florida Historical Quarterly* 25 (July 1946): 1–43.

Pound, Merritt B. *Benjamin Hawkins: Indian Agent.* Athens: University of Georgia Press, 1951.

Power-Greene, Ousmane K. *Against Wind and Tide: The African American Struggle against the Colonization Movement.* New York: New York University Press, 2014.

Powers, William K. *Oglala Religion.* Lincoln: University of Nebraska Press, 1975.

Pratt, Julius W. *The Expansionists of 1812.* New York: Macmillan, 1925.

———. "The Origin of 'Manifest Destiny.'" *American Historical Review* 32 (July 1927): 795–98.

Price, Richard, ed. *Maroon Societies: Rebel Slave Communities in the Americas.* 2nd ed. Baltimore, MD: Johns Hopkins University Press, 1979.

Prude, Jonathan. *The Coming of Industrial Order: Town and Family Life in Rural Massachusetts, 1810–1860.* Amherst: University of Massachusetts Press, 1983.

Ramsey, William L. *The Yamasee War: A Study of Culture, Economy, and Conflict in the Colonial South.* Lincoln: University of Nebraska Press, 2008.

Ranlet, Philip. "The British, Slaves, and Smallpox in Revolutionary Virginia." *Journal of Negro History* 84, no. 3 (Summer 1999): 217–26.

———. "The British, the Indians, and Smallpox: What Actually Happened at Fort Pitt in 1763?" *Pennsylvania History* 67, no. 3 (Summer 2000): 427–41.

Remini, Robert V. *Andrew Jackson and His Indian Wars.* New York: Viking, 2001.

Rensink, Brenden. *Native but Foreign: Indigenous Immigrants and Refugees in the North American Borderlands.* College Station: Texas A&M University Press, 2018.

Reséndez, Andrés. *Changing National Identities at the Frontier: Texas and New Mexico, 1800–1850.* New York: Cambridge University Press, 2004.

Richards, Thomas, Jr. *Breakaway Americas: The Unmanifest Future of the Jacksonian United States.* Baltimore, MD: Johns Hopkins University Press, 2020.

Richter, Daniel K. "Cultural Brokers and Intercultural Politics: New York–Iroquois Relations, 1664–1701." *Journal of American History* 75, no. 1 (June 1988): 40–67.

———. *Facing East from Indian Country: A Native History of Early America.* Cambridge, MA: Harvard University Press, 2001.

Rigau-Pérez, José G. "The Introduction of Smallpox Vaccine in 1803 and the Adoption of Immunization as a Government Function in Puerto Rico." *Hispanic American Historical Review* 69, no. 3 (August 1989): 393–423.

Riordan, Patrick. "Finding Freedom in Florida: Native Peoples, African Americans, and Colonists, 1670–1816." *Florida Historical Quarterly* 75, no. 1 (Summer 1996): 24–43.

Roberts, Justin. *Slavery and Enlightenment in the British Atlantic, 1750–1807.* New York: Cambridge University Press, 2009.

———. "The Whip and the Hoe: Violence, Work and Productivity on Anglo-American Plantations." *Journal of Global Slavery* 6 (January 2021): 108–30.

Rockman, Seth. *Scraping By: Wage Labor, Slavery, and Survival in Early Baltimore.* Baltimore, MD: Johns Hopkins University Press, 2008.

Rodgers, Daniel T. "In Search of Progressivism." *Reviews in American History* 10 (December 1982): 113–32.

Rodriguez, Sarah K. M. "'The Greatest Nation on Earth': The Politics of Patriotism of the First Anglo American Immigrants to Mexican Texas, 1820–1824." *Pacific Historical Review* 86, no. 1 (February 2017): 50–83.

Roediger, David R. *The Wages of Whiteness: Race and the Making of the American Working Class.* New York: Verso, 1991.

Rohrbaugh, Malcolm J. "'A Freehold Estate Therein': The Ordinance of 1787 and the Public Domain." *Indiana Magazine of History* 84, no. 1 (March 1988): 46–59.

Rollings, Willard H. *The Osage: An Ethnohistorical Study of Hegemony on the Prairie-Plains.* Columbia: University of Missouri Press, 1992.

Ronda, James P. "Generations of Faith: The Christian Indians of Martha's Vineyard." *William and Mary Quarterly* 38, no. 3 (July 1981): 369–94.

———, ed. *Thomas Jefferson and the Changing West.* Albuquerque: University of New Mexico Press, 1997.

Roosevelt, Theodore. *The Winning of the West.* Vol. 1, *From the Alleghenies to the Mississippi, 1769–1776.* New York: G. P. Putnam's Sons, 1900.

———. *The Winning of the West.* Vol. 4, *Louisiana and the Northwest, 1791–1807.* New York: G. P. Putnam's Sons, 1896.

Rorabaugh, W. J. *The Alcoholic Republic, an American Tradition.* New York: Oxford University Press, 1979.

———. "The Political Duel in the Early Republic: Burr v. Hamilton." *Journal of the Early Republic* 15, no. 1 (Spring 1995): 1–23.

Rosenberg, Charles E. *The Cholera Years: The United States in 1832, 1849, and 1866.* Chicago: University of Chicago Press, 1962.

———. *Explaining Epidemics and Other Studies in the History of Medicine.* New York: Cambridge University Press, 1992.

Rosenberg, Emily S. *Spreading the American Dream: American Economic and Cultural Expansion, 1890–1945.* New York: Hill and Wang, 1982.

Rothman, Adam. *Slave Country: American Expansion and the Origins of the Deep South.* Cambridge, MA: Harvard University Press, 2007.

Rothstein, William G. *American Physicians in the Nineteenth Century: From Sects to Science.* Baltimore, MD: Johns Hopkins University Press, 1992.

Rowe, David C. "Government Relations with the Fur Trappers of the Upper Missouri, 1820–1840." *North Dakota History* 35 (Spring 1968): 481–505.

Rushforth, Brett. *Bonds of Alliance: Indigenous and Atlantic Slaveries in New France.* Chapel Hill: University of North Carolina Press, 2013.

———. "'A Little Flesh We Offer You': The Origins of Indian Slavery in New France." *William and Mary Quarterly* 60, no. 4 (October 2023): 777–808.

Rusnock, Andrea. "Catching Cowpox: The Early Spread of Smallpox Vaccination, 1798–1810." *Bulletin of the History of Medicine* 83, no. 1 (Spring 2009): 17–36.

Ryan, Mary P. *The Cradle of the Middle Class: The Family in Oneida County, New York, 1790–1865.* New York: Cambridge University Press, 1981.

Sahlins, Peter. *Boundaries: The Making of France and Spain in the Pyrenees.* Berkeley: University of California Press, 1991.

Sampson, Robert D. *John L. O'Sullivan and His Times.* Kent, OH: Kent State University Press, 2003.

Saunt, Claudio. *A New Order of Things: Property, Power, and the Transformation of the Creek Indians*. New York: Cambridge University Press, 1999.

———. *Unworthy Republic: The Dispossession of Native Americans and the Road to Indian Territory*. New York: Norton, 2020.

Saxton, Alexander. *The Rise and Fall of the White Republic: Class Politics and Mass Culture in Nineteenth-Century America*. New York: Verso, 1990.

Schlereth, Eric. "The Privileges of Locomotion: Expatriation and the Politics of Southwestern Border Crossing." *Journal of American History* 100, no. 4 (March 2014): 995–1020.

Schlesinger, Arthur M., Jr. *The Age of Jackson*. Boston: Little, Brown, 1945.

Schob, David E. *Hired Hands and Plowboys: Farm Labor in the Midwest, 1815–1860*. Urbana: University of Illinois Press, 1975.

Schwaller, Robert C. *African Maroons in Sixteenth-Century Panama: A History in Documents*. Norman: University of Oklahoma Press, 2021.

———. "Contested Conquests: African Maroons and the Incomplete Conquest of Hispaniola, 1519–1620." *The Americas* 75, no. 4 (October 2018): 609–38.

Schwarze, Edmund. *History of the Moravian Missions among Southern Indian Tribes of the United States*. Bethlehem, PA: Times Publishing, 1923.

Sellers, Charles. *The Market Revolution: Jacksonian America, 1815–1846*. New York: Oxford University Press, 1994.

Sharples, Jason T. *The World That Fear Made: Slave Revolts and Conspiracy Scares in Early America*. Philadelphia: University of Pennsylvania Press, 2020.

Sheehan, Bernard W. *Seeds of Extinction: Jeffersonian Philanthropy and the American Indian*. New York: Norton, 1974.

Sheriff, Carol. *The Artificial River: The Erie Canal and the Paradox of Progress, 1817–1862*. New York: Hill and Wang, 1997.

Shiels, Richard D. "The Scope of the Second Great Awakening: Andover, Massachusetts, as a Case Study." *Journal of the Early Republic* 5, no. 2 (Summer 1985): 223–46.

Shurkin, Joel N. *Invisible Fire: The Story of Mankind's Victory over the Ancient Scourge of Smallpox*. New York: Putnam, 1979.

Shuttleton, David E. *Smallpox and the Literary Imagination, 1660–1820*. Cambridge: Cambridge University Press, 2007.

Silver, Timothy. *A New Face on the Countryside: Indians, Colonists, and Slaves in South Atlantic Forests, 1500–1800*. New York: Cambridge University Press, 1990.

Skinner, Alanson. *Medicine Ceremony of the Menomini, Iowa, and Wahpeton Dakota, with Notes on the Ceremony among the Ponca, Bungi Ojibwa, and Potawatomi*. New York: Museum of the American Indian, 1920.

Sköld, Peter. "Escape from Catastrophe: The Saami's Experience with Smallpox in Eighteenth- and Early-Nineteenth-Century Sweden." *Social Science History* 21, no. 1 (Spring 1997): 1–25.

Slaughter, Thomas P. *Bloody Dawn: The Christiana Riot and Racial Violence in the Antebellum North*. New York: Oxford University Press, 1991.

Slotkin, Richard. "Nostalgia and Progress: Theodore Roosevelt's Myth of the Frontier." *American Quarterly* 33, no. 5 (Winter 1981): 608–37.

———. *Regeneration through Violence: The Mythology of the American Frontier, 1600–1800*. Middletown, CT: Wesleyan University Press, 1973.

Snyder, Christina. "Andrew Jackson's Indian Son: Native Captives and American Empire." In *The Native South: New Histories and Enduring Legacies,* edited by Tim Alan Garrison and Greg O'Brien, 84–106. Lincoln: University of Nebraska Press, 2017.

———. *Great Crossings: Indians, Settlers, and Slaves in the Age of Jackson.* New York: Oxford University Press, 2017.

Spann, Edward K. *Brotherly Tomorrows: Movements for a Cooperative Society in America, 1820–1920.* New York: Columbia University Press, 1989.

———. *Hopedale: From Commune to Company Town, 1840–1920.* Columbus: Ohio State University Press, 1992.

Spector, Janet, and Eldern Johnson, eds. *Archeology, Ecology, and Ethnohistory of the Prairie-Forest Border Zone of Minnesota and Manitoba.* Lincoln: University of Nebraska Press, 1985.

Spicer, Edward H. *Cycles of Conquest: The Impact of Spain, Mexico, and the United States on the Indians of the Southwest, 1533–1960.* Tucson: University of Arizona Press, 1962.

Spitzer, Leo. "Spanish Cimarron." *Language* 14 (April–June 1938): 145–47.

Stagg, J. C. A. *Mr. Madison's War: Politics, Diplomacy, and Warfare in the Early American Republic, 1783–1830.* Princeton, NJ: Princeton University Press, 1983.

Stannard, David. *American Holocaust: The Conquest of the New World.* New York: Oxford University Press, 1993.

Stansell, Christine. *City of Women: Sex and Class in New York, 1789–1860.* New York: Knopf, 1986.

Stearn, E. Wagner, and Allen E. Stearn. *The Effect of Smallpox on the Destiny of the Amerindian.* Boston: Bruce Humphries, 1945.

Steinberg, Theodore. *Nature Incorporated: Industrialization and the Waters of New England.* New York: Cambridge University Press, 1991.

Stephanson, Anders. *Manifest Destiny: American Expansion and the Empire of the Right.* New York: Hill and Wang, 1995.

Stewart, Mart A. *"What Nature Suffers to Groe": Life, Labor, and Landscape on the Georgia Coast, 1680–1920.* Athens: University of Georgia Press, 1996.

St. John, Rachel. *Line in the Sand: A History of the Western U.S.-Mexico Border.* Princeton, NJ: Princeton University Press, 2011.

Stokes, Melvyn, and Stephen Conway. *The Market Revolution in America: Social, Political, and Religious Expressions, 1800–1880.* Charlottesville: University of Virginia Press, 1996.

Stoll, Steven. *Larding the Lean Earth: Soil and Society in Nineteenth-Century America.* New York: Hill and Wang, 2002.

Strang, Cameron. "Violence, Ethnicity, and Human Remains during the Second Seminole War." *Journal of American History* 100, no. 4 (March 2014): 973–94.

Strong, Pauline Turner. *Captive Selves, Captivating Others: The Politics and Poetics of Colonial American Captivity Narratives.* Boulder, CO.: Westview Press, 1999.

Sundstrom, Linea. "Smallpox Used Them Up: References to Epidemic Disease in Northern Plains Winter Counts, 1714–1920." *Ethnohistory* 44, no. 2 (Spring 1997): 305–43.

Swanson, John R. *The Indian Tribes of North America.* Washington, DC: Government Printing Office, 1953.

Sweet, Jameson. "Native Suffrage: Race, Citizenship, and Dakota Indians in the Upper Midwest." *Journal of the Early Republic* 39, no. 1 (Spring 2019): 99–110.

Taylor, Alan. *The Civil War of 1812: American Citizens, British Subjects, Irish Rebels, and Indian Allies.* New York: Vintage, 2010.

———. *The Internal Enemy: Slavery and War in Virginia, 1772–1832.* New York: Norton, 2013.

———. "'Wasty Ways': Stories of American Settlement." *Environmental History* 3, no. 3 (July 1998): 291–310.

———. *William Cooper's Town: Power and Persuasion in the Early Republic.* New York: Vintage, 1995.

Taylor, Amy Murrell. *Embattled Freedom: Journeys through the Civil War's Slave Refugee Camps.* Chapel Hill: University of North Carolina Press, 2018.

Taylor, George Rogers. *The Transportation Revolution.* New York: Rinehart, 1951.

Tejada, Vivien. "Unfree Soil: Empire, Labor, and Coercion in the Upper Mississippi River Valley, 1812–1861." PhD diss., Duke University, 2024.

TePaske, John J. "The Fugitive Slave: Intercolonial Rivalry and Spanish Slave Policy, 1687–1764." In *Eighteenth-Century Florida and Its Borderlands,* edited by Samuel Proctor, 1–12. Gainesville: University Presses of Florida, 1975.

Thernstrom, Stephen. *Poverty and Progress: Social Mobility in a Nineteenth-Century City.* Cambridge, MA: Harvard University Press, 1964.

Thompson, Angela T. "To Save the Children: Smallpox, Inoculation, Vaccination, and Public Health in Guanajuato, Mexico, 1797–1840." *The Americas* 49, no. 4 (April 1993): 431–55.

Thompson, Jerry. *Cortina: Defending the Mexican Name in Texas.* College Station: Texas A&M University Press, 2007.

Thornton, Russell. *American Indian Holocaust and Survival: A Population History since 1492.* Norman: University of Oklahoma Press, 1987.

Torget, Andrew J. *Seeds of Empire: Cotton, Slavery, and the Transformation of the Texas Borderlands, 1800–1850.* Chapel Hill: University of North Carolina Press, 2015.

Trennert, Robert A. "The Fur Trader as Indian Administrator: Conflict of Interest or Wise Policy?" *South Dakota History* 5 (Winter 1974): 1–19.

Trimble, Michael K. "The 1832 Inoculation Program on the Missouri River." In *Disease and Demography in the Americas,* edited by John W. Verano and Douglas H. Ubelaker, 257–64. Washington, DC: Smithsonian Institution Press, 1992.

Truett, Samuel. *Fugitive Landscapes: The Forgotten History of the U.S.-Mexico Borderlands.* New Haven, CT: Yale University Press, 2006.

Turner, Frederick Jackson. "The Significance of the Frontier in American History." *American Historical Association Annual Report* (1893): 199–227.

Tutino, John. "Globalizing the Comanche Empire." *History and Theory* 52, no. 1 (February 2013): 67–74.

———. *Making a New World: Founding Capitalism in the Bajío and Spanish North America.* Durham, NC: Duke University Press, 2011.

Tyrell, Ian, and Jay Sexton, eds. *Empire's Twin: U.S. Anti-imperialism form the Founding Era to the Age of Terrorism.* Ithaca, NY: Cornell University Press, 2015.

Ulrich, Laurel Thatcher. *A Midwife's Tale: The Life of Martha Ballard, Based on Her Diary, 1785–1812.* New York: Vintage, 1991.

Usner, Daniel H., Jr. *Indians, Settlers, and Slaves in a Frontier Exchange Economy: The Lower Mississippi Valley Before 1763.* Chapel Hill: University of North Carolina Press, 1992.

Valencius, Conevery Bolton. *The Health of the Country: How American Settlers Understood Themselves and the Land*. New York: Basic Books, 2004.

Valle, Rosemary K. "James Ohio Pattie and the 1827–1828 Alta California Measles Epidemic." *California Historical Quarterly* 52, no. 1 (Spring 1973): 28–36.

Vanderwood, Paul J. *Disorder and Progress: Bandits, Police, and Mexican Development*. Lincoln: University of Nebraska Press, 1981.

Van Kirk, Sylvia. "The Role of Native Women in the Creation of Fur Trade Society in Western Canada, 1670–1830." In *The Women's West*, edited by Susan Armitage and Elizabeth Jameson, 53–62. Norman: University of Oklahoma Press, 1987.

Van Zandt, Cynthia J. *Brothers among Nations: The Pursuit of Intercultural Alliances in Early America, 1580–1660*. New York: Oxford University Press, 2008.

Vehik, Susan C. "Dhegiha Origins and Plains Archaeology." *Plains Anthropologist* 38, no. 146 (November 1993): 231–52.

Veracini, Lorenzo. "Introducing Settler Colonial Studies." *Settler Colonial Studies* 1, no. 1 (2011): 1–12.

———. "'Settler Colonialism': Career of a Concept." *Journal of Imperial and Commonwealth History* 41, no. 2 (2013): 313–33.

Vickery, Kenneth P. "'Herrenvolk' Democracy and Egalitarianism in South Africa and the U.S. South." *Comparative Studies in Society and History* 16, no. 3 (June 1974): 309–28.

Violette, Eugene Morrow. *A History of Missouri*. Cape Girardeau, MO: Ramfre Press, 1951.

Vogel, Virgil J. "The Missionary as Acculturation Agent: Peter Dougherty and the Indians of Grand Traverse." *Michigan History* 51, no. 3 (Fall 1967): 185–201.

Walker, Brett. *The Conquest of Ainu Lands: Ecology and Culture in Japanese Expansion, 1590–1800*. Berkeley: University of California Press, 2006.

———. "The Early Modern Japanese State and Ainu Vaccinations: Redefining the Body Politic, 1799–1868." *Past and Present* 163, no. 1 (May 1999): 121–60.

Wallace, Anthony F. C. *Jefferson and the Indians: The Tragic Fate of the First Americans*. Cambridge, MA: Belknap Press, 2001.

———. *The Long, Bitter Trail: Andrew Jackson and the Indians*. New York: Hill and Wang, 1993.

———. "The Obtaining Lands: Thomas Jefferson and the Native Americans." In *Thomas Jefferson and the Changing West*, edited by James P. Ronda, 25–42. Albuquerque: University of New Mexico Press, 1997.

Warren, Louis S. *God's Red Son: The Ghost Dance Religion and the Making of Modern America*. New York: Basic Books, 2017.

Warren, William W. *History of the Ojibway People*. 2nd ed. St. Paul: Minnesota Historical Society Press, 2009.

Warrick, W. Sheridan. "American Indian Policy in the Upper Old Northwest Following the War of 1812." *Ethnohistory* 3, no. 2 (Spring 1956): 109–25.

Watson, Harry. "Andrew Jackson's Populism." *Tennessee Historical Quarterly* 76, no. 3 (Fall 2017): 218–39.

Way, Royal B. "The United States Factory System for Trading with the Indians, 1796–1822." *Mississippi Valley Historical Review* 6, no. 2 (September 1919): 220–35.

Weber, David J. *The Mexican Frontier, 1821–1846: The American Southwest under Mexico*. Albuquerque: University of New Mexico Press, 1982.

———. *The Spanish Frontier in North America*. New Haven, CT: Yale University Press, 1992.

Weber, Max. *Economy and Society: An Outline of Interpretive Sociology*. Vol. 2. New York: Bedminster Press, 1968.

Wehrman, Andrew M. "The Siege of 'Castle Pox': A Medical Revolution in Marblehead, Massachusetts, 1764–1777." *New England Quarterly* 82, no. 3 (September 2009): 385–429.

Weik, Terrance M. "The Role of Ethnogenesis and Organization in the Development of African-Native American Settlements: An African Seminole Model." *International Journal of Historical Archaeology* 13 (June 2009): 206–38.

Weinberg, Albert K. *Manifest Destiny: A Study of Nationalist Expansion in American History*. Baltimore, MD: Johns Hopkins University Press, 1935.

Whelan, Mary K. "Dakota Indian Economics and the Nineteenth-Century Fur Trade." *Ethnohistory* 40, no. 2 (Spring 1993): 246–76.

White, Bruce M. "'Give Us a Little Milk': The Social and Cultural Meanings of Gift Giving in the Lake Superior Fur Trade." *Minnesota History* 48, no. 2 (Summer 1982): 60–71.

White, Richard. "Frederick Jackson Turner and Buffalo Bill." In *The Frontier in American Culture: Essays by Richard White and Patricia Nelson Limerick*, edited by James R. Grossman, 7–65. Berkeley: University of California Press, 1994.

———. *The Middle Ground: Indians, Empires, and Republics in the Great Lakes Region, 1650–1815*. New York: Cambridge University Press, 1991.

———. *The Roots of Dependency: Subsistence, Environment, and Social Change among the Choctaws, Pawnees, and Navajos*. Lincoln: University of Nebraska Press, 1983.

———. "The Winning of the West: The Expansion of the Western Sioux in the Eighteenth and Nineteenth Centuries." *Journal of American History* 65, no. 2 (September 1978): 319–43.

Wiegers, Robert P. "A Proposal for Indian Slave Trading in the Mississippi Valley and Its Impact on the Osage." *Plains Anthropologist* 33, no. 120 (May 1988): 187–202.

Wigmore, Gregory. "Before the Railroad: From Slavery to Freedom in the Canadian-American Borderland." *Journal of American History* 98, no. 2 (September 2011): 437–54.

Wilentz, Sean. *Chants Democratic: New York City and the Rise of the American Working Class, 1788–1850*. New York: Oxford University Press, 1984.

———. *The Rise of American Democracy: Jefferson to Lincoln*. New York: Norton, 2005.

Willand, Jon. *Lac qui Parle and the Dakota Mission*. Madison, MN: Lac Qui Parle County Historical Society, 1964.

Williams, Michael. *Americans and Their Forests: A Historical Geography*. Cambridge: Cambridge University Press, 1989.

Williams, William Appleman. *Empire as a Way of Life: An Essay on the Causes and Character of America's Present Predicament along with a Few Thoughts about an Alternative*. New York: Oxford University Press, 1980.

Williamson, Stanley. *The Vaccination Controversy: The Rise, Reign, and Fall of Compulsory Vaccination for Smallpox*. Liverpool: Liverpool University Press, 2007.

Wilson, Terry P. *The Underground Reservation: Osage Oil*. Lincoln: University of Nebraska Press, 1985.

Wilson, Woodrow. *A History of the American People*. Vol. 4. New York: Harper and Brothers, 1903.

Winn, Kenneth H. "The Frown of Fortune: George Sibley, Breach of Promise, and Anglo-Francophone Conflict on the Missouri Frontier." In *Missouri Law and the American Conscience: Historical Rights and Wrongs,* edited by Kenneth H. Winn. 35–61. Columbia: University of Missouri Press, 2016.

Wishart, David J. *The Fur Trade of the American West, 1807–1840: A Geographical Synthesis.* Lincoln: University of Nebraska Press, 1979.

Witgen, Michael. *An Infinity of Nations: How the Native New World Shaped Early North America.* Philadelphia: University of Pennsylvania Press, 2012.

Witt, John Fabian. "Law and War in American History." *American Historical Review* 115, no. 3 (June 2010): 768–78.

Wolf, Eric R. *Europe and the People without History.* 2nd ed. Berkeley: University of California Press, 2010.

Wolfe, Patrick. "Land, Labor, and Difference: Elementary Structures of Race." *American Historical Review* 106, no. 3 (June 2001): 866–905.

———. "Settler Colonialism and the Elimination of the Native." *Journal of Genocide Research* 8, no. 4 (December 2006): 387–409.

Wood, Gordon. *The Creation of the American Republic, 1776–1787.* Chapel Hill: University of North Carolina Press, 1969.

Wood, Peter. *Black Majority: Negroes in Colonial South Carolina from 1670 through the Stono Rebellion.* New York: Norton, 1974.

Wood, W. Raymond. "Plains Trade in Prehistoric and Protohistoric Intertribal Relations." In *Anthropology on the Great Plains,* edited by W. Raymond Wood and Margot Liberty, 98–109. Lincoln: University of Nebraska Press, 1980.

Wright, Gavin. *The Political Economy of the Cotton South: Households, Markets, and Wealth in the Nineteenth Century.* New York: Norton, 1978.

Wright, J. Leitch. "Blacks in British East Florida." *Florida Historical Quarterly* 54, no. 4 (April 1976): 425–42.

———. "Creek-American Treaty of 1790: Alexander McGillivray and the Diplomacy of the Old Southwest." *Georgia Historical Quarterly* 51, no. 4 (December 1967): 379–400.

———. *William Augustus Bowles: Director General of the Creek Nation.* Athens: University of Georgia Press, 1967.

Wunder, John, and Pekka Hämäläinen. "Of Lethal Places and Lethal Essays." *American Historical Review* 104, no. 4 (October 1999): 1229–34.

INDEX

Page numbers in italics refer to illustrations.

Abihka (town), 35

abolitionism: and colonization, 137, 152, 154, 195–96; different strategies for, 128–33, 135, 143–44; and Florida, 31–32, 61; and Mexico, 13–14, 21, 149–50; and United States, 17–19, 83, 159, 162, 164–65, 167. *See also* antislavery advocacy; emancipation

Abraham (Black Seminole leader), 52, 60–62, *60*, 193

Abraham's Town, 60

Abram (Patty's son), 27–29, 61, 194. *See also* Abraham (Black Seminole)

Acton, MS, 199

Adams, Henry, 196

Adams, John, 78

Adams, John Quincy, 1–6, 8–9, 11–12, 14, 20, 24, 59, 144, 154–55, 193

Adams-Onís Treaty, 2, 3, 6, 11–12, 29, 59

Africa, 33, 129–30, 132, 137, 140–42, 215n12, 226n16

Ahaya (Seminole leader), 36–37, 39. *See also* Cowkeeper

Ainu, 100, 119

Alabama, 1, 8, 17, 29, 133, 143

Alabama River, 35

Alamo, 153

Alaska, 167, 188

Alibamu (language), 35

Allen, James, 119

Almonte, Juan Nepomuceno, 151, 153

Amelung, Ferdinand, 52, 55

American Anti-Slavery Society, 154

American Board of Commissioners for Foreign Missions, 158, 164

American Colonization Society, 129–31, 136–37, 139–42

American Convention for Promoting the Abolition of Slavery, 130, 133, 135, 142–44

American Fur Company, 93, 95, 97, 172, 175–76

American Revolution, 5, 7, 18, 28, 31–32, 42–43, 48, 81, 108

Amherst, Jeffery, 111, 123

Amherst Female Seminary, 165

Anawanymane, Simon, 177–78, 185, 199

Anderson, Gary C., 158–59

Andes mountains, 5

Andover, MA, 161

Angola, 59–60

Anishinaabe, 35, 108, 117, 160, 170

An-paye-too-o-kee-tan In-win, 179

anti-Catholicism, 164, 166, 183

Anti-Masonic party, 18, 167
antislavery advocacy: and Canada, 141–42; different strategies for, 127–37; and Haiti, 139–40; and Mexico, 13–14, 148–55; and United States, 8, 18–19, 20, 83, 163–64, 167, 187, 188. *See also* abolitionism; emancipation
Anti-Slavery Society of Maryland, 134
Apaches, 191, 194
Apalachees, 34
Apalachicola River, 50–51, 57
Appalachian Mountains, 6
Aranama, 148
Arbuthnot, George, 58, 60
Arikara, 100, 103
Arkansas (Indigenous nation), 34
Arkansas (state), 8, 130, 152, 198
Arkansas Band of the Osage, 69, 73, 75–76
Arkansas River, 68–69, 73, 89, 198
Armbrister, Robert, 58, 60
Ashley, William, 94
Assiniboine, 232n46
Astor, John Jacob, 65, 93, 95, 98, 175
Athens, Greece, 81
Atlantic coast, 27, 34, 65
Atlantic Ocean, 36, 90, 107
Audrain, Francis, 85
Augusta, GA, 32
Austin, Moses, 127, 146
Austin, Stephen, 125–28, 133, 146, 148–50

Bahamas, 43–45
Baillio, Paul, 95
Bajío, Mexico, 5, 208n6
Baltimore, MD, 64, 94, 127, 134, 138–39
Baltimore Emigration Society, 139
Baptist missionaries, 113
Barbados, 29
Barber, Elizabeth, 102
Barber, John Warner, 102
Barnard, Timothy, 52
Bartram, John, 40
Bartram, William, 37–41, 44

Battes (fugitive slave), 33
Bayley, Christopher, 204n9
beans, 37
beaver, 65, 69–71, 87, 121, 172, 232n53
Beecher, Lyman, 164
Belgium, 10
Ben (fugitive slave), 33
Bent, Charles, 98
Bent, Silas, 91
Bent, William, 98
Benton, Thomas Hart, 91–93, 95, 98
Berkhofer, Robert F., 158
Berthold, Bartholomew, 93
Bethlehem, IN, 165
Bewlie, 27, 29, 194
Big Osage, 69, 75–76
Billy (Black Seminole), 46
bison: and Comanches, 97; and Dakota, 171–72, 174, 176, 180, 183, 185, 198; and Lakota, 99–100, 114, 232n46; and Osages, 69–70, 198; and US expansion, 79
Bissett, Robert, 43
Blackfeet, 189, 197–98
Black Hills, 99–100, 114, 170
Blaine, James G., 22
boarding schools, 114, 200–202
Boggs, Lilburn, 95
Bogotá, Colombia, 122
Bolek (Payne's brother), 48, 57–58, 62, 196, 213n124
Bolek's Town, 58
Bonne, François, 92
Boone, Daniel, 71, 77, 120
Boone, Nathan, 71, 77, 82
Boston, MA, 223n32
Bouquet, Henry, 111
Bourke, Joanne, 223n23
Bourne, George, 128
Bowles, William Augustus, 40, 44–48, 45, 62, 197, 211n76, 211n86
Boyer, Jean-Pierre, 139
Brazil, 5, 132
Brim (Lower Creek leader), 36–37, 42
Britain, 90, 128, 189

British Empire, 22, 50, 81, 144, 204n9;
  in North America, 3–6, 8, 9, 10, 13,
  16–17, 28, 35–36, 38, 50, 58, 63, 66, 69,
  78, 82, 100, 102–3, 106–7, 116–17, 119,
  123, 170, 194, 197
Brown County, OH, 162
Burgess, Dyer, 165, 167
Buckland, MA, 165
Burke County, GA, 32

Caddoan languages, 68, 72
Caesar (fugitive slave), 32
Calhoun, John, 56, 58–59, 79–80, 116–17
California, 4, 21, 22, 23, 98, 100, 105,
  120–23, 190–92, 221n8
Calvinism, 83, 161, 166
Cambridge, MA, 135
camels, 24, 191–92
Cameron, Charles, 213n124
Canada: Black flight to, 28, 141–42, 144;
  fur traders in, 116–17, 119, 172, 176;
  Indigenous people fleeing to, 192;
  Lundy in, 155; possible annexation of,
  by US, 24, 49, 223n25
Canary Islands, 146
captivity narratives, 105, 108–11
Caribbean region, 5, 22, 27–28, 30–31, 34,
  46–47, 68, 72, 132, 190, 192
Carlisle Indian Boarding School, 200
Carolina, 30–31, 33–36, 39, 49. See also
  North Carolina; South Carolina
Carondelet, Francisco Luis Héctor de,
  72, 75
Carson, Kit, 188–89
Carver, Jonathan, 170
Cashesegra (Osage leader), 75–76
Caso y Luego, Francisco, 58
Cass, Lewis, 103–4, 113–14
Cass Lake, 118
Cassville, MO, 167
Catholicism, 18, 184, 208n7
cattle, 37–38, 41, 55, 79, 178, 209n42,
  233n72
Cayuse, 158
Cazneau, Jane McManus Storm, 19

Chardon, Francis, 104
Charles IV of Spain, 122
Charlestown, SC, 36, 72
Cher-a-ta-reesh, 89
Cherokees, 8, 15–17, 34–35, 44, 50, 78,
  101, 104, 115–16, 185, 198
Chesapeake region, 31, 39
Chester County Society for Preventing
  Kidnapping, 135–36
Cheyenne, 97, 189
Chicago, IL, 21, 78
Chicago River, 49
Chickasaw Bluffs, 78, 95
Chickasaws, 17, 78, 101, 205n35
Child, David Lee, 152
Child, Lydia Marie, 152
Chile, 61
China, 93, 165, 189
Chivington, John, 189
Choctaws, 17, 34, 36, 50, 78, 101, 185
cholera, 116
Chouteau, Auguste, 69, 75, 79, 82, 84, 92
Chouteau, Pierre, 73, 75–76, 79, 81–82, 84,
  86–87, 91–93
Chouteau, Pierre, Jr., 93
Cincinnati, OH, 141, 164–65
Civil War, 10, 13–14, 18, 21–22, 90, 128,
  160, 188–89, 194–95, 202
Clark, William (explorer), 73, 77–78, 80,
  82, 85–86, 88–92
Clark, William (planter), 32–33
Clavin, Matthew J., 212n117
Clay, Henry, 20, 130
Clemson, Eli, 86, 91
Cloe (daughter of Ned and Sue), 33
Coahuila, Mexico, 14, 154, 196
Coahuila y Tejas, Mexico, 1, 125–26, 145,
  147–51, 153
Coffin, Aaron, 140
College of New Jersey, 107
Colombia, 131–32
colonialism, settler, 12, 102, 158, 190–91
colonization, 126–31, 135–43, 153–55,
  195–96, 201
Colorado, 189

Columbia Fur Company, 93–94, 175
Columbia River, 89
Comanches, 5, 12, 67, 72, 97–98, 110,
    112–13, 125, 146, 191, 194, 198
Confederate States of America, 21, 155,
    191, 194–95
Congarees, 34
Connecticut, 112, 162–63
Constitution of the United States, 83
conversion, religious, 83, 157–58, 161–63,
    181–84
Cook, Sherburne F., 121–22
Coosa River, 35
corn, 11, 37–39, 69, 100, 112, 170, 176–77,
    182, 184
cotton, 22, 27, 36, 41, 90, 126, 146, 153
Council of Three Fires, 117. See also
    Odawa; Ojibwe; Potawatomis
Coweta, 35–37, 49
Cowkeeper, 36–38, 43, 46, 194, 196–97
Cowley (fugitive slave), 32
Crawford, William H., 52–53, 56
Creeks, 8, 12, 15–16, 28–30, 32–38, 41–42,
    46–47, 49–55, 78, 193–94, 197–98,
    207n3; Lower, 35–36, 40, 44, 49–50,
    57; Upper, 35–36, 42, 44, 47, 49
Crees, 192
Crooks, Ramsay, 93
Crosby, Alfred, 100
Cuba, 21, 60, 132, 192
Cudjo (free Black man), 46
Cuffe, Paul, 139
Cusabos, 34
Cuscowilla, 37–38, 40, 46, 58, 62
Custis, Peter, 89

Dakota (language), 157, 179–83, 200–202,
    232n46
Dakota (Indigenous nation), 14, 19, 76,
    108, 114, 117–19, 157–59, 168–86,
    188, 192, 198–202; Dakota country,
    168, 177, 181, 186, 198
Dakota Territory, 199–200
Dakota War, 158, 198–200
Daniel (fugitive slave), 27–29, 61, 194

Danish West Indies, 226n87
Dartmouth College, 201
Davenport, IA, 166, 200
Davis, Jefferson, 191, 196
Dearborn, Henry, 73
deer, 36–38, 65, 69–70, 87, 99, 170–72,
    174, 180
DeLacy, John Devereux, 38
Delaware (state), 112
Delawares (Indigenous nation), 77
del Valle, Santiago, 150
Demere, Raymond, 32
Democratic Party, 15, 95
Democratic-Republican Party
    (Jeffersonian Party), 81, 83, 94
Des Moines River, 172
Detroit, MI, 141
Dexter, Horatio, 59
Dhegihan Sioux, 68–69
Dominican Republic, 192, 196
Dougherty, John, 103–4, 112, 114
Dumont, Alexander, 55, 212n117
Dunning, William, 22
Durango, Mexico, 196

East Asia, 165
East India Company, 215n12
Eastman, Charles, 200–201
Easton, Mary, 91–92
Easton, Rufus, 91
East River, 22
Echeandia, José Maria, 121
ecological imperialism, 100
Economy, PA, 143
Edwards, Jonathan, 83, 107, 109
Eitwans, 34
elections: 1824 election, 8, 130; 1828
    election, 1, 8, 15; 1832 election, 8, 15,
    130; 1836 election, 15; 1840 election,
    15; 1844 election, 20, 130, 188
Electoral College, 20
Ellis, Edward, 21
Ellis, William, 196
emancipation, 3, 8–9, 29, 130–36, 141,
    150; compensated, 128; gradual, 126,

128–30, 132–33, 195; immediate, 126, 128, 131, 136, 154–55, 195

Emancipation Proclamation, 194

empresario, 125–26, 146, 148–51

Eshkibagikoonzhe, 119

Esten (free Black man), 46

Europe: and North American empires, 4, 5–6, 12–13, 28–29, 33–34, 36–37, 40, 42–43, 47–48, 68–69, 71–73, 158, 169, 187; smallpox in, 99–100, 102, 105–7, 111, 222n14

expansion, US, 4, 7–9, 12–13, 14, 16, 19–20, 21, 22–26, 48–49, 61, 67, 102, 185, 188–90; arguments against, 2–3; rationalization of, 207n58

experiments, 8, 17, 23–24, 112, 143–45, 152, 187, 191–92

factory system, xi, 66–67, 77–87, 89–95, 98, 197–98, 215n12

Faragher, John M., 63–64, 233n72

Fatio, Francis, 43

Fayetteville, NC, 83, 218n79

Federalist Party, 3, 78

Fenn, Elizabeth, 110–11, 123

Fernández, Antonio, 32

Fernández, Francisco Vital, 125, 151

Fire Prairie, 77, 80

First Congregational Church (Newport, RI), 83

Flat Mouth, 119

Flint, Timothy, 120

Florida, 13, 31, 36, 38–39, 43–44, 49, 50, 61–62, 130, 144, 187–88, 193–94, 196–97, 202, 207n3; British province of, 31, 33, 40–42; East, 8, 10, 25, 29, 32, 41–42, 47–48, 52, 54–56, 58; Jackson's 1818 invasion of, 3, 8, 11, 56–61, 196, 213n124; as refuge from chattel slavery, 33, 37–38; Spanish province of, 3, 4, 5, 6–7, 11, 15, 27–34, 42, 46, 50–61, 193–94, 208n6, 209n42, 213n124; US annexation of, 12–13, 59; West, 7, 33, 41–42, 44, 47–48, 58

Fifty-Fourth Massachusetts, 195

Finiels, Nicholas de, 72

Finney, Charles Grandison, 161–62, 165

Floyd, John, 191

Folch, Esteban, 47

Folch, Juan Vicente, 47

Fond du Lac, 117

Foner, Eric, 63

Forbes, John, 47–48

Forbes and Company, 50–51

Fort Clark, 104

Fort Dearborn, 49

Fort Detroit, 78

Forten, James, 139

Fort George, 49

Fort Jessup, 11

Fort Madison, 49

Fort Osage, 49, 67–68, 77–78, 84–91, 94–95, 101, 116

Fort Pierre, 169

Fort Pitt, 111

Fort Ross, 121–22

Fort Scott, 57

Fort Snelling, 11, 169, 200

Fort St. Stephen, 78

Fort Wayne, 78

Fowltown, 55–57

France, 63–64, 189

Frank (enslaved man), 30

Franklin, Benjamin, 107

free Black people, 25, 154, 202, 226n16; and antislavery, 18–19, 25, 129–32, 135–45; in Florida, 13–14, 30–32, 39, 44, 46, 48; in Mexico, 13, 147–48, 152, 192, 194; in Spanish colonies, 208n7

Freeman, Thomas, 89

Free Soil Party, 18

French empire: in North America, 5, 28; and Louisiana Territory, 8, 35–36, 63–64, 66, 68–69, 72–75, 78, 92, 108; and Great Lakes, 117, 160, 170–72, 219n88

French Fur Company, 93

fugitive slaves. See maroons

fur trade, 87; and cultural exchange, 159–60, 169–70, 171–77; and Great Lakes, 185–86, 219n88; and Missouri River, 65–82, 84, 91–95, 197–98; in Southeast, 36, 40; in Southwest, 97–98; and vaccination, 100, 114, 116, 122. *See also names of individual fur trade companies*

Gabaret Island, 73
Gaines, Edmund, 52, 54–56, 58–59, 214n136
Gainesville, FL, 37
Galena, IL, 166
Gallatin, Albert, 65–66, 76
Galveston, TX, 191
Galveston Island, 146
Garçon (ex-slave leader), 51
Garrison, William Lloyd, 131, 141, 154
Georgia, 41, 48, 78; and Indigenous removal, 8, 17, 185; and Indigenous–white violence, 1, 55–57; and slavery, 5–6, 15, 27, 29–30, 32–33, 35, 49, 51–52, 54, 61–62, 194; and vaccination, 112
Germany, 17, 144
Ghost Dance, 192
Gibraltar, 29
Giddings, Joshua, 61–62
Gila River, 121
Gould, Eliga, 211n76
Gracia Real de Santa Teresa de Mose, 30
Grand Ecore, 83–84
Grant, James, 41
Grant, Ulysses S., 195–96
Granville, Pierre Joseph Marie, 139
Great Awakening: First, 23; Second, 128, 161–63, 166
Great Cypress Swamp, 197
Great Lakes: as borderland, 9, 11, 13, 25, 108–9, 232n49; and fur trade, 76, 78, 159–60, 171, 176; and US expansion, 4; and vaccination, 114, 116–18
Great Plains: as borderland, 10–13; and Dakota, 169–72, 232n46; and fur trade,

65, 74, 159, 176, 197–98; and smallpox, 112; and US expansion, 4, 67–68, 97–99; and vaccination, 114, 116–17
Greenberg, Amy, 19–20, 206n46
Greeneville, TN, 127, 133, 138
Guadalajara, Mexico, 97
Guanajuato, Mexico, 48, 103, 122
Guano Islands Act, 192
Guatemala, 61, 195
Guaymas, Mexico, 121
Guerrero Saldaña, Vicente, 149
Guianas, 28
Gulf of California, 121
Gulf of Mexico, 4, 41

Haiti, 63, 130–31, 137, 139–44, 155
Haitian Philanthropic Society, 140
Haitian Revolution, 131, 139–40
Halttunen, Karen, 113
Harmony, IN, 143
Harrison, William Henry, 15, 16, 65, 77
Harry (free Black man), 46
Harvard University, 1, 111
Haudenosaunee, 108, 117
Havana, Cuba, 31, 44
Hawkins, Benjamin, 47, 51–54
Hazelwood Republic, 185
Hempstead, Edward, 91
Henderson County, KY, 108
Henry, Andrew, 94
Herculaneum, MO, 127
herd immunity, 103
Herrenvolk democracy, 15–16
Herring, Elbert, 115
Heyrick, Elizabeth Coltman, 128
Hidalgo, Miguel, 48
Hispaniola, 28. *See also* Dominican Republic; Haiti
Hitchiti (language), 35
Hokkaido, 100, 119
Holata Micco, 196–97
Holmes, David, 51
Homestead Act, 196
Honduras, 195
Hopkins, Samuel, 83

Horn, Sarah Ann, 110
Horse, John, 13, 16, 193–94, 201
Horseshoe Bend, 50
Houghton, Douglas, 113, 117–20
Houston, Sam, 153
Hudson's Bay, 107
Hudson's Bay Company, 100, 116, 119, 175, 232n53
Huggins, Alexander, 161, 164, 167, 176–77, 180, 185, 199
Huggins, Amos, 199
Huggins, Frances, 161, 164, 185
Huggins, Lydia, 161, 164, 185, 199
humanitarian reform, 112–13

Illinois, 71–72, 92, 108–9, 133, 152, 154, 162, 165
immigrants, 13, 18, 137, 144
India, 189
Indian Affairs, Office of, 86, 101, 103, 115, 117
Indiana, 162
Indiana House of Representatives, 130
Indiana Senate, 130
Indiana Territory, 65, 78, 193, 197
Indian Removal Act, 8
Indian Territory, 3, 13, 17, 188, 193, 196–98
Indian Trade, Office of, 93–94
Indian Vaccination Act, 101–2, 113–14, 117
Indigenous people, 158, 165; autonomy of, 11–12, 24–25; diplomatic relations between European empires and, 5–6, 117, 187; population of, 100, 221n8, 222n13; removal of, 3, 7–8, 19, 90, 101, 113, 197; reservations, 7, 197–99, 201; violence between US and, 1, 7, 8, 199–200; white Americans' racist views of, 7, 100–101, 120, 122
indigo, 27, 41
influenza, 74
Innerarity, John, 48, 55, 212n117
inoculation, 103–4, 107–9, 122, 223n32

intermarriages, 15, 84, 109, 160, 171–72, 177, 219n88
Intertribalism, 15, 17, 198
Iowa (state), 166, 200
Iowas (Indigenous nation), 73, 77, 114
Ipswich Female Seminary, 165
Ireland, 18, 146
Iroquois. *See* Haudenosaunee
Isaac (fugitive slave), 32
Isanti, 170–71
Ishtahba, 178, 184

Jackson, Andrew, 7, 16, 21, 66, 79; as general, 3–4, 8, 11, 15, 50–62, 193, 196, 214n136; as president, 1; as presidential nominee, 15, 62
Jackson, James, 113
Jamaica, 28
Jams, Edwin, 116
James, Thomas, 97–98
James River, 34
Japan, 21, 100, 103, 119
Jefferson, Thomas: and commerce, 80–81, 98; and Florida, 38; and Indigenous people, 65–68, 73, 76–81, 87, 171; and Louisiana Purchase, 3, 63; and US empire, 106; and vaccination, 111–12, 116–17
Jefferson College, 163–64
Jenner, Edward, 108, 115–16
Jessup, Thomas, 193
Johnson, Richard Mentor, 15
Juba (fugitive slave; wife of Isaac), 33

Kansas, 196
Kansas River, 18
Kaposia, MN, 175, 185
Kashita, 35
Kaw, 69, 71, 76, 88, 96
Keating, William, 10, 173
Kelton, Paul, 104
Kentucky, 8, 65, 71, 84, 108–9, 112, 126, 130, 133, 164, 167–68
Kickapoos, 77, 101, 105, 108–11, 113

Kinache (Seminole leader), 46–48, 54–55, 57, 60, 213n124
King Philip's War, 223n23
Kiowas, 97, 100
Kloppenberg, James, 81
Knight, Isaac, 108–11, 113
Koasati (language), 35

La Bahia, TX, 148
Lac qui Parle, xi, 157–64, 166–70, 172, 174–86, 198–99, 200–201
ladinos, 208n7
Lafitte, Jean, 146
Lafitte, Pierre, 146
Lake Champlain, 49
Lake Erie, 49
Lake Superior, 10, 117
Lakota, 5, 12, 73, 76, 99–100, 102–4, 114, 169, 171–72, 189, 192, 197–98, 232n46
Lane Theological Seminary, 164
Lassus, Charles de Hault de, 73, 75
Latin America, 21, 27, 128, 132
Lawrence, Lorenzo, 199
Leavenworth, KS, 112, 114
LeBeaume, Louis, 91
Le Conte, John, 42
Leech Lake, 119
Lenape, 101
Lepore, Jill, 223n23
Leslie, John, 43
Lewis, Meriweather, 73, 77, 86, 88–89, 116–17
Lewis, Reuben, 77, 82, 86
Liberia, 129, 137, 141. See also American Colonization Society
Liberty Party, 18, 20
Lincoln, Abraham, 194–95
Lipans. See Apaches
Lisa, Manuel, 75
Little Crow, 199
Little Osage, 69, 73, 75–76
Little Rapids, 175
London, England, 44
London, Canada, 141–42
Long, Stephen, 10, 116–17

Lorimer, Louis, 86, 219n88
Lorimer, Pierre-Louis de, 219n88
Lorr, Ellen, 85, 90–92
Lorr, Pierre, 85
Lorr v. Sibley, 91–92
Los Angeles, CA, 121
Louisiana (US state), 3, 5, 8, 133, 136, 140, 146–47, 196
Louisiana Purchase, 3, 8, 10, 48, 63–65, 68, 70, 73, 75, 78, 81, 88, 91–92, 98
Louisiana Territory, 3, 8, 22, 28, 44, 63–67; Lower, 68, 77, 79, 82–83, 86, 88–89, 98; Upper, 71–75
Loup River, 72
Lower Mississippi region, 68, 72, 146
Lower Missouri region, 68–69, 72–79, 81–82, 88, 90, 171
Lower Sioux Agency, 199
Lucas, Charles, 91–92
Lundy, Benjamin, 125–45, 138, 147–55, 158, 195–96, 228n60

Madison, James, 50, 64, 66, 130
Madrid, Spain, 30, 44
Maine, 112
malaria, 116
Mandans, 103–4
manifest destiny, 4, 9, 19–25, 61, 65, 102, 127, 187–88, 193, 201, 206n46
manumission, 128–30, 136, 140, 144
market revolution, 17–18, 64–67, 81, 162–63
maroons, 18; and Civil War, 194–95; in Florida, 4–5, 7–8, 12–13, 15, 27–33, 38–39, 46, 50–55, 59–61, 63, 187–88; in Mexico, 146, 148; in Ohio, 164
Marsh, George Perkins, 191
Manumission Society of North Carolina, 140
Manumission Society of Tennessee, 127–28, 133–34, 143
mariage à la façon du pays, 15, 84, 109, 160, 171–72, 177, 219n88
Martha's Vineyard, MA, 112
Martin, Meriwether, 99–101, 103–4, 114–15, 120

Maryland, 112, 127, 132, 134, 138, 141

Mary Lyon's Female Seminary, 165

Massachusetts, 3, 102, 112, 120, 135, 161, 165, 195

Mason, John, 79, 82, 85

Masot, José, 58

Matamoros, Mexico, 151–52

Mather, Cotton, 223n32

Maumee River, 113

McCall, James, 39

McCoy, Isaac, 113

McGillivray, Alexander, 15, 42–47, 49, 210n68

McIntosh, William, 15, 53–55, 57

McKenney, Thomas, 80, 87, 92–93, 117

McQueen, Peter, 15, 49

Mears, William, 91

measles, 106, 122

medicine, 115–16. *See also* inoculation; vaccination

Meigs, Joseph, 112

Melgares, Facundo, 89

Meskwaki. *See* Sauk and Meskwaki

Métis, 172, 176, 186, 232n49

Mexico, 145; and free Black people, 13–14, 17–18, 187, 194, 196, 202; and Benjamin Lundy, 125–27, 132–33, 144–55, 158; and northern territory, 4, 67, 95–96, 98, 190–92; and silver mines, 5; and smallpox, 107; and Texas rebellion, 1–3, 23, 128, 153; and United States, 10, 19, 21, 24–25, 48–49, 188–89; and vaccination, 100–103, 106, 120–23

Mexico City, 122, 126, 146, 149, 151, 153

Meyer, Roy W., 158–59

Mde Wakan, 170–72, 174

Mdewakanton, 170–71, 175, 185, 199

Miamis, 78, 101, 108

Micanopy (Seminole leader), 62

Michigan (state), 162

Michigan Territory, 78, 167

Michilimackinac, 78

Middle Atlantic states, 163

Mikasuki (language), 35, 37, 40

Mikasuki (town), 46, 57–58, 60

Minge, David, 140

Miniyuha (Mdewakanton woman), 175

Minnesota (state), 158, 185, 188, 198–99

Minnesota River, 11, 13, 157, 159, 169–70, 172–76, 185, 187. *See also* Upper Minnesota River

Minnesota Territory, 19, 180, 185

Miró, Esteban Rodriguez, 71

missionaries: and borderlands, 17, 24–25, 113; in California, 121–22; and Cherokees, 115–16; and Dakota, 13–14, 19, 157–69, 176–86, 188, 198–201; and mission schools, 115, 178; in Texas, 148; and US expansion, 7, 230n2

Mississippi, 17, 51, 78, 87, 133, 143, 191, 196

Mississippi River, 49, 92, 118, 166; and Dakota, 159, 175, 180; and emancipation, 131, 142; and fur trade, 71, 77–78, 172; and Indigenous removal, 90, 101; Lower Mississippi River region, 68–69, 72, 146; Upper Mississippi region, 11, 99, 117, 159–60, 163–64, 167, 170–71, 176; and US expansion, 23, 42, 63–65, 158, 189; and US sovereignty, 6–7, 9, 88

Missouri, 8, 16, 67, 83–84, 90–92, 95–98, 113, 122, 126–27, 133, 146, 152, 198

Missouri Fur Company, 82, 93

Missouri junto, 91–92

Missouri River, 10, 13, 18, 49, 65, 67–71, 73, 77, 80, 85, 89, 95, 97, 100, 103–4, 116, 142, 167, 169–70, 176, 180, 197–98; Lower Missouri region, 12, 68–69, 72–79, 81–82, 88, 90, 171; Upper Missouri region, 13, 76, 93, 99, 114, 171

Mobile, AL, 36, 42

Mobile River, 78

Modoc, 189

Mohave Desert, 121

Monclova, Mexico, 148, 150–51

Moniac, David, 16

Monk, George, 172
Monroe, James, 3, 50, 56–57, 79, 144
Monterrey, CA, 122–23
Monticello, 81, 112
Montreal, Canada, 82, 93
Mooney, James, 221n8
Moore, James, 34
Moravian missionaries, 115–16
Morel, John, 27, 30
Morelos, José María, 151
Morel, Peter Henry, 27–28, 30
Mount Vernon, 136–37
Moyamensing, PA, 38
Muskogean (language), 35, 37, 40
Muskogee, State of, 44–48, 211n76, 211n86
muskrat, 65, 70, 87, 172, 232n53

Nacogdoches, TX, 147
Nakota, 232n46
Nancy (fugitive slave), 33
Nantucket, MA, 112
Napoléon, 63–64, 139
Narbona, Antonio, 96
narratives: as alternatives to manifest destiny, 24; blank-slate, 127; of borderlands, 4, 9, 19–25, 187–88; and camels, 24, 191–92; of captivity, 105, 108–11; colonization, 129–30; and emancipation, 127, 131, 132–33; and evangelization, 181–83; and Andrew Jackson, 57; language of humanity as, 112–13; manifest destiny as, 4, 9; and republicanism, 80–81; and salvation, 166; smallpox, 105, 110, 120; as tool to legitimize US expansion, 120–23
Natchez (Indigenous nation), 35
Natchitoches, LA, 78, 83–84
National Republican Party, 95
National Vaccine Institution, 112
Navajo, 12, 189
nativism, 13, 18, 164
Nebraska, 199–200
Ned (fugitive slave), 33
Nero's Town, 60

Neutral Ground, 146
New England, 162–63, 165, 223n23
New Granada, 61
New Hampshire, 112
New Jersey, 126
New Mexico: and Indigenous people, 12, 82, 189, 221n8; and James Pattie, 120, 122; and Pueblo Revolt, 69; and United States, 67, 88–89, 95–97, 113, 190, 219n99
New Orleans, LA, 7–8, 44, 47, 49, 54, 63–65, 72, 120
Newport, RI, 83
New Spain, 5–6, 28, 61, 97, 122, 145–46, 208n6
New York, 112, 134, 161–63, 223n23
New York City, 22, 64, 111, 129, 152
New York Manumission Society, 131, 134
Nez Perce, 189
Nezuma (Osage leader), 76
Niangua River, 71
Nicaragua, 192
Nicolls, Edward, 58
North Carolina, 30, 83–84, 112, 140
Northeast states, 163
North West Company, 6, 93, 172
Northwest Ordinance, 132–33
Northwest Territory, 7, 16, 78, 87, 132–33
Nuéces River, 153, 191

Oberlin, OH, 141
Oceti Sakowin Oyate, 170
Oconee, 35–38, 49
Odawa, 101, 108, 112–13, 117
O'Fallon, Benjamin, 93
Ogeechee River, 33
Ohio, 112–13, 127, 141, 148, 162–64, 167–68, 204n18, 228n60
Ohio River, 132–33, 163–65
Ohio Valley, 69, 110
Ohiyesa. See Eastman, Charles
Ojibwe, 4–5, 12, 76, 103, 105, 113, 117–19, 118, 192
Omahas, 69, 73, 76, 112

Onís, Luis de, 6, 59
Oregon, 4, 6, 19–20, 98, 158–59, 185, 188
O'Reilly, Alejandro, 72
Ortiz, Tadeo, 146
Osage River, 69
Osages, 12, 17, 18, 65–66, 68–77, 70, 80–81, 84–97, 108, 171, 197–98. *See also* Arkansas Band of the Osage; Big Osage; Little Osage
Osceola, 40
Ossabow Island, 27
O'Sullivan, John L., 19–25, 188
Otoes, 88, 112, 114
Ottoman Empire, 22, 191, 207n51

Pacific Ocean, 7, 10, 20, 22, 100, 190, 191–92
Pacific Railroad, 189
Panama, 28
Panton, Leslie, and Company, 42–44, 46–47, 210n68
Panton, William, 43
Parliament, British, 44, 132
Pate (fugitive slave), 33
Pattie, James O., 120–23
Patty (fugitive slave), 27–29, 61, 194
Pawhuska (Osage leader), 76
Pawnees, 68, 72, 82, 88–89, 96, 100, 112–13
Payne (Seminole leader), 46, 48
Pearce, Richard, 151–52
Pearson, J. Diane, 103, 221n8
Pensacola, FL, 31–32, 38, 42–44, 50–54, 56, 58–61, 214n136
Pennsylvania, 38, 112, 143, 163–65, 173, 200
Pennsylvania Manumission Society, 133–34
People of the Seven Council Fires, 170
Pérez, Manuel, 71
Peter (fugitive slave), 32
Phebe (fugitive slave; wife of Pate), 33
Philadelphia, PA, 40, 64, 107, 111, 138, 143
Philippines, 44

phrenology, 16, 100–101
Pierce, Franklin, 191–92
Pike, Zebulon, 6–7, 70, 74–75, 88–89, 171, 175, 219n99
Pilaklikaha (town), 60
Pincas, Steven, 204n9
Pittsburgh, PA, 164
Platte River, 88
Poinsett, Joel, 11, 96
Polk, James K., 20–21, 188, 191
Poncas, 69, 112
Pond, Elnathan, 163
Pond, Gideon, 157–58, 161–63, 166–67, 177–78, 180–82, 185, 199–200
Pond, Sarah, 163
Pond, Sarah Poage, 161–62, 164, 167, 185, 199
Pond, Samuel, 159, 161, 163, 166, 168–69, 180–81, 183, 185, 199
Pond, Samuel, Jr., 177, 186
Portuguese empire, 5
Potawatomis, 49, 73–74, 78, 101, 108, 112–13, 117
Potosí, Bolivia, 5
Powell, John Wesley, 159
Prairie du Chien, 87
Pratte, Bernard, 91, 93
Pratt, Julius, 23
Pratt, Richard, 200
Presbyterianism, 13, 14, 157–58, 163–64, 184, 192
Princeton University, 107
Progressive Era, 23
Prospect Bluff, 50–55, 58, 60
Protestantism, 7, 18, 81, 83, 160, 162, 167, 187–88
Pueblos, 69
Puerto Rico, 122
Puget Sound, 107

Quahobe (fugitive slave; wife of Battes), 33
Quakers, 127–28, 141
Quapaws, 69
quarantine, 73, 104
Québec, Canada, 172

racism, 12–16, 120–21, 129, 135–38, 142–44, 147–48, 150, 154, 201–2
Rainville, Joseph de, 175
Rawle, William, 133–35
Rawlings, Isaac, 85
Red River (North), 169
Red River (South), 68, 73, 78, 89
Red Sticks, 49–51, 58, 193
Renville, Joseph, 93, 175–76, 181–82, 199
Renville, Joseph, Jr., 183
republicanism, 80–82, 84
Republican Party, 22
Republican River, 112
Republic of West Florida, 48
Rhode Island, 83, 112
rice, 27, 41
Riggs, Alfred, 179, 200–201
Riggs, Mary Longley, 161, 165–67, 179, 199–200
Riggs, Stephen Return, 157–59, 161, 164–69, 177–82, 184–85, 198–200
Rio Bravo de Norte. See Rio Grande
Rio de la Plata, 61
Rio Grande, 14, 89, 152–54, 194
Ripley, OH, 164
Rocky Mountain Fur Company, 94
Rolette, Joseph, 172–73
Rome, Italy, 81
Roosevelt, Theodore, 22–23
Royal African Company, 215n12
Russia, 22, 135, 189

Saami, 100–101
Sabbatarianism, 17, 159, 166–67
Sabine River, 3, 5, 146
Sacred Dance. See Wakan Wacipi
Salcedo, Manuel de, 75
San Antonio, TX, 146, 191
Sand Creek, 189
San Diego, CA, 121–22
San Felipe de Austin, TX, 150
San Francisco, CA, 121
San Luis Obispo, CA, 121
San Luis Potosí, Mexico, 97

San Marcos de Apalache, 41–42, 46, 50, 57–60. See also St. Marks
Sans Oreille (Osage leader), 74, 76
Santa Anna, Antonio López de, 150, 153
Santa Barbara, CA, 121
Santa Fe, NM, 82, 95–97, 120–21, 154
Santa Fe Trail, 67, 97–98, 113, 122
Santee Normal Training School, 200–202
Santees (Minnesota), 171
Santees (South Carolina), 34
Santo Domingo, 61, 196. See also Dominican Republic; Haiti
Savannah, GA, 27, 33
Savannah River, 30
Savannahs (Indigenous nation), 34
Sauk and Meskwaki, 11, 16, 77, 101, 108
Saunders, Prince, 139
Schoolcraft, Henry, 117–19
secession, 155
Seminoles, 3–4, 6, 11–12, 13–14, 16, 28–29, 36–40, 43–46, 48, 50, 55–62, 101, 188, 193, 196–98, 202, 207n3, 213n124; Black, 13, 28–29, 38–40, 46, 48, 52, 55, 57–62, 188, 193–94
Seminole Wars, 3, 14, 15–16, 57–59, 193, 196–97, 202
settler colonialism, 12, 102, 158, 190–91
Seven Years' War, 31, 40, 110–11
Sewees, 34
Schlesinger, Arthur M., Jr., 7
Shakopee, MN, 185
Shawnees, 15, 16, 35, 49, 72, 77, 101, 114, 219n88
Shone-gee-ne-gare, 96
Shuttleton, David, 105
Sibley, Elizabeth, 83
Sibley, George, 11, 67, 69–70, 82–98, 101, 116, 218n79
Sibley, John, 82–84
Sibley, Samuel, 83, 94
Simmons, William, 39, 207n3
Sioux, 73, 77, 108, 170, 172, 173. See also Dakota (Indigenous nation); Dhegihan Sioux; Lakota; Yanctonai
Sisseton, 170–71

slavery, 7–8, 9, 12, 13–14, 15, 17–18, 25–26, 27–35, 55, 81, 83–85, 126–55, 161, 187–88, 193–96, 222n14, 225n87; among French people, 68, 72; among Indigenous people, 15–16, 33–34, 38–39, 49, 53, 62, 68–69, 72, 74, 102; among Spanish people, 30, 32, 126, 208n7; in Mexico, 126, 146, 148–50

slaves, escaped. *See* maroons

slave revolt, fear of, 3, 5, 24, 51, 140, 187

smallpox, 17, 24–25, 34–35, 37, 73, 99–116, 122–23, 192, 201, 221n8; narratives, 105, 110, 120

Smyrna, 191

Sonora, 192

South Atlantic coastal plain, 12, 33–37, 104

South Carolina, 30, 32, 39, 112, 163, 167, 208n14, 209n42

South Dakota, 192, 200

Spalding, Lyman, 152

Spanish-American War, 23, 211n86

Spanish Empire: in North America, 3–6, 7, 8, 10, 11, 17, 28, 35–36, 38, 44–46, 50, 61, 66, 68–69, 72, 74, 78, 82, 92, 126, 194–95, 208n7; in South America, 5, 28, 61

St. Augustine, FL, 29–31, 35–36, 40–43, 46, 56, 58–59

Steubenville, OH, 164

St. John's River, 42, 47

St. Louis, MO, 64, 77, 85, 86, 90–95, 99, 189; and antislavery, 128; and fur trade, 65, 68, 70–72, 75, 84, 87, 176; and smallpox, 73, 112

St. Marks, 41–42, 52, 59, 213n124. *See also* San Marcos de Apalache

Stono Rebellion, 208n14

Stork, William, 40–41

St. Paul, MN, 199

St. Peter's River, 172. *See also* Minnesota River

Strathy Hall, 33

St. Simon, 41

Sue (daughter of Ned and Sue), 33

Sue (fugitive slave; wife of Ned), 33

sugar, 5, 34, 41, 144, 151, 153

Suwanee River, 58–60

Sweden, 100–101, 103

Swinton, William, 21

Taensas, 34

Talamanca Branciforte, Miguel de la Grua, 122

Tallapoosa River, 35

Tallushatchee, 50

Tamaulipas, 125–27, 147–48, 151–54, 158

Tampa Bay, FL, 59–60

Taos, 96

Taylor, Alan, 223n23

Tecumseh, 15, 49

Tehuantepec, Mexico, 122, 191

temperance, 18, 22, 159, 161–62, 164, 166–68

Tennessee, 17, 58–59, 62, 78, 112, 127, 133–34, 138, 143

Tennessee militia, 15, 50, 57, 60

Territory of East Florida, 48

Tetonwan, 170–71. *See also* Lakota

Texas, 1–3, 4, 10, 12, 23, 192–93, 196, 221n8; American migration to, 125–26, 146, 149–50; as Mexican province, 122, 125–28, 144–53; rebellion in, 1–3, 126–28, 153; as Spanish province, 29, 61, 146, 208n6; US annexation of, 3, 8, 13, 14, 20–21, 133, 154, 188

Thames, Battle of, 15

Thornton, Russell, 102, 221n8

Timucuas, 34

Tippecanoe, Battle of, 15

Tisné, Claude du, 69

Titus (enslaved man), 27

Tlahualilo, Mexico, 196

tobacco, 37

Tombigby, 87

Tory Party, 204n9

Toteedootawin (Dakota woman), 177, 184

Toyne, Patrick, 43

Traverse des Sioux, MN, 185

Treaty of 1818, 5, 90

Treaty of Amiens, 47

Treaty of Fort Osage, 80, 92
Treaty of Ghent, 90, 94
Treaty of San Ildefonso, 6
Trimble, William, 112
Trinidad, 144
Trist, Nicholas, 190–91
Trudeau, Jean Baptiste, 172
Trudeau, Zénon, 71–72, 75
Tukabatchee, 35
Tunicas, 34
Turner, Frederick Jackson, 23
Turner, Nat, 194
Tuscaroras, 34
Tustunnuggee Hopoie, 54
Tyler, John, 20

United Nations of Creeks and
    Cherokees, 44
United States, 3, 13; borders, 1–5; power of
    federal government, 9–10, 12, 188–89,
    204n18; territorial expansion of, 3, 4,
    7–9, 12–13, 14, 19–20, 22–26, 48–49,
    61, 67, 102, 185, 188–90; weakness in
    borderlands, 4–5, 7, 9–18, 24–25, 73,
    102, 104, 119, 187, 196–97
United States, diplomatic relations of:
    with Britain, 5–6, 24, 90, 188; with
    Indigenous people, 16, 18, 24, 44–45,
    66, 74, 77, 102, 105, 119, 187; with
    Mexico, 96–97, 190–91; with Spain, 3,
    5, 11, 23, 45
US Army, 10–11, 17, 57, 77, 189, 194–97
US Congress, 4, 11, 20, 56–57, 64–65, 82,
    91–93, 101, 112, 128, 139, 144, 196
US Constitution, 130
US House of Representatives, 1–4, 8, 23,
    60, 130, 154, 193
US Independence Day, 147
US-Mexico War, 10, 16–17, 20–21, 49,
    188, 190–91
US Navy, 191, 195, 211n86
US Senate, 3, 8, 20, 55–56, 60–62, 130
US Supreme Court, 82
University of Pennsylvania, 173
Upper Louisiana, 71, 75

Upper Minnesota River, 170, 172
Upper Mississippi region, 11, 99, 117,
    159–60, 163–64, 167, 170–71, 176
Upper Missouri region, 76, 93, 99, 114, 171
Upper Sioux Agency, 185, 199
Utah, 21, 98
Ute, 189
utopianism, 18, 143, 160–161

vaccination, 13, 17, 25–26, 99–106, 108,
    111–23, 187, 192, 201, 221n8, 225n63,
    225n87
Venezuela, 57, 61, 132
Verdigris River, 69
Vermilion River, 108
Vermont, 112
Victoria, Mexico, 125–26
Vidaurri y Villaseñor, Juan José de, 150
Viesca y Montes, José María, 149
Vietnam War, 55
Vilemont, Louis, 76
Virginia, 34, 112, 126–28, 140, 146, 194

Wabash River, 108–9
Wahpekute, 170
Wahpeton, 170, 175
Wakanmane, 199
Wakan Wacipi, 173–74, 179, 184
Walker, William, 192
Wallace, Anthony F. C., 66
Wamdi Okiye, 182
War Department, 101
War of 1812, 10, 98; and Florida, 48; and
    Fort Osage, 85, 89–90, 117, 144; and
    free Black people, 14, 49–53, 58, 140,
    144; and Indigenous people, 5, 6–7, 10,
    16, 49–50, 55, 117, 175; and
    Spain, 82
Washington, Bushrod, 130, 136–37
Washington, CT, 163, 166
Washington, DC, 1, 61–62, 76, 114, 130,
    154, 191
Washington, George, 78, 130, 150
Waterhouse, Benjamin, 111
Wa-za-ku-te-ma-ni, Paul, 185

Weatherford, William, 15–16, 49
Weber, Max, 162–63, 231n15
Weld, Theodore Dwight, 164
West: trans-Appalachian, 6, 162, 165, 204n18; trans-Mississippi, 8, 10, 64, 90, 101, 128, 130, 142, 158, 189, 196, 202
Western Theological Seminary, 164–65
Westos, 34
West Point, 16, 219n88
Whig Party (Britain), 204n9
Whig Party (US), 9, 15, 18, 94, 162
White, Richard, 160
White River, 69
white supremacy, 22, 129, 135–36, 154
Whitman, Marcus, 158–59, 185
Wichitas, 68
Wilberforce, Canada, 141–42
Wilberforce, William, 141
wild rice, 170, 172
Wilkinson, Benjamin, 82
Wilkinson, James B., 74–76, 82, 175
Williams, William Appleman, 206n46
Williamson, Jane, 161, 164
Williamson, John, 200
Williamson, Margaret Poage, 161–62, 164, 167, 185, 199–200

Williamson, Thomas, 161–64, 166–67, 178–79, 181, 185, 199–200
Willson, Marcius, 21
Wilson, Woodrow, 22
Winslow, John, 218n79
Winthrop, John, 102
Winyaws, 34
Wirt, William, 144
Woodward, Thomas, 207n3
Wounded Knee, 192

Yale University, 163
Yamasees, 34–35, 38
Yamasee War, 35–36
Yancton, 170, 200
Yanctonai, 114, 170
Yellowstone River, 176
York, 49
Yuchi, 35, 52

Zacatecas, 97, 153
Zéspedes, Vicente Manuel de, 42–43, 210n68
Zitkadan Washtay, 179. *See also* Riggs, Alfred
Zuñiga, Mauricio de, 52–55